CLASSICAL PHILOSOPHY

PETER ADAMSON

CLASSICAL PHILOSOPHY

a history of philosophy without any gaps

volume 1

OXFORD
UNIVERSITY PRESS

OXFORD
UNIVERSITY PRESS

Great Clarendon Street, Oxford, OX2 6DP,
United Kingdom

Oxford University Press is a department of the University of Oxford.
It furthers the University's objective of excellence in research, scholarship,
and education by publishing worldwide. Oxford is a registered trade mark of
Oxford University Press in the UK and in certain other countries

First Edition published in 2014

Impression: 1

Published in the United States of America by Oxford University Press
198 Madison Avenue, New York, NY 10016, United States of America

British Library Cataloguing in Publication Data
Data available

Library of Congress Control Number: 2013956024

ISBN 978–0–19–967453–4

Printed in Italy by
L.E.G.O. S.p.A.—Lavis TN

For Johanna and Sophia

CONTENTS

Part III. Aristotle

PREFACE

I wrote this book because my back hurt. Well, not only for that reason, obviously. But back-pain did make a significant contribution. It led to me trying to get in shape, by taking up running. The thing about running, especially running every day through the same neighborhood (or if you live in London, as I did then, "neighbourhood"), is that it gets boring. Seeking a diversion, I discovered podcasts. These are basically radio shows you can download from the internet, and they make for an excellent distraction while exercising. Being a bit of a philosophy buff, as you might already have suspected, I started listening to several fine podcasts on this subject. But it struck me that there was no podcast series that covered philosophy from a historical angle, telling the story of philosophy in chronological order the way other podcasts had tackled topics like ancient Rome. Since I am a historian of philosophy, it seemed to me that such a series would be a good thing. It would form a continuous narrative, and it would leave nothing out. It would cover the story of philosophy starting at the beginning, and, to steal a phrase from my esteemed colleague Richard Sorabji, "without any gaps."

And the rest is, in several senses of the word, history. The podcast launched in the autumn of 2010 and is still going strong, having covered all of ancient philosophy and now the philosophical tradition of the Islamic world. Although the podcast version includes episodes with experts on various topics, the core of the series has been a series of scripts. The scripts on classical philosophy form the basis of the book you are holding in your hands, revised for this new format. It is the first of several planned volumes which will offer a continuous history of philosophy, which will be distinctive in paying attention to less commonly explored figures and movements. In this volume I cover several topics you wouldn't expect to encounter even if you studied philosophy intensely at university level: some of Plato's less popular dialogues, for instance, and the Hippocratic corpus. This will be even more obvious in the next volume, when I will look at relatively obscure movements in Hellenistic philosophy like the Cyrenaics. I hope that I've managed not just to include these "minor" topics but to make them accessible for a broad readership, and show their historical and philosophical interest. My goal in this series of books, then, is to tell the *whole* history of philosophy, in an entertaining but not over-simplified way.

We philosophers like to define our terms before we begin, so let me start by explaining what I mean when I talk about the "whole history of philosophy." Let's start with the word "whole." Ultimately my hope is that the series will deal not only with "Western" philosophy (to use a designation I don't particularly like) but also the philosophical traditions of India and China. As already mentioned, philosophy in the Islamic world, a subject dear to my own heart, will also be covered. But of course, dealing with any of these traditions "without any gaps" is doomed to remain more an aspiration than a promise. Some readers may occasionally feel that I've left out a figure or an idea deserving of mention or even lengthy discussion. The point of the "without any gaps" approach is more to avoid skipping from highlight to highlight, the way a lot of university courses on history of philosophy have to do—where one jumps straight from, say, Aristotle to Descartes, vaulting over a gap of two thousand years or so. Rather, I want to show how each thinker built on those who came earlier, while also striking out in new directions.

That brings me to the word "history." Obviously the history of philosophy isn't quite like other areas of history. It is not mostly about events, when and why they happened, and which important people were involved. Nor is it the sort of history that paints a picture of another time, maybe by focusing on people who weren't so important—peasants instead of potentates. On the other hand, the historian of philosophy can't ignore these things. We're going to see that political, social, and religious forces had a lot to do with the way philosophy progressed, and even the fact that philosophy could happen at all. It's an obvious, but easily overlooked, fact: philosophy occurs only in a society that can produce philosophers. Usually this has meant that philosophy happened in close proximity to wealth and power. It's naive to think that philosophy can be practiced, and preserved, without some degree of economic and political stability and support. Yet it's cynical to think that philosophy is never anything more than an expression of political and economic power.

For the period we'll be studying in this volume, historical forces didn't only help to determine who the philosophers were and what they thought. They also determined whether and how their ideas reached us. For most of the time between the ancient Greeks and ourselves, it was extremely laborious, and therefore expensive, to transmit philosophical writings: they had to be copied by hand. We know about Greek ancient philosophy only thanks to manuscripts written in the medieval period—a "manuscript" being, as the word literally says, a text that is handwritten. In order for us to read the earliest works of philosophy from the Western tradition, texts needed to be copied and re-copied over many generations. Even this process has given us only indirect access to the ideas put forward in the sixth century BC, by a man who has some claim to be the first philosopher and is at any rate going to be the first thinker covered in this volume: Thales of Miletus.

But before we get to him, a few remarks about the last word in the title "history of philosophy." (I'm assuming you will have no trouble with the word "of.") The question of what "philosophy" is, is of course itself a philosophical question. It is a question that has been answered differently in different ages. As we'll be seeing, the ancient understanding of philosophy was rather more broad than ours, and included many disciplines we now think of as "science." Hence this book contains, for instance, chapters on how the medical tradition related to philosophy, and on Aristotle's contributions to zoology. This too is part of what I mean by telling the history of philosophy without any gaps. Beyond that, the best way I can tell you what philosophy is, or has been at various times in the past, is to invite you to read this book and subsequent volumes in the series as they appear—but not to stop there. My hope is to whet your appetite for ancient philosophy, and to inspire you to read (or re-read) Plato, Aristotle, and the rest. At the end of the book I've given some advice on further reading, in which I recommend quite a bit of scholarly literature. Still, I would much rather you went and read the works of these ancient thinkers. You might, in fact, think of this volume as being akin to a guidebook to a foreign country. You probably wouldn't read a guidebook to Munich without intending to visit Munich. Likewise, this volume is intended as a guide and invitation for those who want to explore the history of philosophy, without any gaps.

ACKNOWLEDGEMENTS

This book, and the podcast series on which it is based, have been assisted by a number of benefactors. The podcasts received financial support from King's College, London, the Leverhulme Trust, and most recently the LMU in Munich. A number of friends and colleagues also appeared in the series for interviews; guests who spoke to me about classical Greek philosophy were Hugh Benson, Fiona Leigh, M. M. McCabe, Malcolm Schofield, Dominic Scott, Frisbee Sheffield, Richard Sorabji, and Raphael Woolf. I would encourage the reader to listen to the interviews, which provide a range of perspectives on this material additional, or alternative, to the ones I'm presenting in this book. The interviews are available online at <www.historyofphilosophy.net>.

Special thanks are due to an anonymous reader for OUP, and to Dirk Baltzly and Fiona Leigh, all of whom made extremely useful comments on the manuscript. Plato's *Sophist* was covered in the podcast series by an interview with Fiona Leigh. My thanks to her for persuading me to write a new chapter on the *Sophist* for the book version, and similarly to Sandrine Berges for suggesting the idea of adding a chapter on women in ancient philosophy.

I am also grateful to the following people who helped enormously with the production of the podcasts, book, or both: Fay Edwards, Stefan Hagel, Hugh Havranek, Falk Hilber, Andreas Lammer, Dominik Lehmann, Rory O'Connell, Richard Palmer, Julien Rimmer, Ian Rossenrode, and Brett Trewern. I also got supportive and constructively critical comments from many podcast listeners. Thanks are due also to Peter Momtchiloff of Oxford University Press for his encouragement to produce this book, and to Jeff New for his help with the editing. I must also mention the constantly stimulating atmosphere for the study of ancient philosophy I've been fortunate to enjoy, first, in my former home London, and now at the LMU in Munich. There are too many people to mention in this regard, but for London I should at least again name Fiona Leigh, M. M. McCabe, Frisbee Sheffield, Richard Sorabji, and Raphael Woolf, as well as Charles Burnett, Ursula Coope, Verity Harte, John Sellars, the late Bob Sharples, and Anne Sheppard. Now in Munich I have the privilege and pleasure of working with Oliver Primavesi and Christof Rapp.

Finally, there is my greatest debt, which is to my family: my brother, fellow podcaster and faithful listener Glenn Adamson; my supportive parents and grandfather; and above all the people who have to share me with philosophy, my wife Ursula and my daughters Sophia and Johanna. This book is dedicated to the two of them, in the hope that they will want to read it a few years from now.

A NOTE ON REFERENCES

B asic references to the primary texts are included within the chapters. For the chapters on the Pre-Socratics, the citations within the text (marked with §) refer to sections of G. S. Kirk, J. E. Raven, and M. Schofield, *The Presocratic Philosophers* (Cambridge: Cambridge University Press, 1983). The page references to Plato and Aristotle are standard. They allude to pages in early printed editions, and are called "Stephanus pages" in Plato's case and "Bekker numbers" for Aristotle. Thus the citations should help you find the relevant passage in any edition or translation of their works. For English translations of the Hippocratic corpus and the Sophists, see the first footnote in the relevant chapters.

A guide to further reading is found at the back of the volume. In the notes to the chapters I have also given occasional indications of key scholarly disputes over the interpretation of these antique thinkers. In these cases I provide relatively abundant citations of scholarly literature. These are just meant to be examples, to alert the reader that there are such controversies, and that the views I present here are themselves controversial. (Pretty much anything you say about a thinker like Heraclitus, Parmenides, or Plato will be controversial.) These references are thus not intended as anything like an exhaustive survey of relevant secondary literature. My hope is that they may nonetheless be useful for some readers, for instance students who want to write a paper about the topic in question. For other readers they can safely be ignored (well, you could *safely* ignore the whole book, to be honest, but please don't).

DATES

All dates given here are BC. The abbreviation "fl." stands for *floruit*, "flourished," i.e. probably wrote at about that time, while "ca." stands for *circa*, "approximately."

Philosophers and other authors		Selected events in ancient history	
		Dorian invasion, emigration to Ionia	ca. 1050
		Poems of Homer	8th century?
		Poems of Hesiod	8th century?
Thales	fl. early 6th century		
Anaximander	fl. ca. 580–570		
		Peisistratus and sons tyrants of Athens	560–514
		Death of Solon	558
Anaximenes	fl. ca. 550		
Xenophanes	fl. ca. 540		
Themistoclea	fl. mid-6th century		
Pythagoras	fl. ca. 540		
Theano	fl. ca. 540		
Heraclitus	fl. ca. 500	Greco-Persian wars	499–449
		Ionian revolt against Persia	499
		Defeat of Ionians	494
		Defeat of Persians in battle of Marathon	490
Parmenides	fl. ca. 480	Battles of Thermopylae and Salamis	480
		Founding of Delian League	477
Zeno of Elea	fl. ca. 460	Death of Themistocles	459
Anaxagoras	fl. ca. 460	Aeschylus' *Oresteia*	458
Melissus	fl. ca. 450		
Empedocles	fl. ca. 450		
Leucippus	fl. ca. 440	Pericles becomes general in Athens	443
Aspasia	fl. ca. 440		

Protagoras	fl. ca. 440		
Democritus	fl. ca. 430	Peloponnesian War	431–404
Philolaus of Croton	fl. ca. 430		
Diogenes of Apollonia	fl. ca. 430		
Gorgias	fl. ca. 430	Death of Pericles	429
Herodotus	died ca. 425	Sophocles' *Oedipus Rex*	428
Prodicus	fl. ca. 420	Aristophanes' *Clouds*	423
Hippias	fl. ca. 420	Most of Hippocratic corpus written	ca. 420–350
		Euripides' *Trojan Women*	415
		Sicilian expedition of Athens	415–413
Euthydemus	fl. ca. 410		
		Reign of Dionysius I in Syracuse	405–367
		Death of Alcibiades	404
		Thirty Tyrants in Athens	404–3
		Restoration of democracy in Athens	403
Phyntis	fl. ca. 400	March of the Ten Thousand	401–399
		Writing of *Double Arguments*	ca. 400
Socrates	469–399	Trial and execution of Socrates	399
Thucydides	died ca. 395		
Gorgias	483–375		
Archytas	ca. 420–350		
Xenophon	ca. 430–350		
Plato	429–347		
Eudoxus	ca. 390–340		
Speusippus	ca. 410–340		
Isocrates	436–338		
Arete of Cyrene	fl. 350		
Aristotle	384–322	Reign of Philip of Macedon	359–336
Xenocrates	395–313	Death of Dion in Syracuse	354
Theophrastus	ca. 370–286	Alexander the Great	356–323

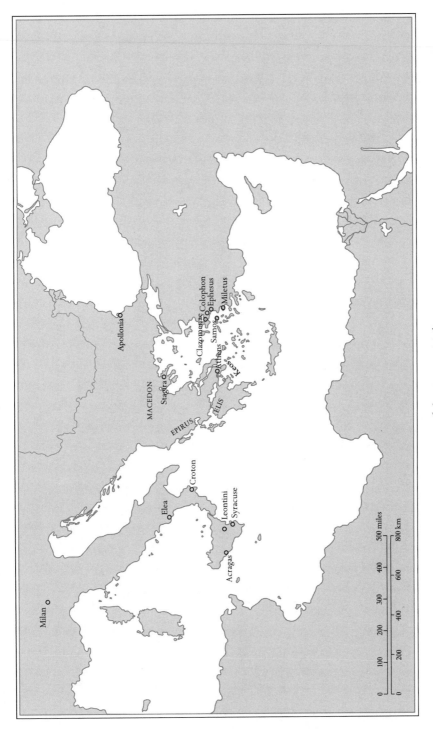

Map of the Ancient Mediterranean

PART I

EARLY GREEK
PHILOSOPHY

1

EVERYTHING IS FULL
OF GODS
THALES

O ur story begins in the sixth century BC, and not, you might be surprised to hear, in Greece. The first ancient philosophy was written in Greek, but in the territory called Ionia, on the western coast of modern-day Turkey. You would reach it if you started in Greece and went around or across the Aegean Sea, towards the east. Which is exactly what Greek-speaking peoples had done well before the sixth century BC. The ancient Greek historians tell us that in about 1100 BC, in response to an invasion of mainland Greece by a people they called the Dorians, many inhabitants of mainland Greece crossed over to Ionia. That name, Ionia, comes from a legendary leader of the colonists, Ion. These refugees set up a number of colonies, some of which became extremely successful. One of the earliest colonies was Miletus, the city Thales called his home. It was founded by a group who came from around Athens, the future home of Plato and Aristotle and one of the few places in mainland Greece not to fall to the Dorians. At least that's what the ancient historians tell us, and the claim is supported by similarities between the Ionian dialect and the dialect they spoke near Athens— called "Attic" Greek, Attica being the area surrounding Athens.

Miletus was a rich and successful city. Just like Australia in the nineteenth century, Miletus went from colony to independent economic power on the back of sheep: their wool was exported across the Mediterranean. Miletus and other Ionian cities became wealthy enough to found colonies of their own, as far away as Italy, but also around the Black Sea, which was an area of strength for the Milesians in particular. Miletus was fairly far south in Ionia, and their location and success as traders meant that someone living in Miletus could easily be exposed to ideas and people from further inland to the east, and from Egypt. So it's always been tempting to say that Thales and the other Milesian thinkers got some of their ideas from Eastern or Egyptian traditions. For instance, Thales was famous for having predicted a solar eclipse in 585 BC (§74), and if he really did that he may have been using Babylonian astronomical tables to pull off the trick. There's also some evidence that Thales went to Egypt in person (§68).

Miletus, then, was a good place to be in the early sixth century BC if you wanted to become the first ever philosopher. But even Miletus wasn't the sort of town where you could just relax and gaze at the stars, trying to figure out when the next eclipse might be coming along. It would be a while before a Greek author would describe full-time contemplation as anything like an ideal or desirable life. On this point Aristotle makes particularly good reading for us philosophers. He explains that we are not, contrary to appearances, just leeching off society when we sit around reading books and having ideas. To the contrary, we are the highest achievers, the ones who realize human potential most fully. But a life of pure speculation was not Thales' style anyway, or so it would seem. He was no detached contemplator, more of an all-purpose wise man. In fact he was named as one of the so-called "Seven Sages" of the early period of Greece. (Another one of the Seven whose name is still remembered nowadays is Solon, who set down many of the laws governing Athens.) Thales' political engagement is best shown by a report that he urged a political union between all the Ionian cities so that they could resist their neighbors to the east, a policy which, had it been adopted, might have enabled the cities to remain independent for longer than they did (§65). In fact, only a few decades after the time of Thales, Miletus and other Ionian cities fell under the dominion of the Persians.

More fun, and also showing a practical turn of mind, is the story about Thales and the olive-presses (§73). Supposedly, Thales' knowledge of weather conditions enabled him to predict a bumper crop of olives in the coming season. He went around and cornered the market on olive-presses, so that he could make a fortune when the predicted crop came in and everyone needed to turn their olives into oil. On the other hand, Plato tells a story about Thales walking along looking at the sky, and falling into a well because he isn't watching where he's going (§72). Conveniently for the anecdote there's a servant-woman on hand to laugh at him, underscoring the point that philosophers don't notice the world at their feet because they're so busy looking at the sky. Since I myself am capable of smashing my toe into a stone step while trying to go into a house and read a book at the same time, I have a lot of sympathy for the Thales who fell down a well. But the evidence we have suggests we should instead imagine Thales as a well-rounded fellow, engaged with the world around him as well as with the nature of the world as a whole.

What kind of evidence do we have about him, then? Thales and the other earliest Greek thinkers are called the "Pre-Socratics": the ones who lived before Socrates, even though, as we'll see, some so-called "Pre-Socratics" actually lived at about the same time as Socrates. For this reason, and because it seems a bit rude to label these thinkers with reference to a future philosopher, I have titled this section of the book

"Early Greek Philosophy." This expression seems to be gaining ground in scholarly works on the subject. Still, for ease of expression I'll mostly use the still-common phrase "Pre-Socratics" to refer to the early Greek thinkers.

For all of these figures, our knowledge is really based on nothing more than tantalizing scraps. People who work in the field call these scraps "fragments." But even this makes the situation sound better than it usually is. What we've actually got is works by later ancient authors—or rather copies of copies of works by later ancient authors—who tell us something about, say, Thales or Heraclitus. Occasionally we're in luck and they quote the early Greek thinkers verbatim, or even better, *say* they are going to quote them verbatim and then do so. Some of these thinkers wrote in poetic verse, which has meter—this, of course makes it much easier to tell if it is a direct quote. But often, what we've got is a much later thinker telling us what an early thinker thought, and we have to decide for ourselves how close this might be to the original wording or idea. Technically these paraphrase reports are called testimonies rather than fragments. But it isn't always easy to tell the difference.

Even if you are lucky enough to have an authentic fragment, it isn't necessarily obvious where the useful information starts and stops. One of our richest sources for the Pre-Socratics is Aristotle, and he has a tendency to mix reports of what they thought with educated guesses about what else they must have thought, and why they thought what they thought. Furthermore, he's almost always forcing the Pre-Socratics into the framework of his own theories, trying to make his predecessors look like they were groping towards the sublime insights of Aristotle himself. Some of what I've already mentioned shows the problems we're facing here: that story about falling in the well is a nice story, but maybe it's a little *too* nice. It sounds more like an amusing anecdote that's been assigned to Thales because he's a famous philosopher, the way witty remarks get ascribed to Oscar Wilde or Dorothy Parker even though they didn't say them. In the case of Thales, the problem is particularly difficult, and I should admit before we go any further that almost nothing can be said about him for sure. But we'll do the best with what we've got.

Some of the things I've already mentioned give a flavor of one major dimension of his achievement: he was a scientist, in something like the sense we would use the term. If we know anything about him for certain it's that he was interested in astronomy. The story about the olive-presses also shows that Thales had expertise in what we would call the physical sciences, or at least had a reputation for having that expertise. This is confirmed by other evidence. There's a story about him diverting a river into two branches so that it would be possible to cross it—because each of the two branches would be shallower than the single river (§66). And although Thales may in fact have written nothing at all, some sources tell us that he did write a book about navigation at sea. All this is typical of early Greek philosophy, and in fact of philosophy right up until the modern period. As I mentioned in the Preface, the tendency to separate philosophy from what we call "science" is a recent phenomenon, and certainly not one most Greek thinkers would have recognized.

So this is one reason to say that Thales was the first "philosopher": he was the first person to gain a reputation for the sort of independent analysis of nature we describe as "scientific." For this reason it's traditional to describe Thales and the other Pre-Socratics as being rational, as opposed to the presumably irrational culture that went before them. But this is not a very useful way of looking at it. The main texts we have to illustrate Greek cultural beliefs before the time of Thales are the works of Homer and Hesiod. Homer's *Iliad* and *Odyssey* would in fact have been, already for the Pre-Socratics, the greatest touchstones of Greek culture. In the ancient Greek world they played the sort of role that the Bible did in medieval Europe, and that Shakespeare does for us—or used to when people knew their Shakespeare. Clearly the *Iliad* and *Odyssey* aren't philosophical texts, but neither is Homer *irrational*. The *Iliad* is, among other things, a reflection on the sources and consequences of (as it says in the first line) the wrath of Achilles. Indeed, you could argue that Homer has a greater insight into cause and effect in the human sphere than most Pre-Socratics have into the cause and effect of the world around us. The fact that Homer often invokes the agency of a god or goddess to explain what is happening in the Trojan War or Odysseus' long voyage home only counts as irrational if you think it's irrational to believe in the gods.

Closer to the aim of Pre-Socratic philosophy is Hesiod's *Theogony*, a poem setting out stories about the origins and natures of the gods, probably in part by collecting previous material. Some of this looks more or less explicitly cosmological, in a way that is not too distant from the kind of Pre-Socratic cosmology we'll be talking about over the coming chapters. Sure, Hesiod equates his gods and goddesses to his cosmological principles—the Greek word *ouranos* means "heaven" and is also the name of a god in Hesiod, for instance. But again, it's hard to make a good case for Hesiod being "irrational." He's laying out a theology, and that theology is at least meant to be consistent and explain something, or even explain everything. If you think theology can't be rational, just wait until we get to Aquinas.

I think a better way of understanding the Pre-Socratics would be to say that their views were, at least implicitly, grounded in *arguments*. This, to me, is the difference between early Greek philosophy and other early Greek cultural productions. We mostly have too little evidence about Thales to reconstruct the arguments that gave rise to his views, but Aristotle was probably right to try to reconstruct arguments of some sort or another. We can follow his example by turning finally to Thales' few attested philosophical claims. The best known is that he thought water was really, really important. It's a little unclear, unfortunately, in what way exactly he thought water was important. Aristotle tells us that Thales believed the world floats upon water, like a piece of wood (§84). Here we seem to have a cosmological view that would be at home in a non-philosophical religious or theological tradition: the heaven, as even Homer says, is like a dome above us, and the world is a disc floating upon the sea under that dome.

However, Aristotle tells us something else about Thales and water: he thought that water was a cosmic *principle*. Here Thales may well have been anticipating arguments that would be made by his immediate successors. As we'll see very soon, various Pre-Socratics thought that the materials the world is made of were formed out of the condensation or rarefaction of other materials. So perhaps Thales, observing the importance of water for life in plants, animals, and humans, or the earthy residue left after water evaporates into air, decided that in the first instance everything comes from water. Now, probably you are not thinking, "My God, he's right, everything *does* come from water!" But if Thales got to his water principle in this kind of way, then at least it would show him giving a novel explanation of the cosmos, and using a process of argument to get to that explanation. Whether, as Aristotle implies, Thales also thought everything is literally *made* of water seems more doubtful (§85). To think this he would have to have believed that something like rock, which seems eminently dry and solid, in fact consisted of water. And there is no reason to believe he attempted such an account, though an explanation like this would be given not much later by another philosopher from the same city, Anaximenes.

Another philosophical claim ascribed to Thales is that a magnet has a soul, and so does amber (§§89–90). (When you rub amber, it attracts things just as a magnet does; this is due to static electricity.) What sense can we make of this? Well, Aristotle tells us about Thales and the magnet in the process of asserting that all philosophers associate soul with motion. Aristotle may be right to say that Thales was already onto this point: there must be soul in a magnet, otherwise it could not initiate the motion that pulls it and a piece of iron towards one another. Aristotle tells us also that, according to Thales, "all things are full of gods" (§91). This is a classic bit of Pre-Socratic philosophy, philosophy in the form of a catchphrase. As we'll see, Heraclitus is the master at this style of philosophy. But let's take seriously the claim that all things are full of gods, by putting it together with the other idea about magnets. What you get is a nice little argument, which would go something like this: everything is full of gods, and I'll show you this using the example of the magnet.

It seems to be lifeless, but it must have soul, because it can initiate motion. So by extension, you should at least be open to the idea that everything has soul, which is divine. That's obviously doing a lot of Thales' work for him, by combining two fragments and filling in the gaps. But that, as I hope you'll come to agree over the following chapters, is what makes the Pre-Socratics so much fun.

2

INFINITY AND BEYOND
ANAXIMANDER AND ANAXIMENES

Thales was not the only Pre-Socratic thinker to hail from Miletus. He was followed by two thinkers with wonderful, albeit confusingly similar, names: Anaximander and Anaximenes. We know a bit more about them than we do about Thales, but don't get your hopes up too high: our evidence about them is pretty thin. I have already mentioned how amazing it is that information about these earliest Greek philosophers has reached us at all. Maybe it's worth dwelling on this just a bit longer. Remember, these figures lived in the sixth century BC. To get some idea of how much time has elapsed since the birth of philosophy, take someone else who lived a long time ago: Charlemagne, the conqueror who founded the Holy Roman Empire. He was born in the mid-eighth century AD, which is early in the medieval period. But that still puts him slightly closer to us in time than to the birth-date of Thales. Even for ancient philosophers like Aristotle, Thales and his immediate successors were far enough in the past that it was hard to know much about them. So we should really marvel that we, more than two millenia after Aristotle, know anything about the earliest Greek philosophers at all.

Even if Aristotle wasn't necessarily all that well informed about the first Pre-Socratics, he is still one of our most important sources of information about them. Another main source is Aristotle's student Theophrastus, who made it his business to collect and interpret bits of information about the history of philosophy up until his time. This is the sort of thing Aristotle and his followers loved to do: they were great collectors of information, and threw themselves into it zealously, whether they were dissecting shellfish or trying to piece together the ideas of someone like Anaximander. Unfortunately there are a couple of pitfalls for us here. In the last chapter, I mentioned that Aristotle often recast Pre-Socratic ideas in terms of his own ideas and vocabulary. A good example is the first book of the *Physics*, in which Aristotle tries to classify a whole range of Pre-Socratic thinkers in terms of how many "principles of nature" they recognized. As you would expect, given that he was Aristotle's student, Theophrastus seems to have followed Aristotle in this respect.

A second problem is that Theophrastus' own works, like the writings of the Pre-Socratics themselves, are mostly lost. Apart from Aristotle, the most useful surviving reports on the Pre-Socratics come from late antiquity. Like Aristotle and Theophrastus, the late ancient reporters were rarely interested in neutral presentation of Pre-Socratic theories. Certain very informative works known as "doxographies" itemize the characteristic doctrines of these long-dead thinkers, drawing in part on Theophrastus. These follow the Aristotelian tendency to force the Pre-Socratics into schematic contrasts and systems.[1] Other important sources include late ancient Platonists, especially Simplicius, a commentator on Aristotle who lived in the sixth century AD, and the Church Fathers. Simplicius does have some philosophical axes of his own to grind, but is unusually interested in accurate reporting of "the ancients" because he worries that information about them is becoming increasingly difficult to find already in his own day. Predictably, the Christian Fathers have a somewhat less positive attitude towards these long-dead pagan thinkers. The upshot is that, when we read through a collection of testimonies and fragments from the Pre-Socratics, we are nearly always seeing them filtered through multiple layers of interpretation and distortion. The task of reconstructing Pre-Socratic thought is beginning to look pretty daunting.

Despite all this, as I say, we do know more about Anaximander and Anaximenes than we do about Thales. The tradition claims that Anaximander was actually Thales' student, and Anaximenes was then Anaximander's. We don't need to take this too seriously, because ancient authors loved to construct chains of teacher–student relationships whether they existed or not. All you really need to know is that Anaximander was just a bit younger than Thales, and that Anaximenes was the generation after that. So let's tackle Anaximander first. Like Thales, he could claim some expertise in physical science: he's credited with setting up a *gnomon*, a device like a sundial, in Sparta back in mainland Greece (§94). Remember that Miletus is on the western coast of what is nowadays Turkey, so it's notable that he would have traveled from there as far as Sparta. Another scientific achievement was his production of a map which showed, we are told, both the earth and the sea (§§98–100). This would have been an appropriate activity for someone from Miletus, which as we've seen was a vibrant economic center with trading connections all over the Mediterranean and up into the Black Sea area.

Anaximander is best known for saying that the principle of all things is what he called "the infinite." The word in Greek is *apeiron*, which means, literally, "that which has no limit." Several different English words have been used to translate this: not only "infinite," but also "boundless," "unlimited," and "indefinite." These different translations bring out different connotations which really do apply to

Anaximander's principle. He did apparently think that the *apeiron* was infinitely *big*, in other words, that it stretched out in space indefinitely far, and surrounds the cosmos in which we live. And we also know that he thought it was eternal—so, infinite in time as well as space. On the other hand, Theophrastus thought it was important to contrast Anaximander to Thales, by saying that whereas Thales' principle was water, Anaximander's principle was nothing in particular: it was, in other words, *indefinite*, having no one nature. Rather, Anaximander said, things with definite nature like air or fire were, as he put it, "separated out" from the *apeiron* (§§104, 119).

This takes us to a rather exciting moment, which is the opportunity to quote the first substantial surviving fragment from Pre-Socratic philosophy. It was reported by Theophrastus, and then preserved by Simplicius, the aforementioned commentator on Aristotle. Here it is: things come to be and are destroyed, Anaximander said, "according to necessity. For they mete out penalty and retribution to one another for injustice, according to the ordering of time" (§§101, 110). After citing this, Simplicius adds that Anaximander was expressing himself rather poetically, even though he was writing in prose and not verse. The fragment isn't a lot to work with, and in fact it's not even certain how it is supposed to relate to the principle called the infinite or indefinite. But taking up the idea of "separating off," what interpreters tend to think is that the different substances separated out of the *apeiron* generate and destroy each other, and that over the long haul this process balances out, so as to restore what Anaximander calls "justice." The idea about the "ordering of time" might suggest that this all happens according to some kind of cycle, which is a popular idea in early Greek thought, and found also in Hesiod.

We can make this a bit more concrete by looking at further evidence about Anaximander, which again comes ultimately from Theophrastus (§121). This evidence bears on the way Anaximander thought the world around us was formed, and in particular how the sky and heavenly bodies come about. He said that, through a process which is unfortunately rather obscure, a ball of fire came to exist around the air surrounding the earth. This ball of fire surrounded the air, Anaximander said, like bark surrounding a tree. The flame then burst apart into rings or circles, which were again enveloped in some kind of air or mist. Round holes in the mist allow us to see the circles of fire, but only partially: and these circular glimpses of the fire are the heavenly bodies. The moon waxes and wanes because the holes in the mist are closing and opening.

Now, this is clearly pretty cool, but how does it relate to the business about the infinite, and things being separated, paying retribution to one another, and all that? Well, the report I've just been describing starts by saying that in Anaximander's scheme something separates hot and cold out from the eternal—the eternal is presumably his first principle, the *apeiron*. The cold part is probably the air or mist, and the hot part is obviously going to be the fire. Notice how they then interact with one another, the mist first being hugged tight by the fire, like the bark on a tree, and then shrouding the rings of flame out in the heavens. All of this suggests that Anaximander was fascinated by the opposed forces we see in nature around us. These countervailing forces, which are things like mist and flame, with opposing characteristics, are what pay retribution to one another. The infinite is indefinite—it has no characteristics that could be opposed to one another. But it is somehow the source of what does enter into opposition. And, because it is infinite in the sense of being inexhaustible, the process of mutual opposition will never cease.

This theme of constant and dynamic opposition, which takes place against the background of an underlying unity, is one of the most enduring features of Pre-Socratic philosophy. We'll find it most strikingly in Heraclitus, but the same idea will appear too in Empedocles and Anaxagoras. Even Aristotle will try to explain nature in terms of opposition and unity. Also typically Pre-Socratic is the attempt to explain something huge and complicated—in fact, the whole cosmos—by invoking fundamental constituents and forces. The ambitions of the theory may go further still: some evidence suggests that Anaximander had in mind more than just our cosmos. Theophrastus tells us that in Anaximander's theory it wasn't just stuffs like air and fire that are separated out from the infinite, but also whole worlds (§§113–14). If this is not entirely misleading—and some think it is—then this could mean either an infinite number of worlds like our own, scattered out through the infinity, or it could mean an unending series of cycles for our own cosmos. Both ideas would, again, have resonances in later Pre-Socratic thought.

The notion that at least our own cosmos does operate in cycles is supported by a bit of testimony which says that Anaximander believed our world is drying out, the seas gradually retreating as the sun heats them and turns the moisture into wind (§132). Maybe the idea is that we live within a part of the cosmic cycle where heat is gradually overwhelming what is cold and moist: a sixth-century BC version of global warming. The idea that things were wetter in the distant past would go well with another scrap of information, which preserves what is probably Anaximander's most memorable idea apart from the infinite principle. He claimed that the first animals were gestated inside moisture and then broke out of it, as if through the bark of a tree—he seems to have had a thing about bark, one can't help noticing (§133). He also suggested that man couldn't originally have been the way he is now, since the first generation of children would not have survived (far too helpless).

Rather, they were formed inside of fish, and full-grown adults burst out of them (§135). This shouldn't be taken as some kind of proto-theory of evolution, because there's no idea here that fish gradually become more and more human over many generations. Rather, it looks more like an attempt to take the idea of Thales that all things come from water or moisture and flesh it out, if you'll pardon the pun. (If you won't pardon the pun, this book may not be for you.)

Overall, it looks like Anaximander had a more abstract approach—one is tempted to say, more philosophical approach—than Thales did. His infinite is a conceptual leap, and seems to be derived from pure argument rather than empirical observation. Some have seen another impressively philosophical approach in his explanation of why the earth stays where it does. He thought the earth is a squat cylinder, shaped like a drum, and we live on the flat upper surface (§122). Aristotle tells us that Anaximander then wondered why this cylindrical earth doesn't move around. The reason, he decided, is that the earth is right in the middle of the cosmos. So no direction would be a more appropriate way for it to move than any other (§123). This is interesting because it shows Anaximander demanding that there be a good *reason* for the earth to move in a particular direction, if it is going to move. The mere equivalence of all the directions it could move is enough to keep it in place.

We might have expected things to develop further in this way, getting more abstract and conceptual. Indeed they will, when we get to Heraclitus. However, the very next thinker on our itinerary is Anaximenes, who seems to go in the other direction. He agreed with Anaximander that the principle of everything is infinite, but he was happy to go ahead and identify it with a particular substance: not water this time, but air. It would, however, be wrong to think that Anaximenes was just ignoring his similarly-named predecessor and retrenching to a view like that of Thales. His philosophy actually builds on Anaximander's in at least one important way, by explaining how the different stuffs that make up the cosmos are generated out of one another.

If you start with air, Anaximenes said, you can change it by making it thicker or thinner (§§140–1). When it gets thinner, more diffuse, it gets hotter and becomes fire. But when it gets thicker, it gets colder and becomes wind, then cloud, then water, and finally earth and rocks. Why does he start with air and not fire, the thinnest stuff—or for that matter, rocks, the densest stuff? Three reasons, I'd guess. First, the sources suggest that Anaximenes was impressed by the fluidity of air. So perhaps he selected air as his principle because he wanted to emphasize the dynamism of the natural world, like Anaximander with his constantly opposed forces. Second, a related point: just like Anaximander's *apeiron*, Anaximenes' air is that from which other things are separated out. The nice thing about air, at least on his theory, is that you can either thin it out and make fire, or thicken it and make cold things like water and earth. It is an in-between kind of stuff, and so can be the principle for both hot and cold things. Third, there's the fact that air is invisible, unlike fire, clouds, seas, and rocks. So if there is some infinite, unbounded substance surrounding us in all directions, it must be air. Otherwise we would be able to see it.

Like Thales and Anaximander, Anaximenes wanted to explain the whole cosmos in terms of these basic constituents. He said that the earth we live on is shaped not like a drum, but like a disc (§§150–1). It forms by the aforementioned process of thickening air, and then rides on the air that is still in its original state. The obvious comparison is to a frisbee, although I haven't seen any secondary literature about Pre-Socratic philosophy that is frivolous enough to draw this particular analogy. His earth, then, is held up by the air, the way Thales' earth floats in water like a piece of wood. That similarity is not likely to be a coincidence. Certainly, here Anaximenes was closer to Thales than to Anaximander, since he agreed with the earlier thinker both about the disc-like shape of the earth, and the need for it to be borne up by something. He furthermore said that the stars, planets, sun, and moon are made of fire. In a lovely image, Anaximenes apparently compared them to fiery leaves which are floating up in the airy, boundless heaven (§154). In a more amusing comparison, he said the heavens rotate around the disc of the earth like a felt hat being spun around on somebody's head (§156).

Anaximenes also had something to say about the soul. Unsurprisingly, he said that the soul is made of his favorite stuff: air, which in this case is breath (§160). This idea of the soul as breath, or in Greek *pneuma*—that's where we get the word "pneumatic"—is going to have a long career in later ancient philosophy. It makes a certain amount of sense, given that if an animal stops breathing, it stops living. This also allows Anaximenes to make a comparison between the human body and the body of the cosmos: both are sustained by the most fundamental substance, namely air. Again, this is an idea with a long afterlife. Right down through the medieval period it will be popular to say that the human is a little version of the physical cosmos, literally a microcosm. Though some doubt that Anaximenes was making this point, I find it plausible to believe that he already had something like the idea of man as a microcosm. Before too long Heraclitus will set out a very similar theory, according to which both the soul of man and the principle of the universe are made of the same stuff, in his case fire. Remember that Thales too said that magnets have a soul, possibly because he wanted to argue that the whole physical cosmos is permeated by soul just like we are. So during the early generations of Pre-Socratic philosophy, this parallel between man and the cosmos seems to have been, if you'll pardon another pun, in the air.

Both Anaximander's infinite and Anaximenes' air are characterized as divine (§§108, 144). Anaximander also says that the infinite, as he puts it, "steers" everything. It's not quite clear how it could do so. Perhaps by enforcing the reciprocal justice between the things separated out of it? In any case, it is important to realize that these early Greek thinkers were not giving up entirely on the notion of the divine. Anaximenes in fact is reported to have said that there are gods, just as Greek religion taught, but that these gods too came from air. What we see here is a subtle, but nonetheless pivotally important, feature of Pre-Socratic philosophy: these are thinkers who want to hold onto a sense of religious awe in the face of the dynamically changing cosmos they describe. They are not discarding religion, but rather throwing down a challenge to previous conceptions of the divine. The way they do this is fairly nuanced. But things are about to get a lot less subtle with the next philosopher we'll discuss, Xenophanes. He staged a direct attack on the conception of the gods that we find in Homer and Hesiod. In doing so, he inaugurated a not-always-friendly rivalry between Greek religion and Greek philosophy that will persist right through Plato and Aristotle.

3

CREATED IN OUR IMAGE
XENOPHANES

In Homer's *Iliad*, there's a rather steamy bit in which Hera decides to seduce her husband Zeus. The reason Hera wants to do this is that she's backing the Greek invaders against the Trojans, but Zeus is on the Trojans' side. So in order to help the Greeks, she needs to get Zeus to stop paying attention for a while. And a sure-fire way to get a man's attention is to seduce him. With a little help from Aphrodite, and the god Sleep, whom she bribes by promising to let him marry one of the divine Graces, she persuades Zeus to lie with her, after which he falls into a deep, post-coital snooze. While he's asleep Hector, the Trojans' mightiest warrior, is badly wounded. On waking, Zeus reacts to this as any betrayed husband might, especially if the betrayed husband happened to be Father of the Gods. He says to Hera: "impossible creature, it is surely your vile scheming that has put godlike Hector out of the battle and panicked his army. [You may] soon be the first to feel the benefit of your troublesome mischief, when I flog you with blows of the whip."[1]

Now, you may find it odd to think that the ancient Greeks told racy stories like this about the *gods*: the very same gods that they sacrificed to, prayed to, built temples to. But there are plenty of tales like this. For example, according to Hesiod, Zeus' father Kronos cut off the genitals of Zeus' grandfather Ouranos with a sickle, and then Kronos' mother threw them into the water. It was out of the resulting froth that Aphrodite was born. In another tale Aphrodite and Ares get caught committing adultery. The Greeks found it possible to recount such stories while still finding their gods worthy of worship. Their understanding of the gods found full expression in the poems of Homer and Hesiod: for the Greeks these poems were something close to sacred texts. The philosophers of ancient Greece couldn't avoid engaging with Homer and Hesiod, any more than the philosophers of medieval Europe could have avoided engaging with the Bible. Greek philosophers, however, took a considerably more critical approach to religion than anything we can find in medieval Europe. And none more so than Xenophanes.

Before we get to him, let's look briefly at the gods in Homer, or rather, in one of the two poems ascribed to him, the *Iliad*. I have already complained about how little we know about the Pre-Socratics, and we know even less about Homer. In fact, there isn't even agreement about whether the two poems are the work of a single person, as opposed to compilations that emerged over the course of generations. The *Iliad*, as you probably know already, is the story of the Trojan War, in which the Greeks, led by Agamemnon, lay siege to Troy in order to recover the beautiful Helen, of her-face-is-so-beautiful-it-launched-a-thousand-ships fame. The thousand ships her face launched were the ones carrying the Greeks to Troy.

The *Iliad* covers only a little bit of the Trojan War. As it says in its opening lines, it focuses on the "wrath of Achilles": the story of how Achilles is offended and refuses to fight, leading to a stalemate between the two armies, until his anger is roused and he comes out and kills Hector, the Trojans' main hero. Although the climax is a duel between Hector and Achilles, there are many heroes on both sides, including on the Greek side Odysseus, whose voyage home will be the subject of the *Odyssey*. There are also many side characters who aren't mighty heroes, even an occasional commoner or woman. The aged Priam also gets a good part as a grieving father, after Achilles slays his son Hector and drags him around the city tied to his chariot. But aside from the heroes, the main characters are the gods. The gods are involved whenever anything significant happens to the human characters. We've already had an example of this: Homer shows us that Hera needs to distract Zeus by getting him to go to sleep, so that she can arrange for Hector to be wounded without Zeus' interference.

The overall effect of this, from a philosophical point of view, is that Homer's gods are the explanations of last resort, or even of first resort. Nothing can happen without the gods being involved. At the very least, they need to allow humans to act. More often it seems like human agency is just an extension of divine agency. When the warriors are brave, it's because the gods have put courage into their hearts; when they retreat, it's the gods who have drained away their willingness to fight. On the one hand, this makes the humans seem like mere playthings of the gods. But on the other hand, the Homeric gods are a lot like humans, and not even particularly well-behaved humans. They get angry, they quarrel, they deceive and seduce one another. So one might look at it from the other point of view, and say that the human sphere has been extended to include the ultimate explanatory principles, namely the gods.

Now let's turn to the other main text which tells us about Greek religion before the Pre-Socratics—what you might call Pre-Pre-Socratic belief about the gods. This is by a farmer named Hesiod, from the rustic area of Boeotia in mainland Greece. Hesiod wrote a poem called *Works and Days*, which has a lot to say about farming as well as the gods, though Hesiod also finds time to complain about his lazy jerk of a brother. But the more important text for us is his *Theogony*, which as its title says is a poem about the generation or birth of the gods.[2] After a long opening prayer to the Muses, Hesiod tells us that the first of all things to come into being was the god Chaos, who seems to represent some kind of void or gap between the earth and the underworld. Then comes Gaia. Gaia is the earth, and she gives birth to the god Ouranos, which means "heaven." They mate to produce a whole generation of gods, including Zeus' father, Kronos. This is a theme commonly found in other early religions: the mating of the earth and heaven which produces other cosmic principles.

So far this sounds a bit like some of what we've seen in the Pre-Socratics: Thales says everything comes from water, Anaximenes that it all comes from air, Hesiod that it all comes from Chaos and earth. Of course in Hesiod's story the cosmic principles are gods, but still, he's giving you a cosmology. But there are some big differences between Hesiod and the early philosophers of Miletus. Like the Pre-Socratics, Hesiod is trying to explain things. But the things he tries to explain tend to be rather different. For instance, he tells a story in which Prometheus tricks Zeus into taking the bones and skin of an animal rather than the meat. This is supposed to explain why the Greeks sacrifice animals to the gods, but are allowed to eat the meat rather than offering up the whole animal. This incidentally is a common refrain in Homer: the gods are often pleased or annoyed with our heroes because they do or don't sacrifice properly. But in general, Homer is much more interested in the human sphere than Hesiod is, at least in the *Theogony*. That makes the *Theogony* a more vivid comparison and contrast to our early Pre-Socratic philosophers.

Another important difference between Hesiod and the Pre-Socratics is that Hesiod isn't giving us arguments, even implicitly. Instead he's declaiming, telling an epic tale that will convince with its power and instill awe as well as belief. Despite this, his gods turn out to be much like the gods of Homer. They trick each other, they sleep with each other, they get angry and fight wars. This may strike us as distinctly un-philosophical. But we should remember that all Greek philosophers, from Thales to Neoplatonists in the fifth century AD more than a thousand years later, knew their Homer and Hesiod inside out. These poems were the definitive works of not only religion but also literature and history, in the Greek world. They were a shared culture which bound together Greek civilization. Unsurprisingly, Plato and Aristotle often quote from both Homer and Hesiod, and they are happy to ascribe various philosophical doctrines to these great poets. For instance, in a dialogue called the *Theaetetus* Plato associates Homer with Heraclitus' doctrine that everything is constantly changing. Aristotle, meanwhile, is always pleased if he can quote a line of Homer to illustrate a certain view—it shows that wise people tend to take the view seriously, Homer being the ultimate example of a wise person. This way of treating the poets is disconcerting. Did Plato and Aristotle really not know the difference between poetry and philosophy? As we'll see later in this book, they certainly did, and in fact Plato has quite an axe to grind with Homer. But they were open to the idea that Homer or Hesiod might be addressing some of the same issues as the ones philosophers tackle, even if not in exactly the same way.

It's really this that makes it possible for there to be a clash between the philosophers and the poets. If Homer had only talked about the wrath of Achilles and Odysseus' journey home, if Hesiod had only talked about farming and his useless brother, then Xenophanes would have had no complaints. The reason he went after the poets is that they dealt with a further subject on which Xenophanes had very firm views, namely the gods. Xenophanes was a poet himself, albeit not an author of epic verse. His philosophical fragments are in poetic meter, and our longest fragments from him are from elegies, poems he would probably have performed at banquets. He lived a long time—in one fragment he says that at the time of writing his poem he's 92 years old (§161). This, plus the fact that it's hard to know when he was born, means that he could have been a contemporary of several philosophers we haven't yet discussed, including Heraclitus, who criticized Xenophanes by name. But basically we're looking at a man who lived most of his long life in the sixth century BC. We do know where he was from: Colophon, a coastal city in Asia Minor, on the Mediterranean coast of what is now Turkey. It's a bit further north up the coast from Miletus, where Thales, Anaximander, and Anaximenes lived. Xenophanes seems to have traveled extensively: he went west, as far as Sicily. Some later sources tell us that he went to Elea in mainland Italy, but they might have invented this because they want us to connect Xenophanes with Parmenides, who was from Elea (§§163–4).

Xenophanes represents a new development in Pre-Socratic philosophy, because he's the first explicitly to attack the authority of the poets. Of course the Milesians, the philosophers we've looked at in the previous two chapters, were departing from the poets also, by replacing the gods with more complicated physical accounts of the cosmos. But Xenophanes was the first to really lay into Homer and Hesiod. One of his complaints was something I've already mentioned: the poets say scandalous things about the gods, telling stories of their adultery, thefts, and mutual deception. These gods aren't just *like* humans, they are all *too* human. And no wonder, says Xenophanes in another couple of fragments, because the conception we have of the gods is really a projection of human nature. The poets describe the gods as being born from parents, just like humans; they wear clothes; they talk. In fact, points out Xenophanes, it isn't just the poets. The Ethiopians think that the gods have black skin, like people from Ethiopia, whereas the fair-haired people from Thrace think that the gods have, you guessed it, fair hair (§168). In what may be the first joke in the history of philosophy, albeit a joke with a serious message, Xenophanes sarcastically remarks that if cattle or horses could depict the gods, they would show them looking like cattle or horses (§169).

At first this seems to be the sort of thing a skeptical atheist of modern times might say. God didn't create man in His image, rather we create God in our image. But Xenophanes was no atheist. Rather, he was motivated by respect for the gods, and thought it appalling to say they engaged in adultery and theft, or even wearing clothes. Even in one of his non-philosophical poems, he said poets should devote pious hymns to the gods and not speak of war or the clash between giants and titans, a favorite theme of mythic poetry. So part of Xenophanes' point was plain old moral outrage: depicting Kronos castrating his father isn't appropriately reverential. It's just not sending a good message to all the kids out there. But he also has his own positive conception of God, which he thinks *would* be consistent with divinity and appropriately reverential.

Xenophanes seems to have come up with this conception by reversing the approach of Homer and Hesiod. His God won't be like humans; instead, he'll be as much unlike humans as possible, and better in every way. Unlike us, God needs nothing, despite what the poets would have you believe. So you can stop sacrificing those animals. God doesn't move at all—there's nowhere he needs to go—and maybe he doesn't even have a body. On the other hand, like the Homeric and Hesiodic gods, He is very powerful. In fact He can "shake everything" just by thinking, as Xenophanes puts it (§171); this phrase echoes his nemesis Homer, who says in the *Iliad* that Zeus shakes Olympus. Another fragment of Xenophanes says that God sees, thinks, and hears as a whole—in other words, He does nothing but think and perceive (§172). Perhaps most strikingly of all, Xenophanes says that "God is one among gods and men, incomparable to mortals in body or thought" (§170). This fragment is a little confusing: "God is one among gods"? Is he saying that there is only one God, or one God who is greater than all the other gods? If it's the former, then Xenophanes is abandoning not only the anthropomorphic conception of the gods we find in the poets, but even the idea that there are many gods. We might see this as another move in the direction of simplicity, as we found in the Milesians: they each had their single principle, be it water, air, or the infinite. Xenophanes has his one God.

So what about all the things that the poets explained by referring to their many gods? A nice example is what Xenophanes says about the rainbow. The Greeks had a goddess, named Iris, who was identified with the rainbow. Total rubbish, says

Xenophanes: a rainbow is nothing but a cloud with some colors in it (§178). As for the sun, it's not a god called Helios, it's a bunch of fire that has been gathered together (§175). Here we can see Xenophanes extending the ideas of his Milesian predecessors as a way of replacing the poetic world-view. It's almost irresistible to call his new approach "scientific," because it refers to physical stuff like clouds, rather than gods and goddesses. But again like the Milesians, he hasn't gotten rid of religious sentiment. If anything, he's saying that proper respect for the divine should lead us to adopt his conception of a single God who does nothing but think, and has nothing in common with us apart from this ability to think. But why is God thinking, and not moving or any of the other things we do? Maybe because thinking is the one thing humans can do that is worthy of God. But even here, Xenophanes insists that God is nothing like us: he is incomparable to us both in body *and* in thought. You'll notice, for instance, that we can't shake all things just by thinking about it.

You can only imagine what Xenophanes' contemporaries must have thought about all this. Where does this arrogant dude from Ionia get off, telling us everything we believe about our cherished gods is silly? And certainly Xenophanes, as I've presented him so far, seems, if not arrogant, then at least blessed with tremendous self-confidence. He's taking on the poets, the biggest target around. But other fragments give a different impression. In these fragments he shows that he has a cautious, and maybe even skeptical, attitude towards what humans (including himself) can know. He says that no one really knows about the gods and other things he is telling us about; rather, even if you are lucky enough to *believe* the truth, you won't *know* (§186). This is just as revolutionary as his ideas about God. He's distinguishing between believing something and really knowing it, a distinction which will be tremendously important down the line when we get to Plato, for example. In fact, this is important for philosophy as a whole: the attempt to sort out what we can know from what we merely believe.

But it's not clear exactly what Xenophanes is saying here: what are the things no one can ever know? He's at least claiming that the nature of God, or the gods, is beyond human grasp. In another fragment, in which it looks like he's talking about his own teachings, he says, "let these things be believed, as being *like* the truth" (§187). Where's that tremendous self-confidence now? It seems to have been replaced by a deep modesty about human powers of understanding. The best any of us can do is to find the most plausible and appropriate beliefs. But that doesn't stop Xenophanes from being pretty tough on people who fall short of these most plausible and appropriate beliefs, especially on a topic as important as the divine. We don't *know*, maybe, that God thinks and can shake all things by thinking, but we should *believe* it. Whereas we sure as heck shouldn't believe that God commits adultery.

These themes from Xenophanes are going to reverberate throughout Pre-Socratic philosophy, and also in Plato and Aristotle. Other Pre-Socratics will also distinguish between what we can merely believe and what we actually know; but they'll tend to be a lot more confident about their own views than Xenophanes was. We'll also keep seeing a kind of rivalry between the philosophers and the poets. That's true of Heraclitus, for instance, who we'll get to shortly. Heraclitus insults Hesiod and Xenophanes in the same breath, saying they both show us that learning many things doesn't make you intelligent. But first we'll be turning to another philosopher whom Heraclitus insults in that same passage. This next philosopher will be one whose relationship to traditional Greek religion was much friendlier than Xenophanes'—indeed, he wasn't so much a friend of the gods, as a family member.

4

THE MAN WITH THE GOLDEN THIGH
PYTHAGORAS

Philosophers have always loved mathematics. It's not hard to see why: one of the things philosophers are most interested in is knowledge. We just saw one of the earliest Greek philosophers, Xenophanes, making a contrast between really having knowledge of the truth and having mere beliefs. And if you're looking for a nice, solid example of knowledge, mathematics is just about the best example there is. You don't merely believe that 2 + 2 = 4, you actually *know* it. Or at least, this is what most people think: that mathematics is a kind of gold standard against which other supposed examples of knowledge can be measured.

This way of looking at mathematics goes back to Greek philosophy, even though of course mathematics itself goes back much further. I'm not just talking about counting or adding simple sums, here. The Babylonians and Egyptians were accomplished in the sorts of mathematics required for land-measurement and astronomy. We saw already that Thales, the first Pre-Socratic philosopher, did some astronomy and that he may have got some of his astronomical knowledge from the Egyptians. Pythagoras too, according to legend, traveled to Egypt and may have picked up some knowledge of mathematics there. So mathematics is older than philosophy, but the two have been close companions ever since philosophy came on the scene. Plato is famous for emphasizing the links between philosophy and mathematics. Supposedly he had a sign over the entrance to his Academy, reading: "Let no one enter who has not studied geometry." Although mathematics is one of the few disciplines in which Aristotle was not a pioneering genius, he did get permission to enter the Academy, and he often treats mathematics as a paradigm example of knowledge. We can find similar attitudes much later in Greek philosophy. For instance, Galen, the great doctor of the second century AD, once fended off an attack of skepticism by taking refuge in the certainties of mathematics. His contemporary, the equally great astronomer Ptolemy, says that among the theoretical sciences, mathematics is the only really certain discipline.[1]

But long before Galen and Ptolemy, in fact long before Plato and Aristotle, there was Pythagoras. Pretty much everyone has heard of Pythagoras, if only because of the Pythagorean theorem. I may as well break the news right away: there's no good evidence that Pythagoras himself discovered the Pythagorean theorem. It was, however, known to his followers, the Pythagoreans. That rather sets the tone for the rest of our discussion of Pythagoras. We know a great deal about the tradition of Pythagoreans which takes its name from him, but we know hardly anything about the man himself. Among the Pre-Socratics, all of whom are surrounded by a good deal of misinformation and legend, he stands out as the one figure who is more myth than man. But what a myth! He's credited with being the first to fuse philosophy and mathematics, with being a worker of miracles, being divine or semi-divine, the son of either Apollo or Hermes. The beliefs ascribed to him range from arcane metaphysical and religious ideas, for instance reincarnation, to homely ethical teachings, for instance that you shouldn't eat beans or meat. Typically, there are other ancient texts that say he did eat meat.[2]

But before we get carried away with the myth—and don't worry, we'll be getting carried away shortly, since the myth is too good to pass over in silence—let's start with what we do know about the man. We've seen that the first Pre-Socratics hailed from Miletus, on the coast of Asia Minor in modern-day Turkey. Xenophanes too was from there, but traveled west. The same is true of Pythagoras: we have good evidence that he was from Samos, an island off the same coast (§264). But he too traveled across the Mediterranean, possibly having left his birthplace because he didn't see eye to eye with the local tyrant, Polycrates (§266). The place he's most associated with is therefore not Samos but Croton, a city in southern Italy (§§269–70). In fact ancient authors liked to give him credit for founding a distinctive philosophical tradition, the so-called "Italian school" of philosophy. Here it might be worth mentioning again that Sicily, Italy, and other parts of the western Mediterranean had been settled by Greek colonists in the centuries previous to the emergence of the Pre-Socratics. The Greeks held on in southern Italy for quite a long time, until the Romans finally pushed them out of this region, which they called Magna Graecia. Pythagoras himself would have lived there in the sixth century BC, about two centuries after the settlement of Croton in the late eighth century.[3] But getting really clear about his dates is not an easy matter. We know that both Xenophanes and Heraclitus refer to him by name, meaning that he's a rough contemporary of these thinkers, which is good enough for our purposes.

So there's Pythagoras, in southern Italy, not discovering the Pythagorean theorem. Another thing he was not doing is writing books. In fact, it's striking that Pythagoras and Socrates are, arguably, the most famous philosophers prior to Plato and Aristotle, and yet neither of them wrote anything. Maybe they are so famous precisely *because* they never wrote anything. Socrates, like Pythagoras, became a literary character—a vessel for the ideas and imaginings of other people. And while we like to think we have some reasonably vivid idea of the real Socrates, thanks to Plato and other authors like the historian Xenophon, in the case of Pythagoras we are really just sifting through legends and myths. Not only is Pythagoras quite a bit earlier than Socrates, but his way of doing philosophy—if he did philosophy at all—was a lot less public than Socrates'. Whereas Socrates would walk up to people in the marketplace and harass them by asking them to define virtue, Pythagoras and his young students in Croton supposedly observed a code of silence, to prevent their secret teachings from being divulged to the uninitiated. Of course, maybe that code of silence is just another legend, but the fact remains that we have very little idea what Pythagoras himself said or thought, not only because of a lack of reliable evidence, but because the stray bits of reliable evidence often seem to be deliberately obscure.

To make things worse, these bits of reliable evidence are buried under an avalanche of more dubious evidence from people who thought of themselves as "Pythagoreans." This tradition of Pythagoreanism is one of the most durable in ancient Greek philosophy. It begins, obviously enough, with Pythagoras himself and his immediate followers. There was then a reasonably well-defined Pythagorean movement in the fifth century; and Plato and Aristotle in the fourth century had associates and students who styled themselves as Pythagoreans. Aristotle found this phenomenon interesting enough that he wrote a book about Pythagoras and his followers, but unfortunately this is lost. It's really the fifth-century Pythagoreans, after Pythagoras himself was dead but before Plato comes along, who should get the credit for fusing philosophy with mathematics. Ideas like the harmony of the spheres—the notion that the proportions of the celestial bodies are arranged according to some kind of musical ordering—probably emerged in this period. Still, all ancient authors assume that Pythagoras himself had an intense interest in mathematics, and we may as well go along with this, while remembering that his interest may have been more religious or symbolic than technical.

The ancient authors who talk about early Pythagoreanism build up a probably fictitious contrast between two types of followers of the divine Pythagoras (§280). There are the ones who are interested in the religious and ethical precepts that he laid down, the so-called *acusmata* (§§275–6); and then there are the math geeks. It's in the ethical precepts that we get the instruction, for instance, not to eat beans or meat. Oh, and don't ever touch a white rooster. Did I mention, don't bury corpses wearing woolen clothing? These rules are hard for us to explain, and they weren't much easier for the ancients: various symbolic explanations are given by later authors who are well disposed towards Pythagoreanism. As for the math geeks, these are the Pythagoreans who really interest Plato and Aristotle. They get mentioned in Aristotle's existing works as well as his lost work on the Pythagoreans, which we only know in fragments. These were thinkers who went so far as to say that things in the physical universe are somehow *made* of numbers (§§430–2). Aristotle claims to find this idea barely comprehensible, but if we're feeling generous we might want to see here an anticipation of the modern idea that mathematical concepts are at the foundations of physics. We'll see later that in his dialogue the *Timaeus* Plato suggests that the elements of physical objects are literally made of triangles, which come together to form solid shapes. That is the sort of idea that the Pythagoreans inspired, even if isn't something they thought of themselves.

The mathematically inclined Pythagoreans had a deeply symbolic, maybe even mystical, understanding of number. These were people like Philolaus, from Pythagoras' adopted home Croton. Philolaus and other Pythagoreans made genuine advances in mathematics, but they also used to say things like this: 2 and 3 symbolically represent woman and man, so 5 is the number of marriage, because it is 2 + 3. A particularly important number for them was 10, which among other things is the sum of the first four numbers, which they called the *tetraktys*; in other words, 1 + 2 + 3 + 4 = 10. Aristotle, in fact, tells us that the Pythagoreans thought there must be a heavenly body which is always hidden from us, the so-called "counter-earth," because the visible heavenly bodies including the sun and moon counted 9, but there must be 10 of them because 10 is the most important number (§§446–7).

After Aristotle and Plato's immediate followers the Pythagoreans fade away a bit, but they make a big comeback in the first century BC. At this point we begin to see a powerful tendency to combine Plato's ideas with Pythagorean ideas like number symbolism. This tendency lives on until the end of pagan Greek philosophy, with the tradition we nowadays refer to as "Neoplatonism": we call the late ancient philosophers of the third to sixth centuries BC Neoplatonists because they were followers of Plato, but also had a lot of "new" ideas which modern scholars do not find in Plato. For them one of the biggest influences was the tradition of Pythagoras, whom they saw as an ultimate source of Plato's own ideas. Thus Pythagoras, one of the very earliest Greek thinkers, became one of the most important authorities and intellectual heroes of the Greek thinkers in late antiquity, a full millenium later.

One of the Neoplatonists who most admired Pythagoras was Iamblichus, who lived in the third to fourth century AD. We'll get to him as a philosopher in his own right in a future volume of this series. I mention him now because he wrote a work called *On the Pythagorean Way of Life*, which shows the way Pythagoras was perceived by that much later period of Greek philosophy.[4] By Iamblichus' day the legend of

Pythagoras has blossomed so that he is seen as the definitive sage, able to work miracles and apparently inexhaustible in his wisdom. At one point Iamblichus says that there are three kinds of two-footed beings: birds, humans, and Pythagoras. And well he might, in light of the miraculous events he ascribes to this ancient sage and wonder-worker. (Some were already reported much earlier, for instance by Aristotle.) For example, Pythagoras is said to have had a thigh made of gold, which he once exhibited at Olympia. He's able to see the future, for instance, by predicting an earthquake. He can talk to animals, and even give them instructions: Iamblichus has him confronting a bear who had been attacking people in the local area, and persuading the bear to mind its manners. If that's not enough to impress you, he can also talk to geographical features: both Aristotle and Iamblichus tell us that he was once greeted by a river (§273).

This sort of thing may strike us as somewhat amusing now, but it had a serious purpose at its time. It's been suggested that the Pythagoras legend was emphasized by authors like Iamblichus because they lived in a time when their pagan religious beliefs were under pressure from the rapid spread of Christianity. For a Platonist pagan like Iamblichus, or his teacher Porphyry, who wrote venomous attacks on the Christians, Pythagoras could serve as an ideal holy man to rival Jesus. His piety and religious teachings are emphasized throughout, and we hear Pythagoras' advice about how to behave towards the gods and their temples. For instance, he says you should never visit a temple unless it is the primary reason for your journey; just stopping off at a temple on the way to somewhere else is inappropriate, even if you are walking right by one. On the other hand, Iamblichus most definitely sees Pythagoras as a philosopher. He sees him, in fact, as *the* philosopher: the founder of Iamblichus' own intellectual tradition and even the first man to call himself a *philosophos*, which means "lover of wisdom," *sophia* being the Greek word for wisdom. On this account, Pythagoras was the first to make the love of wisdom into a way of life.

As we might expect, Iamblichus also emphasizes Pythagoras' connections with mathematics, especially music. From very early on in the Pythagorean tradition music and mathematics were intimately related. And no wonder, because the relationships between notes are just examples of mathematical ratios. In fact, you would make a Greek lyre by stretching numerous strings at the same tension: the different lengths of the strings give you the different notes. Iamblichus tells a picturesque story, in which Pythagoras hits upon this insight when he's walking by a blacksmith's shop and hears the hammer beating against the metal, ringing out at different tones. Pythagoras then goes home and experiments with stretching strings on weights, to get the different musical ratios such as the octave. Iamblichus adds the exceedingly implausible idea that Pythagoras actually invented a whole range of musical instruments.

The Pythagoreans believed that the musical harmonies had some kind of affinity with, and effect on, the human soul. Another feat ascribed to Pythagoras—one you can try at home—is using different kinds of music to induce different emotional states. Iamblichus tells how Pythagoras once managed to calm down a ragingly drunk man just by having someone play the right sort of music on a set of pipes. The idea that the soul and its states would somehow resonate to music, if you will, chimes with the idea that the soul itself might be a kind of harmony. This idea is mentioned, but rejected, by both Plato and Aristotle.[5] The theory may seem to us strikingly plausible, in its way. On this view, the soul is not some entity separate from the body, but is rather the attunement or proportion that keeps the body in functioning order. Just as a lyre will play badly, or not at all, if its strings are taken out of the correct harmonic tension, so a body will become defective (for instance, ill) or just die if its attunement is disrupted.

But there's something of a puzzle here. Although in a sense it isn't surprising to see the music-and-mathematics-obsessed Pythagoreans setting forth this sort of theory about the soul, it is almost certainly not the theory of soul Pythagoras himself adopted. For, according to Pythagoras, the soul can leave one body and go on to reside in other bodies, including the bodies of animals (§285).[6] In other words, Pythagoras believed in reincarnation. Part of his legend is that, unlike the rest of us, he was able to remember who he had been in his former lives: for example, he was the chap who killed Patroclus, the bosom companion of Achilles in the Trojan War. But again, there's more here than just legend. I mentioned that Xenophanes refers to Pythagoras by name (§260): he says that Pythagoras heard a puppy whining as it was beaten, and cried out: "Stop, for I recognize that its voice belongs to a friend of mine!" This is a little joke at Pythagoras' expense, one that only makes sense if he was already known to believe in reincarnation.

Perhaps you're not convinced that this counts as philosophy. I guess if you met someone at a party who was convinced that she used to be Marie Antoinette and then, after a trip to the guillotine, a giraffe, you wouldn't think, "Aha! A philosopher." But this theory of reincarnation at least relates to, and maybe even inaugurates, a philosophical theory with a grand lineage: dualism. Dualism is simply the view that the soul and the body are two distinct things. Many dualists draw the further inference that one can therefore exist without the other. This is implied by reincarnation, obviously: the soul survives the death of one body, namely Marie Antoinette's, before entering the next, namely that of a giraffe. Perhaps Pythagoras' view was even stronger—and certainly, later Pythagoreans wanted to interpret him in this stronger way—and he held that the soul and the body are completely different metaphysical entities. They would be more different than, say, your nose and my nose. These are distinct things, and one can exist without the other, but they are the same sort of thing. By contrast, according to most Pythagoreans in ancient philosophy, the soul and the body are utterly different sorts of thing. The soul is immaterial and probably indestructible. The body is material and will inevitably be destroyed. This view is what philosophers usually mean when they use the word "dualism," and it will be defended by many famous philosophers. Plato and Descartes especially leap to mind. In fact there's good reason to think that Plato had Pythagoreanism in mind when he developed his particular version of dualism. So we've taken a big step in the direction of understanding Plato's background, or at least the background of one major theme in his philosophy.

And now, if you'll again pardon a pun, we've come full circle, back to the Pythagoreans' interest in things like circles: numbers, shapes, and all the other objects studied in mathematics. It's no coincidence, I think, that Pythagoreanism is associated both with dualist theories about the soul and with an emphasis on mathematics. The soul postulated by the dualist has a great deal in common with numbers. Both are abstract, immaterial entities and look like they will always exist, assuming they exist at all. How are you going to kill an immaterial soul, or assassinate the number seven? One reason Platonism and Pythagoreanism were able to combine together so easily is that both Plato and the followers of Pythagoras were interested in these stable, immaterial objects. They wanted to get away from the messiness of physical things, with their constant change and their being subject to an infinite number of various features. That certainly isn't the only idea that drives Plato, but it seems to be one of the most important; and it is even more important for later thinkers who see Pythagoras as the inventor of Platonic philosophy, like our friend Iamblichus. In all this, the Pythagoreans are very different from our next thinker, who once remarked that the things he values most are things he can see, hear, and learn about. His name was Heraclitus.

5

OLD MAN RIVER
HERACLITUS

Heraclitus of Ephesus is, you might say, the ultimate Pre-Socratic. He brings together many of the features we associate with Greek philosophy before Socrates, Plato, and Aristotle came along. For instance, most of the thinkers we've looked at so far wanted to reduce the whole cosmos to one fundamental principle: Thales chooses water, Anaximenes chooses air, Anaximander has his more abstract principle, the unlimited. Heraclitus too has his basic element, namely fire. Another example: these thinkers also wanted to explain change and opposition, and once Heraclitus comes along their forays in this direction seem like a mere prologue to his theory of the unity of opposites. But of course, the most obvious fact about the Pre-Socratics is that we read only fragments of their thought. We know them only through intriguing quotations and paraphrases found in later authors. Heraclitus, though, more or less *wrote* in fragments. His body of work is not unlike that of a comedian from the 1950s: it consists mostly of one-liners.

Heraclitus did apparently write a book. Like most of the Pre-Socratics he's credited with having written a work called *On Nature*. That title doesn't mean he was a natural scientist, or only a natural scientist. The Greek word for "nature" is *phusis*, which is where we get the word "physics." As used by these early thinkers it had a very broad meaning. Nature was just everything there was, and that was the topic of the book Heraclitus wrote. In it, he reportedly dealt with the cosmos itself, political questions, and the gods. We have fragments on all these topics. But with one major exception, the fragments we have from Heraclitus don't look like excerpts from a book, really. They look, as I say, like one-liners; like philosophical riddles. For example, "The road up and down is one and the same" (§200). Or, to paraphrase slightly: "Sea-water: healthy for fish, unhealthy for men" (§199). Or the most famous of all, "You can't step into the same river twice" (cf. §214). Often, his sayings involve wordplay. The most obvious example is: "The bow: its name is life, its work is death." This is a pun, which doesn't work in English but does in ancient Greek: the words for bow and life are both spelled *bios*. It is with good reason, then, that the ancients referred to him as "the riddler" or "Heraclitus the obscure." He didn't make himself popular with this sort of philosophy in his home-town of Ephesus, yet another city in Ionia like Miletus, Colophon, and Samos, where our philosophers have come from so far. Unlike his contemporaries in the sixth century, Pythagoras and Xenophanes, Heraclitus didn't travel to the west. It seems he was quite happy to stay in the east and provoke people into deep thought, or more likely just plain annoyance, with his riddles.

As I said, there is one fragment that does look like an excerpt from a book, indeed, like the beginning of his book (§194). Nonetheless, it displays his characteristic penchant for wordplay. In the opening sentence of this fragment, Heraclitus writes: "Of the *logos* which is always men prove not to understand." Here he carefully places the word "always" (*aei*) so that it can be read either with what comes before: the *logos* always is—or with what comes after: men always prove not to understand. (Aristotle notes this as an example of bad Greek writing, because of its ambiguity—not his most insightful moment.) But what is this word "*logos*"? It's a term that is always difficult to translate in Greek philosophical texts; in this case, it's even harder. Basically *logos* means "word," but it expands to mean many other things too, like "account" and "reason," or even "proportion" or "measure." It's where we get all those English words that end in "-ology." For example, "theology" is giving an "account," a *logos*, of "god," *theos*; "anthropology" is giving an "account," a *logos*, of "man," *anthropos*; and we just saw that *bios* means "life," hence our word "biology." So, quite an important word, and it's here in Heraclitus that it first becomes really crucial in philosophical Greek. At the beginning of his book, Heraclitus tells us that the *logos* he speaks of is something nobody understands, even once they've heard it. People go through life blissfully unaware of the *logos*, even though evidence of it is staring them in the face. Which is a shame, because the *logos* Heraclitus is trying to get you to listen to is one that he claims explains absolutely everything; and here he uses that word "nature" or *phusis*. This will be an account of everything there is.

What was contained in this account? Another fragment from early in the book, which has the familiar one-liner form, says, "Hearing not me, but the *logos*, it is wise to agree that all things are one" (§196). A lot of ink has been spilled over this sentence.[1] For one thing, why is he distinguishing between hearing the *logos* and hearing him, Heraclitus? Isn't this his account, his *logos*? Maybe the idea is: we shouldn't believe this because he's saying it, but because it is true. Other explanations have been offered, for example that *logos* doesn't really mean "account" here, in a sense the views being put forward in Heraclitus' book, but rather the proportion that binds together all things so that they turn out to be one. On the other hand, this *logos* needs to be something you can hear or listen to. Actually all these interpretations may have something of the truth. Heraclitus liked to play around with the double-meanings of Greek words, and it seems likely that he had several different aspects of the word *logos* in mind when he wrote this.

What about the other part of this fragment, that we should agree all things are one? This is pretty exciting because it makes Heraclitus the first philosopher to endorse what is called "monism": the idea that everything is, in some sense, a unity. Here Heraclitus is anticipating the theory of Parmenides, the subject of our next chapter. Parmenides, as we'll see, thought that unity is all there is, and he accordingly rejected our experience of the world that tells us there are many things. Heraclitus wasn't going this far, though. Indeed, it's typical of him that he says that all *things*, plural, are one. His idea isn't that reality is one and not multiple; his idea is that reality is both a multiplicity *and* a unity. Heraclitus stresses the unity here because he thinks this is the aspect of reality that tends to escape us. We go through life not hearing the *logos* because our limited vision only takes in one little bit of the world at a time. Heraclitus' philosophy is designed to teach us to see all of nature—everything there is—as one unified whole, but a whole which includes many different things.

And that brings us to Heraclitus' core idea, the so-called "unity of opposites." We've already seen examples of this idea in some of Heraclitus' one-liner riddles. For example, sea-water poisons humans, but fish need it to live. It's the same water, but it has opposite properties. The bow is both "life" (because of its name, *bios*) and death (because of its function, to kill). A similar Heraclitean proverb says that donkeys prefer garbage to gold. The gold is valuable for us whereas garbage has no value for us, but for the donkey things are the other way around. The clearest example is when Heraclitus says the road up is the same as the road down. His point here is not that whether it is the road up or the road down depends on your perspective, namely whether you are headed to the peak of the mountain or to the foothills. Instead, his point is that the same thing really is the road up, and it really is the road down, at the same time. The gold really is both valuable and worthless, as is the garbage. Our different perspectives are relevant only insofar as they cause us to grasp only one of the opposed aspects of each thing. Again, we're not listening to that *logos*. With our limited understanding, we're only aware that we can buy things with gold, need to avoid drinking sea-water, and are walking uphill.

Of course, not everything in the world so obviously unites opposites in this way. But Heraclitus has something else up his sleeve to persuade you, the thing he's most famous for: his attention to the phenomenon of change. One of his nicest sayings is about a popular beverage drunk by the ancient Greeks, made of wine, barley, and cheese. He said that this barley drink stands still, but only when it moves. For an example we're more familiar with, think about a salad vinaigrette: how you have to stir it and then pour it over the salad quickly after stirring it, before the oil separates from the vinegar. The nature of the drink or the dressing depends on the fact that it is in motion, or changing. Like the vinaigrette, the unity of the world consists in what Heraclitus called a constant "war" or "strife" between all things (§211). Maybe we see here why Heraclitus decided to express his philosophy in these mysterious, fragmentary riddles: the truth he was trying to express was itself paradoxical, that stability resides precisely in change, that unity resides precisely in opposition.

This goes against what we're usually told about Heraclitus. The thing people tend to associate with him more than anything else is the idea that everything is always changing and that there *is* no stability, no unity. This version of Heraclitus is epitomized in his most famous statement, "You can't step into the same river twice" (§214).[2] The world is like the river. It doesn't persist, but is constantly flowing; there is only change and nothing ever remains the same from one moment to the next. One nice thing about this interpretation of Heraclitus is that it provides a clear contrast to Parmenides, who thinks that change is an illusion. He thinks this, as we'll see, because all things are one: for change to happen one thing would need to become something else, and there is nothing else. So we'd have Heraclitus, who believes in constant change or flux, and Parmenides, who believes change is impossible. Nice and easy to remember.

I'm all for making things easy to remember, so remember this: the flux interpretation of Heraclitus is wrong, and it's all Plato's fault. It's Plato, in his dialogue the *Theaetetus*, who sets up this neat opposition between the unity theory of Parmenides and the radical flux theory of Heraclitus. He may have been doing so honestly. We know of people who lived in Plato's day who styled themselves as followers of Heraclitus, and did apparently believe in this flux doctrine. One of them was Cratylus, a philosopher after whom Plato named a dialogue, as we'll see. Cratylus is famous for having held that it's impossible to name anything, because it is always changing, flowing away before your eyes. Instead, you can only point. Rather wittily, he tried to outdo Heraclitus by saying that you can't even step into the same river *once*.

But this supposed improvement on Heraclitus shows how badly Cratylus, and perhaps as a result Plato, understood Heraclitus, because Heraclitus *did* believe that there was one and the same river on different occasions. We can see this from a different version of the famous saying, which from its language and point seems more likely to be what Heraclitus actually said (or maybe he said both). In this version he said, "Different waters flow over those who step into the same rivers" (§214). It is the *same* river on different occasions, but with different bits of water each time. This illustrates the point we've already been talking about, the unity of opposites: just like the gold is both valuable and worthless, the river is both the same and different. So maybe he did think that all things were constantly changing, and in flux, while also being the same and stable. This would explain his making war or strife a kind of universal principle. But it leaves standing his idea that all things are one; in fact, it explains *why* he thinks all things are one.

It's perhaps because he was so impressed by change and destruction that Heraclitus chose fire for the fundamental element of his cosmology. In another fragment he says: "All things are exchanged for fire, and fire for all things; like gold for goods and goods for gold" (§219). His idea here is in part that fire will consume things and actually turn them into itself—think of a small blaze engulfing a whole forest and seemingly transforming it into flame, until it is all used up and the conflagration dies out. But Heraclitus thinks it can go the other way too, with fire being turned into water and earth. In fact he sees a fundamental opposition between fire and water. One is transformed into the other, like Anaximenes' air which can become the other elements. We can find a parallel to Heraclitus' image of paying out fire, like gold, in Anaximander's idea that all things pay retribution to one another. Here we have the same basic thought, even if Heraclitus uses an economic analogy instead of a legal one.

Another reason that Heraclitus emphasized fire was, it seems, that he was very impressed by the heavenly bodies and wanted to give them a primary place in his cosmology. He said that the sun, moon, planets, and stars are actually bowls full of fire turned towards us so that we're looking into the bowls (§224). Rather charmingly, he suggested that the reason the moon waxes and wanes each month is because that bowl is slowly turning, so we can only see some of the fire from the side. Thus Heraclitus, despite his obvious interest in the fundamental principles of things, continues the Pre-Socratics' interest in specific phenomena of the natural world, and especially the stars—remember, this goes back to Thales, with his expertise in astronomy. Their interest in the stars isn't so surprising. After all, these philosophers lived in a time before electricity, and hence before light pollution. If you walked outside at night, even within the walls of a big city like Athens, you would see a stunning night sky, with more stars than most Europeans ever get to see nowadays. If anything in the world of the ancient Greeks cried out for explanation, it was the heavens. So: overturned bowls of fire. Why not?

Another area of Heraclitus' philosophy where fire plays a major role is his theory of the human soul. Actually, he thinks that the human soul is just *made* of fire. When we die, it is because our souls have turned into water (§229). The most fiery souls— Heraclitus calls them "drier" souls—are the ones which are wisest (§230). And here's my favorite thing Heraclitus said: we can explain the pathetic behavior of drunk people by the fact that their souls are moist (§231), presumably from the wine they've been drinking. This idea that the soul is made of fire makes more sense than you might at first think. After all, when humans and other animals are alive they are warm, and it's easy to notice that they cool down fast as soon as they die. Heraclitus won't be the last Greek thinker to suggest that the soul has some fiery aspect. He adds—and again this is something later philosophers will agree with—that our breath is closely related to the soul, suggesting even that we take fire in from the cosmos by breathing it in along with the air. This shows that his conception of fire is not just flame, such as you'd see in a fireplace; it's a more abstract conception of some dry, warm, fast-moving stuff that is the most exalted substance in the universe. Notice also how he makes both the stars and our souls fiery, suggesting that we share a nature with the divine heavenly world.

A final aspect of Heraclitus' thought is one that usually doesn't get much emphasis. I mentioned that later sources have him writing on politics, though a mischievous ancient anecdote claims that Heraclitus was approached by the people of his city of Ephesus and asked to write a set of laws for them, as Solon did for Athens. He declined, saying he'd rather play with the town's children. That's actually quite charming, but unfortunately it's not a story with much plausibility. In any case, we don't have a great deal of his political thought, but what we do have emphasizes obedience to the laws of the city: one should protect them as one protects the walls in a siege (§249). He also says that human laws are given sustenance by the laws of the god (§250). Whether this reference to law should be connected to Heraclitus' *logos* and the unity of opposites is not clear, but it's tempting to think that these are the absolute rules of justice which our laws imitate.

A final story about Heraclitus I'd like to mention likewise lacks historical plausibility, but makes up for it by being rather amusing. According to this tale, Heraclitus was so misanthrophic that he eventually withdrew from the city and lived in the hills outside it, subsisting on wild plants. This diet caused him to suffer from a watery build-up, or dropsy, in his body. Returning to town, he riddlingly asked the doctors if they could make a drought out of a rainstorm. They found this bewildering, so Heraclitus took matters into his own hands and went to the stables, where he buried himself in dung in hopes that the heat would sweat out the excess moisture. When this failed, he died (§190). Of course this is a legend, but one that cleverly links together different aspects of Heraclitus' philosophy: the riddles, the severity towards human society, the association of heat with health and life.

In a sense, the legend is then faithful to Heraclitus, who had already forged links between the different parts of philosophy. The ideas we find in the Pre-Socratics belong to areas of philosophy that we now distinguish. It was really Aristotle who first got into the business of distinguishing them. Nowadays it's common, even expected, that a professional philosopher might work only on ethics, for example, or only on the philosophy of mind. Heraclitus, though, had something to say about every philosophical subject, and the different things he had to say all tied together. Indeed, his various sayings are probably meant to resonate with and be read alongside one another. Thus, "Hearing not me, but the *logos*, it is wise to agree that all things are one" should be read alongside the opening line, "Of the *logos* which is always..." A fragment I haven't mentioned yet could almost be taken as a commentary on the pun about "bow" and "life," making more explicit the relevance of the example for the unity of opposites. In this other fragment, Heraclitus remarks that people fail to notice the way things are "brought together" by being "pulled apart," and gives the examples of the lyre and bow, which are held together by being in tension (§209).

So, despite his one-liner puns and emphasis on opposites, Heraclitus' own thought also holds together rather nicely. In this he anticipates the systematic ambitions of Plato and Aristotle, who, for instance, connect the question of what it is to be a human being to the question of how humans should conduct themselves. In other words, for them ethics and the study of human nature are intimately related. As far as we can tell it was Heraclitus, a riddler with his ready-made fragments, who first really begins to indulge in this systematic way of doing philosophy. But in this he is outdone by Parmenides, who offers not one but two systems: the true system, which tells you that everything you think you knew was wrong; and the system which consists of mere opinion, but is still pretty different from what you thought you knew. Parmenides has much more in common with Heraclitus than Plato would have us believe, but there's little doubt that, with him, we are really stepping into a new era of philosophy, which we might call the era of metaphysics. It's an era that still hasn't ended.

6

THE ROAD LESS TRAVELED
PARMENIDES

The systematic and all-encompassing style of philosophy pioneered by Heraclitus, and carried on by Plato and Aristotle, has fallen out of fashion nowadays. Perhaps it's just that philosophy has gotten too big for any one person to pursue as a whole, or that more virtue is nowadays seen in specialization than systematicity. At least in the English-speaking world, philosophers tend to value depth over breadth. And not without good reason, since philosophy is a whole of parts, and each of its parts looks pretty challenging on its own. Of course there are the parts of philosophy that tell us what to do: ethics and political philosophy. Both the word "ethics" and the word "political" come from Greek: in ancient Greek *ethos* means custom or character, and *politike* means, well, "political," because *polis* means "city." The other two main areas of philosophy are epistemology and metaphysics, and you'll never guess where these words come from. Latin! No, just kidding, it's ancient Greek again. Epistemology is from *episteme* meaning "knowledge"; and so epistemology is the study of knowledge. For instance, epistemologists want to know what the difference is between knowledge and mere belief, or whether it is possible to know anything at all.

Metaphysics is a bit stranger in its etymology. It really means "after physics," and many later ancient and medieval philosophers took it that metaphysics is quite literally the discipline one studies after studying physics: you graduate from studying the physical world to studying the "metaphysical" world of immaterial things, like god. Another possible derivation for the word is that Aristotle's book on metaphysics came to be called that because it was studied, or even just placed on the shelf, after his books about physics. In any case, the science of metaphysics is first explicitly marked out by Aristotle in his book of that title, even if it is not a title he gave it. Aristotle calls metaphysics "first philosophy," "first" not because it is the first one you would study, but because it is the most fundamental philosophical inquiry. He tells us that what metaphysics studies is *being*. In other words, it studies whatever there is, insofar as it is. This means that many of the traditional problems of philosophy are metaphysical problems: does God exist? Does the human soul exist? Does anything exist apart from physical bodies? Other topics, like the problem of free will, are usually taken to belong to metaphysics even if they also relate to ethics.

Our next Pre-Socratic thinker, Parmenides, was the first philosopher who we can say had a clear interest in metaphysics, the study of being—the study of what exists. Certainly we do find metaphysical ideas in some of the Pre-Socratics we've already covered, especially Xenophanes with his criticism of the traditional Greek gods. Partly for that reason some ancient authors try to convince us that Xenophanes was Parmenides' teacher. Even though this is possible chronologically, we probably shouldn't take it too seriously, since the ancients were always trying to say that every famous philosopher was the student of some other famous philosopher. Of course, Socrates really was Plato's teacher and Plato really was Aristotle's teacher, which sort of undermines the point I'm trying to make here. So ... maybe I'll just say that this is the exception that proves the rule, whatever that means, and move on.

I just referred to chronology, and that brings us to another thing about Parmenides, which is that he is the first philosopher we'll discuss who was active in the fifth century BC rather than the sixth century BC. Plato wrote a dialogue which depicts an older Parmenides meeting a young Socrates in Athens. That, again, is something we probably shouldn't take too seriously, but unless Plato is really messing with the chronology it means that Parmenides would have been a teenager when the fifth century began. The fifth century was going to be a time of upheaval for the Greeks, what with the Persians trying to invade mainland Greece on more than one occasion, and the two alliances led by Athens and Sparta facing off in the Peloponnesian War, which raged towards the end of the century. But it was going to be a good time for Greek philosophy and science. Not only did this century see the mature careers of both Parmenides and Socrates, but it was also the period when the Pythagoreans built up their mathematical systems, as we discussed already; when Greek medicine really started to get going; and when Empedocles, Anaxagoras, and the atomists developed the ambitious cosmologies which will be occupying us in the next few chapters. This century of philosophy ended with a bang one year late, when Socrates was put to death by the Athenians in 399 BC. By the way, that's a good date to remember, if you are the kind of person who likes to remember dates: 399 BC, the death of Socrates.

Given the chaos and war that was gripping mainland Greece, and the domination of Ionia by client kings of the Persians, it's perhaps unsurprising that in the fifth century BC the philosophical action largely moves west, to Italy and Sicily—although even these places too were dragged into the conflict between Athens and Sparta in the later part of the century. Parmenides and his pupil Zeno were from Elea in Italy, and as we've already seen, Italy was also strongly associated with the Pythagoreans. Empedocles was born and active in Sicily. Anaxagoras is the main exception, since he was from Ionia, like most of the philosophers we've looked at thus far. From there Anaxagoras came to Socrates' city, Athens. In any case, Parmenides was strongly identified with his city of Elea, and his followers were often called the "Eleatics." When Plato created a character in one of his dialogues (the *Sophist*) to represent the Parmenidean approach to philosophy, he called him the "Eleatic Stranger."

But it's hard to get much stranger than the original philosophy of Parmenides himself. Systematic thinkers like Plato and Aristotle may try to persuade us that all of philosophy is one. That's nothing compared to what Parmenides claims: that reality itself is one.[1] Nothing ever changes or moves. Multiplicity of every sort is an illusion, whether it be the multiplicity of different objects, different colors, or different events happening at different times. All this is shown by way of a poem written in hexameter verse, whose first half consists of a relentless chain of argument that proceeds on the basis of pure reason, rather than observations about the world around us. In this first half of his poem Parmenides is the original armchair philosopher: he thinks that he can establish the nature of all reality with a purely abstract argument. In this he makes an interesting contrast to Heraclitus, who in some of his fragments emphasizes that he is using his eyes and ears to observe the world and to learn the laws that govern that world. But Parmenides and Heraclitus do agree about one thing: everyone else apart from them is completely confused, unaware of the nature of reality. Pre-Socratics were rarely short on self-confidence.

Perhaps because Parmenides knows that what he has to say is rather flabbergasting, he begins his poem by assuming the trappings of divine revelation. He tells us that he rode a chariot in the company of young maidens, up to the gates leading to the paths of night and day (§288). The goddess Justice is persuaded by the maidens to allow Parmenides to ride his chariot on through, and then the goddess congratulates him for finding his way to a road that mortals do not travel. She tells him he will learn two things: first, the truth, and second, the mere opinions of mortal men. These correspond to the two halves of the poem that follows. In the first half we are given the so-called "way of truth": Parmenides' arguments for the unity of being. In the second part, the so-called "way of opinion," we get a cosmology very similar to what we find in the earlier Pre-Socratics from Ionia.

I'm going to concentrate on the way of truth, since that's the famous and more exciting bit, but first let me say something about this division of the poem into two halves. I've been talking about Parmenides as the father of metaphysics, but with this division we can also see him making a major contribution to epistemology. You might remember that Xenophanes already distinguished between mere belief and genuine knowledge. But Parmenides goes much further here, by devoting half his poem to knowledge and half to belief. What's interesting is that he spends so much time on the mere beliefs. The second part of the poem, which dealt with cosmology and other issues in natural science, is not preserved as completely as the first part, but it was clearly quite extensive and, as far as we can tell, was offered with serious intent. Parmenides seems to be setting out the beliefs that one should adopt if one isn't capable of grasping the more fundamental, underlying truth of the unity of being. We have a fragment which apparently formed a transition from the way of truth to the way of opinion (§300), and in that fragment he warns us that the way of opinion is not to be trusted: it is not as firmly grounded as the way of truth. It is still, though, the second-best way, because according to Parmenides it is the most plausible explanation of things like the heavenly bodies and human body, these being the sorts of topics he tackled in the way of opinion (§301). In the way of truth, rational argument has shown us that things like heavenly bodies are mere illusions. Yet Parmenides seems to think it is worthwhile to give an account of them. He seems to tell us: if you are going to reject the way of truth and believe something false, then at least believe the falsehoods I offer in the way of opinion.[2]

The primary message of Parmenides' poem, though, is that we should not trust the senses, but follow philosophical argument wherever it leads. Let's follow it, then, down the path less traveled: the way of truth. Parmenides begins by making a distinction between two possible paths of inquiry: either "is, and must be" or "isn't, and can't be" (§291). The second path is rejected, because it involves trying to think about what is not: non-being is not something we can think or speak about meaningfully. There is actually a third path, mentioned a little later on, which is even worse: according to this path, we say both "is" and "is not." This has the same problem that we would need to grasp non-being, but in addition leads to a contradiction: both is and is not. Parmenides says this is the path most people try to follow, and this is why most people are totally confused (§293). Actually, they're worse than confused: they are unwittingly engaged in self-contradiction.

It's at about this point that most readers begin to suspect that they haven't the foggiest notion what Parmenides is talking about. "Is and must be"? "Isn't and can't be"? *What* is, and *what* isn't? In the Greek there is no explicit subject for the verb "is," it just floats free.[3] Probably, though, the idea is that we can apply the argument to anything we like: take a giraffe. Either the giraffe is, in which case we can think and speak about it, or there is no giraffe, in which case Parmenides is right that it's at least difficult to understand how we could think or speak about it. He seems right again when he says that the worst approach would be to say that the giraffe both is and is not. Thus the path recommended to us is the path no one has yet taken, until Parmenides passes through those gates: to allow only being, while completely avoiding any attempt to think about or refer to non-being.

Once we head off down this path, we find ourselves in unfamiliar territory. For starters, Parmenides points out that being cannot *begin* to be. After all, it would have to start being after there is no being—but non-being is something we promised not to contemplate (§296). Nor can being be destroyed, for the same reason: it would have to become non-being (§298). Parmenides infers from this that change is impossible. If there were change, whatever changes would have to go from non-being to being, or being to non-being. Since in either direction we would have the involvement of non-being, this is impossible. But like a giraffe, Parmenides seems to be sticking his neck out a bit too far here. Not all change involves creation and destruction, after all. I can change a giraffe without killing it, for example by painting it blue, if I can get it to hold still for long enough and if I have enough paint. And that's a change that doesn't involve non-being. Parmenides would beg to differ. Either because the blue of the painted giraffe replaces the non-being of blue in the giraffe, or, what amounts to the same thing, because the blue giraffe comes to be after there is no blue giraffe.

The same kind of argument will work for any supposed change, or even any supposed difference between one thing and another. To contrast our blue giraffe to a giraffe that *is not* blue, we would need to use the banned concept of non-being. So we can think of this as an argument for the unity of being over time. Being isn't one thing at one time and another thing at a later time, because it can't change. Furthermore, being must have unity at any given time, because if there were variety in it then one part of it would be different from another, but we just saw that you need to think of non-being to grasp the notion of difference, and that's not possible. Parmenides gives a further argument for the unity of being at one and the same time. He points out that if being were divided up, it would need to have gaps or divisions in it. These gaps or divisions would, of course, consist of non-being, because they are different from being. So being is also continuous (§297). Any part of it will be just the same as any other part.

Obviously it's starting to sound like Parmenides is not talking about giraffes, and not only because they were thin on the ground in ancient Italy. In fact it's almost impossible to imagine this being that Parmenides is talking about, until he compares it to a sphere (§299). He says that it is spherical because it must have some kind of limit or determination. This is maybe the most puzzling passage in the way of truth, against the admittedly strong competition offered by every other passage in the way of truth. For one thing, if being is a sphere, won't there be non-being outside the sphere, the non-being we aren't allowed to think or speak of? For this and other reasons, some interpreters want to see this idea that being is spherical as a kind of metaphor: maybe the idea is to emphasize that it is determinate because we can think and reason and talk about it successfully. But he may mean it more literally, and be thinking that it is a sphere because it must be some shape, and the sphere is the most perfect shape—shades of Pythagoreanism here, perhaps. In any case, he does go on to argue that being is perfect, and here his argument is a bit easier to follow. Being must be perfect, because if it were not it would lack something it could have: and in that case it would contain some kind of non-being, namely the absence of whatever it is lacking.

Let's take stock. The passages I've just discussed represent the core argument of Parmenides' way of truth, which has come down to us pretty much in its entirety. This is, incidentally, thanks to a commentator on Aristotle named Simplicius, who wrote a good thousand years later. He remarked that Parmenides' poem was hard to get hold of in his day—so that it was worth copying out at length into his commentary. He's also a major source for the other Pre-Socratics. So let's take a moment to be thankful to good old Simplicius. In any case, we have these extensive fragments from the way of truth, and what they show is that Parmenides was offering a rational deduction. He starts from a basic principle—that you can have "is," but you can't have "is not"—and then proceeds to explore the consequences, whatever they might be. Whatever we make of his argument, this is a real quantum leap in the history of philosophy. Parmenides is not just offering explanations of what he can see around him, though he goes on to do that in the way of opinion. Rather, he puts all his trust in reason itself, and trusts the power of argument more than he trusts the evidence of his own eyes and ears. This is not to say that Parmenides is the first Pre-Socratic to offer arguments. Already with Thales, I suggested that he may have had implicit arguments for his views on water and the claim that everything is full of gods. Nonetheless Parmenides does represent something new. He tries to settle an abstract philosophical issue—the nature of being itself—with an explicit and complex deductive argument.

But as you might expect, not many people have been persuaded by Parmenides' argument that all reality is nothing but a single, unchanging sphere. On the other hand, plenty of philosophers since Parmenides have, knowingly or not, given arguments that are reminiscent of his way of truth. For instance, the argument for the perfection of being reappears in the medieval period as a way of trying to understand the perfection of God. And certainly Plato and Aristotle take Parmenides very seriously. Aristotle, for instance, devotes considerable energy to explaining how change is after all possible, despite Parmenides' point that it would involve non-being. Closer to Parmenides himself were his immediate followers, the other Eleatics. They worked hard to defend the astonishing conclusions of their master. It was in pursuit of this aim that Zeno of Elea developed the most brilliant set of paradoxes in ancient philosophy. Zeno's paradoxes try to undermine the possibility of change and multiplicity, making good on Parmenides' claim that no one can contemplate non-being without ending in self-contradiction. These paradoxes will be—and certainly will not not be—the topic of our next chapter.

7

YOU CAN'T GET THERE FROM HERE
THE ELEATICS

Imagine you're standing at the baseline of a tennis-court. That's the line at the back, where you serve from. It's time to change sides, so you are about to walk straight across to the other end of the court. You set off, undertaking a journey of almost twenty-four meters, the length of a regulation court; it doesn't seem particularly daunting. When you get halfway, of course, there will be a net blocking your path, but you figure you'll cope with that problem when you get to it. Maybe you can leap over it jauntily, the way tennis-players used to do at the end of the match. But before you get to the net, which looms some twelve meters in the distance, you'll be arriving at the line drawn halfway across your side of the court—as those of you who are tennis experts know, this is called the service line. At that point you will have completed a quarter of your trip, having walked about six meters. But of course, to do *that*, you've first got to get halfway to the service line: you need to walk three meters forward. And to do *that*, you've got to walk half of those three meters. It's starting to look a bit more daunting now, isn't it? In fact, now that you think about it, there is quite literally an infinite number of things you need to do to walk to the far side of the court: to get to any point, you will need to travel halfway to that point, and halfway to that halfway point, and so on. There is no end to the halfway points you'll need to visit. You'd better bring a packed lunch.

This thought experiment, obviously without the tennis-court, was invented by a man named Zeno of Elea, who was born in the early fifth century BC. He was an associate and student of Parmenides, and along with Melissus of Samos, his most important follower. Zeno is renowned for the paradoxes he invented in support of Parmenides' theory that being cannot change or be more than one. The word "paradox" is another one of these English words that comes from ancient Greek. *Para* means, in this case, "against," and *doxa* means "belief": so if something is *para doxon* it is contrary to our beliefs. Zeno's paradox of the halfway points, usually called the Stadium or Dichotomy paradox (§§318–20), is paradoxical in this sense. It shows you that it's impossible to move, and yet of course you still believe you can move. In fact you move all the time.

Paradoxes are a great way to introduce people to philosophy, because they force us to think hard about things we normally take for granted. There are many kinds of philosophical paradox. For instance, in ethics. There are two burning buildings in front of you: in one is your mother, in the other several innocent children. You can only save the occupants of one building: what should you do? Then there are paradoxes about time and space; for instance, you hop in a time machine, go back, and stop yourself from being born. But then how did you exist in order to go back in time in the first place? This, of course, is the basis of that philosophical classic, the film *Back to the Future*, the only case I know of where the philosophy of time comes together with a DeLorean. There are also logical paradoxes, for instance the barber's paradox: imagine a barber who shaves every man in the village who doesn't shave himself. Does the barber shave himself or not? Or the liar's paradox: if I say, "What I'm now saying is a lie," is this a lie or not? And so on.

Obviously different paradoxes call for different kinds of solutions. You might say the burning building and other such moral puzzles are not really *paradoxes*. It's just that there is no right answer. The world sometimes lands us with tragic situations that cannot be resolved morally. In the case of *Back to the Future*, we might simply say that such paradoxes show time-travel to be impossible. Similarly, we might say the barber in the logical paradox can't exist. In each case the paradox forces us to stop and think about the subject at hand, whether it be walking across tennis-courts, the nature of time, or moral dilemmas. But we have to assume that the paradox is meant to be resolved in one way or another. Hardly anyone wants to say that it both is and is not possible to walk across the tennis-court, or that the sentence "this is a lie" is both true *and* false.

When people think about the Dichotomy paradox, they naturally enough assume that the task is to spot the error in Zeno's reasoning. This approach assumes that the philosopher's job is to defend common sense against the paradox. Since we clearly *do* walk across tennis-courts, there must be a mistake somewhere. Of course this is a perfectly reasonable response, but it isn't what Zeno was hoping for. What he wanted to do, as a follower of Parmenides, was to show that motion really is impossible. Parmenides, as we saw, had argued that all motion and change are impossible, because they would involve non-being in some way. Parmenides argued positively, starting out from first principles—in particular, that one can speak and think only about being but never non-being. From this principle he established that being is unchanging and eternal, a perfectly balanced sphere. Zeno takes a different approach, which is more destructive. With his Dichotomy paradox he tries to show us that the concept of motion is itself beset by contradiction. That this was Zeno's method is confirmed by Plato, who makes Zeno a character in a dialogue starring, and named after, Parmenides. In the *Parmenides* (127d–128a = §314), Plato shows Socrates discussing Zeno's book with Zeno himself. Socrates asks whether he has understood the goal of Zeno's book rightly: to show that belief in change and multiplicity leads inevitably to self-contradiction. Exactly right, says Zeno.

There is some uncertainty about exactly how Zeno's book was structured, and whether all the paradoxes ascribed to him were contained in this one book. But we know that he did produce a whole series of paradoxical arguments, some of which were apparently paired together. For instance, he used one argument to show that if things are many, then things are finite. Then he had another to show that if things are many, then things are infinite. Taking the two arguments together, we can conclude that if things are many, they must be both finite *and* infinite—a contradiction (§315). Thus, things are not many; instead, being is one, just as Parmenides taught. We have information about a number of Zeno's paradoxes. Some are rather complicated, so I'll discuss only a few of them, especially since I'm already almost halfway through this chapter (Zeno, I refute you thus).

First, let's return to the Dichotomy paradox. Here it is again, without the tennis-court: whenever you move from A to B, you have to move to C, the point halfway between A and B; to do that, you have to move to D which is halfway between A and C; and so on. There will be an infinite number of such points, meaning that to move from A to B you have to perform an infinite number of tasks, which is impossible. Or, to put it as Aristotle does when he relates the paradox (§320), you have to come into contact with infinitely many things (namely the halfway points). But why is this impossible? It's either because you only have a finite time to visit all these points, or simply because no one can do an infinite number of things. Another of Zeno's paradoxes makes pretty much the same point. We imagine Achilles racing a tortoise, with the tortoise getting a head start. The much faster Achilles tries to catch up. But every time he reaches the point where the tortoise just was, the tortoise has moved on at least a little bit further. And when Achilles reaches that new position, the tortoise has moved on again. Achilles can't overtake the tortoise, no matter how fast he runs (§322).

Can we refute Zeno, other than by getting up and walking away, and thus proving that motion is possible after all? It's often thought that somehow modern mathematics, and especially our modern notions of infinity, have solved the Dichotomy paradox. The idea would be, I guess, that we now have no problem in accepting that the series one-half, one-quarter, one-eighth, one-sixteenth, and so on adds up to one. In fact we might say that the number represented by that series just *is* one. So that's how the distance is covered. But this is no solution: after all, Zeno's paradox relies precisely on this fact, that the whole distance is equal to the sum of the infinite series. That's not to say that Zeno's understanding of infinity is the same as ours. But this may not be the decisive issue: the question is not only about mathematics, but about time and space. Certainly we can now mathematically model the idea of dividing up a space or a motion into infinitely small parts. But Zeno's paradox isn't only about a mathematical model, it's about time, space, and motion. His question to us will be, okay, you've got your mathematical model: but how does it relate to what is really going on?[1]

Aristotle offers what I think is a more relevant response to Zeno (*Physics* 233a). He says that one can divide the time needed to move from A to B right along with the distance from A to B. For instance, if it takes you twenty seconds to get from A to B it will take ten seconds to get halfway there, five seconds to get a quarter of the way there, and so on. It's simply a mistake on Zeno's part to think that one needs an infinite amount of time to visit this infinite number of points, because the divisions will apply to both the time and the distance. This response, though, assumes that Zeno was worried about the motion taking an infinite amount of time. But perhaps his point was rather that it is impossible to perform an infinite number of partial motions in the finite amount of time it takes to perform the whole motion. In that case, Aristotle's response does not really solve the paradox.

This mention of time brings us to another argument of Zeno's: the paradox of the Arrow (§§323–4). Here we consider an arrow, in mid-flight on its way from archer to target. Now consider how things are with this arrow at any one moment during the flight—imagine it captured by a stop-motion camera. In this freeze-frame moment it isn't moving at all, because at least a little time has to pass for anything to move. As Zeno says, it is at rest, because it is "against something equal." What he means by this is, I suppose, something like this: at this instant, the arrow is exactly aligned with the bit of space it is occupying, so it is at rest with respect to that space. Of course this will be true for any instant during the flight of the arrow. This, then, is the paradox: at any instant during the arrow's flight it seems to be hovering motionless in the air. Yet over the whole time of its flight the arrow apparently moves from bow to target. Again, we naturally assume that there's something wrong with the way Zeno has described the situation. This is how Aristotle reacted (*Physics* 239b). He complains that time is not made up of instants, which he calls "nows," that have no duration; rather, if you divide time you have to divide it into periods of time. Maybe very short periods, like a millionth of a second; but even a millionth of a second takes some time to elapse, and the arrow will move a little while that little time passes. Of course Zeno would disagree. He would say that if motion cannot happen *now*, it cannot happen at all—even if "now" is understood as having no duration. And this is the intended conclusion. As a follower of Parmenides, he simply doesn't believe that anything can move.

Not all of Zeno's paradoxes concern motion. Some have to do with our even more basic assumption that there is more than one thing in the world. As we've seen, Parmenides claimed that all being is unchanging, eternal, continous, and one. This would mean, for instance, that you and I are the same thing, unless neither of us exists at all. Pretty hard to believe, either way. But Zeno's paradoxes try to persuade us that if we assume that *more* than one thing exists, the results are just as bad. For instance, he tried to show that, between any two distinct things, there must be an infinity of other things (§315). As with the Dichotomy and the Arrow, we need to speculate about exactly how this argument should work, but I think the idea is something like this. Imagine you've got two objects, call them A and B. Well, they must be separated from one another, because they aren't just one continuous object. So there must be some third object, C, which is separating A and B. But now why is C distinct from A on the one hand, and B on the other hand? There must be some fourth thing separating A and C, and a fifth thing separating C and B. As with the Dichotomy, we can repeat this argument over and over. The only way to escape is to give some explanation of how two things can be touching each other directly, without being a single object because they form a continuous body. Of course, one could try to give such an explanation. Again Aristotle is the first to try: he devotes a whole discussion to what it means for two distinct things to be in contact (*Physics* 226b–227a). In a way, Aristotle's response is a tribute to the fruitfulness of Zeno's paradoxes. Even if they do not really tempt us to believe that all being is one, they do force us to ponder the nature of such things as motion, time, and physical contact. This is why philosophers still find his paradoxes useful. Like Aristotle, they can formulate their positive ideas about motion and so on by explaining how Zeno's paradoxes should be resolved.

We find a rather different approach to Parmenides' legacy in the other great Eleatic of the fifth century BC, Melissus of Samos. Attentive readers will recall that Samos is also the island that gave us Pythagoras, in the eastern Mediterranean off the coast of Ionia. So when we call Melissus an "Eleatic," we mean that he followed the philosophy of Parmenides of Elea, not that he was from Elea. Unlike Pythagoras, Melissus played a major role in the history of Samos. The historian and philosopher Plutarch tells us that Melissus led his people in a naval battle against the Athenians, and won handsomely (§519). This battle was fought around about the middle of the fifth century BC, which probably means that Melissus was, like Zeno, a generation younger than Parmenides. He may have been younger still than Zeno. In any case, his philosophy is clearly an attempt to develop and defend Parmenides, but not without departing from the master on some points.

Melissus follows the method of Parmenides rather than Zeno. That is, he argues positively that all being is unchanging and one, instead of inventing paradoxes to undermine motion and multiplicity. Like Parmenides, he starts from the idea that being cannot have *started*: to do that it would have to come from non-being, which is absurd (§525). He now applies this point to space, as well as time (§§526–8). Whereas Parmenides had said, apparently quite seriously, that being is spherical in shape, Melissus denies that being has any limits at all. After all, if it had limits there would have to be non-being beyond those limits, and there is no such thing as non-being. Thus he calls being "unlimited" or "infinite": it's the revenge of Anaximander's principle, the *apeiron*. These developments of Parmenides' ideas show that the Eleatic philosophy wasn't just a static, received doctrine. Rather, the theory of unchanging being itself changed, and was taken in different directions by Zeno and Melissus, even at the price of contradicting the teachings of Father Parmenides.

Another one of Melissus' ideas, though, would no doubt have delighted Parmenides. This is his argument against the possibility of motion (§534). Again, he starts by ruling out non-being. In this case, the sort of non-being he discusses is emptiness: there cannot be a place with nothing in it, again because there is no such thing as nothing. To put it another way, void is impossible. Now Melissus points out that if there is no void, then that will make motion impossible. After all, there will be no empty place for anything to move into. The whole of being will be like a train compartment packed so tightly that no one can budge. In the wake of this argument of Melissus', anyone who wants to defend the common-sense idea that motion *does* exist has two possible responses. One would be to agree that there is no void, but insist that there is motion anyway: whenever one thing moves, something else is displaced. Imagine the people in the train compartment shuffling along, perhaps with difficulty, each moving into the place of their neighbor in front while they give up their place to the person behind. This was Aristotle's view.

The other response would be to say that, except in the London Underground at rush hour, no place is totally full: there is indeed void. Bodies move around in this emptiness, banging into each other. That is, more or less, what we think today. Of course we now know that outer space is empty, or mostly empty. But also, every physical body down here on Earth turns out to consist of more empty space than full space, or at least that's what I was told in high school. Atoms and molecules exist in the void. What I wasn't told in high school is that this conception is a very old one. It was first conceived in response to the Eleatics, and perhaps especially in reaction to Melissus. It was developed by the ancient atomists, Leucippus and Democritus. With apologies to Zeno, let's now move along to look at them.

8

THE FINAL CUT
THE ATOMISTS

We've already looked at some pretty extravagant theories in this book. We started with Thales telling us that the principle of everything is water and that magnets have souls, and just now Zeno was trying to persuade us that it's impossible to walk across a tennis-court. But if you stopped a historian of philosophy in the street, and asked him or her to name one idea from Pre-Socratic philosophy that turns out actually to be true, the answer you're most likely to get is "atomism." After the apparently rather far-out theories of the earlier Pre-Socratics, it's comforting to come across an idea that looks familiar. All bodies are made of particles, so tiny that they are invisible to the naked eye, and the interaction of these particles explains the phenomena we see in the visible world around us. The particles are, of course, atoms. By now I hardly need to tell you where the word "atom" comes from. It's ancient Greek again: *tomein* means "to cut," and *atoma* means quite literally "uncuttables," In other words, atoms are things that cannot be divided into smaller parts. Not because you don't have a sharp enough knife, but because they are by their nature indivisible.

Here we've gone no further than the word "atoms," and already discovered a big difference between ancient atomism and the atomism of modern science. Our modern atoms are misnamed. They do have parts which can be divided from one another. Atoms can nowadays be split, with callous disregard for etymology. Furthermore, the parts of these modern atoms, namely protons, neutrons, and electrons, are themselves made up of smaller particles, all those gluons and quarks and whatnot. The particles of the modern scientist, then, are a pretty poor excuse for "atoms." Maybe someday the scientists will tell us that there is some smallest or most fundamental particle, or a whole bunch of such particles, which really are indivisible. If they do tell us this— maybe they already have, because quite frankly I haven't been paying much attention—then these most fundamental particles will be comparable to Greek atoms.

Of course, the ancient atomists also arrived at their theory in a very different way from that of modern science. No chemical experiments, no periodic table. Instead, the atomism put forward by the fifth-century BC thinkers Leucippus and Democritus was reached by a process of abstract reasoning. Here a useful starting point is provided by Zeno's paradoxes. As we saw in the last chapter, Zeno pointed out problems that result from assuming that distances or bodies can be divided up infinitely. You take a nice familiar object like a tennis-court or a giraffe, and you start cutting: divide it in half, divide the half in half, divide the resulting quarter in half, and so on. Zeno exploited the assumption that there seems to be no end to this process. The distance or the body turns out to be in some sense infinite, and once infinity is on the scene paradoxes are not far away. The atomists stop Zeno in his tracks, by assuming that if one keeps dividing and dividing, one will eventually hit bedrock. The giraffe, the tennis-court, and all other things are made of atoms, the uncuttables. Once you've reached the atoms, you're like a film director sending a movie to be shown in theaters: you've made the final cut.

This is only one side of the atomists' picture of the cosmos. The other side, however, doesn't exist. It's the nothingness in which the atoms move around, in other words, vacuum or void. Here, the atomists were reacting to Melissus' argument that motion is impossible: for something to move it must move into an empty place, but an empty place is nothing, and there is no such thing as nothing. The atomists hijack Melissus' train of thought and drive it in the other direction. Since we can plainly see that motion is possible, there must be such a thing as nothingness, in which things are moving (§545). This nothingness is the void. Now we need to be careful here. It's tempting for us to imagine that the atomists have a conception of three-dimensional space, and that they are saying that space can be either full, in which case we have an atom, or empty, in which case we have void. But our textual evidence doesn't show them working with any third notion like "space" which is independent of both being and non-being. Instead, they are making a direct reply to Eleatic philosophy. In addition to being, they say, we will have non-being. Being consists of atoms, non-being consists of void, and the atoms move into the void, presumably replacing non-being with being as they do so—exactly what never happens, according to Parmenides and friends.

This direct philosophical link to Eleatic thought is well-attested in our sources, for instance in Aristotle. So we have good reason to expect a historical connection between the atomists and the Eleatics. As I've mentioned, the ancient tradition wants every famous philosopher to be the student of some other ancient philosopher, and duly makes Leucippus an associate of Parmenides or Zeno (§539). We don't need to believe this. But it's no doubt true that Leucippus was well acquainted with the Eleatic tradition begun by Parmenides. He was probably responding mostly to Zeno and especially Melissus, rather than directly to Parmenides. The later Democritus then seems to have taken his atomism directly from Leucippus.

Both of them lived in the fifth century BC, but with Democritus we're really getting to the point where it's misleading to talk about these early Greek philosophers as "Pre-Socratics." Democritus was in fact an almost exact contemporary of Socrates. One source claims that he was one year older than Socrates, which is cutting it pretty close if you want to qualify as a Pre-Socratic. (Then again, he was an atomist, so cutting things close was something of a speciality for him.)

We don't know much about the biography of either Leucippus or Democritus, unfortunately. There's even uncertainty about where Leucippus was from. I find it rather suspicious that his home city is reported to be either Miletus or Elea: in other words, one of the two cities most famous for Pre-Socratic philosophy. Sounds to me like an educated, or maybe not so educated, guess. Things are a bit better with Democritus, since we can at least name a home city for him, namely Abdera in Thrace (§542), on the northern coast of the Aegean Sea. As far as their philosophy goes, it's not easy to say where Leucippus stops and Democritus starts. In the ancient sources many of the atomist doctrines are just ascribed indiscriminately to both of them. Democritus' interests seem to have been considerably wider, though, and for him we have fragments on ethics as well as atomism. Another thing that seems to be distinctive about Democritus, and which I'll come back to, is that he draws strikingly skeptical conclusions from his atomic theory. Here it's tempting to make a connection to Protagoras, the relativist or skeptical sophist who, like Democritus, hailed from the city of Abdera. We'll be getting to him and his fellow sophists soon.

But for now, let's get back to those atoms. If I ask you to imagine an atom, I suspect you'll think of a smooth, round sphere like a ball-bearing. These microscopic ball-bearings would bang around, colliding off each other and gathering together to make larger bodies. If that's the image in your head, it isn't far wrong. For the atomists, larger bodies are indeed made of atoms, and atoms do both collide and get collected together. But it turns out that they don't look like microscopic ball-bearings. Or rather, only some of them do. There are in fact atoms of every possible shape (§555). Some have hooks or are curved in various ways, so that they can get tangled together or fit snugly into one another if they encounter another atom of the right sort. Different types of larger, visible bodies are made from atoms of various shapes and sizes. For instance, Aristotle tells us that for the atomists the soul consists of particularly smooth, round atoms which can flow around through the body. These are those ball-bearing-like atoms, which can collect to form a soul, but not necessarily the rest of the body that houses this soul.

There is an infinite number of atoms (§557). This is crucially important for the atomists, and shows again how they are responding to the Eleatics, and especially Melissus. For Melissus, being was one and infinite; for the atomists, being is many and infinite. The difference, as I mentioned already, is that the atomists have integrated void, or non-being, into their world picture. Void separates out being into many things, and these things are infinite. But why do the atoms have to be infinite? Couldn't there be, say, exactly ten billion atoms bouncing around in an infinite emptiness? In answer to this, the ancient atomists could invoke a rule which is sometimes called the principle of sufficient reason. It states that there has to be some good reason or explanation for each feature of the universe. In the present case, atoms must be infinite because there is no reason why there would be any particular finite number of them. Sure, there could be exactly ten billion atoms—but then why not ten billion and one atoms? The atomists could give the same kind of argument to show why the atoms must have every conceivable shape. Why would they only be spherical, or only come in, say, ten varieties? Rather, they will have every shape that atoms could have, because there is no reason why any possible shape should be lacking, especially given that the atoms are infinite in number.

Since the atoms are of different sizes, it seems that by the same reasoning there should be atoms of *every* size, including ones we could see, and still others much bigger than that. There is some uncertainty in the sources here, with some reports saying that all atoms are invisible to the naked eye, and others suggesting that the atomists thought there were atoms big enough to be visible, just not in our part of the universe. But I tend to think that Leucippus and Democritus just assumed that atoms must be smaller than we can see. In fact, they could give a good account of this if they wanted to. They explained vision in terms of sheets or films of atoms being shed from the outer layer of visible bodies, which pass through the air and enter our eyes so as to interact with the atoms that make up our soul. Obviously a single atom can't throw off a sheet of atoms that are part of it, so if there were such a huge atom there's no way we could see it anyway. Of course, it could still collide with us. I quite like the idea that someday an invisible atom the size of an elephant could come hurtling towards us from outer space. In the unlikely event of such an emergency, do not try to deal with the atom by cutting it in half.

Fortunately the cosmology presented by Leucippus and Democritus makes it clear that enormous atoms are not going to be found around here, if they exist at all. They have a nice explanation of how our cosmos formed out of the atoms (§563). There have always been atoms, and they have always been colliding with one another. The atoms don't just bounce off one another, they also get entangled—partly because of their shapes, like I said, but also because the atoms have a tendency to gather together with other atoms of similar size and shape. This might explain why the soul is able to hold together as a single conglomeration, rather than having all its smooth atoms just go ricocheting off into the void. At the level of the whole cosmos, what happens is that huge groups of atoms start to swirl around in a kind of vortex. The heavier and bigger atoms tend to bunch towards the middle and the lighter atoms tend to move to the outside. The former make up the earthy and moist bodies of the earthly world, while the latter turn into the fiery heavens.

And there's more—in fact, infinitely more. It turns out that there isn't only one cosmos. After all, look around: does the visible cosmos look like it has an *infinite* amount of atoms in it? No. There must be a vast number of atoms making up the earth and all the plants, animals, mountains, and so on on its surface, and yet another vast number making up the heavens. But vast plus vast still equals a finite number. Besides which, to invoke that principle again, there's no good reason why there should be only one cosmos. Instead, the atomists said—and this is a respectable entry among the daring ideas proposed by the Pre-Socratics—that there is an infinite number of worlds (§565). Those worlds exhibit every possible combination of atoms. One way of understanding this is that every way that the world could be actually exists out there somewhere. There could be worlds that are very different from ours, maybe a world made entirely out of cheese. (In the next chapter we'll meet another philosopher, who apparently thinks that there is cheese everywhere in *our* universe. Time to invest in crackers.) But this infinity of worlds would also include some that are only slightly different from ours, like worlds where giraffes have wings but everything else is the same. This theory is truly mind-bending, and the atomists don't seem to have explored its implications as fully as we might have hoped. But perhaps we should rein in our imagination just a bit, because there may be a cosmic vortex in all the other worlds too. This would result in many worlds which are a lot like ours, at least in the sense that there is an Earth-like body in the middle with fiery heavens surrounding it.

We seem to have gotten quite far from Parmenides now, even though the theory started out by simply modifying the Eleatic system to allow for non-being, and to allow multiple beings instead of a single, unchanging one. But notice that each atom in itself is similar to the Eleatic single being. Okay, they move, but they are indivisible, unchanging, and eternal. And there's something else about the atomists, or at least Democritus, that may remind us of Parmenides. You might remember that in his poem Parmenides distinguished between the way of truth and the way of opinion. His radical metaphysics of one being is the way of truth—it is the hidden reality that we fail to grasp, because we are caught up with the appearances of the world. Democritus does something similar, which is at first rather surprising. You might think that he's out to defend common sense against the Eleatics. Giraffes and tennis-courts do exist, and he can explain why with his atomic theory, right? But instead Democritus took a more skeptical line, because he was impressed by the fact that the underlying reality of atoms and void is not evident to our senses. Thus he criticized the senses, saying in effect that things in the phenomenal world—the giraffes and tennis-courts—are unreal, because what is really real is the atomic universe we can't see. He put this in a famous aphorism: "By convention sweet, by convention bitter, by convention hot, by convention cold, by convention color, but really atoms and void" (§549). In a less famous fragment he says, perhaps echoing Xenophanes and Heraclitus, that no one knows anything, and instead we make do with belief.

His position, then, is that things may appear to us to be sweet and so on, but that is only an appearance. The atomic interactions explain why things seem sweet to us, but the sweetness isn't real. It's the atomic interactions that are real. Here Democritus has hit upon a perennial issue in philosophy. Scientific theories often tell us that the world is very different from what it seems at first. This has always been the case, as we've seen with the inventive and surprising theories of the Pre-Socratics. The invisible world of quantum particles in modern physics is no less bizarre, probably even more bizarre, than the theories the Pre-Socratics came up with. In both cases one might ask whether the scientific theories *replace* the phenomenal world with another world, grasped through more specialized methods, or whether the phenomenal world is retained, while also getting explained by the scientific theory. Should we say that giraffes are not real, because really all that exists are the atoms that make up the giraffe; or should we say that giraffes are real precisely *because* they are made up of atoms?

Democritus takes the first option.[1] He thinks that science banishes our familiar everyday reality, rather than securing our familiar reality by explaining it. We can see why, if we go back to the different approaches used in ancient atomism and in modern physics. Modern physics, despite the mind-boggling world of atomic and sub-atomic particles it offers us, is still an extension of our everyday experience. The tools of physics, chemistry, and so on are much more powerful than our eyes and ears, but that just means that they *enhance* our experience of the world. The microscope and telescope are good examples: when you use them you are still seeing, but you are seeing things much smaller or more distant than the naked eye could see unaided. Even the most outlandish features of the quantum universe are in principle observable, albeit indirectly so. Ancient atomism is not like this at all. The atomists continued in the tradition of Parmenides and his followers, by applying pure reason to the task of deducing what the world must be like.

Democritus makes this very clear when he contrasts the deliverances of the mind to the deliverances of the senses (§554). Mind tells us about the atomic theory, and thus undermines what the senses tell us, even though sensible reality is supposed to be grounded in events at the atomic level. We can find this deference to the mind elsewhere in Greek philosophy. You might remember that Xenophanes said that his God thinks; later on Aristotle will say that mind is the divine element in us, and that god himself is nothing but a separate mind. But no Greek philosopher pays greater tribute to mind than another thinker who tried to preserve the reality around us from the results of Parmenides' arguments. This was Anaxagoras. In his philosophy, Mind takes central stage not only as an instrument for discovering truth, but as the fundamental principle which steers the universe.

9

MIND OVER MIXTURE
ANAXAGORAS

In a dialogue called the *Phaedo* Plato shows us the last conversation of Socrates. It will end when Socrates drinks the hemlock and bravely prepares to meet whatever the afterlife may hold for him. But first he indulges in a bit of autobiography, telling his friends, soon to be his mourners, about his early philosophical explorations (*Phaedo* 97b–100b). In this story he gives a central role to Anaxagoras. Socrates says he came across Anaxagoras' book, which could apparently be picked up cheap in Athens towards the end of the fifth century BC. At first he found the book promising. Anaxagoras offered an account of how the cosmos is produced and ordered by·Mind, which, Socrates assumed, meant that Anaxagoras would go on to explain why everything in the world is for the best. Instead, the book turned out to consist largely of crude physical explanations, invoking things like the hot and the cold, the rarefied and the dense. Disappointed, Socrates went off on his own way and, at least according to Plato, invented the theory of Forms.

Later on in this book we'll look at the *Phaedo* in its own right. But I wanted to mention it at the start of this chapter because the passage nicely captures a kind of duality in Anaxagoras' philosophy. On the one hand, there is his exalted Mind, the purest and most subtle of things, which plays a central role in forming the cosmos. On the other hand, there is his fascination with physical processes, and above all his startling theory of universal mixture: everything is in everything, according to Anaxagoras, except for Mind. Anyone trying to come to grips with Anaxagoras should try to do what Socrates wasn't able to. That is, they should try to understand not only the theory of Mind and the theory of mixed physical substances, but also how Mind and the physical substances interact.

Anaxagoras was the most notable philosopher of Athens until Socrates came along, so it's not surprising that his book was available there in Socrates' day. We always think of Athens as the capital city of Greek philosophy, but as you may have noticed, so far none of the philosophers we've looked at came from Athens or spent a significant part of their lives there. Anaxagoras was the first to do so, and he is thus something of a one-man symbol for the transfer of philosophy from Ionia to

Athens. He was from Clazomenae on the Ionian coast, and he continued some of the traditions of Ionian philosophy going back to the Milesians in the sixth century BC. Despite this, it was in Athens that he seems to have done his philosophy, and it was in Athens that he became associated with the great statesman Pericles (§§459, 461). As the leading politician of the democracy of Athens in the middle of the fifth century, Pericles helped to build the empire that would face off against Sparta in the Peloponnesian War, starting in 431 BC. But Pericles' career mostly coincided with the more peaceful period of increasing Athenian strength, after the wars with Persia but before the disastrous conflict with the Spartans. It's appropriate that Pericles should have consorted with a philosopher of Anaxagoras' stature, given that it was under his leadership that Athens developed into a pre-eminent power and thus a center for philosophical speculation and other cultural activities. This was the environment in which Socrates was formed.

Anaxagoras has something else in common with Socrates, apart from his association with Athens: like Socrates, he was put on trial for being insufficiently reverential towards the gods. He didn't wind up drinking hemlock, but instead left town, which is safer (§459). Unfortunately, we don't know much about the trial, but it may have resulted from his political connections. Then again, his theory of the cosmic Mind is not much like traditional Greek religion, so it may have been, as they say, a fair cop when he was accused of impiety. That's not to say that Anaxagoras' Mind is anything less than divine. At least, it sure sounds like he is talking about god, or a god, when he describes Mind. He says that it is infinite and controls everything that lives (§476). This may recall to us Xenophanes' version of God or even Heraclitus' version of fire. It seems to me that when Socrates started to read Anaxagoras' book this was probably also the impression that he formed. Mind was going to be described as a powerful, perhaps even all-powerful, god who planned and designed everything so that it would be as good as it can possibly be. He then became disappointed when Anaxagoras didn't invoke Mind constantly, but appealed to various material processes instead.

But I think this was a bit unfair on Socrates' part. There's a grand tradition in both philosophy and religion of invoking god, or the gods, to explain the fact that the world looks so well designed. Think about how the sun moves in just the right way to give us seasons, so that we can plant and harvest food to keep ourselves alive. Think of the giraffe with its long neck, just the thing for reaching those tasty leaves in the trees. Think even of how much it hurts when you step on something sharp. Sure, you don't feel grateful when it happens, but if not for the pain you'd be a lot less careful in the future and you'd probably wind up with cuts all over your feet, and then where would you be? So even the bad things in life seem to be designed to make life better. Socrates assumed that this is, roughly, where Anaxagoras was heading when he put Mind in charge of the cosmos. There may have been something like this thought in Anaxagoras' book, but the evidence we have suggests that he had other fish to fry.

For one thing, the fragment that tells us about Mind controlling things says that it controls *living* things, so maybe giraffes and people who can step on rocks, but not the rocks that the people are stepping on. His idea seems to be not that Mind is responsible for how well designed things are, but for the special abilities of things like people, animals, and perhaps plants. He says that of the things that have Mind, some have a greater share and some a lesser share. Presumably humans have more than dogs, which have more than insects. Perhaps some humans have more than others. Now, none of this sounds anything like the Creator God we know from religions like Christianity, Judaism, and Islam. Anaxagoras' Mind is not there to explain why everything is designed as well as possible, but to explain why some things can think, see, and so on, whereas others can't. We humans get a healthy portion of Mind, rocks don't get any. In short, it sounds more like Anaxagoras' Mind is an ingredient or a power which is distributed unequally through the universe.

But if Mind is an ingredient, then it is a very special ingredient. Anaxagoras reserves a unique place for it when he explains how the world is put together. This takes us to his other most famous idea: universal mixture. Before the cosmos was formed, Anaxagoras says, there was nothing but Mind and another infinite substance in which all other things were mixed together (§467). However, there were, in amongst this mixture, what he calls "seeds" (§468). These seeds were the beginnings of later, distinctive substances like, for example, air or water. Only Mind stands outside this mixture. It must be over and above the things it is going to control, so it alone is, as he says, "unmixed" (§476). Furthermore, Mind has the important job of kicking off the formation of the cosmos. It somehow initiates a cosmic rotation, in which the infinite mixture of stuff starts to spin around (§§476–8, 488–90). As the rotation goes on, the seeds of lighter things are sifted out towards the edges, and become air and the fiery stuff of the heavens, while the seeds of moist and dense things stay towards the middle. At a certain point some large stones go spinning out of the central portion and become the visible heavenly bodies, like the sun and moon, burning white with heat.

So far this sounds a lot like what we've found in the earlier Ionian philosophers. In particular, we already saw in Anaximenes this idea that the bodies in the middle of the cosmos, where we are, collect there because they are dense, whereas air and fire are rarefied and light. It's almost as if Anaxagoras has put this together with Xenophanes' God, who just by thinking "shakes all things." But Anaxagoras is adding something of his own as well. Even though the seeds are separated out by the rotation that Mind sets in motion, nothing apart from Mind is ever completely separated. Instead, as he puts it in his most famous slogan, "everything is in everything" (§§481–2) The oceans may look to us like they are made only of water, but actually they also contain things other than water, for instance, air and fire. In fact, all things contain all other kinds of thing. So when soul-singers from the 1970s to the present have informed us that "everything is everything," they were broadly speaking in agreement with Anaxagoras. As far as I'm concerned, that alone makes it worth trying to understand what he was up to with this theory.

As usual, Aristotle has an explanation of what Anaxagoras was thinking, and as occasionally happens, Aristotle's explanation may actually be right. He puts Anaxagoras' theory squarely in the context of the Parmenidean denial of change (§485). You might remember that for Parmenides and his followers motion and change were impossible, because for anything to come into being it would have to come from non-being, but there is no non-being. Aristotle suggests that Anaxagoras accepted part of this reasoning. He agreed that nothing could come from absolute non-being, and yet, like the atomists, he refused to accept that nothing ever really changes or moves. The atomists go in one direction here, and Anaxagoras goes in the other. For the atomists, in one sense there is no change because all the atoms are eternal: they never come to be and are never destroyed. So nothing comes to be from non-being, but the atoms can come together in different configurations, which underlie the world we see around us.

Anaxagoras, rather ingeniously, suggests instead that absolute change is not required because everything is *already* everything else. He gave the example of food. You eat a loaf of bread with a hunk of cheese on it, and this manages to restore the flesh, bone, and blood in your body. Clearly, there must be flesh, bone, and blood in the bread and cheese. After all, there is nowhere else for it to come from. And there's another contrast between Anaxagoras and the atomists. He's happy to accept, in the face of Zeno's paradoxes, that you can take any material body and divide it, divide it again, and so on and so on infinitely (§472). But every portion of that body, no matter how small, will still contain all things. Even the tiniest particle of cheese has some bone in it. Anaxagoras, then, would have us believe that every single material object or part of an object, no matter how small or large, contains all the ingredients that make up the universe. You can't separate out any one ingredient to get, say, pure and unmixed bone or flesh. As we saw, only Mind is ever unmixed. Rather, what you'll get if you start cutting up bone is smaller and smaller bits which still contain all the ingredients. It's not, mind you, that the cheese can be *turned into* bone. The idea is that there is *already* bone in the cheese, and in everything else.

Now, this raises a couple of obvious questions. First, will any of us ever want to eat cheese again? Second, if all the ingredients are in every portion of everything, why doesn't everything look the same? It should all be one homogeneous mass, with no differentiation between cheese and bone, or anything else. But this objection is easy to answer. Even if all ingredients are present in a given chunk of the world, they might be present in different proportions. A chunk of earth, for instance, has all the ingredients in it, but the earth in the chunk predominates over all the other ingredients. We might say that there are "trace elements" of other things like water and fire in the earth. Similarly, there are trace elements of flesh, blood, and bone in the cheese. The process of digestion pulls these trace elements together to build up our body, which is made of portions which likewise have all ingredients but are predominantly flesh, or predominantly bone (§496). Apparently this sort of pre-dominance has always been present, because there were "seeds" of things already in the infinite mass that Mind began to rotate. These seeds were portions which were already predominantly cold or hot. Of course, it had to be like this if the rotation begun by Mind was going to achieve anything. After all, the hot bits can hardly get spun out towards the edges if no one bit is hotter than any other bit.

Another thing we might wonder is, what exactly is the list of the ingredients? Is it really the case that *everything* is in *everything*? Do we really want to say that inside every particle of a giraffe there is just a hint of Eiffel Tower, and vice-versa? Here we've reached a somewhat controversial area of Anaxagoras' philosophy. Some have thought that he was working with a very short list of "ingredients," which in fact don't look much like ingredients at all.[1] These would be things like hot, cold, rare, and dense. If this is his theory, it isn't quite as surprising as it first seemed. His point would only be that nothing is so hot that it has no admixture of cold, or vice-versa. Rather, there would be a kind of continuum between hot and cold. And similarly for other basic oppositions, like perhaps moist and dry. We might envision this by imagining a measurement scale with no top or bottom (so, no absolute zero in the case of temperature). He would then explain this idea in the more concrete terms of a physical mixture. This would be in keeping with other Pre-Socratic philosophers, and even some later thinkers like Aristotle, who speak of things like "the hot" and "the cold" as kinds of stuff rather than measurable properties.

Other interpreters find this version of Anaxagoras harder to swallow than bony cheese. After all, ancient authors, including Aristotle and others who could probably have read Anaxagoras' own writings, seem happy to speak of things like bone and flesh among the ingredients that are always present.[2] This doesn't need to mean that the ingredients included more complicated things, like plants, animals, and humans, to say nothing of man-made things like tables and the Eiffel Tower. Rather, he seems to have had in mind the simplest materials out of which such things are made. In the case of the Eiffel Tower this would be metal, in the case of a giraffe it would be good old bone, flesh, and blood. In fact, though, Anaxagoras could afford to be relaxed about the list of ingredients. He could say to us: "I've given you the theory of universal mixture, which is my breakthrough insight. We'd need a detailed investigation to find out what the basic constituents of the universe are. But my theory could turn out to be true, whatever those exact ingredients turn out to be." In this spirit we might note that, even though there is no bone in cheese, there is calcium in cheese, and bone is made partly of calcium. Maybe he was onto something after all.

With this theory, Anaxagoras put on the table a philosophical problem which was going to worry philosophers for many generations to come: the problem of mixture. It's not something that leaps to mind nowadays when we think about pressing philosophical difficulties. "Does God exist?" "What is the nature of consciousness?" Sure. But "What is it for one thing to be mixed with another?" Not so much. Yet this problem was at the heart of ancient attempts to understand the nature of material objects. If we don't worry about the problem any more, it's because one answer to the question eventually carried the day. We now think that when two things, like water and wine, get mixed together, what is actually happening is not so much mixture as a very complicated jumbling together. There are wine particles and water particles, and these particles don't literally fuse, they just get juxtaposed. This is, of course, precisely the answer that the ancient atomists would have given, and at least to this extent they were right.

Anaxagoras was proposing a different sort of answer, which would turn out to be more popular among ancient philosophers like Aristotle and the Stoics. According to this second answer, it is indeed possible for one body to be *completely* mixed or fused with another. In fact, the Stoics said it was possible for a single drop of wine to mix with the entire ocean, so that every portion of the ocean, no matter how small, would have some of the wine in it. No one apart from Anaxagoras went so far as to say that absolutely every type of body can be found absolutely everywhere, but his fundamental intuition about mixture is perfectly reasonable. After all, we see wine mix with water and the two seem to suffuse one another completely. Why not think this is happening, as it were, all the way down, including in portions of the mixture too small to see? Once you've gotten to that point you already need to accept Anaxagoras' idea that one ingredient can predominate over another, even if the two ingredients are mixed with one another through and through. Obviously, in the ocean mixed with a wine-drop, water is predominant, even though wine is present absolutely everywhere in the water.

Anaxagoras, then, brings together many of the themes we have seen in other Pre-Socratic philosophers, but he offers a bridge to Socrates and post-Socratic philosophy as well. With Anaxagoras we have brought philosophy to Athens, seen another response to Parmenides, and also been reminded of the grand cosmic theories of the Milesians. Along with the Eleatics and the atomists, Anaxagoras exemplifies the ambitious system-building that we find in fifth-century BC philosophy up until Socrates, and even during Socrates' own lifetime, for instance with the development of Leucippus' atomism at the hands of Democritus. But there's one major Pre-Socratic from the fifth century whom we haven't examined yet: Empedocles. There are some signs that Anaxagoras was responding to Empedocles, rather than the other way around, even though Anaxagoras seems to have been born slightly earlier. Aristotle is constantly presenting the two of them together, comparing their two cosmic schemes in various ways. Like Anaxagoras, Empedocles was very influential, responsible for systematizing the four elements of earth, air, fire, and water. He was also a wonderfully over-the-top wise man, in the style of Pythagoras. He claimed to be an incarnate god capable of working miraculous healing, and he supposedly died by hurling himself into a volcano. Like Socrates, this was a philosopher who knew how to make an exit.

10

ALL YOU NEED IS LOVE, AND FIVE OTHER THINGS EMPEDOCLES

What you would have held in your hands if you'd picked up a work of ancient philosophy in the ancient world? I just mentioned that Socrates was, according to Plato, able to buy a copy of a book written by Anaxagoras. But the word "book" conjures up the wrong image. What Socrates would have read was not a stack of pages fitted between two covers. Rather, it would have been written on a long scroll. You would unroll the book as you read it, and the writing would be in vertical columns which you would read from left to right. There would have been no punctuation, no separation between words, and no difference between capital and lower-case letters—these things were invented later. Ancient "books" were made either from papyrus, which is an Egyptian invention, a writing surface made from plants, or from parchment, which is made from animal skins. The first thinkers who had access to both Greek ideas and paper lived in the Islamic world, which imported the Chinese technology of paper-manufacturing in the eighth century AD. And of course, whether they were on papyrus, parchment, or paper, all ancient and medieval philosophical works had to be written and copied out by hand.

The reason I mention this is to help you picture an exciting event which occurred twenty years ago in the library of the French city of Strasbourg. A scholar named Alain Martin was examining some scraps of papyrus, which had been lying around in this library for quite some time, and he made a discovery: these bits of papyrus had verses of a poem on them. The poem was written by Empedocles. This could be verified, because some of the verses matched fragments of Empedocles known from other sources. Thus, in the early 1990s, the extant remains of Empedocles got a bit bigger. In ancient philosophy that's about as exciting as it gets. Thanks in part to the Strasbourg fragments, we have a surprisingly large amount of evidence for the writings of Empedocles.[1] So you might think that, whereas with other Pre-Socratics we've been having to work hard to fill in the gaps, we would have a really firm understanding of Empedocles' philosophy. We should be so lucky. In fact, Empedocles is at least as controversial among scholars of early Greek philosophy as any of the thinkers we've looked at—maybe because all that evidence just gives the historians more to argue about.

Even without this relative abundance of evidence, Empedocles would be hard to resist. He combines the religious mystique of Pythagoras, the pithy inscrutability of Heraclitus, and the cosmic vision of Anaxagoras. Let's start with the religious mystique. Empedocles informs us, modestly enough, that he is a god, who is decorated with wreaths wherever he goes, worshipped by the people, who beg him to bestow prophecy and healing upon them (§399). Diogenes Laertius, a later ancient author who preserves a lot of juicy biographical material about Empedocles and other philosophers, claims that he did indeed make quite an impression. In part this was because of the miracles he performed, not unlike Pythagoras: he raised a woman from the dead and cured one city of the plague. Then there was the way he looked, affecting long, flowing hair and a purple robe, and wearing distinctive bronze-soled shoes. Those shoes appear in the most famous bit of Diogenes' report. This has Empedocles dying by throwing himself into a volcano, in order to vanish without a trace and thus prove that he had become a god. The trick was discovered when his bronze sandal was discovered on the edge of the volcano's mouth.[2]

You have to love this stuff, even though, as usual with Diogenes, we're in the realm of legend rather than biography. Even Diogenes, not the most critical of historians, also reports the more sober story that Empedocles simply went off to the Peloponnese and was never heard from again. But there's a grain of truth in the volcano story, which is that the volcano named is Mount Etna in Sicily, and Sicily really is where Empedocles was from. To be more specific, he hailed from Acragas on the south-western coast of Sicily (§332). His proximity to Italy, where Pythagoreanism was in force during the fifth century BC, may help explain the distinct Pythagorean flavor of some of his ideas, including the boast about his own divinity. Among his doctrines, the most obviously Pythagorean element is his belief in reincarnation. You might remember that the followers of Pythagoras believed that after death we return as other people and animals. Empedocles apparently was able to confirm this from personal experience. He tells us in one fragment that he has been a boy, a girl, a bird, and a fish, even a bush (§417). (One can't help asking oneself what it is like to remember being a bush, but let's pass over this and move on.) In another fragment he describes the father who raises up his own son in prayer before brutally slaying the child, heedless of his screams (§415). The idea being that the son has previously died, and been reincarnated as an animal who is being sacrificed on the altar. Like the Pythagoreans, Empedocles figures that if reincarnation is possible, you'd better not eat meat. You might wind up eating your family! What's really remarkable, though, is the chilling vividness with which Empedocles imagines this gory scene. It's one of only two images from Pre-Socratic philosophy that would be at home in a horror movie. The other one is also from Empedocles, and we'll get to it in a moment.

The power of Empedocles' imagery is in part due to the way he wrote, namely in hexameter poetry, following the lead of Parmenides. Parmenides looms large over Empedocles' philosophy, as too for the other philosophers we've been talking about in the last several chapters. As with the atomists and Anaxagoras, one of the main worries for Empedocles is how change is possible, despite the arguments that Parmenides and his followers gave for the impossibility of change. We've seen that, in their own ways, the atomists and Anaxagoras sort of agreed with the Eleatics that absolute change can't happen: nothing comes to be from complete and utter non-being. Rather, what happens is that the things which already exist, whether this means Anaxagoras' infinite mixture or the atomists' infinity of unchanging atoms, alter or recombine in different ways. This is Empedocles' solution too. He says, echoing Parmenides, that in a way nothing ever changes. The basic building-blocks of the cosmos, which Empedocles called "roots" but which Aristotle and later philosophers will call "elements," are always the same. They just get separated and combined in different ways, which yields the universe we see around us (§349).

The roots, or elements, are air, earth, fire, and water. Even people who have never really encountered ancient Greek philosophy know about these four elements—you might hear people talk about them when discussing astrology, for instance. Well, Empedocles was the first person to establish these as the basic ingredients of the world. Mind you, he doesn't always just call them air, earth, fire, and water; that would be too straightforward for his style. Instead, he uses the names of gods to refer to them; for instance, in one fragment water is the goddess Nestis and fire the god Hephaestus (§374). These, combined in certain proportions with earth, result in bone. He even gives a numerical analysis, which sounds something like a bartender describing a mixed drink: four of eight parts are fire and two are water. Empedocles also gives a more artistic analogy. To those who doubt that the world, in all its complexity, could emerge from only these four "roots," he points out that painters can fashion images of all things from just a few pigments (§356).

We might well think Empedocles is onto something here. Varied and complex things can indeed come out of only a few basic elements; just think of the periodic table. What we'll want to know next, though, is how and why the elements come together in the way they do. The analogy of the painter suggests that someone is controlling this process. As it turns out, there are two someones, or two some-things, in charge. Empedocles calls them Love and Strife. These two principles, which we might think of as cosmic forces, are ultimately responsible for the formation of plants, animals, stars—the whole cosmos—out of the four roots (§§349, 355, 360). They play something like the role that Mind plays in the cosmology of Anaxagoras, except that, of course, in Anaxagoras Mind has no other force opposing it. The fact that Empedocles has two principles gives him the opportunity to put forward a grandiose and influential idea: his theory of cosmic cycles.

According to this theory, there is a kind of waxing and waning in the power of both Love and Strife. When Love is completely dominant, all the four elements are mixed together in total peace and harmony. Empedocles describes the cosmos in this condition as a sphere (§§357–8), which might remind us of the spherical one being in Parmenides. Unlike Parmenides' being, though, this sphere is going to change: as Strife begins to exert its influence, the elements are sifted out from one another (§360). Ultimately the elements become completely separate, so that all the fire is gathered together, all the water gathered somewhere else, and the same for air and earth. Obviously, when the cosmos is dominated totally by Love or by Strife, there will be no people, animals, or plants. It's only when we are somewhere in between these moments of total domination that things get really interesting. A cosmos like ours results when Strife has broken down the unified oneness of Love (the "sphere"), but not pulled it apart completely. Such a cosmos will arise again when the cycle is moving in the opposite direction—away from the separated elements and towards the sphere. Thus, in each cycle it happens twice that you get sunflowers, giraffes, humans, and indeed the structured physical universe as a whole. Indeed, all things other than the four elements themselves are joint productions of Love and Strife that arise at the appropriate stages of the cosmic cycle.

This brings us to the second image in Empedocles that wouldn't be out of place in a horror movie. It's one thing to say that somehow plants, animals, and people arise from the four elements. It's quite another to explain how this happens. Empedocles, true to form, has quite a bold theory about this. He says that animals emerge in stages. At first, you don't get whole animals but only individual limbs and organs. In what is surely a contender for his most fantastic fragment, he describes the situation: "here sprang up many faces without necks, arms wandered without shoulders, unattached, and eyes strayed alone, in need of foreheads" (§376).[3] So here you have these eyeballs cruising around, occasionally bumping into a shoulderless arm. The eyes don't apologize, since they have no lips. The next thing that happens is that the limbs come together.[4] But they do so in an apparently random fashion, which produces, as he says, things that look like they come from dreams (§375)—the dreams must be nightmares, I guess, though I personally don't have many nightmares that feature shoulderless arms sporting eyes.

Next, things progress still further and you get whole animals. But these aren't necessarily the animals we know and love. Since they come together randomly, the results are still monstrous—for example, an ox with the face of a man (§§379–80). But these monsters, says Empedocles, always die out, and still die now when they are occasionally born. They perish, he says, because they are unsuitable. It's only in a fourth phase that we get animals which are able to reproduce. Now, I know what you're thinking: holy cow! Or rather, holy man-faced ox! Empedocles invented the theory of evolution! At least, that's what a lot of people have thought. I don't want to take anything away from Empedocles' audacious theory, but I do want to point out that it does not really anticipate the theory of evolution. To have a theory like Darwin's, you need the idea that species carry on by means of inherited features; and the idea that inherited features are selected because they make the animal or plant more likely to survive. Empedocles has neither of these ideas. Reproduction comes in only in the final stage, when the "suitable" animals, namely the ones we have now, have been produced. Fitness for survival is what makes reproduction possible, not the other way around. Without an explanation of inherited features, Empedocles cannot really tell us why it is the so-called "suitable" animals that survive. Perhaps it's true that the man-faced ox will die a quick death, whereas the ox-faced ox will prosper and get to mate with the other ox-faced oxen. It's not quite clear why that should be; maybe the lady beasts find the man-faced ox less than appealing. Let's just grant it to Empedocles, for the sake of argument. But still, why does the ox-faced ox produce an animal that looks just like it? This cannot be explained simply by appealing to chance, a point emphasized by Aristotle, as we will see later.

A long-standing point of debate among Empedocles scholars is what, if anything, his story of cosmic cycles and organic generation might have to do with his theory of reincarnation.[5] The former looks like Anaxagorean natural philosophy, the latter like Pythagorean religion. As we've seen, Empedocles claimed to be a god banished to this world. He believes that he and other gods have become lesser beings, called "spirits" or "demons" (*daimones*). These spirits then come to be trapped in fleshly bodies (§§402–7). Ultimately they can rise back to divine status, by becoming outstanding humans (like "prophets" or "doctors") and then escaping from this world of mortality. One of the reasons that the new Strasbourg evidence for Empedocles is important is that it confirms a link between the reincarnation cycle and the cosmic cycle. It would seem that Empedocles was trying to describe the same process, in which unity is lost and then regained, from two points of view. On the one hand there is the material process undergone by the elements, on the other, the more spiritual process each spirit undergoes, which was vividly described by Empedocles as personal experience.

Like other Pre-Socratics, Empedocles thus married religious trappings to a rational account of the cosmos. Yet his fascination for the physical world seems to outstrip that of any other Pre-Socratic, though this could also just be because we have more evidence for Empedocles. He uses the resources of his cosmic theory to explain in detail such things as the anatomy of the eye. In one fragment he describes how the eyeball is fashioned by Aphrodite, comparing it to a lantern which shields a fire from the wind (§389). The fire of the eye is surrounded by water, but never doused because of the membranes that separate the flame from the moisture. Vision is possible because of tiny pores that allow fine material to pass through, so that the membrane around the fire inside the eye is like a kind of screen, both protecting it and letting it interact with the world outside. But why does there need to be fire in the eye? The reason is that Empedocles thinks that colors are fiery, and only fire can be affected by something fiery. This principle, that in sensation only like can affect like, is one we will revisit when we get to Aristotle's theory of the soul.

But for now I want to emphasize something else, which is the careful way Empedocles has thought about the eye—you might even say, dissected the eye. Perhaps literally, when we think about those membranes. Remember Empedocles claimed that, everywhere he went, people flocked around him asking to be healed—and "doctors" are among the men who are close to being freed from the cycle of reincarnation. His enthusiasm for things medical is confirmed by other ancient authors who tell us about Empedocles' expertise in this field. But was there really medicine at this early period in ancient Greece? You bet there was. In fact, ancient medicine and ancient philosophy were in constant interaction, since at least the fifth century BC if not earlier. Hippocrates, the "father of medicine," was a near-contemporary of Plato's, and Hippocrates was already able to draw on generations' worth of ideas about the human body, including the sort of thing we find in Empedocles. Of course, these days we don't think of medicine as being a part of philosophy, and even in ancient Greece and Rome medical doctors were considered to be something of a separate profession. But as we'll see now, Greek philosophy and medicine were, like Empedocles' elements, seeds that became mixed with one another.

GOOD HUMOR MEN
THE HIPPOCRATIC CORPUS

"First of all, do no harm." This fundamental precept of medical ethics goes back to the man known as the Father of Medicine, Hippocrates of Kos. Well, more or less. The phrase is found in a work called the *Epidemics*, a fascinating text which gives detailed medical observations about outbreaks of disease in the ancient world. It instructs the medical practicioner "to help, or at least not to harm," and this phrase has come down to us along with the idea that doctors should take an oath. Even today, we talk about doctors taking their Hippocratic oath. And in fact we do have an ancient Greek text called the *Oath* which, like the *Epidemics*, is ascribed to Hippocrates. These are just two of the more than sixty writings ascribed to Hippocrates in antiquity; we now call them the Hippocratic corpus. But the way Hippocrates relates to this body of texts is a bit like the way Homer relates to the *Iliad* and the *Odyssey*. Hippocrates certainly did exist; in fact, we're more sure of this than we are that Homer existed. But we can't say which, if any, parts of the corpus Hippocrates wrote.

Not only did Hippocrates exist, but he became famous very quickly. It's because of his fame that all these writings about medicine were attached to his name. Plato and Aristotle already refer to him as a pre-eminent doctor. Plato also says that he accepted students for a fee, and taught them medicine. As with most Pre-Socratics, we don't have a firm idea of when Hippocrates lived, though of course he must have been on the scene in time for Plato to have referred to him. For our purposes it's enough to say that he was younger than Socrates, perhaps a rough contemporary of Plato's. Was he the Father of Medicine? Definitely, in the sense that the Hippocratic corpus, that is, the works supposedly written by Hippocrates, represents our first really important medical literature from the Greeks. As we'll see shortly, there is plenty of evidence that there was medical activity before Hippocrates, or perhaps we should say, before even the earliest works from his corpus were written. But it's in the Hippocratic corpus that we have our earliest surviving treatises on medicine. They discuss everything, from the way a doctor should behave—as in the *Oath*—to theories about the causes of disease, to the techniques that the doctor should use to cure and prevent diseases.

This is a book about the history of philosophy, so why am I talking about medicine? Well, as I said at the end of the previous chapter, philosophy and medicine were very closely related in the Greek world. This is an example of something I've mentioned before: the close relationship between ancient philosophy and science in general. Medicine makes a particularly good example, because it was a preoccupation of so many philosophically-minded authors, and because we can actually trace the impact of philosophy on medical ideas. Medicine and philosophy in the Greek world went hand-in-hand, especially in the generations leading up to the time of Socrates, Plato, and Aristotle—the same period as gave rise to the understanding of medicine enshrined in the Hippocratic corpus.

Medicine, in the sense of a technical expertise claimed by certain experts, goes way back in the Greek world—in fact, pretty much as far as our evidence does. In the *Iliad*, Homer depicts the gods healing wounds, and also includes two human characters who are both soldiers and healers: they learned their art of medicine from their father, Asclepius. In Homer, Asclepius seems to be a human, albeit one whose father was a Centaur. Later on in Greek history, though, Asclepius will be seen as a god of medicine. This is already one way that medicine is like philosophy: the seeds of a tradition are already planted in the Homeric poems. Another striking parallel is that Greek medicine is associated with the same region of the Greek world as gave birth to philosophy: the far eastern Mediterranean. Hippocrates hailed from the island of Kos, off the coast of Ionia where the Milesians and Heraclitus devised the first philosophical thoughts. It's revealing that, even though the dialect of Greek spoken in Kos was Doric—the kind of Greek they spoke in Sparta, for instance—the Hippocratic corpus is written in the Ionic dialect. So that's another hint of the connections between Hippocratic medicine and Pre-Socratic philosophy. We can also point to the attitude that Hippocratic authors take towards religion. As with Pre-Socratic philosophy, it's commonly said that Greek medicine distanced itself from religion, and thus became "scientific" and "rational." But also as with Pre-Socratic philosophy, the situation is actually a bit more complicated.

An interesting case here would be a Hippocratic work on epilepsy, which the Greeks called the "sacred disease": epilepsy was thought to be sent by the gods, and sometimes to involve inspired visions on the part of the epileptic person. But the author of the Hippocratic treatise titled *The Sacred Disease* doesn't have much time for this notion.[1] He explains that epilepsy, like other diseases, has natural causes—it isn't a curse, or for that matter a blessing, that comes willy-nilly from the gods. He makes fun of people who claim that certain kinds of epileptic fits are caused by certain gods. Instead, he says, epilepsy is no more sacred than any other disease. But he goes on to add that epilepsy is no *less* sacred than any other disease. In a sense all diseases are sacred, because they are brought about in our bodies by natural forces like the winds or the sun, and these forces are themselves divine. He concludes with an aphorism worthy of Heraclitus: all diseases are divine, and all are human. If anything, the author is claiming to be *more* pious than those who blame epilepsy on the gods. Respect for the gods doesn't mean thinking that they intervene randomly in human life to strike certain people down with an illness. It means seeing all of nature as divine, or as having a divine source. This might remind us of Xenophanes, who attacked Homer and Hesiod for making the gods too much like humans, with human emotions and irrationality. Xenophanes, like the author of *The Sacred Disease*, saw rationality as the correct religious attitude, not as a complete departure from religion.

In fact, Greek medicine was closely related to religious practice. There were elaborate cults which involved asking the gods for healing. An example would be the cult of Asclepius, which was introduced in Athens in the late fifth century BC. At this point Asclepius is seen as a god. He has a dedicated temple, with a staff of priests who are apparently also doctors. When you're sick, you go sleep in or near the temple. If you are favored by the god you will have a dream, during which the god will either heal you or give you instructions on how to be cured. Asclepius' cult became strongly associated with Hippocrates' island of Kos, and a large temple was built there in his honor. In the ancient world there was a legend that Hippocrates learned his medical wisdom by reading the inscriptions on the walls of the temple, but this is impossible for chronological reasons. Still, there's every reason to think that Hippocrates himself, and the sort of doctors who wrote and read the Hippocratic treatises, would have accepted the religious practices around disease. At the same time, they sought to bring human understanding to bear on the causes and cures of those diseases. As one Hippocratic author says, "prayer is good, but in addition to calling on the gods, one should lend a hand."[2]

So religion was one part of the world that generated Hippocratic medicine. But a still bigger influence came from Pre-Socratic philosophical and scientific ideas. We've already seen philosophers making claims that border on the medical—for instance, Heraclitus saying that drunkenness relates to being moist, or Anaxagoras explaining nutrition with his theory of universal mixture. But for medicine in the proper sense, Empedocles was the most important of the famous Pre-Socratics. Not only did he boast about his powers of healing and knowledge of drugs, but his medical interests are borne out by details of his theory of nature. As we saw, for Empedocles everything is made of the four elements, air, earth, fire, and water; for instance, bone or the eye: in both cases, he explains how these body parts arise out of the four elements. And for Empedocles, blood and flesh are made of nearly *equal* proportions of the four elements. That makes blood and flesh something like an ideal physical stuff, from Empedocles' point of view.

The medical application for this idea is obvious: if you're sick, it's because your proportions are out of balance. We find another thinker, the much more obscure Philistion of Locri, making precisely this point. Locri is at the tip of the Italian boot, so not far from Empedocles' home in Sicily—and Philistion takes up Empedocles' four-element theory. He says that since your body is made up of those four elements—fire, air, earth, and water—we get sick because some of the elements dominate so that our bodies become too hot, cold, dry, or wet. The trick is to get these qualities into balance. What Philistion says is based on Empedocles' theory, but it also has some common-sense plausibility—just think of what it's like when you have a fever. The idea will be applied for centuries and centuries to come. For instance, Hippocratic doctors already made extensive use of drugs, and this sort of theory—in its general outlines, if not its details—could provide a theoretical basis for how the drugs worked. As the medical tradition carries on, theories about pharmacology tend to explain that the ingredients in the drugs will adjust the heat, cold, moisture, or dryness of your body. The same thing goes for another major area of ancient medicine: diet. If you consulted a doctor in the ancient world, whether in fourth-century Greece or centuries later in the Roman empire, the doctor would almost certainly give you advice about what to eat, how much exercise to get, and so on.

This advice was based on long observation, and on trial-and-error. But if you pushed the doctor to give a theoretical explanation for why these things worked, he would most likely say something involving Empedocles' four-element theory. Empedocles gave more to medicine than this general theory, though. I just mentioned that he was a big believer in blood, with its perfectly balanced proportions. He also put a lot of emphasis on breath—the Greek word for breath is *pneuma*, which is where we get words like "pneumatic." Aristotle explains that, according to Empedocles, there is a kind of interplay between breath and blood (§392). There are passages through the flesh of our bodies which fill with blood and then with air, in alternation. To judge from other authors, like Philistion, the point of this was apparently that taking in air keeps the innate heat of our bodies more moderate. Again, it's all about proportion and balance.

Another Pre-Socratic philosopher who was fascinated by breath was Diogenes of Apollonia. Ancient authors tended to see him as somewhat derivative (§598). His big thing was the principle of air, which seems to be a throwback to Anaximenes

(§§602–3). Diogenes was more influenced by Anaxagoras than Empedocles, and identified his airy principle with the cosmic Mind of Anaxagoras. Air is an intelligent principle flooding the universe, and it turns into the other elements when it changes in density. As a proof of this, he points to the fact that the intelligent beings of the cosmos, namely we humans and other animals, live by taking in air as they breathe. Dying is, quite literally, running out of breath, and being intelligent is basically a matter of having more air in your physical make-up—so that he explains the fact that plants can't think in terms of their not taking in and retaining air (§612). Again, there are medical, or at least anatomical, applications. For instance, he has a theory of reproduction which I'll describe delicately, since this is a book for the whole family. The basic idea is that the human seed produced by men is blood which has been thinned and made foamy by mixing with air (§§615–16). He even made observations about the network of blood-vessels which were supposed to support this theory.

Diogenes was not a major thinker, but his idea that there is a close association between life and breath, or *pneuma*, is almost irresistible, at least once someone else has thought of it. After all, it can't be a coincidence that living people breathe and dead ones don't, right? Many later thinkers will go further, and say that the soul itself is made of some kind of breath which pervades the body, and perhaps even circulates through what we now know to be blood-vessels or nerves. These theories will get quite sophisticated. For instance, the second-century AD doctor Galen distinguished several different types of *pneuma* which animate the body. I'm not saying we should try to trace all this directly back to Diogenes of Apollonia or Anaximenes. But certainly the foundations of the idea were laid by the Pre-Socratics.

Now, these sorts of theoretical considerations were certainly not the main concern of the authors of the Hippocratic corpus. The treatises cover a range of issues, from medical ethics to drugs, gynecology, you name it. One text, called *On Ancient Medicine*, actually defends what the author considers to be traditional medicine against newfangled theories which invoke the contrary properties hot, dry, cold, and wet.[3] In fact, this author refers explicitly to Empedocles. Instead of these simplistic theories, the Hippocratic author says, we must follow the teachings of the medical tradition, which are gleaned from long and careful experience. Medicine is a large and complex body of knowledge, which is especially required in order to prescribe the correct diet for each patient. The author thus anticipates arguments in the late ancient world, where we will find Galen criticizing rival schools for saying that medicine is easy and simple to learn on the basis of a few theoretical principles. To quote another famous Hippocratic saying: "Life is short, but the art is long."[4]

And yet the Hippocratic corpus does recognize certain theoretical principles. Of course, given that the various Hippocratic treatises aren't all by the same person, the theoretical basis can change from one text to another. But something we find frequently in the Hippocratic material is the idea that what makes our bodies healthy is the same thing that preserves the cosmos as a whole: balance and proportion. In particular, the Hippocratics talk about the well-balanced proportion of bodily humors, meaning the various fluids in the body. You may well have heard of the four humors: blood, phlegm, yellow bile, and black bile. The parallel with the four elements of Empedocles is not a coincidence—and the humors could likewise be associated with the elemental properties, heat, cold, and so on.

This version of the four-humor theory was in the process of developing at the time the Hippocratic corpus was produced, so we don't find the corpus consistently referring to these as the canonical four humors. But we do often find the idea of keeping the humors in balance, that is, whichever humors are recognized in a given treatise. The humors are already starting to be associated with specific diseases. The best example is "melancholy": the word comes from the Greek words for "black bile." When you have too much black bile you are melancholic—which for the ancients involves a complicated set of symptoms, and not just sadness, as the word has come to mean in English. The meanings of the English words "sanguine" and "phlegmatic" also refer to humors recognized by ancient and medieval thinkers— "sanguine" is an allusion to blood and "phlegmatic" to, well, phlegm. The fact that these English words refer to personality traits, and not diseases, shows that the tradition extended the humoral theory to explain not just disease but a wide range of human behavior. Some of the notorious practices we associate with medieval medicine, like blood-letting, can also be explained as an attempt to restore balance to the body by draining out one humor that has become excessive.

Hippocratic doctors did practice blood-letting, as well as cupping, which is where you make a small incision and place a heated glass over it; when the glass cools this creates negative pressure inside the glass, which draws out the blood. But the Hippocratic authors caution us to use such techniques sparingly. In general, they show an admirable reluctance to engage in what we would now call "invasive procedures": they knew that their art had serious limits. The *Oath* has the doctor promise to avoid using the knife—though the idea here may just be that surgery should be left to real specialists, whereas the *Oath* was for doctors who were what we might call "general practicioners."[5] It's possible to look back at Hippocratic practices and see many attractive features that make an interesting contrast to modern medicine. For instance, there is not only their reluctance to intervene, but also their attention to preventative medicine, especially in the form of dietary advice.

There is the Hippocratic insistence that medicine is an art, not a set of rules to be applied automatically, so that the doctor must learn to size up each patient as an individual case. There is the commitment to holism, which is mentioned as a signature doctrine of Hippocrates by none other than Plato. Hippocrates taught that one should treat the whole body, not just the one part of the body where we find an ailment.

But let's leave to one side the implications of Hippocratic practices for modern medicine, and ask instead where all this leaves us in terms of early Greek philosophy. For one thing, it reminds us that the Pre-Socratics applied their general theories to very specific problems. As I mentioned earlier, they saw the body as a "microcosm," a little version of the whole universe. The rules that apply to the cosmos apply to the human body as well, an idea which is used to explain even things like respiration and the ingredients of blood and bone. Something else we've learned is that the Pre-Socratics managed to influence their culture more broadly. They didn't see philosophy as a narrow, cloistered discipline, and their breadth of vision meant they could influence authors with other interests, like these doctors, who took Pre-Socratic ideas seriously and put them to use.

This integration of philosophy into wider Greek culture is only going to become more important as we turn our attention to the big three: Socrates, Plato, and Aristotle. But before we get to Socrates, I want to continue exploring this wider cultural context. Next I'll be looking at a group of thinkers who fascinate and infuriate in equal measure. Plato will make them a foil for Socrates and for true philosophy; he will make their very name synonymous with dubious, devious argument. Yet among these same authors we'll find the roots of some fundamental philosophical ideas, such as relativism. Who are these many-faced, slippery characters? If you haven't already guessed, you'll just have to turn the page.

12

MAKING THE WEAKER ARGUMENT THE STRONGER THE SOPHISTS

The word "sophist" is, nowadays, a term of abuse. If you call someone a sophist, you're accusing them of using bad arguments, arguments which are deceptively plausible but in fact totally bogus. Worse still, sophistry is arguing badly on purpose, trying to pull the wool over people's eyes by weaving a web of confusing and misleading words. How can this be, given that the word "sophist" derives from the Greek word for wisdom, *sophia*? The word *sophistes*, or "sophist," originally meant something like "a wise man." So how did it come to have these fraudulent associations—to the point that a sophist is almost the reverse of a wise person, someone who is out to undermine the search for wisdom? As usual, the culprits are Plato and Aristotle, who permanently tarred the Greek sophists with the brush of duplicity and underhandedness. For them, and hence for us, sophistry means using rhetorical techniques to induce persuasion without regard to truth, or using argumentative tricks to embarrass an opponent. Aristotle even wrote a work called *The Sophistical Refutations*, in which he warns the reader about the sophists' tricks, teaching us how to diagnose and avoid their chicanery.

But despite their poor reputation, the sophists made a major contribution to the history of philosophy. This isn't to say that they were philosophers, exactly, though they did put forward ideas which we might see as philosophical. It's more that their impact on Socrates and, especially, Plato was enormous. A truly great philosopher benefits from a truly provocative opponent. There's no greater philosopher than Plato, and he got the most provocative opponent he could have asked for in the shape of the sophists. It's interesting to note that, whereas only one Platonic dialogue came to be titled with the name of a Pre-Socratic philosopher, Parmenides, Plato wrote dialogues named after *four* of the most important sophists: Protagoras, Gorgias, Hippias, and Euthydemus. Another dialogue is called simply the *Sophist*. In it the characters try to define the word "sophist," and discover that the sophist is, even in this sense, difficult to pin down. Sophists play a major role in several other dialogues, including two of Plato's greatest works, the *Republic* and the *Theaetetus*. In short, Plato was obsessed with the sophists, and returned to them again and again, treating them with a mixture of humor, fascination, dismay, and disdain.

To understand Plato, then, we need to understand the sophists. And to understand the sophists, we need to understand a little bit about Athens in the fifth century BC. We've actually been talking about the fifth century for numerous chapters now, because Pre-Socratics like Empedocles, Anaxagoras, the Eleatics, and the atomists were all working in this period. But I haven't said much yet about the historical situation. There would be a lot to say, since this is the most eventful century of ancient Greek history. But to make a very long story very short: in the first part of the century the Greeks faced down the threat of invasion from the Persians in 480 and 479 BC. In the wake of this famous victory, Athens stepped to the forefront of power in the Greek world. As we've seen already, much of the Mediterranean Sea was an arena for Greek power, which extended itself through the establishment of colonies stretching from the Black Sea region, to modern-day Turkey, to Italy and Sicily. Athens' pre-eminent position in the middle of the fifth century was based on its dominance of the sea. As the greatest maritime power, it could intimidate other Greek cities and grow extremely rich. The Athenians formed an alliance with other city-states, in theory for defensive purposes, called the Delian League—the name alludes to the island of Delos, where the treasury of the League was kept before it was moved to Athens. Ultimately, Athens' overweening power provoked a backlash from an alliance of city-states led by Sparta: this was the Peloponnesian War, a protracted conflict which finally led to the breaking of Athenian hegemony in 404 BC.

Democracy was at the core of the Athenian domination of the Greek world in the middle of the fifth century. Athens preferred to ally with other democratic city-states, and liked to contrast itself to non-democratic Sparta. Even Athens' naval power may have been linked to its democratic institutions. You needed a lot of people to row the Greek boats called triremes, whereas the Greek hoplite army, which fought on land, was made up of richer citizens who could afford the armor and weapons. So it's plausible to think that Athens' investment in naval power went hand-in-hand with its democratic practices. I'll leave it to proper historians to evaluate this idea; the main point is that Athens was indeed "democratic," albeit not quite in the sense we would use the term today. For one thing, of course, this was a democracy of male citizens, excluding women and slaves. Also, the democratic institutions of Athens left a surprising amount to chance. Citizens representing the various territories in and around Athens would form a decision-making assembly. Membership of this and other political offices was decided by lot, and the randomly appointed assembly was then empowered to choose certain directly elected officials, including the military leaders.

It was this mechanism which allowed individual men to achieve, and retain, lasting political power even in Athens, with its lottery-based democratic system. In the middle of the fifth century Athens was ruled above all by one man: Pericles. He led Athens through years of peace and then into the Peloponnesian War, which began in 431 BC, two years before Pericles died in 429. Pericles is important not only for plain old history but also for the history of philosophy, because he associated with both philosophers and sophists. From among the philosophers he was connected especially with Anaxagoras, who, as we saw, seems to have been a kind of mentor for Pericles. Anaxagoras' trial for impiety, which I also mentioned briefly, may well have been in part due to his political associations as well as his genuinely challenging beliefs. (For instance, he denied the divinity of the heavenly bodies, and most Athenians would have found this scandalous.) From among the sophists, Pericles was associated especially with Protagoras, whom he appointed to write the laws for an Athenian colony in southern Italy.

Like several other major sophists, Protagoras wasn't from Athens. He came from Abdera, the city that also gave us Democritus the atomist. Protagoras and other sophists naturally flocked to Athens, sometimes carrying out political embassies from their native cities. It was a perfect place for them to ply their trade. Because of its wealth and political dominance, the city's elite was flush with cash, an attractive proposition for sophists who could apparently command startingly large fees for their services. Just as important was Athens' democratic constitution. In this regime persuasion was the key to political power. If you wanted to advance in Athenian society and become an influential gentleman, you needed to be able to speak well in order to sway the assembly. This is what the sophists taught their students to do: to speak persuasively on any topic. The skills they offered could also be of great use in the law-courts where, similarly, what was needed was a facility for convincing an audience.

According to Plato, this is what sophistry was all about: teaching persuasive techniques for an exorbitant fee. And there's plenty of other evidence that the sophists did teach their students to speak persuasively, both in public and in private, at length or in the cut-and-thrust of debate, on any and all topics. But we should not reduce sophistry to the mere production of bad but convincing arguments. The sophists were part of the more general flowering of Greek culture in the fifth century BC, which produced great historians like Herodotus and Thucydides, great artists like the sculptor Phidias, and great playwrights like Sophocles, Euripides, and Aristophanes. The sophists contributed to this culture, pioneering in the literary analysis of

Homer and other texts, and reaching a new sophistication in the use of language. That was especially true of a sophist named Prodicus. His speciality was carefully distinguishing the meanings of words; for example, Plato depicts him insisting that in order to be civil one should "debate" but not "argue," with the result that the audience is "gratified" but not "pleased" (Plato, *Protagoras* 337a–c). Plato also mentions that Prodicus was a teacher of Socrates. In another dialogue, Socrates says that he could unfortunately only afford to attend Prodicus' cheap one-drachma lecture and so missed out on the full version, which cost fifty drachmas (*Cratylus* 384b).[1] There's some fun being had at Prodicus' expense here, but Socrates' constant search to define what virtue is, what courage is, and so on, could be seen as a development of the linguistic precision urged by Prodicus.

Beyond language and rhetoric, we know that the sophists were active in a wide variety of fields, including mathematics, for example. The best example of the sophist as an all-around wise man was Hippias. Plato has some fun with him too. He tells us that Hippias once attended the Olympic games having personally made everything he brought with him: he wove his own clothing, cobbled his own shoes, even made the rings he wore on his fingers (*Hippias Major* 368b–d).[2] And of course he brought speeches, ready to talk on any subject. He was, in short, an expert in all human wisdom—as he announced proudly to anyone who would stand still long enough to listen. So it would be wrong to think that the sophists were narrowly concerned with the practice of persuasive speech-making. Still, from a philosophical point of view the sophists' most relevant ideas all relate somehow to the value of persuasion. They were not dispassionate seekers of truth, but advocates and word-smiths, more akin to political advisors or spin-doctors than to academic researchers. At their most radical, the sophists could occasionally be moved to suggest that there is no absolute truth to be found, and that persuasion is all we have.

This idea is associated especially with the greatest of the sophists, Protagoras. Like other major sophists, he received a high fee for his services, and in return he claimed to teach something of enormous value. If you wanted to know how to make a convincing speech, he could certainly help. But he offered more: he offered virtue. Our most substantial piece of evidence for Protagoras' teaching on these matters is, unfortunately, in Plato's dialogue the *Protagoras*. The reason I say "unfortunately" is that Plato was a genius of earth-shaking proportions, and therefore thoroughly unreliable. He used historical figures as characters, and did with them whatever his artistry demanded. We can't trust Plato to give us the straight story on Socrates or Protagoras, any more than we can trust Shakespeare to give us the straight story on Richard III or Henry V. Still, we might optimistically hope that the so-called "Great Speech" put into Protagoras' mouth by Plato represents the real Protagoras' attitudes

(*Protagoras* 320d–328d).[3] In it, Protagoras portrays political virtue as a gift from gods to men, which is shared out equally to all—that is, everyone can partake of virtue, unlike more specialized skills, like flute-playing. It's for this reason, says Protagoras, that we punish people when they fall short of what virtue would demand. On the other hand, not everyone is equally virtuous, and this is where Protagoras comes in—he, after all, is able to teach people how to be more virtuous than they are by nature. So confident was Protagoras that he would accept as payment whatever his students felt that the tuition was worth. On this note I can't resist repeating the following anecdote, even if it has the whiff of legend about it: a pupil of Protagoras refused to pay him, and they were to meet in court to settle the matter. Protagoras said the pupil should simply cough up the fee in advance. After all, the student would either win or lose his case. If he lost, he would have to pay the fee. But if he won, he would thereby prove that Protagoras had earned his fee by teaching the student to argue effectively in court; so he should pay either way.[4]

But if you remember just one thing about Protagoras, don't remember that story. Remember his famous remark that "man is the measure of all things, of the things that are, that they are, of the things that are not, that they are not."[5] In this brief statement we have the roots of an ancient and, to many, disturbing philosophical tradition: relativism. This is how Plato understood Protagoras: he was saying that each man judges what is true for him, but no one is in a position to judge what is true for anyone else. On this interpretation, Protagoras was saying that truth is always something's being true *for someone*, so that it could be true-for-me that the wind is cold, and true-for-you that the wind is warm. There is no such thing as the way the wind really is in itself. There is only the way things seem to us. On the face of it, this doctrine looks hard to square with Protagoras' claim to be a teacher of virtue. After all, if virtue for me is whatever I think it is, then why do I need Protagoras to teach me about it? In Plato's *Theaetetus*, Socrates imagines Protagoras answering that virtue is really what is *advantageous* to me. What Protagoras teaches me is not what would be best absolutely, but what would be best for me, meaning from my point of view.

This assimilation of virtue to what is advantageous is a key tenet of the sophists, and a somewhat different version of it shows up repeatedly in Plato. In yet another dialogue, the *Gorgias*, Socrates battles against the claim that virtue is the advantage, not of just anybody, but of those who are naturally stronger. Yet another sophist, named Thrasymachus, defends the same idea in the first book of Plato's *Republic*. Here we have an application of Protagoras' position to the sphere of morality: if there is no absolute truth, then there is nothing but advantage, and by rights what should happen is that the strongest people should get the best rewards. But why think the strongest people should get more than the weak? In fact, how can the sophists even use the word "should" if they reject absolute morality? Here the sophists could turn to a distinction they liked to draw between custom and nature. It is only by custom that there are social rules and laws of justice, and these laws may or may not reflect the natural order of things. It's natural for the strong to dominate the weak, whereas it's a mere custom for the weak to band together and restrict the power of the strong. Thrasymachus and other radical sophists saw themselves as speaking up for nature, and unmasking morality as nothing but social convention.

Protagoras himself probably drew more benign conclusions from his "man is the measure" doctrine. For Protagoras, the point was to educate people so as to make their lives seem better, that is, more advantageous. If he could make your life seem better to you, then would you really care whether there was anything real behind the seeming? He was willing to bet his fee that you wouldn't. Furthermore, Protagoras had ways of showing that you aren't going to get at reality even if you insist on trying. He was a pioneer in the paradigmatically sophistic activity of making arguments on both sides of a question. We have a later text, by an anonymous sophist, called simply *Double Arguments*, which shows how to argue on both sides of several philosophical issues—for instance, whether there is any difference between justice and injustice.[6] There's a disturbing implication here: if one can always argue with equal plausibility on both sides of any question, then arguing won't get us to the truth. We're only going to be persuaded by whichever argument is presented more effectively. The sophists were duly renowned for claiming they could "make the weaker argument the stronger." This boast was the sort of thing that made Plato shudder, but it makes a certain amount of sense. After all, you don't need an expensive lawyer, or sophist, to help you win a court-case when you're clearly innocent. You need one when it looks pretty certain that you're guilty.

That brings us to a final great sophist, and perhaps the most philosophically interesting of the lot: Gorgias. There is a connection here with Pre-Socratic philosophy, as he came from Sicily, and it seems that he was influenced by his fellow Sicilian Empedocles. Gorgias, like Protagoras, was more interested in persuasion than philosophy. Unlike Protagoras, however, Gorgias went out of his way to deny that he could teach virtue, and in fact stressed the moral neutrality of his art of rhetoric. In the dialogue named after Gorgias, Plato has him say that rhetoric is a bit like boxing: if a trainer teaches someone to box and he goes out and beats people up, this is not the trainer's fault (*Gorgias* 456c–457c).[7] Similarly, if Gorgias teaches a politician to argue effectively, then it's not his fault if the politican uses his newfound power for evil instead of good. On the other hand, Gorgias emphasizes that the ability he teaches is a lot more potent than boxing. For an expert rhetorician, like himself, can speak persuasively on *any* topic. He is the one who can persuade the patient to take medicine, even when the doctor can't (*Gorgias* 456a–b).[8]

We might distrust Plato here: isn't he just trotting out his favorite accusation, that the sophists were abandoning knowledge for the sake of persuasion? Well, yes. But we do have another, non-Platonic source where Gorgias speaks about the almost magical power of rhetoric. He wrote a display speech, which happily survives today, showing how he would defend the notorious Helen, who allowed herself to be seduced and thus triggered the Trojan War.[9] The central part of the speech argues that if Helen was *persuaded* to go off to Troy, then she was helpless to resist. Persuasive speech, says Gorgias, is like a drug. If a skilled user of words really wants you to do something, you will do it, as surely as if someone were to come along and use physical force on you. An equally fascinating surviving text by Gorgias is called *On Not-Being*. It seems to be a mind-bending parody of the Eleatic philosophers.[10] Whereas they showed that being is one and unchanging, Gorgias argues, with a series of absurdly complicated proofs, that there is no such thing as either being or non-being; and that if there were being or non-being, we could neither know about it nor say anything about it.

While this was probably intended at least in part as a mockery of Parmenides or his followers, Gorgias doubtless had a serious point too. Like Protagoras, Gorgias was hoping to pull the rug out from under philosophers, with their ambitious theories of underlying reality. If there is no reality to get at, and in fact no unreality either, as Gorgias argues in *On Non-Being*, then we are left only with the way things seem to us. This kind of world, of course, suits the sophist, who operates always at the level of seeming, of plausibility and persuasion. You can now begin to understand why Plato found the sophists so alarming—the sophist outlook was the diametrical opposite of Platonism. But of course, before there was Platonism there was Socrates. Because Socrates is now seen as a martyred saint of philosophy, we find it obvious to cast him in the role of the sophists' greatest adversary. Plato too puts Socrates in this role. So it may come as a surprise to discover that at least one other contemporary, who knew more about both Socrates and the sophists than we do, saw little distinction between them. This was the comic poet Aristophanes, one of two authors who will provide us with some context for the more famous portrayal of Socrates we find in Plato.

PART II

SOCRATES AND PLATO

13

SOCRATES WITHOUT PLATO
THE PORTRAYALS OF
ARISTOPHANES AND
XENOPHON

S ocrates is without doubt the most influential and famous philosopher who never
wrote anything. With no book to his name, Socrates owes his renown to the
impression he made on the people he met face to face, and above all to the fact that
one of those people was Plato. It is mostly through the dialogues of Plato that Socrates
lives on today. In those dialogues, Socrates appears as one of the great literary
characters of the ancient world—humorous, ironic, thoughtful, courageous, seductive, outrageous, and remarkably ugly. His personality stays relatively consistent
through the many dialogues in which he appears, but there are also shifts of emphasis
and doctrine. It is clear that Plato admired Socrates greatly, yet this did not stop him
from using Socrates for his own purposes. As I remarked in the last chapter, Plato is
anything but a straightforward witness as regards his predecessors, whether they were
sophists or his own teacher. That's one reason why, before I get into the Platonic
depiction of Socrates, I want to look at Socrates without Plato. In particular, I want to
talk about the way Socrates was portrayed by two very different authors from Athens,
who like Plato couldn't resist using him in their literary productions.

Most of us start by picturing Socrates at his end, the philosopher sitting calmly in
his jail cell, cheerfully draining a poisonous brew of hemlock after being sentenced
to death by a jury of his peers. As with Anaxagoras' trial, these events may have been
politically motivated. Socrates was executed in 399 BC, several years after Athens had
capitulated to Sparta at the end of the Peloponnesian War. In 404 BC, the same year
that the war ended, Athens was taken over by a group of thirty oligarchs or tyrants.
One of these tyrants was Critias, an associate of Socrates. A more famous friend of
Socrates was Alcibiades, a man as good-looking as Socrates was ugly, talented and
ambitious in equal measure. Alcibiades was, to say the least, a controversial figure.
He'd been exiled from Athens after a scandal involving the defacement of religious
statues, and he'd subsequently switched sides more than once in the long war

between Sparta and Athens. So it's possible that the citizens of Athens had Socrates executed in part because he had unpleasant and anti-democratic friends. On the other hand, we know that Socrates refused to carry out an order from the Thirty Tyrants, when he was told to arrest someone unjustly. And in fact, if ever anyone was his own man, it was Socrates—it's rather difficult to imagine him promoting any one political faction in Athens. As we'll see, Plato makes it clear that Socrates was quite capable of annoying people all on his own. Maybe the citizens of Athens just got fed up with him.

Socrates was constantly in conversation, with both friends and more hostile interlocutors such as the sophists. The classic image of Socrates, enshrined in more than one painting and sculpture, shows him taking the hemlock.[1] But a better image to hold in your mind is of Socrates in the marketplace, a group of young men gathered around him, discussing the nature of virtue. His young friends were not exempt from the razor-sharp edge of Socrates' wit: friends and foes alike were cut down to size. The classic Socratic approach is, of course, to ask questions: what is virtue? What makes a good leader? Do you really think you are justified in what you are doing? Once you answer this first question, you're done for. Socrates will expose the thoughtlessness of your assumptions—he will show you that you quite literally don't know what you are talking about. But this isn't to say that Socrates did nothing else in his life. He fought against the Spartans, and was involved in several battles, including a major loss at the battle of Delium in 424 BC. In one dialogue Plato has Alcibiades tell of Socrates' amazing performance in battle and on military campaign generally. He was, says Alcibiades, so imposing in his fearlessness that no one from the enemy army wanted to come anywhere near him.

Of course we're used to this sort of admiring portrait of Socrates as an almost superhuman hero and martyr of philosophy. Yet the earliest portrayal of Socrates shows him as anything but heroic. It was written by the comic poet Aristophanes, a younger contemporary of Socrates who died in 385 BC. Aristophanes was the greatest writer of comedy in Athens, and makes Socrates an important character in a play called the *Clouds*.[2] Anyone who found out they were to feature in a play by Aristophanes would have known they were in for some rough handling. His plays are full of brilliant wordplay and political satire. In them one can find deep and powerful protest against war and injustice. On the other hand, the plays are also brimming with toilet humor and sex gags, and the *Clouds* is certainly no exception. Aristophanes was a great poet, but a *comic* poet, and he never strays far from his central task of getting the audience to laugh. And for good reason: Aristophanes was quite literally competing for the approval of that audience. At the festival of the god Dionysus in Athens each year, celebrated over several days, numerous plays were performed. Aristophanes' productions were pitted against those of other play-wrights. He won the prize several times, albeit not with the *Clouds*, which was voted third and last in the year 423 BC.

Aristophanes' ignominious defeat on this occasion would no doubt have allowed Socrates a wry smile, if it weren't for the fact that Socrates was surely above such pettiness. Indeed, "above" is precisely where Aristophanes puts Socrates. He called for Socrates to enter on a kind of crane normally used in other plays for depicting gods and heroes in the sky, looking down on the action of the drama. Socrates quite literally has his head in the clouds. He explains to the main character, one Strepsiades, that he is engaged in meteorology, which in Greek meant study of things in the sky generally, not just weather. Strepsiades is there to get Socrates and the other philosophers he consorts with to teach him how to win arguments. He wants to be able to make speeches and wield bewildering wordplay in order to get out of some financial debts that are pressing down on him. Socrates assures Strepsiades that he can teach him arguments to prove any point, and along the way teaches him to give up belief in the traditional Greek gods and to worship the clouds instead. These clouds are played by the chorus of the play. Also along the way, as I say, is a healthy serving of those toilet and sex jokes.

All this is something of a shock, not just because we don't normally associate Socrates with this sort of lowbrow frivolity, but because Aristophanes is making it crystal clear that he thinks Socrates is a sophist. Surely this is wrong? As we'll see, both Xenophon and Plato show Socrates clashing repeatedly with sophists. But of course, sophists could and did clash with one another. So Aristophanes evidently saw little distinction between Socrates and his sophistic contemporaries. After all, both Socrates and the sophists left their opponents dazed by raining down argu-ments on them, and both traded in fine attention to the meanings of words. Of course we want to insist that Socrates' motives were different—pure, virtuous—but that seems to have been lost on Aristophanes. Plato too, by the way, more than once suggests that Socrates was widely seen as a sophist. In one dialogue he describes a kind of "noble sophistry" (*Sophist* 231b), which eliminates false belief rather than encouraging it. It seems clear Plato has Socrates in mind here. But to less subtle observers the most obvious difference between Socrates and the sophists would have been his poverty. Unlike them, he never asked a fee from his associates—he considered them to be his friends. Whereas Xenophon and Plato emphasize this and think it puts clear water between Socrates and the sophists, for Aristophanes it's just more material for jokes: he has great fun with Socrates' voluntary indigence, his barefooted, ragtag appearance.

Still more confusing is that Aristophanes uses Socrates to represent not only the sophists, but also the Pre-Socratic philosophers. Socrates' fascination with meteorology is a case in point, and the worship of clouds is evidently designed as a dig at philosophers who thought that air was a divine principle, like Diogenes of Apollonia. This too is directly contradicted by Plato and Xenophon, who go out of their way to stress that Socrates did *not* engage in physical sciences, except perhaps early in his career.[3] His concern was virtue, not clouds. Again, Aristophanes was not interested in these fine distinctions. For him Socrates was useful because he was a very visible and notorious character to put in a play. It's even been speculated that Socrates was chosen in part because he was famously ugly. His protruding eyes and snub-nose would have made him an ideal person to put on the Greek stage, where all the actors wore masks. (An actor playing the part of a real person like Socrates would wear a mask caricaturing his features.) Still, it's telling that Aristophanes selected Socrates, of all people, to stand in for the whole movement of sophists and philosophers in Athens in the late fifth century. For Aristophanes, and no doubt for most of his audience, Socrates was just one more intellectual who peddled the same impious sophistry as the others.

The fact that Aristophanes depicts Socrates as rejecting the gods makes it hard to laugh at the *Clouds*—at least, if you know why Socrates was put to death a quarter-century later. The charge leveled at him was that he invented new gods and corrupted the youth. When Aristophanes showed him on stage telling Strepsiades that the traditional gods don't even exist, he was, presumably unwittingly, helping to prepare the case for the prosecution. By contrast, our other witness, Xenophon, was out to defend Socrates. He defended him posthumously, because by the time Xenophon wrote Socrates had been dead for some years. Xenophon was a close contemporary of Plato, born at around the same time (ca. 430 BC; he died about 350 BC). Like Alcibiades, Xenophon was exiled from Athens, and spent many years away from his home before finally returning to spend the last decade of his life there. Xenophon actually left Athens voluntarily before being exiled *in absentia*, and his choice to leave was a fateful one—Socrates advised him to think twice before doing so, but he went anyway. He left to join an attempt to overthrow the ruler of Persia, working as a mercenary on the behalf of the would-be deposer Cyrus, among a large cohort of Greek soldiers. When this failed, he underwent a harrowing journey as the leader of the Greeks, trying to bring as many as possible back alive to Greece. He later wrote a record of this experience, his most famous work, the *Anabasis*—which means "going up," in other words, back to Greece.

In addition to this tale of adventure and some other broadly historical works, Xenophon wrote several pieces about Socrates.[4] Sometimes he was imitating his fellow Socratic admirer, Plato: for instance, he wrote a dramatization of a drinking-party or "symposium," like the *Symposium* of Plato, with Socrates sitting and discussing love with other men. His longest Socratic work, the *Memoirs of Socrates*, is also reminiscent of Plato, with Socrates shown in discussion with a succession of characters, most of whom get put firmly in their place. And again like Plato, he wrote an *Apology* of Socrates, describing what Socrates said at the trial where he was condemned to death. Yet Xenophon's Socrates is very different from Plato's. As Xenophon himself tells us, his primary motivation is not to exploit the philosophical potential of Socrates as a character—as Plato did—but to vindicate Socrates and his way of life, and in particular to undermine the accusations that had been made against Socrates in the fatal trial.

As I said, these accusations were twofold: Socrates departed from traditional religion, and he corrupted the youth. Where Aristophanes stoked these slanders for humorous effect, Xenophon strenuously rejects both. For him, Socrates was a paragon of virtue, albeit one who few if any people could hope to imitate. He duly emphasizes Socrates' piety—rather than rejecting the gods, his Socrates goes on at length about divine providence, and says we must be grateful to the gods who show their benevolence by designing humans and the world around them so well.[5] Xenophon also emphasizes Socrates' hot-line to god. This was Socrates' famous "divine sign," something also mentioned more than once by Plato. Socrates could not exactly see the future, but he claimed that the gods would warn him to avoid certain activities when he began to undertake them.[6] For instance, he did not prepare a defense speech for his apology because, when he was about to write it, the divine sign warned him off.

As Xenophon stresses, the moral of the story here seems to be that it was better for Socrates to die. Certainly, Xenophon agrees with Plato that Socrates did nothing to avoid death once he'd been brought to trial. Far from it: in fact he went out of his way to outrage and offend the jurors in his impromptu defense speech. In both versions, but especially that of Xenophon, Socrates is stunningly arrogant. Xenophon shows him bragging about his perfect virtue—modesty not ranking very high among the character-traits valued by the Greeks. He also shows Socrates claiming to be specially favored by the gods, in particular because of the divine sign. As Xenophon says, this was the last thing Socrates should have said if he wanted to save his skin, because the jury was outraged, either with incredulity or envy at Socrates' special favor from the gods. But Socrates was, it would seem, not trying to save his skin—he was trying to die as he had lived, with perfect and uncompromising virtue.[7]

That brings us to the second accusation, Socrates' supposed corruption of the youth. Xenophon has Socrates argue that this could hardly be the case, because he was always perfectly virtuous and so should serve as a good, not a bad, example for his young friends.[8] If these boys' fathers objected to Socrates hanging about with their sons in the marketplace, it was no doubt due to envy: the fathers were not well pleased that the boys sought education at the feet of Socrates rather than with them. But what would such boys have seen in Socrates? He was, after all, ugly, poor, and apt to mete out biting criticism to anyone unlucky enough to pass by. That last habit was no doubt part of the attraction, though: these young men liked learning to catch out their elders. Xenophon, in a scene hardly designed to solidify our admiration of Socrates, shows Alcibiades imitating Socrates' argumentative style as he deftly refutes the great statesman Pericles.[9] This is no doubt fictional, but there is also no doubt that Socrates' young friends did imitate him, mightily annoying a good many powerful men in the process.

Socrates was also seductive for these young men because they could admire his sort of virtue. His virtue was, in essence, independence and freedom. He was poor not because he had to be, but because he knew that an utterly destitute man can, paradoxically, be more self-sufficient than a man who has to worry about his wealth and hangers-on. For Socrates, the greatest slaves were tyrants, who had many enemies but also friends who might turn on them. As for sophists, they were nothing but whores who sold their supposed wisdom for cash. Socrates took no money for the wisdom he dispensed, and secured something more valuable: friendship. Beholden to no one, Socrates was his own man, and followed the dictates of no one apart from his divine sign. A young Athenian gentleman could see much to admire here. Socrates' total freedom was precisely what they sought, freedom and self-sufficiency, even though they planned to pursue this goal through a political life. They might not follow Socrates' path, because it was too ascetic, too self-denying— but they could see the point of it. And Socrates knew how to play on the ambitions of such men. In one scene, Xenophon shows us how Socrates could use the desire of a young man for honor and political success by showing him that knowledge is the only sure route to these ends.[10]

Socrates is being quite cunning here, because for him, of course, honor and political success were nothing to be prized. For him, it is knowledge itself which is valuable—success as a political leader is something he dangles as bait, to get his young friend to pursue what Socrates offers. Xenophon agrees with Plato that Socrates did, indeed, teach that knowledge is the most important thing in life, and that knowledge is "virtue itself." This idea will be explored in much greater depth by Plato, but Xenophon gets across the basic point: to do anything virtuously is to do it well, and to act well means to act with knowledge. Again, Xenophon's Socrates appeals to the political interests of his audience in making this point: he says that choosing an ignorant man to be the leader of a city would be like choosing an ignorant man as one's doctor. We don't let untrained men experiment on our bodies, and neither should we let men without knowledge experiment on the body politic. Here Xenophon doesn't sound much different from the Plato of the *Republic*.

But in many other respects Xenophon gives us a very different Socrates from the one we find in Plato. As we'll see, in Plato Socrates makes a big deal of proclaiming his own ignorance. Plato's Socrates is puzzled when the oracle at Delphi pronounces him the wisest man in Athens, because he knows that he knows nothing—how can he be wise? By contrast, Socrates in Xenophon is swaggering with confidence in his own perfection. He tells the jury at his trial that the oracle at Delphi proclaimed him to be the wisest and most free of men, but in Xenophon's telling this comes as no surprise. It simply confirms what Socrates knew all along, which is that he is the most virtuous man walking the earth. He does add, modestly, that the oracle stopped short of calling him a god.[11]

Instead of claiming ignorance, Xenophon's Socrates feels free to dispense advice on a wide range of topics. Often Xenophon puts rather banal ethical advice into the philosopher's mouth. We see him chastising a man for being unable to bear his hectoring mother—just remember, says Socrates, that she means well. We see him telling a man that spending time with beautiful women is as dangerous as somersaulting through knives. We see him telling off a man who complains that the drinking-water in his house is too cold—after all, Socrates points out, it's better for taking baths, and the slaves don't complain about the water; do you really want to be more choosey than one of your slaves?[12] In such passages, Socrates seems more like an advice columnist than a philosopher. It's hard to escape the conclusion that Xenophon is using Socrates as a mouthpiece, just as Plato does—but putting much less interesting ideas into his mouth.

Yet, we should not underestimate Xenophon, or Aristophanes for that matter. They both made careful choices in their use of Socrates, and made this most extraordinary of men subordinate to their authorial purposes. Aristophanes gives us valuable insight into the late fifth-century perception, not just of Socrates, but of the whole intellectual blossoming of that period—the sophists, the philosophers, and Socrates as the ugly face of the whole phenomenon. Xenophon, meanwhile, manages to capture many of the themes that will be associated with Socrates by Plato and for centuries thereafter. Some of the ideas I've highlighted—for instance, the ideal of self-sufficiency and the focus on virtue as the only thing worth having—will be carried on by the philosophical schools of the Hellenistic period, especially the Stoics and the Cynics. We should give Xenophon credit for already seeing these aspects of Socrates. If it wasn't for Plato, we might see his record of Socrates as a milestone text in the history of philosophy. But that's a bit like saying that if Shakespeare hadn't written *Romeo and Juliet*, then *West Side Story* would be the classic tale of doomed lovers. Our Socrates is inevitably the Socrates we read about in Plato, and it is to this Socrates that we turn next.

METHOD MAN
PLATO'S SOCRATES

Anyone who has spent time in a classroom, whether as a teacher or a student, has probably encountered the Socratic method. It means, of course, teaching someone by asking them questions—perhaps leading questions, but questions nonetheless. When practiced rigorously, the Socratic method requires that the teacher never says *anything* apart from questions. This can descend into parody pretty quickly. The student asks for the dates Plato was born and died, and instead of saying that he was born in 427 BC and died in 347 BC, the teacher says, "Well...when do *you* think he was born and died?" But practiced in moderation, the Socratic method is an excellent way to teach. It forces the students to figure things out for themselves, rather than passively sitting there waiting to be filled with knowledge, as if teaching were like pouring wine into the empty vessels that are the students' heads.

Socrates was of course a prominent user of the Socratic method, if not its inventor. According to Plato, he had a very good reason for using the method, namely that he had no wisdom of his own to impart anyway. Socrates claimed to be ignorant about the things he was out to discover. The reason he gave for cornering the good people of Athens in the marketplace, and pestering them to tell him what courage or piety or virtue in general might be, was that he himself really didn't know what courage or piety or virtue was. He was desperate to find someone who could help him answer these most important questions, questions that became the basis for many of Plato's dialogues. In Plato's *Laches*, Socrates asks military men to explain what courage is (190b–d). In the *Euthyphro*, he asks a man who is prosecuting his father for murder to explain what piety is (5d)—after all, anyone who would prosecute his father for murder must be pretty confident in his own moral judgment.

Socrates likes to ask questions more than he likes to answer them. In the *Meno*, for instance, Socrates is asked whether virtue can be taught, and replies that he can't rightly say, because he doesn't even know what virtue is, so he can hardly know whether it can be taught (70a–71b). But perhaps Meno would be willing to help out, by first saying what virtue is? When faced with Socrates' questions, Meno and the other interlocutors say what they think about virtue, and Socrates gently, or not so gently, shows them that they have no idea what they're talking about. They contradict themselves, get into logical muddles, and wind up seeing that their ideas lead to outlandish and unbelievable results. Socrates ends up disappointed, and the interlocutors go away, perhaps angry, certainly puzzled, and with any luck realizing that they don't know quite as much as they thought.

This is the classic version of Plato's Socrates, as he emerges from a whole series of works which are often called the "Socratic dialogues." These dialogues were probably written early in Plato's career, and many people have thought that they are a faithful record of the real historical Socrates—perhaps even reports of actual discussions Socrates had. As I've admitted, I'm pretty skeptical about this. I think that from day one Plato was using Socrates for his own philosophical purposes, and that there's not much use in trying to extricate a portrait of the historical Socrates from some supposedly reliable Socratic dialogues. Besides, why should we try to do this anyway, when the Platonic Socrates is so interesting? We can watch as Plato develops Socrates as a *character*, in dialogue after dialogue, confronting him with various other characters, many of them also based on real people, like generals, poets, sophists, young lovers, scoundrels, politicians, and in the case of the *Republic* even Plato's own brothers. Of course, these portraits must have been inspired by the historical figures in question. Any resemblance to persons living or dead was not merely coincidental. But as students of the history of philosophy, what we are really interested in is what Plato did with the characters, not how close his versions were to the real people.

The best place to start if we want to understand Plato's Socrates is a dialogue called the *Apology*. As I mentioned last time, Xenophon also wrote a Socratic apology; and these were not the only two men writing Socratic literature around this time. Socrates had many admirers, and quite a few sought to rehabilitate his reputation after his execution in 399 BC. At that time Plato was twenty-eight years old. In his *Apology* he has Socrates mention that he, Plato, is there in attendance at the trial (34a). We shouldn't leap to the conclusion that the *Apology* is therefore an accurate record of what Socrates said, though. After all, in another dialogue, the *Phaedo*, we are told that Plato was sick and couldn't be present at Socrates' deathbed (59b). But this doesn't stop Plato from telling us what was supposedly said in Socrates' final hour. Nor are these the only dialogues set in the days leading up to Socrates' death. Between the *Apology*, in which we see Socrates' trial, and the *Phaedo*, in which we see his death, there is the *Crito*, in which Socrates' friend Crito unsuccessfully tries to persuade Socrates to save his own life by escaping and fleeing Athens. The *Euthyphro*, which I've already mentioned, is also set in the days leading up to the trial, as are several more dialogues. By setting so many dialogues in this short time-frame, Plato makes sure we don't lose sight of the high stakes we play for when we do philosophy. Socrates is trying to discover how best to live, and he's doing it even as he has only hours left to do any living.

But let's return to the *Apology*, which, as I say, is a good way of approaching Plato's take on Socrates. The first thing to say is that in it Socrates is anything but apologetic. It consists mostly of a defense speech, though he does engage in some typically Socratic cross-examination of one of his accusers, Meletus. The speech he gives isn't so full of swaggering arrogance as the one Xenophon wrote, but Plato's Socrates certainly makes little effort to ingratiate himself with the jurors. He does begin by making one apology, namely that he is a poor public speaker (17a–18a). This, of course, is a classic ploy used by good public speakers, and Socrates goes on to offer a *tour de force* of argument after claiming to be incompetent in rhetoric. Yet Plato's point isn't really to show Socrates trying to soften up the jury; it's to dispel the widespread notion that Socrates was a sophist. Socrates alludes directly to Aristophanes' play the *Clouds*, which as you'll remember from the last chapter portrayed Socrates both as a sophist and a kind of composite Pre-Socratic philosopher. Given the way he highlights the *Clouds* here in the *Apology*, it seems that Plato blamed Aristophanes for helping to create Socrates' ultimately lethal reputation.

Like Xenophon, Plato has Socrates demolish the official accusations against him, that he rejects the gods and corrupts the youth. There is, however, less focus on these specific charges here than in Xenophon. In Plato's version, Socrates' main theme is the story of how he made himself so unpopular in Athens. The story is as follows. As also reported by Xenophon, Socrates' friend Chaerephon went to the oracle at Delphi. What the oracle tells Chaerephon, in Plato's version, is that there was no man wiser than Socrates (*Apology* 21a). Socrates is stunned at the oracle's pronouncement, because he knows that he is not really wise at all. Such wisdom as he has is only "human wisdom," the nature of which he doesn't really explain (20d). But he lacks what would be really valuable, namely divine wisdom—this would be absolutely certain knowledge of the most important things, such as virtue.

Thus Socrates sets out to discover the sense in which the oracle's pronouncement might be true. Since he knows nothing of any value, one would expect it to be easy for him to find someone wiser than he is. So he tries to do so. He goes to the obvious candidates: politicians, poets, and craftsmen. He finds that they do know some limited things—for instance, the carpenters know how to make things out of wood—but none of these people possesses true wisdom, the knowledge of the most important things that Socrates is after. Worse still, they get carried away with the little understanding they do possess, and assume that they must have true wisdom in addition to their little bit of expertise. Their false pretentions of wisdom far outweigh the value of whatever it is they do know. The poets, for instance, claim all sorts of exalted insight, whereas actually they can't even explain the poems they have written themselves (22b). Socrates gradually realizes what the oracle at Delphi meant: he is the wisest of men not because he is so wise, but because he at least knows that he is *not* wise. His condition is something we have come to call "Socratic ignorance." This ignorance is, paradoxically, a kind of knowledge: it is knowing that one does not know.

This gives us a context for understanding what goes on in other Socratic dialogues. In questioning people from all walks of life, Socrates is giving them a chance to show that they do know, for instance, what courage or piety is. Maybe he'll finally strike lucky and find the man or woman who refutes the Delphic oracle by being wiser than Socrates. But if that doesn't happen, at least Socrates will reduce the interlocutor to a state of Socratic ignorance. He is doing them a great favor, really. He is disabusing them of the impression that they know things they don't really know. As Socrates says in the *Apology*, he is like a gadfly who buzzes around a horse, annoying it (30e)—but the annoyance is helpful and productive. Even though he can't do what some sophists like Protagoras claimed to do, namely teach people how to live, he can at least show people that they do *not yet* know how to live. That will put you in the same boat as Socrates, still looking for wisdom; but until he's purged you of your confidence in false beliefs, you won't even bother looking. Socrates firmly believes, therefore, that he's been doing the Athenians an important service. After he has been found guilty, he is asked what sentence he proposes for himself, and he suggests that he should receive free meals at state expense for the rest of his life (36d). Here it's hard to avoid the impression that Socrates is deliberately goading the Athenians into putting him to death. Yet Plato's Socrates does genuinely seem to believe that he ought to be rewarded by the Athenians he has served so faithfully.

On the other hand, the question of what Socrates genuinely believes is a bit tricky. Alongside Socratic ignorance, another of his trademarks is Socratic irony.[1] For instance, surely when Socrates tries to get a definition of piety from Euthyphro, a man who is about to prosecute his own father for murdering a slave, this is meant ironically? That is, Socrates knows full well that Euthyphro hasn't the foggiest idea what piety is, as shown by the fact that he's in the midst of doing something completely impious in hauling his father before a court. Similarly, Socrates would know that Laches the general has no clue what courage is, that Meno cannot define virtue. There's nothing to be gained from asking them, really—except to show *them* that they are ignorant. But it's far too easy to take just about anything Socrates says as being "ironic." No doubt experience has taught him that, as a rule, you don't get a good answer when you ask Athenian citizens to define the virtues. But this doesn't mean he expects to get nothing out of the process himself. More than once in the Platonic dialogues Socrates makes an impassioned plea that we should never stop inquiring into these questions—and he himself never gets tired of doing so. When accused of always saying the same things, he says, "Yes, and about the same subjects!" (*Gorgias* 490e). Though reducing people to Socratic ignorance is a genuine public service, Socrates also does it out of self-interest, because he believes that through this constant inquiry he has some hope of reaching true wisdom.

We might think, though, that this project of Socrates' is a bit odd. Why would anyone think that providing an account or definition of virtue is a good way to prove you are virtuous? Surely someone could be virtuous without being able to explain virtue? Socrates would disagree. After all, experts in other domains are indeed able to give accounts: a carpenter can explain to you what is involved in building tables. So a virtuous person should be able to give an account of virtue. Even if we concede this point, we might still complain that it is not *enough* to have an account or definition of virtue. One can explain football without being able to play it, and in the same way, knowledge about virtue doesn't seem to guarantee virtuous conduct. Again, Socrates thinks otherwise. One of his fundamental assumptions is that anyone who knows what is good will choose it. Why would anyone deliberately choose what is bad? When it's put like that, this doesn't sound so paradoxical. But we do think, don't we, that people deliberately choose things even though they are bad? Maybe even *because* they are bad, given the perversity of human nature? For Socrates this idea was absurd. For him, something's being "good" obviously implies that it is worth choosing. So for someone to think that something is good is for them to think it worth choosing. To put it another way, it's incoherent to imagine someone thinking: "This is good, but goodness doesn't really do much for me. I'm going with what's bad instead."

This Socratic position, which he argues for in several dialogues, is usually summed up in the phrase "no one does wrong willingly" (for instance, *Gorgias* 475e, *Protagoras* 358d). If I always want to do what is good, then my doing bad can only be the result of incomplete information. If I steal or kill, I must think stealing or killing is good, when really it is bad. This gets us closer to understanding Socrates' strange way of conducting his search for the virtuous life. For him vice and wrongdoing are always the result of ignorance: not the benign Socratic ignorance of knowing one doesn't know, but the really dangerous, insidious kind of ignorance, where you are utterly convinced you know what is good, but actually you have no idea. Without naming names, you might think of politicians who have displayed this kind of ignorance, and see that Socrates has a point.

The next step is obvious: if vice is ignorance, then perhaps virtue is knowledge. And indeed, in seeking knowledge of virtue, Socrates takes himself to be seeking virtue itself. He argues for this in other ways too. For example, he points out that things are only good or beneficial when used with knowledge (*Euthydemus* 281b). Consider medicine: use it with the guidance of a knowledgeable doctor and it can save your life. Use it without such guidance and you'll be lucky to survive the experience; that's why there's such a thing as prescription drugs. The same point applies to anything we might take to be good—for instance, money. Money is very handy, we all agree on that, but only if used wisely. If you use money the wrong way you can do immense harm to yourself and others. Or take health, which looks like an uncontroversially good thing. Is the health of a brutal tyrant really good? No, because the tyrant uses his continued vigor to oppress and exploit the people. In every case, the apparently good thing becomes good only when you add wisdom.

So virtue is knowledge or wisdom; and Socrates says that he lacks knowledge and wisdom. He merely knows that he knows nothing. Should we conclude from this that Socrates is not virtuous? In a sense, probably so. If he were already virtuous, presumably Socrates could stop rushing about Athens asking people to help him find out what virtue is. But his special, Socratic brand of ignorance gives him an important advantage over his peers: he at least knows that his beliefs about virtue are deeply fallible. And there's no reason to deny that he does have beliefs about virtue—perhaps this is what he means by the "human wisdom" he mentions in the *Apology*. For example, he believed it was wrong to arrest an innocent man at the behest of the Thirty Tyrants, and believed it was right to fight bravely against the Spartans at Delium. In fact, for all his efforts to show people that they lack a general understanding of virtue, he's often quite happy to accept their beliefs about particular cases of virtue. For instance, when Meno says that virtue is, for a woman, tending the home well and being obedient, Socrates doesn't criticize Meno for being sexist. He simply insists that Meno give him a *definition* of virtue, and not just *examples* (*Meno* 71e–72c).[2] What the interlocutors lack, when it comes to virtue, is the big picture—they lack general and consistent knowledge about virtue, even if they often get it right on particular occasions.

Plato's Socrates, and Plato himself, worried that such people would also get it wrong on particular occasions, precisely because they lack general and consistent knowledge. When the chips are down, you want to follow the person who has knowledge, not the person who has some true beliefs. So again we can ask, why doesn't Socrates make mistakes too, since he too lacks such wisdom? Well, he has another advantage: his divine sign. Plato confirms Xenophon's report that Socrates could hear a divine voice, which would speak up and warn him against those actions which would be wrong (*Apology* 31d). Socrates, then, was given a way to cheat his way to virtue. His true beliefs, tempered by the modesty of Socratic ignorance, were augmented by a divine sign which pointed him towards virtue or at least away from vice. He was not only the wisest man in Athens, he was also the most blessed. No wonder that Plato took him as the hero for most of his dialogues, especially since this was a man who loved conversation, and as a writer of dialogues, conversation was Plato's business too.

15

IN DIALOGUE
THE LIFE AND WRITINGS OF PLATO

The fact that the earliest Greek philosophers are called the Pre-Socratics shows the extent to which Socrates is seen as the pivotal figure in the history of Greek philosophy. Yet some of Socrates' predecessors could claim to represent a turning-point. How about Xenophanes, with his rational skepticism towards traditional religion? Or Heraclitus, arguably the first man to be primarily a philosopher rather than an all-around polymath and scientist? And what about Parmenides, the first thinker to pursue a path of pure rational argument, and the inventor of metaphysics? Of course, Socrates did add something new to the tradition, above all a new focus on ethics. With his relentless questioning of his fellow citizens, demanding that that they account for their choices and values, Socrates invented the notion that philosophy is primarily an inquiry into how we should live.[1] That conviction is not so popular nowadays, but was shared by all ancient philosophers after Socrates. Still, if Socrates is a transitional figure in Greek thought, it's not so much because of his ideas, but rather because without Socrates there would be no Plato.

In fact, while I yield to no one in my admiration for Socrates and the Pre-Socratics, I'm willing to say that it's with Plato that philosophy really gets going. The philosopher and logician Alfred North Whitehead famously remarked that the history of philosophy is "a series of footnotes to Plato."[2] This has become such a cliché that I thought I'd get it out of the way here in the first chapter on Plato. But cliché or no, Whitehead had a point. Philosophy did not begin or end with Plato; but it did come of age with him. Many central issues of philosophy are found for the first time in Plato, such as the nature of language or the immortality of the soul. But Plato wasn't only a philosophical genius, he was also a literary genius. The Greeks admired him as one of the foremost stylists of Attic Greek, and even in translation he is one of the philosophers who is most pleasurable to read. In the Platonic dialogues we can find everything we expect from great literature—suspense, humor, foreshadowing, symbolism, subtle allusions to other texts, and of course memorable characters. His most enduring literary creation is Socrates, but Plato was a brilliant mimic, able to produce scintillating parodies of historical figures like

Protagoras and Aristophanes. In many cases the mimicry is so compelling that it becomes almost impossible to imagine the historical person separately from the Platonic portrayal. As we've seen, that is certainly the case with Socrates.

As for Plato himself, he remains elusive. He is removed from us not only by almost two-and-a-half millenia, but also by his choice to write dialogues. We saw in the previous chapter that in one of those dialogues, the *Phaedo*, a character remarks that Plato was not present at Socrates' death, because he was ill. This passage reminds us that Plato is in a way absent in every dialogue. Plato never made himself a character in one of his dialogues, and he never wrote philosophy in anything other than dialogue form. He does not speak to us directly, which leaves us wondering which, if any, of the ideas expressed by Plato's characters represent his own views. In many cases, it's almost irresistible to think that Plato is using one or another character as the mouthpiece for his own ideas. But just take the case of Plato's most famous doctrine, the theory of Forms. It turns out to be surprisingly difficult to find passages in Plato's dialogues where this theory is expounded and defended. In fact, one of the few explicit discussions of the Forms is immediately followed by a powerful, and unanswered, series of objections to Plato's own theory.

More on this later. For now, I want to say a little bit more about the man himself. Who was this elusive genius I've been describing in such rapturous terms? Let's start with some basics. Born in 427 BC and dying in 347 BC, Plato hailed from Athens. Indeed, he could supposedly count among his ancestors the great lawgiver of Athens, Solon. The central event in Plato's own life was, we can safely assume, his encounter with Socrates when he was still a young man. When Socrates was put to death Plato was almost thirty years old. Yet Socrates must have made a big impression on the young Plato, enough for him to make Socrates the main character in most of his dialogues. After Socrates' death, Plato spent time away from Athens, in southern Italy, where he could have encountered Pythagorean ideas, a further source of inspiration. One shouldn't exaggerate the importance of this, I think. Plato's dialogues show that he had a wide knowledge of most of the Pre-Socratics. He was especially interested in Heraclitus and Parmenides, who were at least as important for him as Pythagoras. An ancient tradition tries to convince us that Plato was really an inheritor of higher Pythagorean truths. But in fact Pythagoreanism was only one of the many strands of Greek philosophy up until Plato's time, and Plato wove his cloth from all the strands he could find.

After his foreign travels Plato returned to Athens and set himself up as the head of a philosophical school. The school was situated in a grove outside the city—the Akademeia, named in honor of a mythical Greek hero named Hekademus. (This, of course, is where we get our word "academy.") Plato and his colleagues engaged not only in the pursuits we would think of as properly philosophical, but also practiced dialectical reasoning and argument, classification and division, and mathematics. You may have heard the legend that a sign at the entrance to the Academy said "Let no man enter who has not studied geometry,"[3] and indeed it's clear from the dialogues themselves that Plato had a deep interest in mathematics. He also had colleagues who did serious mathematical research, in particular Archytas, a Pythagorean philosopher. Another contemporary was Isocrates, not to be confused with Socrates: Isocrates was a brilliant rhetorician, and heir to the sophistical tradition Socrates had confronted in the fifth century. As we'll be seeing, Plato devotes a lot of attention to the question of rhetoric, and Isocrates may be one of his targets. But of course Plato's most famous contemporary, apart from Socrates, will be his own student Aristotle, who learned his trade at the Academy before setting up his own rival school after Plato's death.

As with other famous ancient philosophers, we can get some further information about Plato from a collection of biographies written by an author of the early third century AD—Diogenes Laertius.[4] Diogenes tells us that the name "Plato" was actually a nickname. It relates to the Greek *platus*, which means "broad" or "wide." Supposedly Plato got his name because he was so well-built, being an accomplished wrestler. Alternatively, Diogenes adds, it may have been because of the expansiveness of Plato's writing—or, more mundanely, because Plato had a wide forehead. Whatever the reason for the nickname, we should be grateful to whoever came up with it. Plato's real name was Aristocles, and it would be mighty confusing if the two leading ancient thinkers were called Aristocles and Aristotle.

In terms of Plato's biography, the most important information in Diogenes concerns Plato's three visits to Syracuse in Sicily. We also have some letters, supposedly written by Plato himself, which discuss Plato's involvement in Sicilian politics.[5] To make this long story short, Plato went to Syracuse for the first time in the 380s BC, when he was about forty years old. Diogenes Laertius tells us that while he was there Plato criticized the way that the tyrant Dionysius was running his city. The tyrant became irate, as tyrants tend to do. He was tempted to have Plato put to death, but settled for having him sold into slavery. Plato was eventually ransomed and able to return to Athens, but returned to Syracuse to meet with the tyrant's son and namesake Dionysius when the young man inherited his father's position. Plato hoped to persuade this young tyrant to adopt philosophy and rule with justice and by the laws, rather than through violence and fear. Unfortunately this trip too was a failure: Plato and a friend of his named Dion were sent packing. Plato made a third and final trip to Syracuse, for the sake of getting the tyrant Dionysius to look more favorably on his friend Dion. Yet again, Plato's mission failed. In due course the exiled Dion returned to Sicily with an invading army. Dion deposed Dionysius, but was murdered. The whole sorry tale provides a striking example of a philosopher trying and failing to exert influence in real-world politics. I suppose many readers have found some amusement in Plato's ineffectual idealism, his hope of turning the young Dionysius into one of the philosopher kings from the *Republic*. But I'm always happy to speak up for Plato. So I say we should commend him for trying to put his theories into practice rather than just sitting in the Academy, writing dialogues and doing mathematics.

The most famous passage in Plato's letters discusses the younger tyrant Dionysius. It appears in the so-called *Seventh Letter*, which like the others may or may not be by Plato. The passage discusses a rumor that the young tyrant Dionysius tried his hand at writing some philosophy. The letter's author says that if Dionysius did write such a book, then you can be sure that that book was not based on teachings that Plato delivered to him in Syracuse (341c). Any good philosopher knows that philosophy is not a body of doctrines which can be laid out by a teacher, so as to be ingested and then written out by the student. True philosophy consists in a discussion between teacher and pupil, and the insights one achieves in this way cannot just be stated in so many words. The author of the *Seventh Letter* gives a kind of metaphysical argument for this (342a–344c). Words are distant echoes or images of true reality, so that it is impossible to capture reality perfectly in language. Still worse is putting one's thoughts into writing rather than live speech, since the written words will inevitably be vulnerable to distortion and misunderstanding. As the definitely real Plato says in one of his dialogues, the *Phaedrus*, written words cannot explain or defend themselves the way we can explain and defend ourselves in conversation (275d–e).

Many readers have been tempted to connect these passages in the *Seventh Letter* and *Phaedrus* to the fact that Plato wrote dialogues instead of treatises full of doctrines. As I've said, Plato never speaks to us in his own voice. He is not one of the characters, he is the intelligence that lurks unseen behind the characters. Why did he write philosophy in this way? Diogenes, in his biography of Plato, says that Plato invented the use of dialogue form in writing philosophy—and he seems to be right about this. Perhaps some earlier philosophers, like Parmenides' student Zeno, had written in the form of opposed arguments. But Plato was original in using the form of dramatically realistic, literary dialogues with vivid characters taken from real life. The *Seventh Letter*, if it is really by Plato, would help to explain this choice. The letter suggests that Plato didn't think it was possible to state philosophical truth in a book—hence his preference for dialogues over didactic treatises. Alternatively, Plato may have thought that although it is possible to state philosophical truth in theory, in practice he was unable to do so. Perhaps he was always working through his ideas, and never reached a doctrine that satisfied him. Then again, maybe Plato was perfectly confident of his insights but worried about the vulnerability of words, especially *written* words. In face-to-face discussion one can explain oneself, respond to criticism, clear up confusions, and so on. But written words are like orphans, at the mercy of the reader who comes along and finds them. In any case, it seems plausible that, for Plato, philosophy occurs above all in discussions, not written works. When he did put pen to papyrus, he sought to re-create this context on the page.

I think we can go further, if we consider what it is like to read a Platonic dialogue. The dialogues are entertaining, but they can also be frustrating. Why are the people talking to Socrates, his interlocutors, letting him get away with apparently bad arguments? Why aren't they asking him to explain certain points more fully? Above all, why do so many dialogues end in a frustrating impasse, with Socrates and his interlocutors agreeing that they haven't achieved any insight into the topic at hand? These stalemate endings no doubt relate to Socrates' admission of ignorance: he knows only that he does not know. But Plato isn't telling us to settle for ignorance, even Socratic ignorance. When the participants in the dialogue overlook important objections, or fail to explore seemingly obvious avenues of inquiry, we are meant to notice. He wants his readers to engage actively with his dialogues. The readers should be alert to spot those overlooked alternatives, to see that some solutions are only being hinted at. You might say that the written text is one partner in a further dialogue, a dialogue between the reader and the text.

This also would help to explain why Plato's dialogues are so *literary*. By this I mean not only that they are beautifully written—though they frequently are—but that Plato deploys a full arsenal of allusions, metaphors, and cross-references such as we might expect from a novelist or playwright. This again invites the reader to think about the subtext as well as the surface meaning of the dialogue. The dramatic bits of stage-setting that surround Plato's philosophical arguments are as important as the arguments themselves. He might, for instance, show us his characters exhibiting, or not exhibiting, a virtue like courage in the very way that they pursue a philosophical discussion about virtue. Similarly, Plato set dialogues about piety and respect for the law within days of Socrates' execution. We should read these dialogues with Socrates' fate in mind.

Perhaps there is no single, general explanation for why Plato wrote dialogues.[6] He seems to have seen many possible advantages in the dialogue form, and to have exploited different advantages in different works. Consider a short dialogue like the *Euthyphro*, in which the title character is shown by Socrates to be unable to define piety. This and other so-called "Socratic" dialogues are very different from the much longer and more complex *Republic*, which still uses Socrates as the main character but in a more didactic mode, as he lays out theories about knowledge, Forms, the soul, and politics. Both dialogues are intensely literary, with strong and memorable characters in addition to their philosophical content. Yet it would be foolish to assume that the *Republic* is simply a much longer attempt to do the sort of thing Plato was trying to do in the *Euthyphro*. So rather than asking simply why Plato wrote dialogues, it may be more fruitful to consider how he uses the form for different effects in different dialogues.

This brings us to the more basic issue of how many dialogues there are. Collections of Plato's works go back to the first century AD, when a man named Thrasyllus produced an edition of the dialogues. His edition divided thirty-five dialogues, plus the Platonic letters as a final text, into nine groups of four. These were the works Thrasyllus himself thought were really by Plato. Nowadays, though, we accept only between twenty-five and thirty dialogues as being authentic. Several of the dialogues, like the Platonic letters, are of uncertain authenticity, and others are agreed by everyone to be forgeries. Also, Thrasyllus' division of the dialogues into groups of four has been abandoned. Instead, scholars now usually group the dialogues into early, middle, and late.

According to this division, Plato began writing his dialogues in the shadow of Socrates' execution. The dialogues he wrote in this early period adhered more or less closely to Socrates' actual practice in discussion. As I've mentioned, they usually end with an impasse—in Greek the word is *aporia*—where everyone in the dialogue agrees that they can't answer the question at hand. The aforementioned *Euthyphro* is an example: the question of the dialogue is "What is piety?" Some suggestions are made and refuted, and Socrates and Euthyphro part company without having successfully defined piety. A famous example from the *Euthyphro* is the title character's proposal that what is pious is simply that which all the gods love (9e). The difficulty with this idea is that it may get the direction of explanation wrong: are things really pious because the gods love them, or is it rather the reverse, and the gods love things because they are pious? The problem uncovered here by Plato is destined to become a mainstay of debates in the philosophy of religion. Do the gods, or God, dictate morality and goodness, in which case apparently anything could have been good? Or does God want us to do things *because* they are good? Although this difficulty goes under the title of the "Euthyphro dilemma," here Plato is at least as interested in the methodological question of how explanations work as in the application to piety as such.

This is typical of the early or "Socratic" dialogues. These tend to depict Socrates inquiring with partners into a certain concept, usually a virtue like piety or courage, and failing to achieve clarity in the end. Then comes the "middle period," during which Plato wrote more ambitious, longer works, and moved away from representing typical Socratic encounters. The *Republic*, Plato's best-known dialogue, is the star example for this period. Finally, there are the "late" works. We know that a hugely long and, most readers tend to feel, hugely boring work called the *Laws* was not yet completed when Plato died.[7] So this was his very last work. Other late works tend to be more technical and less dramatic in their setting. Often there is one lead character who controls the discussion by taking advantage of an interlocutor who doesn't give him much trouble. In many dialogues of this later period Plato removes Socrates from center-stage and allows other characters to take the leading roles.

How true is this story about the three periods of Plato's career? Well, some dialogues refer forward or back to others, which is a hint of relative chronology. Scholars have also used statistical analysis of Plato's evolving writing style, which could help put the various dialogues in order.[8] These indications tend to confirm a rough version of the scheme I just described. So we can say with some confidence that, for example, most of the so-called "Socratic dialogues" are earlier than the *Republic*. Still, there is no general agreement about the exact chronological order of the dialogues. And even if we did know the order in which the dialogues were written, it's not clear what this would mean for our understanding of Plato's ideas. Even if we accept that Plato's views evolved over time, that doesn't mean the evolution was a simple one. Plato was a self-critical philosopher, and liked to explore the same problems from numerous angles. No doubt he did change his mind, consider objections to ideas he'd discussed earlier, and so on. But there are no simple trajectories along which Plato's mind traveled over the course of his career.

A much better way to read Plato is one dialogue at a time. Every dialogue is a world unto itself and should be considered on its own before bringing it into relation with other dialogues. This is true not only of a long, famous work such as the *Republic*, but also of shorter and lesser-known dialogues. To illustrate this, I'll turn now to two such dialogues. They are not on the reading-lists of many undergraduate courses, but they will introduce us to many of the themes that are central to Plato's writings—his humor, his rivalry with the sophists, his fascination with the erotic, and his puzzlement over the nature of knowledge.

16

KNOW THYSELF
TWO UNLOVED PLATONIC
DIALOGUES

For many years BBC's Radio 4 in the UK has had a show called "Desert Island Discs." They invite famous people on, and ask them to say which music they'd want to have with them if they knew they were going to be stranded on a desert island. At the end the guests also get to say which book they'd want to have with them, not counting the Bible and Shakespeare. This is something I've never understood. Surely the answer is blindingly obvious: if you were going to have only one book on a desert island, why would you consider taking anything other than the collected works of Plato? My copy of the collected dialogues is 1,745 pages long, not counting the index.[1] That's enough to keep you company through many a lonely desert island night. If you were trapped on a desert island, and started reading Plato's dialogues one after another, I predict you'd be impressed at how deep his back catalogue is. Once you look past Plato's greatest hits, like the *Republic* and the *Phaedo*, you'd find plenty of other dialogues that are not just worth reading, but worth reading a few dozen times—you might as well, after all, since you're stuck on a desert island. In this chapter I'm going to look at two such dialogues: the *Charmides* and the *Euthydemus*. These aren't famous works, but they show Plato at his best, or close to his best.

Like most of Plato's dialogues, the *Charmides* is named after one of the main characters who appears in it. In the dialogue Socrates tells the story of how he first met Charmides, a young man of charm and devastating good looks. In fact the whole dialogue is narrated by Socrates, so that as we read it's as if we were sitting with him in the marketplace, listening to the story. He tells us that at the time of his meeting with Charmides he himself has just returned from a military campaign. Everyone wants to hear news of the war, but Socrates quickly shifts the conversation to his two favorite subjects. How is philosophy doing in Athens? And are there any promising young men around? An older man who is present, Critias, says that Socrates is in luck: here comes the most beautiful youth in Athens, his cousin Charmides (153a–154b).

Charmides enters, with other men fawning over him because of his good looks, a situation which Plato exploits for some slapstick comedy. Everyone wants to sit next to the enticing young Charmides, and there's such a struggle to make space for him on a long bench that the guy at the end falls onto the floor. Socrates wins the contest for Charmides' attention with a trick suggested by Critias: Charmides, it would seem, has been having headaches. Socrates pretends to know the cure, a certain leaf. But to cure the headache, it turns out you need to cure the whole body—a reference to the holistic medical theories of the Hippocratic corpus (156c). Not only that, but you need to make sure that the soul is healthy in order to cure the body. And we're off and running with a philosophical discussion, intended to discover whether or not Charmides has the virtue the Greeks called *sophrosune*, usually translated as "temperance" or "moderation." If so, his soul is healthy, and we can proceed to curing his body. But presumably, if Charmides has this virtue, he will be able to explain what it is. Thus Socrates invites Charmides to define *sophrosune* (159a), and the attempt to do so occupies their attention for the rest of the dialogue.

So far, so typically Socratic, with a bit of slapstick thrown in. But hang on a moment. You may remember the name Critias? I've mentioned him as a relative of Plato's and a leader of the Thirty Tyrants who overthrew the Athenian democracy just at the end of the fifth century BC. And you'll never guess who was another member of the Thirty Tyrants: yes, Charmides. It's rather unclear what Plato himself thought about the episode of the Thirty Tyrants. As we'll see later, he was no enthusiastic supporter of the restored Athenian democracy that executed his teacher Socrates. But obviously, when we read the *Charmides* we need to bear in mind the controversial histories of these two characters. What Plato has done here is a bit like an author of today staging a philosophical conversation about international law, and casting George W. Bush and Tony Blair as leading characters. Immediately, we see that Plato's choice to write in dialogue form gives him the opportunity to produce literary effects we don't expect from philosophy. When Socrates asks whether Charmides is as beautiful in soul as he is in body, we are supposed to know what became of the real Charmides, and that affects the way we read the arguments.

Of course, within the dramatic setting Socrates doesn't know what will become of either Critias or Charmides. Plato does have Critias behave in a rather bad-tempered way throughout the dialogue. But Charmides is as charming as he is beautiful. For instance, Socrates asks him point-blank whether he has the virtue of temperance, and Charmides replies that it would be boastful to say yes, but he would bring shame on himself if he said no (158d). This shows quick wit, while neatly sidestepping the question of his virtue. We readers, however, know how Charmides will turn out. Charmides will become the follower of the tyrant Critias, not the philosopher Socrates. All of this is more than a literary game. It adds resonance to the dialogue's fundamental question, which is not so much "What is temperance?" as "How we can know whether someone is temperate?" and "How can we know whether we ourselves are temperate?"

Here we arrive at Plato's favorite themes: knowledge of others, and knowledge of ourselves. The theme becomes explicit after some more Platonic theater. Young Charmides suggests that temperance is doing one's own business. Socrates finds this perplexing. Is he saying everyone should make their own shoes? No, no, says Charmides, that's not what he means...but on the other hand, he isn't quite sure what he does mean. It emerges that this is a definition of temperance he heard from his older relative Critias, who is annoyed at having his cherished definition refuted by Socrates (162b–d). Taking over the conversation, Critias says that, *obviously*, the definition means that temperance is doing one's business in the sense of doing what one should. In other words, doing good things (163e). Knowingly or unknowingly, asks Socrates? For instance, if I help a man without knowing whether it will benefit him, is this temperance? No, no, says Critias, that's not what I mean. Really, what I mean is the same thing as a famous slogan that appeared as an inscription at the oracle of Delphi. And yes, that's the same oracle that proclaimed the wisdom of Socrates.

You've no doubt heard the oracular inscription, even if you don't know where it comes from. It read *gnothi seauton*: "Know thyself." So there's my definition, announces Critias. Temperance is self-knowledge (164d–165b). He exudes confidence throughout all this, acting as if it's Socrates who is fumbling along, even though it's he, Critias, who leaps from one attempted definition to another as if they were all obviously the same. As ever, Socrates is patient and calm, albeit perplexed: he just wants to understand, if only there is something worth understanding. He doesn't quite get what it would mean to have self-knowledge. Medicine is knowledge of health, and house-building is knowledge of building; what is self-knowledge knowledge *of*? Here Critias makes a surprising move. He says that temperance, or self-knowledge, is knowledge *of knowledge* (166b). This leaves Socrates more confused than ever. There's no such thing as vision which sees vision, or hearing that hears hearing. How could there be knowledge that knows knowledge?

At this point Critias is ready to admit that he, too, is perplexed. Plato gives us a nice image for this perplexity: he has Socrates say that, just as a man who yawns tends to make everyone else around him yawn, so one man's confusion tends to infect others with confusion (169c). As always with Plato, there's more here than literary byplay. With the surprising shifts in discussion, he's managed to transform the dialogue from a jocular discussion of temperance into something rather different. The dialogue now becomes an inquiry into the nature and usefulness of knowledge. Nowadays we would say that the dialogue has gone from dealing with ethics to dealing with epistemology—the study of knowledge.

In particular, we're wondering what it means to have knowledge of knowledge. What does this amount to? On the one hand, as Socrates points out, it seems that if I know something, I should know that I know it. For instance, since I know that 2 + 2 = 4, I also know that I know 2 + 2 = 4. In fact, you might even suspect this is a good test of whether I know something. If I'm not sure whether or not I know that 2 + 2 = 4, isn't that enough reason to say I *don't* know that 2 + 2 = 4? On the other hand, as Socrates also points out, it's hard to see what good it does to know that I know. If I know that 2 + 2 = 4, that's good enough for all practical purposes. When would I ever need to *know that I know* that 2 + 2 = 4? Thus we have something of a paradox. On the one hand, knowledge of knowledge seems to be absolutely essential. On the other hand, knowledge of knowledge seems empty and useless.

If this all seems too abstract, consider instead the case where I am trying to figure out whether somebody *else* has knowledge. Suppose, for instance, I'm trying to decide whether to let someone give me open-heart surgery. Suddenly it's looking pretty urgent to decide whether the would-be surgeon knows what he is doing. If at all possible, I'd like to know *for sure* whether or not he knows. So now knowledge of knowledge looks vital. But for me to be absolutely certain whether or not the would-be surgeon is qualified, it seems plausible that I would need to have some grasp of medicine myself. Indeed, perhaps I would even need to be a qualified surgeon myself. Otherwise I'll have to take other people's advice to find out whether the would-be surgeon knows what he's doing. I might get lucky, and get good advice. But I wouldn't be certain that the would-be surgeon is knowledgeable. To be certain, I would need the same kind of knowledge the surgeon (hopefully) has: I need to know about surgery. What I don't need, on the other hand, is some further knowledge which is about knowledge (instead of being about surgery). So from this perspective too, knowledge of knowledge looks essential from one point of view and useless from another.

Once Socrates and Critias have banged their heads against this problem for a while the dialogue ends in a stalemate, without any agreement as to what temperance, or for that matter self-knowledge, really is (175a–176d). But it would be wrong to say that they, and we, have learned nothing. At the very least, we've been presented with numerous possible routes for further inquiry. Some of what has been said looks extremely Socratic: in particular, Socrates might agree with Critias that temperance, and all the other virtues, are kinds of knowledge. This allows Plato to use one of his favorite tricks: he diverts the discussion away from virtue, toward a more general inquiry into the nature of knowledge. As I said, we go from talking ethics to talking epistemology. On the other hand, in other dialogues we've seen suggestions that for Socrates virtue is the *same thing* as knowledge. So perhaps this is no diversion at all. Plato is simply working through the implications of this Socratic thesis. If virtue is knowledge, then discussion of virtue and discussion of knowledge are one and the same. Epistemology and ethics are nowadays taught and studied as separate parts of philosophy. But if virtue is knowledge, then this firm separation is a big mistake.

We can find similar ideas in another unloved Platonic dialogue, the *Euthydemus*. As with the *Charmides*, the dialogue is narrated by Socrates. This time we know who he's telling the story to: his good friend Crito, who in another dialogue named after him is shown trying to persuade Socrates to flee Athens before he is executed. In that dialogue Socrates refuses to escape, saying he has a duty to obey the laws, even if they put him to death unjustly. Are we meant to think about this episode when we read the *Euthydemus*? Should we think, perhaps, about Socrates' trial and the charge against him that he corrupted the youth? This would be appropriate, because as in the *Charmides*, the *Euthydemus* shows Socrates struggling to exert influence over a young man. In this case, the beautiful young man Socrates speaks to is named Clinias. In the *Charmides* Socrates seemed to be competing with Critias to see who would manage to exert influence over Charmides. The same sort of thing happens here in the *Euthydemus*. But this time Socrates' opponents are more fearsome than the rather doltish Critias. They are two sophists, brothers named Euthydemus and Dionysodorus.

The two brothers, it emerges, used to make a living as experts in the martial arts. They could teach you to fight wearing armor, to lead men in battle, to devise strategies in war. But they've diversified since then, and become specialists in verbal instead of physical violence (271c–272b). They boast that they can teach wisdom and virtue, but what they actually do is bamboozle people with their bewildering wordplay and arguments. Socrates asks for a demonstration—he wants them to use their amazing wisdom to persuade Clinias to become a philosopher and a seeker of virtue. "No problem," they say, and then the sophistical fireworks begin. Euthydemus and Dionysodorus take it in turns to refute poor Clinias. They ask him questions, and show that whichever answer Clinias gives he will wind up contradicting himself. For instance, who is it who learns, wise people or ignorant people? Presumably wise people, and Clinias says so. But the brothers point out that wise people already have knowledge, so they don't need to learn. So it must be the ignorant people, Clinias says. Wrong again. The ignorant students in any group are precisely the ones who don't learn, otherwise they would hardly be ignorant (275d–276c).

Socrates takes all this to be mere tomfoolery, and chastises the brothers for not being serious. He offers to show what he means by persuading Clinias to develop an interest in philosophy. He questions Clinias in such a way as to lead him to the classic Socratic conclusion that anything that seems to be good—money, food, power, health—turns out to be good only if you use it with knowledge (281d–e). You remember this point: money is useful, but only if you use it on things that will be good for you, and this requires knowledge. Socrates hopes that with this good example, the sophistical brothers will buckle down and lead Clinias to wisdom rather than to bewilderment. Instead, they reach back into their bag of tricks. A typical argument goes like this. The brothers ask you whether you know anything at all. Sure, you say, there are some things I know. So if you're knowing, say the brothers, then you must know *everything*. Otherwise, you'd be knowing and not-knowing at the same time, which is a contradiction (293b–d). Now, this is clearly a bad argument. It's perfectly possible to know one thing—for instance, how to tie your shoes—while not knowing another thing—for instance, how to look after a giraffe. But the brothers insist on leaving out these qualifications. That's cheating, they complain, and they ought to know, because they put themselves in charge of setting the rules of debate. And so it goes: for instance, the brothers argue that if you have a dog, then the dog is yours; if the dog has puppies, then he's a father; and if the dog is yours and he's a father, then the dog is your father (298d–299a)!

Again, it isn't terribly difficult to see that this is a bad argument, though spelling out in detail where the mistakes are made would require some subtlety. Perhaps Plato's goal here is partly to train the reader to see what goes wrong in such fallacious arguments. But that isn't the only fish he's out to fry. Some of the arguments made by the brothers have deep philosophical implications. This is a dialogue in which fundamental questions of metaphysics and epistemology underlie apparent silliness. To give just one example, the brothers argue that it's impossible for two people to contradict one another (285d–286b). If you say that the horse is white, and I say that the horse is black, then we can only be talking about two different things: you're talking about a white horse and I'm talking about a black horse. If you're right and there *is* no black horse, then I'm not talking about anything at all—so I'm saying nothing. And how can I contradict you without saying anything? This argument too seems trivial at first, until we reflect that the brothers sound a lot like Parmenides. If you remember, he too said that it is impossible to think about or speak of that which does not exist. The sophists are exploiting this thought for their own nefarious purposes—to show that it is impossible even to disagree.

The *Euthydemus* does, then, have serious philosophical bite. To a large extent it is a reflection on the nature of knowledge, just like the *Charmides*. Indeed, many of the puzzles that arise here, in an apparently frivolous way, return in other dialogues and are considered at greater length. One example is the question about whether it is the wise or the ignorant who learn—this is remarkably similar to Meno's paradox, which we'll be looking at shortly. Equally fundamental to the *Euthydemus* is the question of how we should treat other people in philosophical argument. The point of philosophical argument is not winning at all costs, like these verbally pugilistic sophists do. It is to seek wisdom.

This makes the dialogue another attempt to show us that Aristophanes was wrong: Socrates is no sophist. He wants to lead young men like Clinias to virtue and wisdom, rather than to perplexity. On the other hand, Plato's Socrates leads young men into perplexity too. Of course Socrates looks good compared to the sophist brothers. But don't the *Charmides* and the *Euthydemus* also shed light on the limitations of Socrates? In both dialogues Socrates has a chance to influence a young man and make him virtuous. We know he fails with Charmides, and things don't go very well with Clinias either. This leads us to wonder: can talking to Socrates really make a young man virtuous? That is a question to which Plato returns repeatedly, especially in the dialogues we'll discuss in the next two chapters: the *Gorgias* and the *Meno*.

17

VIRTUE MEETS ITS MATCH
PLATO'S *GORGIAS*

Ancient philosophers spent a lot of time arguing about the nature of the good life. In particular, they usually wanted to show us that the best way to live is to be virtuous. But why be virtuous? You could instead follow the example of, say, Archelaus the king of Macedon, who seized power by killing several of his family members, including his own seven-year-old half-brother, whom he tossed into a well and drowned (471c). Okay, that might bit sound a bit radical. But can we really be sure that Archelaus made the wrong choice? He may have had blood on his hands, but those hands held the reins of power in a mighty state. And let's be honest: we've all performed the odd misdeed to get what we want. So why not go for broke and commit these most outrageous injustices, if it will allow us to fulfill our desires—not just today, but for the rest of our lives?

This is a central question posed in Plato's dialogues, and never with more urgency than in his early masterpiece, the *Gorgias*. We've already met the namesake of the dialogue when we looked at the sophists. Gorgias was a teacher of rhetoric and, as you might recall, the author of several works which still survive today, and which show off his way with words as well as his conviction that words have an almost irresistible power. You might also remember that Plato, in dialogue after dialogue, pits Socrates against opponents who are sophists and teachers of rhetoric. We already saw an example in Plato's *Euthydemus*, and the verbal sparring there is typical of these encounters, which frequently seem more like competitions than dispassionate discussions of truth. In the *Gorgias*, Socrates trades verbal blows not only with Gorgias himself, but also with two of Gorgias' followers, Polus and Callicles. Even though the dialogue came to be named after Gorgias, it is Callicles who cuts the most memorable figure, as a passionate defender of immorality. In no dialogue does Socrates, the champion of virtue, meet up with a more formidable opponent.

In the last chapter we saw how Plato's *Charmides* poses as an inquiry into virtue, but turns out to be an inquiry into knowledge. We'll see another example of that Platonic trick when we come to look at the *Meno*. But in the *Gorgias* something like the reverse happens: Socrates says he wants to discover what rhetoric is, but winds up mounting a defense of the virtuous life. When the action begins, Socrates and his friend Chaerephon are meeting up with Gorgias and his fellow rhetoricians Polus and Callicles. Whereas Polus and Callicles are relative beginners in rhetoric, Gorgias is already accepted as a master. He has just given a display speech, and is an honored guest at Callicles' house. Socrates wants to hear what the famous Gorgias has to say, but not in the form of a finely wrought speech (447c). Instead, Socrates wants, well, what he always wants: he wants to have a conversation about virtue. Happily, Gorgias boasts that he can speak with unequalled brevity if called upon to do so (449c). He's just as good at the cut and thrust of debate as he is at delivering long, ornate speeches. This belongs to his expertise, his art. Socrates proceeds to lock horns with him over this very question: what is the art which Gorgias claims to have mastered and to be able to teach?

The art, of course, is rhetoric. But what's rhetoric, exactly? Carpenters make things out of wood, doctors make us healthy. What do rhetoricians do? According to Gorgias, rhetoric is an art that concerns speech, not just any old speech, but speech about "the greatest of human concerns" (449d–451d). The man who has mastered rhetoric can go into the court or the public council and get his audience to believe whatever he likes. In short, the art of rhetoric is the art of speech which is persuasive. In fact, *very* persuasive. As we saw, the real Gorgias, in his defense speech of Helen, argued that if Helen was persuaded to go to Troy using words, then she was in effect compelled to go, just as surely as if she'd been dragged there by force. Against a truly effective speaker, there is no defense. The Gorgias presented by Plato would agree with this. He tells Socrates that if a doctor and a rhetorician debate in front of an audience about how best to cure a patient, the audience will agree with the rhetorician and not the doctor (456b–c). He gives examples to prove his point: for instance, it was the great orator Pericles who persuaded the Athenians to build a defensive wall, not a bunch of stonemasons, who are experts in wall-building (455e).

So if you teach someone rhetoric, you have in effect given him a powerful weapon. Thus armed, a man can control his city. He can literally get away with murder, by using honeyed words to get himself acquitted of the charge. He could also, as we've just seen, persuade someone to ignore the advice of a doctor. But as we saw when discussing the sophists, Gorgias argues that we shouldn't blame the teacher in a case like this (457b–c). We should blame the student who misuses the art for evil instead of good. A teacher of rhetoric is like a teacher of boxing: sure, he's taught his students to beat people up, but it's not his fault if the students go off and use their newfound prowess to clobber their friends or parents. Socrates is surprised at all this. Surely Gorgias can also teach people how to be good? In which case, the student certainly will not go off and use his rhetorical superpowers for evil instead of good. This is a crucial moment in the dialogue. Gorgias, perhaps embarrassed to say he can't tell someone the difference between good and evil, agrees with Socrates that he could teach goodness as well as rhetoric (460a). Plato is probably playing fast and loose here. The claim to teach virtue is strongly associated with some sophists, like Protagoras. But the historical Gorgias apparently did not make any such claim. Even Plato reports elsewhere that he stuck to teaching excellence in speaking, rather than virtue (*Meno* 95c). Plato has, it seems, had his fictional Gorgias say something the real Gorgias was careful not to say.

In doing so, the fictional Gorgias has left himself open to a series of Socratic punches. Later on in the dialogue Socrates makes the rather cheap, but nonetheless amusing, point that sophists are always complaining that their students cheat them by not paying their fees, which is odd given that the sophists have taught these same students to be good! But there's a deeper problem with Gorgias' position. He's said that the whole point of rhetoric is to make a speaker persuasive, whether or not they know what they are talking about. The rhetorician may be more persuasive than the doctor on the matter of health, for instance (456c). But it's the doctor who can tell you what would *really* be good to do about that nagging cough; the rhetorician has no idea. Similarly, if it's a matter of reaching a decision in the democratic assembly of Athens, the rhetorician can persuade the assembly to do whatever he wants them to do. But this art of persuasion will not give the rhetorician any insight into what the assembly really *should* do. Unless, that is, rhetoric turns out after all to be a knowledge of good and evil, of justice and injustice. In that case it really would be the knowledge of the greatest of human concerns, as Gorgias has boasted. But Gorgias has described rhetoric as producing persuasion in the *absence* of knowledge. Rhetoric is starting to look like the art of convincing people to make mistakes.

Once Socrates gets this far, Gorgias' supporter Polus can no longer restrain himself. He interrupts, and demands that Socrates say what *he* thinks rhetoric is (462b). Socrates explains to Polus that as far as he's concerned, rhetoric isn't really an art at all. It's more like a know-how or a knack. He compares it—and I'll warn you in advance that this next bit may make you hungry—he compares it to knowing how to make pastries (465c). If you ask people to vote on who they'd rather have feeding them, they'll take the pastry-chef over the dietician any time. The pastry-chef offers croissants, including those nice ones with the almond filling; whereas the dietician tells you to eat raw carrots. I don't know about you, but I'm going with the pastry-chef. Rhetoric is the same. The rhetorician can flatter and please an audience, but he can't tell the audience what is really good for them.

At this point Polus is incredulous. Socrates is making rhetoric sound like some mean kind of trickery, when actually we all know it is majestic in its power. A really good rhetorician will rule in his city, as Pericles and Themistocles did in Athens. He can have his enemies put to death, can do whatever he likes, whenever he likes (466b). The art of rhetoric, in other words, confers the sort of power held by a tyrant like Archelaus, the Macedonian king I mentioned at the start of this chapter. Polus gives Archelaus as an example of the sort of untrammeled domination he has in mind (470d–471d). And who cares whether rhetoric can tell us what we should really do, if it gives us this kind of absolute power? The appeal of the rhetorician, his sales pitch if you will, is obvious. If you're a young Athenian gentleman who hopes to grow into a position of eminence and prestige—and all young Athenian gentlemen wanted this—then hire a rhetorician.

Socrates is not impressed. He insists that without knowledge and wisdom the rhetoricians may put to death whoever they want, but that doesn't mean they are really powerful (466b). True power is being able to do what is really good for you. If a tyrant or a rhetorician, blundering in his ignorance, uses his so-called power to put to death those who try to give him good advice, then he is actually harming himself as well as his city. Again, Polus scoffs (468e). As if Socrates wouldn't gladly assume the power of life and death if it was handed to him! Socrates replies that, for him, the power to put someone to death unjustly is no power at all. In fact, he'd far rather be put to death unjustly himself than put someone else to death without good reason.

Here we've come to one of Socrates' most famous doctrines: that it is better to suffer wrongdoing than to do wrong oneself (496b–c). A man like Archelaus may seem to Polus to be the happiest man in Macedonia, but in fact he is the most miserable, and certainly more miserable than a man who is, for instance, unjustly tortured to death. Better to be tortured to death unjustly than to order that this torture be carried out. Polus is incredulous: surely Socrates cannot be serious? Would anyone really prefer to be put to death unjustly than to do wrong himself? Well yes, actually. Socrates for one was fairly cheerful about being put to death unjustly. Not that Socrates *wanted* to be put to death, but it was a matter of relative indifference to him, whereas he put the highest possible value on his own virtue.[1]

But does Socrates have an argument for this attitude, or does he just want to lead by example? He's Socrates: of course he has an argument. He gets Polus to agree that justice is admirable and injustice shameful. But things are admirable either because they are pleasant, or because they are beneficial, or both (474e). Justice is not much fun, as we all know—all that telling the truth and paying back our debts. So if justice is admirable, it can't be because it's pleasant; it must be because it's beneficial (475c). With unjust things it will be the opposite. Since they're shameful, they must be either unpleasant or harmful, or both. Obviously, being an unjust tyrant isn't unpleasant—in fact, it's a non-stop orgy of pleasure, what with all the feasting and chuckling as one devises new and innovative ways to put one's enemies to death. So if injustice is shameful, it can only be because it's harmful. Thus, people who do unjust things are harming themselves, just as much as they are harming other people. It turns out the political power Polus so admires can be a disaster in the wrong hands, even (or rather especially) for the person whose hands hold that power. If a ruler uses his authority to act unjustly, he will only be inflicting ever greater harm on himself.

This Socratic position looks pretty convincing, at least from a certain point of view. When we consider monstrous tyrants like Caligula, we don't think of them as happy: they destroy themselves as well as their people, with their outsized appetites and poor judgment. Without power and wealth Caligula would just have been an over-sexed thug. But as emperor he was in a position to inflict huge damage on everyone nearby. And no one was nearer to Caligula than Caligula himself. Or if you prefer, think of a more down-to-earth example, like a drug addict. A drug addict will be worse off if he has more money, because he will use the money to buy drugs that harm him. On the other hand, there's something that might disturb us about Socrates' defense of just action, and virtue more generally. Do we really think that we should be virtuous because it will *benefit* us? This seems strangely self-centered. We might even want to insist that virtue is admirable precisely because virtuous people are willing to sacrifice their own good for the good of others. We don't think that Mother Teresa was admirable because she had such a good understanding of what was good for Mother Teresa; we think she was admirable because to her the welfare of the poor was at least as important as her own welfare. So, one could perhaps admit that Socrates has mounted a good defense of virtue, but accuse him of failing to defend altruism. In fact, he hasn't even tried to defend altruism. Maybe this is because he's trying to persuade the self-centered Polus that virtue is the right choice; he's appealing to what Polus would find persuasive. But as we'll see as we go along, Socrates was not the only ancient philosopher to put forward a strikingly egocentric argument for the life of virtue.

Be that as it may, the next attack to come at Socrates is not from this direction at all. Instead, when the bell rings for round three Socrates finds himself facing an even more radical opponent: Callicles. Callicles accuses Socrates of exploiting the feelings of shame felt by both Gorgias and Polus (482e). It was shame which led Gorgias to make the tactical mistake of saying he could teach his students virtue. And it was shame that led Polus to make the crucial concession that justice is a good thing and injustice a bad thing. In fact, Callicles says, Polus should have said the exact opposite. It is justice which is bad and injustice good. Justice is merely the set of conventional rules that society uses to keep the strongest people in line. The law of nature says the opposite: the strongest person should get the greatest rewards (483b–484c). What would these rewards consist in? Not the glow of self-righteous justice that Socrates so admires, but what is naturally, rather than conventionally, good: namely, power and pleasure. Callicles thinks, then, that justice is nothing but a trick for getting the strong to surrender their natural right to seize as much pleasure as they can handle.

Socrates rightly recognizes that Callicles is raising a serious challenge, one more difficult to defeat than anything Polus has said. Callicles, in fact, bears a striking resemblance to no less a figure than Friedrich Nietzsche, the great nineteenth-century critic of (Judeo-Christian) morality. However, Socrates focuses on an aspect of Callicles' view that is not particularly Nietzschean, namely its hedonism. The word "hedonism" comes from the Greek word *hedone*, meaning "pleasure"; so hedonism is the view that pleasure is the good. Socrates thinks that the life Callicles describes, in which every desire is constantly being satisfied, sounds more like a life of slavery than mastery.

To explain why, he presents a kind of allegory which he takes from certain Sicilian or Italian wise men—this may be an allusion to Empedocles or the Pythagorean tradition more generally. To simplify slightly, the allegory compares the soul to a jar, like the earthen jars used for holding water or wine in ancient Greece. The hedonistic seeker of pleasures is a man whose jar is full of leaks, so that water rushes out of the jar even as he's desperately pouring it in. The temperate person, by contrast, is like a man with a sealed and watertight jar, which never loses any of its contents (393d–494b). The allegory represents a fundamental flaw of hedonism, which is that pleasure-seeking is an endless task. As soon as you've sated yourself at one banquet, you start getting hungry again. As the next day dawns you have to worry about your next banquet. And the more it takes to satisfy you, the harder it is to get hold of the next round of pleasures. Far better to content oneself with as little as possible, so that one is spared the trouble.

Callicles sticks to his guns, insisting that he'd rather be someone whose jar is full of holes, so that the water can flow out rapidly and he can replace it with new pleasures. He admires the life of insatiable appetite, even when Socrates tries to show him that there is just as much pain involved in such a life as pleasure. The life of the sealed jars, as far as Callicles is concerned, may as well be the life of a stone (494a). As their argument goes on, it becomes clear that Callicles and Socrates are not going to reach agreement. In fact, they share so little common ground, and Callicles is such an intemperate conversational partner, that by the end Socrates is reduced to performing both sides of the discussion (505d–506c). Callicles refuses to speak, and Socrates both asks the questions and answers them. As you might expect, Socrates finds himself to be remarkably cooperative.

With this memorable scene, I believe Plato is drawing our attention not just to the impossibility of reasoning with a radical hedonist like Callicles, but also to the limitations of Socrates and his art of refutation. Socrates can get no purchase on the argument, because he and Callicles share no common ground. Whereas Polus was ready to admit—out of shame or genuine conviction—that justice is good and injustice bad, Callicles is loath to concede any premise that Socrates could use to refute him. When he does make such a concession, he invariably takes it back later in the argument. No doubt Plato expects us to prefer the Socratic life of virtue to the Calliclean life of unrestrained hedonism. But Plato also worries that it could be difficult, or impossible, to refute a consistent immoralist. Socrates fails to land a knockout blow in this bout with the arch-immoralist Callicles. But is this failure due either to his limitations as a moral teacher or something lacking on the part of Callicles, the intended student? This issue will arise again as we turn to our next dialogue, an inquiry into the nature of learning itself.

18

WE DON'T NEED NO EDUCATION
PLATO'S *MENO*

Given that you have not only gotten your hands on this book, but are actually reading it (you're almost halfway through—Zeno, we refute you thus, again!), you are obviously a person of refined taste and good judgment. I imagine that you are slightly above average height, and good-looking, in a mysterious, thoughtful kind of way. You are kind to children and animals, and gladly give up your seat to pregnant ladies and the elderly on public transport. You are, in short, a wonderful specimen of humanity—it's a real privilege to have you along for this tour of the history of philosophy. But, being a philosopher, I must pose the question: how did you get this way? How did you get so darn *virtuous*? Were you born like this? Did you inherit it from your parents, so that virtue comes to you as naturally as it comes naturally to dogs to turn around in circles for no reason before they lie down? If not, then somebody must have taught you to be virtuous. But how would that work? Is virtue even the sort of thing that *can* be taught?

This very question begins Plato's dialogue the *Meno*, one of his most popular and most frequently studied writings. If you've taken an undergraduate course which touched on Plato, chances are pretty good that you were asked to read the *Meno*. And for good reason. It's not terribly long, it's reasonably funny, and it has at the center of it a memorable scene and a memorable theory about learning. At the risk of ruining the suspense, the theory is that we don't ever actually learn at all. Rather, when we seem to be learning, we are in fact remembering or recollecting. We are recollecting knowledge not from some point earlier in our lives, but rather from a time before our lives began. Before we were born, we knew everything that can be known, and the apparent process of learning is just a way of jogging the memory to give us access to this knowledge.

It's an eloquent proof of Plato's genius that a dialogue with this fairly zany-sounding theory right in the middle of it has made it onto practically every undergraduate philosophy syllabus in the English-speaking world. So, what is this much-studied dialogue, the *Meno*, about? It presents itself as a dialogue about virtue. The main characters are Socrates, who is as usual ready to shoot down ill-considered answers to philosophical questions, and an interlocutor named Meno. There are also guest appearances by a slave-boy and Anytus, one of the men responsible for Socrates' being put on trial and executed. But it's Meno who gives most of the ill-considered answers. He kicks off the dialogue by asking this question I've been talking about: can virtue be taught (70a)? Socrates responds, predictably, by protesting that he can't say whether virtue is teachable, because he doesn't know what virtue is. Perhaps Meno can help him out by giving him a definition of virtue? And then they'll be able to figure out whether it's teachable.

You don't have to have read too many of Plato's Socratic dialogues to know what's coming. Meno will propose some definitions of virtue, Socrates will show that the definitions aren't good ones, and in the end they'll be stuck in puzzlement or *aporia*, which (as we saw in Chapter 15) means something like an impasse or unsolved problem. This, in fact, is exactly what happens in the first part of the dialogue. Meno is confident that he can say what virtue is, because he is a student of the sophist Gorgias, whom we've seen in previous chapters. Meno recites a version of what he's heard from Gorgias, saying that each kind of person has their own kind of virtue (71e–72a). For instance, the virtue of a man is to be capable in politics, whereas the virtue of a woman is to look after the house—women's liberation was still a few millenia in the future, although, as we'll see when we get to the *Republic*, Plato was ahead of the curve on this topic, as on so many others. Socrates objects to Meno's answer, complaining that this isn't a definition of virtue but rather a list of the types of virtue. What we want to know is, what do all the types have in common (72c)?

This, along with several other exchanges between Socrates and Meno in this part of the dialogue, asks us to focus on the question of what would be a good definition. That's typical of the dialogue as a whole: we think we are going to get a discussion of virtue, and to some extent we do. But we get something perhaps more important, namely a reflection on what it would be to *know* about virtue. Would knowing what virtue is be the same thing as giving a good definition of virtue? If so, what are good definitions like? They aren't just lists, like the one Meno gave. They also aren't circular, like another definition Meno attempts, when he says that virtue is getting good things in a just way. After all, justice is a virtue, so he's effectively saying that virtue is getting good things virtuously (79a–e). Not very helpful. Notice that these points would apply not just to virtue, but to anything we might want to define. If I am asked to define "ruminant," I haven't done my job if I just say "giraffe, camel, sheep, goat," or if I say that they are things that ruminate. Neither would be a proper and illuminating definition. So what Socrates and Meno are discussing has implications well beyond just the question of what virtue might be. This is particularly clear when Socrates gives Meno a model of the kind of definition he wants, by offering a definition of geometrical figure or "shape" (76a), which is obviously not an ethical concept. Just as we've seen in previous chapters, Plato uses a discussion of ethics as an opportunity to get into a discussion of knowledge.

After several failed attempts to define virtue, Meno admits that he's stumped. He offers a famous analogy for what Socrates is doing to him. He says that, whereas before talking to Socrates he felt very confident in discussing virtue, he's now been paralyzed, like someone who's been stung by a stingray (80a). This paralysis is the condition of *aporia*, or puzzlement, that I mentioned earlier. Socrates remarks that the analogy only applies to him if he's like a stingray who paralyzes himself, since he too is in puzzlement about what virtue might be (80c). At this point one could imagine the dialogue ending—it would be much shorter, and much less interesting, but it would conform to our expectations of a Socratic dialogue. Socrates meets a confident interlocutor; refutes him; the two are puzzled; Socrates resolves that one should keep inquiring nonetheless; the end. But in the case of the *Meno*, the most interesting part of the dialogue is yet to come.

It begins when Meno poses a challenge against the possibility of inquiring into what virtue is, indeed, against the possibility of inquiring into anything. The challenge is what we now call Meno's paradox, or the learner's paradox. It goes like this: either you know something or you don't. If you know it, you don't need to inquire into it, since you already know it. If you don't know it, then you do need to inquire into it. But how can you? After all, you don't know what it is. So how will you go about searching for it, and for that matter, how will you recognize it if you do come across it (80d–e)? Now, there seems to be an obvious way to steer between the two horns of this dilemma. The paradox assumes that you either know something so well that you don't need to learn any more about it; or you know absolutely nothing at all. But in fact neither of these is usually the case. After all, I know a fair amount about Buster Keaton. I know that he was a silent-film actor, that he made several of the greatest films in cinematic history, like his masterpiece *The General*, that he is famous for not showing emotional reactions in his films and was therefore nicknamed "the Great Stone Face." So I'm not completely ignorant about Buster Keaton. But do I know *everything* about him, so that there's no need for further inquiry? I haven't even seen all of his films, because I haven't bothered to sit through all the talkies he appeared in after his time as a silent-film comedian. And I certainly don't know, for instance, what his shoe-size was (judging from the shoes he wears in his movies it was well into the high figures).

So that might be a solution to the paradox: we can know something partially, in addition to knowing it completely or not at all. But does that really help? After all, you might ask how we ever got to know anything *partially* in the first place. Surely, we start out not knowing anything, and from there move to this position of partial knowledge. But then we are impaled on the second horn of the dilemma, because at the point where we knew nothing, we had no basis for inquiry. So there is still a problem here: how do we *get started* when we are trying to get knowledge? Perhaps for this reason Socrates doesn't try to give the solution I just suggested. He does something more surprising: he tells a kind of religious myth, which he says he's heard from some priests and priestesses. According to this myth, our souls are immortal—they will always exist, and they have always existed. Before our current earthly lives, our souls have already existed for an endless time, and during this endless time they have learned all there is to know. Thus, we are never in the position of knowing nothing. On the contrary, we always know everything. It's just that we've forgotten most, if not all, of the things we knew in our previous existence. It follows that when we seem to be learning new knowledge, we are in fact only being reminded of things we already knew (81a–e).

I think you'll agree that, as promised, this does sound pretty zany. Meno isn't immediately convinced either, so Socrates proceeds to demonstrate his theory. In one of the more famous scenes in the Platonic dialogues he summons a slave-boy, whose only intellectual qualification is that he knows Greek (82a–b). Socrates takes the slave-boy through a discussion of a geometrical problem, namely finding the length of the side of a square whose area is eight (82d). He gets the boy to guess, and then to see that his guesses are wrong. This induces puzzlement in the boy, the stingray effect. Then Socrates gets the boy to see the right answer, namely that the side of a square of area eight is the same length as the diagonal of a square whose area is four (85a–b). The nifty part is that he does all this only by means of asking questions. This illustrates the famous Socratic method, teaching by soliciting ideas from the student, instead of directly imparting information. Though people often complain that Socrates is asking leading questions throughout the scene, it's true enough that he never asserts anything. The slave-boy has to figure it out for himself, albeit with the help of Socrates' prompting him. In fact, Socrates leads him down false paths a couple of times, perhaps to warn the boy that he should be on his guard and think for himself. Since the boy is able to get to the right answer in this way, without being given the answer from the outside, Socrates concludes that he must have had the knowledge in him all along, just waiting to be brought out by expert questioning.

This slave-boy sequence ends the presentation of the so-called "theory of recollection," probably Plato's most famous doctrine apart from the "theory of Forms," of which more soon. It's not clear how strongly Plato is committed to the notion of recollection, though. For one thing, he doesn't exactly work it into every dialogue he writes. It turns up here in the *Meno* and occasionally elsewhere, especially in his dialogue the *Phaedo*. Some interpreters, perhaps slightly embarrassed by the religious trappings of the doctrine, don't want to take the mythic story about the soul very seriously. They think that Plato is just trying to set out what we would now call a theory of innate knowledge. In other words, he's saying that humans are born with a great deal of knowledge already built in, so to speak.

Theories of innateness are still current in contemporary philosophy, for instance in Noam Chomsky's theories about how babies learn language—a lot of linguistic structure, according to him, is already hard-wired into our brains from birth.[1] So this way of understanding Plato could help to show that he is relevant to our philosophical concerns today. Now, I'm the last to deny that Plato is relevant. For example, in a moment we'll see that in this very dialogue, the *Meno*, he introduces a distinction that is still fundamental in philosophy today, the distinction between knowledge and true belief. But I don't believe we should take the theory of recollection as a metaphorical endorsement of a theory of innateness. For one thing, as we'll see a bit later in this book, Plato's *Phaedo* invokes the recollection theory to argue for the immortality of the soul. The point made there is precisely that, if we recollect knowledge we already had before we were born, then the soul must have existed before it came to be in a body. So, at least in that dialogue, the whole point would be ruined unless the recollection theory genuinely envisioned pre-existence for the soul. To my mind, this should encourage us to think that the *Meno* too really asks us to believe in an immortal soul which knows everything and pre-existed our birth.

We might wonder whether there is some other, less extravagant way of solving Meno's paradox. Let's go back to a suggestion I made earlier, with the example of Buster Keaton: it's possible to have partial knowledge instead of complete knowledge. We saw that that doesn't really help, because you need to explain where the partial knowledge comes from. But let's try another solution of the same kind: could there be some state which falls between ignorance and knowledge? So, for example, could I fall short of knowing what virtue is, while still doing better than total ignorance of virtue? Plato sees that the answer is yes: I could have mere *beliefs* about virtue, and if those beliefs were true, then that would be better than ignorance but not as good as certain knowledge. We might even think that Meno fits the bill. Although he doesn't know what virtue is, he does have true beliefs about it: for instance, he can give relevant examples (as he did when he attempted to define virtue by listing cases of virtue) and affirm that justice is a virtue.

Socrates introduces this idea at the end of the slave-boy scene, when he says that his questioning has brought only true beliefs out of the boy, but not yet knowledge. To have knowledge, the boy would have to be questioned many times and in different ways (85c). Now it might be our turn to be a bit puzzled. What exactly is the difference between true belief and knowledge? Actually, if I've got true belief, why do I need knowledge? Suppose I have a true belief about who will win tomorrow's horse-race. That is just as good a way to win my bet as if I knew the winner for sure. But you might disagree; you might say that if I knew for sure, I'd put down more money on my horse than if I only had a true belief. That seems wrong, though. After all, people can be incredibly confident in their beliefs without having knowledge.

Plato, as usual, sees this point, and deals with it later in the dialogue. He has Meno raise exactly the puzzle I just mentioned, namely that true belief is just as good as knowledge (97a–d). Socrates agrees that it seems like a puzzle, giving the example of knowing how to get to another Greek city, called Larissa: if I have a true belief about the right way, that will get me there just as well as knowledge (97b). But then he seems to change his mind, and decides that true belief really is inferior to knowledge. He takes true belief to be less reliable than knowledge, because it is not grounded in an adequate "account." By this, Socrates seems to mean that if I know something is true, I should be able to understand and explain why it is true. It is this ability, and not my degree of confidence, that marks the difference between true beliefs and knowledge. In another famous image, Socrates compares true beliefs to magical statues which run away unless tied down (97d–98a). In the same way, our true beliefs are unreliable unless they are tied down by giving an "account" of their truth.

One aspect of this unreliability is that people who have only true belief, and not knowledge, may be unable to impart the truth to other people. Or at least that's suggested by further reflections in the *Meno* on the subject of whether virtue can be taught. (That was, after all, the initial question of the dialogue, and it remains important throughout.) In between the slave-boy scene and the discussion of true belief, Meno and Socrates speculate that virtue would be teachable if it were a kind of knowledge (87c). This rings Socratic bells: as we've seen in previous chapters, Socrates was notorious for thinking that virtue is knowledge. But if virtue were knowledge and were thus teachable, shouldn't there be people around who teach it? This is the cue for the entrance of Anytus, one of the men who had Socrates indicted for corrupting the youth and introducing novel gods. In this scene we get a glimpse of why he might have done so. Socrates asks Anytus whether he supposes that there are people who can teach virtue (91b). The obvious candidates are the sophists. As we saw, some sophists claimed to teach virtue in return for money. But Anytus has nothing but scorn for these supposed teachers. He says that someone who wants to learn to be virtuous is better off asking any Athenian about it (92e). Socrates counters by reeling off a list of famous Athenian statesmen, like Pericles, who were clearly virtuous but had vicious sons (94b). If being virtuous makes you able to teach virtue, wouldn't these men have taught virtue to their sons?

This disrespect towards the great men of Athens is enough to make Anytus furious. He makes the none-too-subtle parting remark that Socrates should watch his step, since the city is apt to mistreat him if he doesn't mind his manners (95a). This was no empty threat, as things turned out. But of course a threat, whether empty or not, is no answer to Socrates' latest puzzle. If virtue is knowledge, as Socrates typically claims, then why are there no teachers of it? Here true belief might come to the rescue: the virtuous men might be the ones who have true beliefs about what to do, rather than knowledge. Socrates even suggests that such men are given their beliefs by divine dispensation, given that they haven't done the philosophical work required to ground their beliefs with an "account"—or whatever it is that makes a true belief knowledge (99c).

Now, here in the *Meno* Plato doesn't say in any detail what you would have to do to turn true beliefs into knowledge. But we should give him credit for discovering a problem that still obsesses philosophers today.[2] He's right that true belief is not the same thing as knowledge. After all, suppose I just believe everything anyone tells me. That would get me a lot of true beliefs, but also a lot of false ones—and it seems obvious that none of the beliefs would count as knowledge. On the other hand, it seems equally obvious that true belief has some close relation to knowledge. If I know something then I must believe it, and it must be true. The question is, then, what you need to add to true belief in order to get knowledge—only one of the issues that will arise in our next dialogue.

19

I KNOW, BECAUSE THE CAGED BIRD SINGS PLATO'S *THEAETETUS*[1]

Those of you who spend time with children will know that, between the adults and the children of this world, a war is raging. Skirmishes in this war are fought across the land, every morning, and both sides use all the weapons at their disposal—tantrums, the silent treatment, withheld treats, even, in extreme cases, the naughty step. I am speaking, of course, about the question of how warmly to dress. The children's perspective on this issue is well entrenched: it is not nearly as cold outside as you parents would claim, and we aren't going to wear that winter coat, though we may be willing to consider a light sweater. The parents' point of view is equally firm: you'll catch your death of cold. I guess that if you are reading this book you are above the age of twelve, and so naturally favor the adult perspective. There is, we quite naturally think, a fact of the matter about how cold it is outside: just look at the thermometer. Yet the children can turn to us and say: "But I don't *feel* cold. So for me, it *isn't* cold." And they've got a point, albeit a point which is undermined slightly when they start shivering even as they're insisting on how warm it is. The point is that it is for each person to say how cold the air feels to them. You might even say that, whatever the temperature may be, the air's being cold is nothing more than the air's seeming cold to each of us.

This prompts an unsettling thought. It's not implausible that the air is really neither cold nor hot in itself, but is cold for you and warm for me—I grew up in Boston, so I'm made of tougher stuff than you are. And we can think of other cases: most of us have been in disputes about whether a certain piece of clothing is blue or green, and maybe it is just green for one person, blue for someone else. Thus the unsettling thought: what if everything is like this? Suppose that there is no truth apart from the way things seem to each person? They may be warm for me, cold for you, blue for me, green for you, *good* for me, *bad* for you, while having none of these features in themselves. In that case, nothing is true absolutely. Rather, truth is relative: something might be true *for me* and false *for you*, but neither false nor true in itself. This relativist theory of truth is one still arises in contemporary philosophy, but it has its roots in the dialogues of Plato. In particular, it is explored in my personal favorite among the Platonic dialogues: the *Theaetetus*.

I've previously mentioned the word "epistemology," which means the study of knowledge—because the ancient Greek word for knowledge or understanding was *episteme*. We just saw that Plato's *Meno* has quite a bit to say about this, and we've found interesting epistemological ideas already in the Pre-Socratics. But the first work to devote itself fully to epistemology is the *Theaetetus*. It explores some of the ideas of the *Meno* but goes well beyond them, investigating not only a relativist theory of truth, but also the question of how false judgment is possible and how knowledge relates to belief. The main characters are our old friend Socrates, Theodorus, a mathematician, and a young man who is a mathematician like Theodorus, and profoundly ugly like Socrates: he shares Socrates' protruding eyes and snub-nose (143e). This is Theaetetus, one of the most admirable characters to engage with Socrates in Plato's dialogues. Despite his youth, he shows much more commitment to the philosophical search than the older Theodorus. He offers several attempts at saying what knowledge might be. As we have come to expect in Socratic dialogues, each attempt is refuted, but he doesn't lose heart—and we learn a great deal about knowledge in the course of the dialogue, even if the characters fail to produce a definition of knowledge that satisfies them.

Theaetetus' first attempt is to say that knowledge is perception (151e). The word for perception here is *aisthesis*, which incidentally is where we get the word "aesthetics." It can mean sense perception—that is, vision, hearing, smell, and so on—or more broadly any kind of perception, including the perception of things with the mind. Especially if we take it in this broader sense, Theaetetus' definition looks plausible: we know something when we perceive it. Or perhaps one might say, we know when we grasp that something is the case. But Socrates shows that Theaetetus' definition could be taken in a more unsettling way: if knowledge is perception, then whatever seems to me to be the case must actually be the case for me (152a). Here he gives the same example I just used: the wind seems warm to me and cold to you, so I perceive the wind as warm and you perceive it as cold. If perception is knowledge, then that means that I know the wind is warm and you know it is cold. How could this be? Well, only if truth is relative: it's true for me that the wind is warm and true for you that it is cold, but there is no such thing as the wind's being truly warm or cold in itself, relative to no perceiver. After all, knowledge is nothing but perception.

Socrates adds that in putting forward such a view Theaetetus would be in good company. In particular, this relativistic theory of truth was asserted by the great sophist Protagoras (152a). As we saw in our previous chapter on the sophists,

Protagoras was famous for saying "man is the measure of all things, of the things that are, that they are, of the things that are not, that they are not." Like Theaetetus' definition of knowledge as perception, this "man is the measure" doctrine could be taken in a lot of different ways. But Socrates wants to take both claims as boiling down to relativism about truth. If I am the measure of whether the wind is warm, then there is nothing more to the wind's being warm than its being warm *for me*, and not cold *for me*. The way things seem to me determines the way the wind is and isn't.

Socrates adds that Theatetus and Protagoras have another heavy-hitter on their side, namely the Pre-Socratic philosopher Heraclitus (160d). You might remember me saying that Plato portrays Heraclitus as believing in a doctrine of total flux. That is, everything is constantly changing in every respect, and there is no stability in us or the world around us. The *Theaetetus* isn't the only dialogue where Plato ascribes this view to Heraclitus, though it is the most prominent one. But why does the flux doctrine go along with relativism about truth? Apparently because, if Protagorean relativism is true, then the things in the world around us will have no stable natures from moment to moment. They will only be whatever they seem to be to various perceivers, and this is changing all the time, according to Heraclitus as he's presented here. So on this view, it would turn out that nothing is cold and nothing is warm; rather, everything is always changing in every way. Actually it might be even worse than this: if we say that what is changing from warm to cold or vice-versa is both warm *and* cold, then the air will always be both warm and cold. It was with this in mind that Aristotle later accused Heraclitus of denying the principle of non-contradiction.

These radical consequences of the flux doctrine give us plenty of reason for rejecting it. And if buying into the relativist theory of truth means buying into the flux theory, then maybe we'll give up on relativism as well. But Protagoras will try to persuade us that the relativist theory isn't as implausible as it seems. If you're interested in which things are good, then obviously what you're interested in is which things are good *for you*. What would it even mean for something to be good, but not for you, or for anyone in particular? This, perhaps, connects the theory Plato is considering to the real historical Protagoras. He claimed to teach virtue, and may have supposed this was possible because the good is the advantageous, and because he could teach people how to get things they would consider to be advantageous, like political power. Whether Protagoras really held the radical epistemological theory that Plato ascribes to him here in the *Theaetetus* is, of course, another matter. But let's leave that aside, and also leave aside the problems about flux, and just consider the problem of how to refute someone who adopts the relativist position on truth.

At first this sounds easy. Just point to a thermometer, which tells us an objective fact about how cold the air is. But here Protagoras can agree with your kids that, whatever the thermometer says, it's up to each of us to say whether that temperature is cold or warm for us. Besides, he can point out that the thermometer is itself something you perceive. If it seems to you that the thermometer reads, say, 30 degrees, then it's true *for you* that the thermometer reads 30 degrees. It's true for you simply because you perceive it to be the case. To insist on there being an absolute truth about the reading of the thermometer is to assume that there is a truth independent of any perceiver, and that's just what Protagoras denies: man is the measure of all things. But Socrates has a couple of other tricks up his sleeve. He starts with abuse: wouldn't it be just as true to say that a pig or a baboon is the measure of all things (161c)? Abuse is always satisfying, of course, but it doesn't carry much argumentative weight. Fortunately he has more philosophically satisfying points to make too. For instance, on this "man is the measure" doctrine there'd be no point consulting experts: why pay to go to the doctor if you are just as good a measure as the doctor is? If it seems to you that taking aspirin will cure that nasty bout of appendicitis, then it's true for you! This sounds like a theory that will reduce the life-expectancy of its adherents—reason enough to reject it. Closely related is an objection about predicting the future. If I expect to recover from my illness, then it will be true for me that I will recover. If it then later seems to me that I'm still sick, then it will seem to me that I have not recovered, and so it will be true for me that I didn't recover (178c). It's hard to see how both of these could be the case.

But Socrates' most interesting objection illustrates a classic, perennially useful philosophical maneuver. Whenever you're presented with a bold new theory, ask whether the theory is consistent with itself. For example, if someone says that nothing is true, you can ask him whether this claim is itself true. Or if someone says that language is meaningless, you can ask her how she is able to convey this idea in a sentence. In the same way, Socrates suggests that Protagoras' relativism doctrine is self-refuting. For, even if Protagoras agrees with the doctrine, Socrates does not. Thus it will be true *for Socrates* that Protagoras' doctrine is false. Indeed, since this follows from Protagoras' doctrine, it will even be true *for Protagoras* that *for Socrates* the doctrine is false (171b). Thus Protagoras is bound by his own doctrine to admit that his doctrine is false. But maybe this trick is a bit too tricky: even if Protagoras has to admit that the doctrine is false *for Socrates*, he doesn't have to admit that it's false *in itself*, or *really* false. Remember, according to him, there's no such thing as something's just being true or false. There is only something's being true or false to you, to me, to Socrates.[2]

Before we get any dizzier, let's leave relativism behind and move on to another major theme of this dialogue: the possibility of false belief. This theme arises when Theaetetus accepts that knowledge is not, after all, perception, and makes another suggestion. Perhaps knowledge is having a true belief (178b). After all, when I know something I have a belief about it, and it obviously can't be a false belief. So why not say I know something when I have a true belief about it? All well and good, says Socrates, but if we want to uphold this definition we need to understand how it could be that some beliefs are true and others are false (188c). And here we will run afoul of those pesky sophists again. Some sophists suggested that it is impossible to say or believe anything false—in which case everything is just a matter of persuasion. This challenge appears in several Platonic dialogues; we've already seen it show up in the *Euthydemus*. But the *Theaetetus* again provides the most prominent example. The argument here for the sophistical view is rather reminiscent of Meno's paradox. It goes like this: either I know something or I don't. If I do know it, then obviously my knowledge will prevent me from making mistakes. But if I don't know the thing in question, then my ignorance will prevent me from even thinking about it; you don't have false beliefs about people you have never even heard of, for instance. So I won't be able to make a mistake then either. In other words, I'll either have perfect knowledge of each thing or no knowledge of it at all, and in neither case will I get things wrong. Therefore, it's impossible to make a mistake, to believe anything false.

As with Meno's paradox, it looks like the way out is to say that there is some middle ground where I know or grasp something well enough to make a mistake about it, but not so well that I am immune to error. Socrates presents two analogies to suggest how this could work. First, he says, imagine that your memory is like a wax tablet—they used to write on these in ancient Greece. When you perceive something, that's like a stamp making an impression in the wax of your mind (191c–d). Some people have tough, dirty wax and are slow on the uptake; others have fluid wax and get impressions quickly, but lose them just as fast. Still others have wax which is ideally suited: easily stamped, but also good at holding the impressions. Quite a nice image of how memory works, really. Now for false judgment: that would happen when there is a mismatch between something you perceive and an existing impression in the wax of your memory (193c). For instance, I think I am watching a silent film starring Buster Keaton, but actually I've made a mistake. That lovable fellow on the screen is in fact Charlie Chaplin, and I'm matching the visual image to the wrong stamped impression in my wax tablet. As Socrates says, it's like putting your right foot into your left shoe (193c).

This does seem to solve the sophistical dilemma: I can make a mistake about something because in a way I know it, and in a way I don't. I know who Buster Keaton is, because I must have got acquainted with him to have an impression of him in my memory. But this doesn't guarantee that I'll be error-free in identifying a given person as Buster Keaton. This is a compelling analogy, and for once the proposal isn't exactly rejected in the dialogue. Rather, the characters realize that even if it works for cases of mistaken identity in perception, there are many cases of false judgment where it will not help. For instance, what is going on when I add seven and five and get eleven (195e–196c)? There's nothing here about impressions being made on our memory by perception, and yet still I've made a mistake. So Socrates produces another image in place of the wax tablet. Imagine, he says, that your soul is like an aviary, a birdcage, with lots of birds flying around in it, each of which represents a piece of knowledge (197c–199c). Then imagine that learning is like catching birds and putting them into your aviary. What happens when you add five to seven and get eleven is that you reach into your aviary and pull out the eleven bird instead of the twelve bird (199b). Again, your knowledge of eleven actually *enables* you to make the mistake, the way your knowledge of Buster Keaton enabled you to mistake Charlie Chaplin for him.

Unfortunately, Socrates and Theaetetus decide that this model too is problematic. It means that when you make a mistake, it is precisely by virtue of knowing that you get things wrong (199d). It is, paradoxically, because of your knowledge of eleven that you are able to have a false belief about five plus seven. The indefatigable Theaetetus has another suggestion, though: what if your aviary contains birds representing ignorance, as well as birds representing knowledge? Then when you make a mistake you've just grabbed the wrong kind of bird (199e). But that ruins the whole point, which was to explain how we can know something just enough to make a mistake about it, without knowing it so well that we are immune to error (200a–c).

So where does all that leave us? Right back where we started: without a general account of false belief, but still thinking that maybe knowledge is the same thing as true belief (200e). Ah, but it isn't, says Socrates. Just consider the case of a jury: the jurors might be persuaded by some fancy lawyer that a certain man is innocent of a crime. And the man really *is* innocent. But we wouldn't say that they *know*, since they only believe this because the lawyer was slick enough to persuade them (201a–c). Thus they have a true belief, but not knowledge. So much for that definition. Yet Theaetetus still feels—and today's epistemologists tend to agree—that knowledge must have *something* to do with true belief. Maybe knowledge is true belief and something else as well, something the jurors are lacking, but which you would have if you were, say, an eyewitness at the murder and know that the accused man is innocent. It's no easy task to say what that would be. As I say, modern-day epistemologists are still struggling with these questions, and for them a central issue is precisely what might separate knowledge from true belief. When they address this topic, they are taking up a challenge first thrown down here in the *Theaetetus*.[3]

FAMOUS LAST WORDS
PLATO'S *PHAEDO*

When a swan is about to die, it sings. It sings more beautifully than it ever has before, for it belongs to the god Apollo, and has the gift of prophecy (85a–b). So the swan knows it will die, and sings with joy because it is finally about to join its divine master. Or so, at least, says Socrates, who likewise dedicated himself to Apollo and met death with hope rather than reluctance. He says as much to his friends who gather around him in prison, in Plato's dialogue the *Phaedo*. It dramatizes Socrates' own swan-song, his final philosophical discussion and his death upon unflinchingly drinking down the hemlock. The *Phaedo* is a great work of literature, whose portrayal of bravery in the face of death has inspired readers from the ancient world down to the present. From a philosophical point of view too, it is one of Plato's greatest dialogues, in part because it is the first dialogue to set out the theory of Forms.

This is usually taken to be Plato's most important doctrine, so you may have been wondering why I haven't dealt with it yet. But as it turns out, Forms are not mentioned explicitly in all, or even most, of Plato's dialogues. They are absent from the dialogues we've looked at so far, like the *Gorgias*, *Meno*, and *Theaetetus*. Even in the *Phaedo* the main topic of the dialogue is not Forms, but the immortality of soul. This is a matter of some concern to Socrates, since each page of the dialogue is bringing him closer to his death scene. In what must be a swipe at Aristophanes, Plato has Socrates say that even a comic poet wouldn't blame him for irrelevant prattling when he takes up this topic at this time and place. It's typical of the way Plato handles the topic of Forms that even here, in one of the handful of dialogues where they are discussed directly, they play only a supporting role.

So let's start, not from Forms, but from this question of the soul's immortality. One might suppose that the first order of business would be to establish that we do have a soul. But Socrates and his friends simply take this for granted. Indeed, they seem to presuppose some kind of dualism as a basis for their discussion. By "dualism," I mean they assume that the soul is one thing and the body another. But this is not to say that they assume the soul is incorporeal in the sense of being immaterial. Socrates even suggests at one point that his friends may think our souls are like smoke that could blow away upon death (70a). And even if the soul is immaterial, it might depend on the body for its existence, so that Socrates' soul will vanish when he drinks the hemlock. As one of his friends suggests, soul could be like the harmony or tuning of a string instrument, which would not be a body but would be destroyed along with the instrument. Socrates' task, then, is to show that the soul is not just distinct from the body, but capable of surviving independently from the body. Along the way, he will show that it is indeed immaterial, invisible, indivisible—all the things we expect a Platonic dualist to believe about the soul.

So how should we prove this? To use a rather lame joke that Plato himself seems to find amusing, you will *recollect* that in the *Meno* Socrates has argued that when we seem to be learning we are actually recollecting things we knew before we were born. After the characters remind each other about this idea ("remind," get it?), they realize that it implies that the soul existed before the body did (73a–76c). So obviously the soul can exist without the body, since it used to do so. Furthermore, the soul must be akin to the things it knew before birth. This is the cue for the Forms to make their entrance. What we knew before birth and now recollect are things like "the beautiful itself" and "the equal itself," or as we would usually put it when talking about Plato, "the Form of Beauty" and "the Form of Equal." These are not physical objects but the natures of which beautiful or equal physical objects partake. So, we already have another way to show the soul's independence of body, the so-called "affinity argument." This argument assumes that the soul must be akin to whatever it knows.[1] Since these things are eternal and immaterial, the soul too is eternal and immaterial.

Notice again that these arguments are intended to prove the soul's immortality, not the existence of Forms. In fact, it looks like we are just assuming the existence of Forms to prove that the soul is immortal. So is the theory of Forms something Plato wants us to take for granted, like the distinction between soul and body? And how does he expect us to know what these Forms are like? It would be pretty disappointing if Plato gave us no reason to believe in them and no explanation of what they are. But wait, there's more. Plato invites us to think more carefully about how recollection of Forms would actually work. It might be helpful to consider other cases of recollection. Imagine being reminded of your best friend (if you don't have a best friend, your worst enemy will do just as well). As Socrates points out, you could be reminded of him or her by something which is nothing like your friend—like a piece of their clothing. Alternatively, you could be reminded by something which *is* like the friend—say, a painting of the friend (73d–e). In this second case it is natural to compare the two things. For instance, you will judge whether or not the painting is a good likeness of your friend.

Now Socrates applies this point to the Forms. He suggests that when you see two equal sticks, and are reminded of the Form of Equal, it is like seeing an imperfect likeness. The sticks do resemble the Form of Equal, because they are equal to one another. But they are also unlike the Form, because in some other respect, *they are unequal* (74a–75b). It's not totally clear what Socrates means here, but to me the most persuasive reading is this: imagine two equally long sticks and a third longer one next to them. The stick on the left is equal to the stick in the middle, and vice-versa. But both are unequal to the stick on the right, which is longer than them. Thus, sticks number one and two are *both* equal *and* unequal. Unlike the Form, which is only equal.[2] As a student of mine once put it to me, with apologies to George Orwell: the Form is equal, and the stick is equal, but some equal things are more equal than others. This sort of example crops up in other Platonic dialogues too. Take, for instance, Helen. You remember her, from the *Iliad*, the one whose face was so good at ship-launching? She is beautiful compared to other human women, but not beautiful compared to a goddess. She is thus both beautiful and not beautiful. Or take the example of repaying a debt. This is normally good. Suppose, for instance, you borrowed an axe from a friend and are going to return it. That sounds good. But suppose your friend has gone insane, and is now an axe-murderer wondering where he might be able to find an axe?[3]

People in the Plato business have a nice bit of terminology to describe such cases: "compresence of opposites."[4] The basic idea is that the things in the world around us often have contradictory features, which especially emerge when we are comparing one thing to another. Things may be in one respect equal, in another unequal; in one respect beautiful, in another not beautiful; in one respect good, in another bad. Plato is convinced that our knowledge of things like equality and beauty is not just directed towards equal sticks and beautiful women, or, for that matter, beautiful sticks and equal women. Rather, equality itself and beauty itself must be somehow separate from the sticks and the women, and we must be judging the sticks and the women by looking to an absolute standard of equality and beauty. When we do this, the Forms are the standard by which we judge. So this, along with the theory of recollection, introduces a further reason to believe in Forms: they are standards of judgment, and thus play a crucial role in our knowledge.

But wait, there's still more. Forms not only play a role in Plato's theory of knowledge (his epistemology). They also play a role in his metaphysics, or to be more specific, his understanding of causation. His idea here is that the Form of Equal somehow *causes* equal things like sticks to be equal, while the Form of Beauty causes

Helen to be beautiful. Socrates presents this idea in a kind of intellectual autobiography. I mentioned this passage in an earlier chapter, because in it Socrates criticizes the Pre-Socratic philosopher Anaxagoras. As you might remember, Socrates was disappointed that Anaxagoras invoked Mind as if he would show that the universe follows a rational design, but then retreated into merely physical explanations (98b). As Socrates says, this would be as if he were to say that he is sitting in jail because his bones and muscles are in jail, instead of saying that he is sitting there because he decided not to run away when he was offered the chance to do so (98c).

The examples show what Plato expects from a causal explanation. Whether we try to explain the cosmos or why Socrates is sitting in jail, we should select a cause which *must* give rise to the effect we're trying to explain. The presence of the true cause shouldn't be compatible with other possible outcomes. So, for instance, Anaxagoras' famous vortex seems on the face of it to be compatible with a badly designed, chaotic world, as well as with the good world we see around us; and Socrates' bones and muscles would be involved in both running away and staying put. Another example: it would be wrong to say that one man is taller than another "by a head," because it's also possible to be smaller by a head—so invoking the head doesn't explain being taller any more than it would explain being smaller. And by the way, there's another problem with invoking the head as a cause of tallness. The head itself is small, and Socrates finds it ridiculous to say that something small could be the cause of tallness (101b).

Plato is making a very strict demand here. To oversimplify a bit, it boils down to the following: the cause of, say, largeness should not be small, nor should it be able to cause smallness. Likewise, the cause of equality should not be unequal, and should never cause inequality. Now, Forms seem to satisfy this demand admirably. If things are equal precisely because they resemble the Form of Equal, it stands to reason both that the Form of Equal is not going to be unequal, and that the Form of Equal never causes anything to be unequal. But if the Form of Equal doesn't cause things to be unequal, what does? Well, maybe there's a Form of Unequal too, or maybe things are just unequal because they fail to be perfectly like the Form of Equal, the way your friend's portrait isn't perfectly like your friend. The same kind of logic will work for other Forms. The Form of Beauty is not ugly, and cannot cause ugliness; ugliness must be caused either by another Form, the Form of Ugly, or a simple failure to resemble the Form of Beauty. Plato seems to be saying not just that each Form excludes its opposite (for instance, the Form of Equal is not unequal), but also that each Form exemplifies itself. For instance the Form of Equal would itself be equal, the Form of Beauty would itself be beautiful. This may sound reasonable enough. But we might worry that the Form of Large, for instance, can't really be large, since it is immaterial. And as we'll see, this assumption that each Form exemplifies itself is going to cause trouble for Plato in another dialogue.

For now, though, let's grant that the Forms do satisfy Plato's demands for proper causation. Still, isn't this, well, cheating? Is it really illuminating to be told that the cause of Helen's being beautiful is the Form of Beauty? This sounds a lot like the uninformative definition we considered in the chapter on the *Meno*, that ruminants are things that ruminate. Plato is sensitive to this objection, and has Socrates admit that when we invoke Forms we are giving what he calls "safe" but "simple-minded" causes (105c). Although it's "safe" to say that Beauty makes Helen beautiful, it doesn't seem to take us very far. On the other hand, it may take us further than we might think. Remember that the Forms are not just causes, but also the objects of our knowledge. So someone who knew the Form of Beauty would know exactly what it means to be beautiful. They would, after all, understand the nature of beauty itself. So they would be able to explain exactly what it is for Helen to be beautiful, and perhaps also why Helen is not beautiful compared to a goddess.

Socrates also recognizes that sometimes we can give what he calls a "clever" cause in addition to a "safe and simple-minded" cause. For instance, if we want to know what has made something cold, we might play safe and say the Form of Cold. But a more clever answer would be snow. After all, snow satisfies the demands Plato has laid down. It is cold without being hot, and it cannot make anything hot. In these respects, therefore, snow is just as good a cause as the Form would be. In other respects though, the Form is a better cause. The Form of Cold will be involved *every* time something is cold. Thus it's always "safe" to invoke the Form of Cold as a cause of things being cold, whereas snow is not involved every time things are made cold. Sometimes the clever cause might be ice, or liquid nitrogen, or an insufficiently generous Valentine's Day present. So, although the Forms may be safe and simple-minded causes, they will be better than at least some clever causes because of their universal application.

Now, I've been talking about Forms for quite a while. What happened to the immortality of the soul, which I was insisting was the main topic of this dialogue? Well, it turns out that what we've just been talking about is directly relevant to this topic. After all, what is the soul, if it is not a cause of being alive? But if it is a proper cause, one that satisfies Plato's demands, then the soul will have to be only alive, not dead—just the way that, in order for snow to be a proper cause of cold, it has to be only cold and not hot. If this is right, then the soul can no more be dead than snow could be hot, or the number three even. The soul will have to be permanently alive by its very nature (105d). This line of argument allows Socrates to ward off an argument which has been troubling him and his friends. Even if we say that the soul can survive the body's death, how do we know it won't wear out eventually? It might be like a weaver who has worn out many cloaks. Just as the weaver survives while one cloak after another becomes threadbare and has to be discarded, so the soul might survive for a long time, wearing out one body after another. But eventually the weaver will die, wearing his last cloak. In this way the soul could perhaps die, after it leaves its last of many bodies (87b–88b). Happily, Socrates is now able to refute this: as a proper cause of life, the soul is by nature immune to death.

Notice again how Socrates is assuming that the soul is distinct from the body, and then asking what this distinct soul is like. He doesn't really pay any attention to the possibility that he is nothing other than his body—which is the very possibility that nowadays leads us to fear we may not survive death. Instead, he worries that the soul itself may be a mortal being, which would expire along with the death of the body. Upon reflection, Socrates decides he does not need to worry after all. All the arguments at his disposal point towards the conclusion that his soul will live on. He might, of course, worry instead that his soul will live on but go to some horrible fate. Here again, though, Socrates is an optimist: he believes that he will be joining good, divine masters, and if there are humans in the afterlife, they too will be good. If there is anything to fear, it is that we might come back into worse bodies after escaping from our current human bodies. But Socrates suggests that we are likely to receive the bodies we deserve: violent people will get the bodies of wolves, orderly people will come back as well-organized insects like bees (82a–b). And Socrates? He doesn't make a prediction, but I like to think that next time around, he was a swan.

Before we move on to another dialogue, let me say just a little bit more about the theory of Forms and the soul. As I've explained, Forms help Plato with at least three interconnected problems. First, they give him appropriate objects of knowledge—when we recollect, it will be Forms we are recollecting. Second, Forms are free of the compresence of opposites: the equal things we experience are actually both equal and unequal, but the Form of Equal is not unequal in any way. Third, Forms will be proper and universal causes of features like equality and beauty. That's a lot of philosophical payoff, but it still doesn't exhaust the usefulness of Forms. For instance, in other dialogues Plato suggests that things in the physical world are constantly changing. Forms allow him to say that some things, at least, are stable and unchanging—a way of avoiding the total-flux doctrine he ascribes to Heraclitus. He makes this point at the end of his dialogue the *Cratylus* (439b–440d). In the same dialogue he invokes Forms to explain the meanings of words, as we'll be seeing in a later chapter. It's easy to assume that Plato thought up his theory of Forms and then engineered these puzzles to convince us of his theory. But if we look at the way he actually uses Forms, in the *Phaedo* and elsewhere, we see that he usually goes in the other direction. Plato was plagued by a whole range of philosophical problems, and he repeatedly found that Forms could help him solve those problems. He was driven by the need to solve philosophical difficulties, not the desire to defend a doctrine for its own sake.

Now finally, back to the soul. To state an obvious but important fact, the soul whose fate is in question here is supposed to be not just a part of Socrates, but Socrates himself. At the end of the dialogue his friends ask how they should bury him, and Socrates laughs, saying that they will do well to catch him (115c). In other words, Socrates is not the body they will bury, but rather his soul. Now the *Phaedo*, and especially its affinity argument, seem to suggest that the soul is a lot like a Form. So if Socrates is his soul, he will be immaterial, indivisible, immortal. But doesn't our experience show that we, or our souls, are riven by conflict? That we are anything but simple, and are instead a mass of conflicting desires, experiences, and ideas? The *Phaedo* does not seem to recognize this fact. But Plato will make up for this omission in what is usually regarded as his greatest work, the *Republic*. There, Plato has Socrates argue that our souls are complex entities, capable of both internal conflict and internal harmony. Harmony in the soul would be nothing less than justice—the topic of the *Republic* as a whole, and of our next chapter.

SOUL AND THE CITY
JUSTICE IN PLATO'S *REPUBLIC*

One of the most famous scenes in the *History of the Peloponnesian War*, by the ancient Greek historian Thucydides, presents a dialogue between the representatives of Athens and the people of a small island called Melos. The Athenians are embroiled in their long-running war against Sparta and its allies. The Melians have preserved their neutrality in this war, but now the Athenians want to persuade the people of Melos to join the fight against the Spartan alliance. When the Melians ask why they should do this, the Athenians admit that they can offer no principled reason. Instead, they point out that they are powerful, whereas the Melians are weak. Their argument is simple: join us, or be smashed. The Melians opted not to join Athens, and were duly smashed. The men of the island were massacred, the women and children sold into slavery, and the island made into an Athenian colony. As Thucydides has the Athenians observe, "the strong do what they can, and the weak suffer what they must."[1]

Actually, this traditional translation of Thucydides' famous aphorism is not particularly accurate.[2] But in any translation, the scene shows Athens giving Melos a brutal lesson in *Realpolitik*. Thucydides has his own reasons for putting this speech into the mouths of the Athenians, because it helps him develop his great theme of Athenian arrogance and expansionism. On his telling, the Athenians reap what they sow when they lose the Peloponnesian War. This shook the political institutions of Athens to their foundations. As I've mentioned already, in the wake of the defeat the democratic constitution of Athens was overthrown by a cabal of men, the so-called "Thirty Tyrants." Once the tyrants were removed and the democracy restored, the good people of Athens indulged in some civic spring-cleaning, including the trial and execution of Socrates.

Thucydides is our most important source for reconstructing the confrontation between democratic Athens and the oligarchic city of Sparta. But the events of the late fifth century have echoes in other ancient Greek writings, such as the plays of our old friend Aristophanes. Those echoes can also be heard in a dialogue that is usually regarded as the founding text of political philosophy, and the greatest work of Plato: the *Republic*. The *Republic* is a work of extraordinary complexity and length. It takes in not only political philosophy, but also moral psychology, metaphysics, epistemology, and aesthetics. In fact, one would be hard pressed to think of an area of philosophy not explored in the *Republic*. I'm going to devote two chapters to it, but I could easily give it ten chapters, one for each book, and still leave out a lot. First, I'll deal with Plato's description of the ideal city, and the parallel he draws between this city and the virtuous human soul. The next chapter will examine the famous images of the cave, line, and sun found in the central books of the *Republic*.

We get a taste of the themes of the *Republic* on its very first page. Socrates is the narrator, and tells us of an encounter he had at the time of the festival of the goddess Bendis. He has seen a religious procession and is returning to Athens, when he is intercepted by a group led by a man named Polemarchus. In a darkly amusing passage which resonates with Thucydides' Melian dialogue, Polemarchus invites Socrates and his friend Glaucon to come home for some hospitality. He points out that if Socrates doesn't want to come, he can be forced to do so, since Polemarchus' companions outnumber Socrates and Glaucon (327c). Polemarchus' group is physically stronger, so it's inevitable that they will get what they want, one way or another. Already in this opening sequence Plato has made us think about the role of strength and compulsion in human affairs, a central issue throughout the *Republic*.

Socrates agrees to go quietly, and winds up back at Polemarchus' house. Among the people gathered there, three are particularly important. There is Thrasymachus, a sophist who locks horns with Socrates in this first book. And there are Glaucon and Adiemantus, who will be the main interlocutors for Socrates for the remaining nine books of the *Republic*. These two characters just happen to be the brothers of Plato. The discussions Socrates has with Thrasymachus, and then with Glaucon and Adiemantus, are about the nature of justice. Thrasymachus holds a view much like the one defended by Callicles in Plato's *Gorgias*. On this view, it is natural for the strong to do whatever benefits them, and justice is simply the "advantage of the stronger" (338c). Thrasymachus admires the man who is bold enough to commit any number of so-called injustices, to take what he can get, to become a tyrant and enslave his enemies. Justice is, if you will, for the strong to do what they can and the weak to suffer what they must. Thrasymachus admits that this is not what people usually mean by "justice." According to the popular view, justice is often a matter of forgoing one's own advantage for the sake of someone else's—for example, keeping the terms of a contract even if it would be more profitable not to (343d). If that's what justice is, says Thrasymachus, you can keep it. One should instead seize whatever is advantageous to oneself, at least if one is strong enough to do so. And in fact, when we look at political rulers across Greece, we see that this is exactly what they do. Just as a tyrant rules for his own advantage, so democracies like Athens pass laws that favor their rulers, namely the people or *demos*, as opposed to the aristocracy (338d–e).

Socrates proceeds to refute Thrasymachus in his inimitable fashion. He argues that political rule must look to the benefit of the ruled, not that of the ruler—just as the art of medicine looks to the benefit of the patient, not the doctor (342d). In fact, in an anticipation of a conclusion that will be reached much later in the dialogue, Socrates argues that a good ruler would rule reluctantly, since it would normally involve looking after the subjects' good rather than his own (347c). After this dialogue between Socrates and Thrasymachus Book One of the *Republic* comes to an end. When Book Two opens, Glaucon and Adeimantus complain that Socrates' refutation of Thrasymachus has left them unsatisfied. They would like to be convinced once and for all that justice really is better than injustice (357a–b). People claim to admire justice, but is this what they believe in their heart of hearts? Glaucon does a good job of playing devil's advocate here. First he suggests thinking of justice as a kind of tacit agreement between people not to harm each other (358e–395a). We would all gladly be cruel to one another, to take what we can and make others suffer what they must. But we agree not to, because a situation in which everyone is trying to harm everyone winds up being bad for most people most of the time.

This is reminiscent of later accounts of morality or political institutions which we call "contract theories." The most famous such theory is found in the work of the English philosopher Thomas Hobbes.[3] You know, of "nasty, brutish, and short" fame. But unlike Hobbes, Glaucon backs up his contract theory with a mythical story in which a farmer discovers a ring that turns him invisible. Using the ring, the farmer manages to kill the local king, seduce his wife, and become a tyrant (359d–360b). And let's face it, says Glaucon: we would all do the same if we were given a ring of invisibility. I note that hobbits would seem to be an exception to this rule. But hobbits aside, the example of the ring is supposed to show that people don't really value justice, because if they could get away with it their actions would prove that they think injustice is more advantageous.

This, then, is the task set for Socrates in the *Republic*: to show that justice is more choiceworthy than injustice, precisely because it is more *advantageous*. For Socrates, the hard-nosed *Realpolitik* which sacrifices justice for the sake of expediency, as the Athenians did at Melos, betrays a crass misunderstanding of our real interests. This will be true at the level of the city, as well as the level of the individual person. Socrates introduces this parallel between soul and city by suggesting that, if we wanted to read some words that were written in small letters, we would be happy to have the opportunity to look at the same words written elsewhere in much larger letters. In the same way, he suggests, we can learn about justice in the soul of an individual by studying justice in the city (368d–369a). Here you might complain that Socrates is simply *assuming* that there is a parallel between city and soul. Shouldn't he be *arguing* for this, if it's going to be so important? Well, we do in fact talk about justice at both the level of societies and of individuals. Unless we're using the word "justice" in two completely unrelated ways, Socrates must be right that political justice and individual justice have something in common. Besides, the proof is in the pudding—if Socrates can discover parallel features and structures in both the soul and the city, then his strategy will show itself to be a good one.

So let's look at justice at the political level. We can start with the very word "political." It relates to the ancient Greek word *polis*, which means "city" or "city-state." As you may know, or already have noticed from my allusions to classical Greek history, the political units of the ancient world were cities like Athens and Sparta, not countries like Greece or Italy. But these units could extend further than a literal city. Athens, for instance, dominated the area called Attica, and its democratic constitution allowed for the sharing of political power among the citizens of this area. Often the various cities banded together in alliances, like those which clashed in the Peloponnesian War or cooperated to repulse the invasions of the Persians. They also came together to celebrate the Olympic games, to sponsor and worship at religious centers like Delphi. Such cooperative, or competitive, activities certainly had a political aspect. Still, when both Plato and Aristotle talk about political constitutions they normally have in mind the workings of a *polis*, a single city, and not an alliance of multiple cities (to say nothing of institutions like the modern nation-state). They do, of course, talk also of "the Greeks," but this has to do with cultural affinity—for instance, common language and religious practices—and not an overarching political unity.

Now, if you wanted to figure out the most just possible way of running a city, how would you do it? An obvious strategy would be by choosing an existing city which seems to do well and modeling your theory on that city; or by learning from the mistakes of cities that do badly. But this is not how Plato does it. In this way he is very unlike Thucydides. As a historian, Thucydides does convey ideas about how cities should be run, how wars should be prosecuted. But he does this by artfully framing actual history, for instance, by showing us the consequences of the swaggering imperialism of Athens. Aristotle, as we'll see later in this book, characteristically takes a middle road: he presents general observations about political structures, yet frequently refers to the ways actual Greek cities are run. In the *Republic*, by contrast, Plato has Socrates start with a blank slate, designing an ideal city from scratch. The lessons for real cities like Athens remain implicit. For instance, when democracy is criticized in Book Eight of the *Republic*, we aren't invited to consider any actual events in Athens or other democratic cities.

Socrates' first attempt to describe an ideal city is strikingly modest. The best city would be fairly small, a cooperative, one might almost say communitarian group of farmers, craftsmen, and traders (369b–372c). They eat a restricted, vegetarian diet, wear simple clothing, and live in peace. Glaucon immediately objects that this sounds more like a city of pigs than a city of men—apparently, he wouldn't have enjoyed living in a 1960s hippie commune (372c). Glaucon's objection here changes everything. Socrates says that if the city is to afford luxuries, it will need to expand, to develop a powerful military for taking and protecting more land than it strictly needs (373d–e). This is the origin of the infamous class system of Plato's *Republic*, since it sets up a division of the city into two types of people, the guardian soldiers and the laborers. The guardians will rule over the craftsmen, and their rule will, as we'll see shortly, be absolute and unquestioned. This aspect of the *Republic* has come in for its share of criticism. Famously, the twentieth-century philosopher Karl Popper accused Plato of being an enemy of what he called "the open society," and saw the *Republic* as a founding text of totalitarianism.[4] Now, I don't want to be an apologist for Plato. Actually, I take that back: I do want to be an apologist for Plato. Part of my defense would be that the introduction of a ruling class is explicitly marked by Socrates as being a departure from the true ideal, which is his more simple, agrarian community. The city which includes luxuries is, as he says, fevered rather than truly healthy.

As the next several books of the *Republic* unfold, we are given much more detail about this feverish version of the ideal city. The guardian class takes center-stage. We get a lengthy discussion of the education that will turn the guardians into a patriotic and disciplined fighting machine (376e–412b). In the course of their education, it becomes necessary to separate out this higher class into two sub-classes. There will be the "true guardians," who actually rule the city, because of their natural gift for self-control. And there will be the helpers or "auxiliaries," who will serve as a fearsome army for defending the city (414b). So in the end the city Socrates is describing winds up with three classes, not two: there are the true guardians, who do the ruling; then the auxiliaries, who do the fighting; then the craftsmen, who do everything else. It's paramount that the right citizens are placed into the right classes. To make this possible, sexual relations between the citizens are highly regulated. People are assigned by a rigged lottery to mate with carefully selected partners (460a). The guardians have no private property but share all things in common, even children, who are taken away from their mothers at birth and raised by the whole community of guardians, so that they form one big, happy family (457c–464b).

These are surprising, not to say wacky, proposals. It's hard to imagine them as a real set of policies that could have been instituted in ancient Greece. Plato's audience would have been particularly shocked by the proposal that there should be women in the guardian class. Women were treated as far less than equal to men in Greece as a whole, and got a particularly bad deal in Athens. But Plato has Socrates argue explicitly that even if women are not actually equal to men, they should be capable of performing all the same roles in society (455d–456a). Of course, for us this is at least to some extent admirable and forward-thinking. (To how great an extent we'll discuss later in this book.) But Socrates' proposals for the sexual politics of the ideal city have some disturbing resonances for us too. These days eugenics doesn't exactly have a good name. Socrates is adamant, though, that without such firm control over the class system and the reproductive arrangements that sustain it the city is bound to degenerate. He invents a mythic story which will be fed to the citizens of the city—the so-called "noble lie." According to this noble lie, the citizens of the city all have an admixture of metal in their blood. The true guardians have gold in them, the auxiliaries silver, and the craftsmen bronze and iron (415a). This will persuade them to see the importance of staying within their own class, or "doing their own," as Socrates puts it (433a–b). The justice of this perfect city consists, in fact, in the various classes' doing what they are meant to do, with the guardians ruling, the auxiliaries fighting, and the craftsmen obeying. Here, admittedly, you can see why Popper and others might have caught a whiff of totalitarianism in the *Republic*. Interestingly, Socrates himself sees the ideal city as unsustainable, since he supposes that the eugenic lottery will inevitably fall short of perfection, and the classes will be mixed up after all (546a–547a).

That, then, is a sketch of Socrates' just city. But what about the just soul? Can we really, as Socrates suggested, understand justice in the city as a larger image of justice in the soul? Socrates argues in the fourth book of the *Republic* that we can. He points out that, like the city, the soul must have more than one aspect. For the soul can be in harmony or tension with itself.[5] Consider, for instance, your desire to drink a beer. Your desire for the beer might be very strong, but you might exercise self-control and refrain from the beer, for instance, if you are going to drive later or need to study for an exam. This shows that the soul is not simple, but has several aspects which can struggle against one another. Socrates argues that, like the city, the soul has three aspects: reason, spirit, and appetite (437b–441c). Reason is the highest aspect, which is directed towards truth. Spirit is directed towards honor, and with this aspect of our soul we are able to feel such emotions as anger and courage. Appetite, finally, is the set of drives we possess for such things as food, drink, and sex. Justice in the soul, then, is very like justice in the city. It is for the three parts of the soul to do what they should, for the ruling part—reason in the soul and the guardians in the city—to rule, with the assistance of the spirit or auxiliaries, over the lowest part, namely appetite or the craftsmen.

Finally, if this is how justice is established in the city and the soul, what about injustice? What happens when a city or a soul degenerates and becomes worse? Plato extends the analogy between soul and city when he comes to consider the degenerate cases. He has Socrates tell us two stories in parallel: in one story we get a sequence of individual men, worse sons born to better fathers (546a–e); in another story worse political arrangements arise from better ones (547a–c). For instance, the best arrangement after the ideal city is a so-called timocracy, in which the city is dedicated to honor and victory (548c). This is basically the ideal city shorn of its true rulers, and guided solely by soldiers who long to distinguish themselves on the battlefield (547d–549a). From this arises an oligarchy, a city of the rich (550c–551c); then democracy, the city ruled by the common people (555b–557a). By the way, all these English words come from ancient Greek: "timocracy" comes from the Greek word for "honor," while "oligarchy" means rule by "the few," and "democracy" means rule by "the people." Finally, Socrates tells us that the natural next step from democracy is tyranny, which is rule by a single, vicious man (565a–566d). On the soul side there are individual personality types, as we might call them, which correspond to these cities. There is the timocratic man who wants nothing but honor, the oligarchic man who wants wealth, the democratic man who wants freedom. Worst of all is the tyrannical man, whose lust for power ironically winds up enslaving him to his own desires (579b). Just as it's natural for, say, an oligarchic city to degenerate into a democratic one, so it's natural for a father with an oligarchic character to have a son who goes bad and develops a democratic character.

We may find it shocking that Plato sees democracy as the second-worst form of government. For him only tyranny, rule by the worst of all possible rulers, is worse than democracy. There's little doubt that Plato is here registering his dissatisfaction with the performance of democratic Athens. They did, after all, execute Socrates. On the other hand, his critique of democracy is rather nuanced. When the people, the *demos*, are in charge there is total freedom for all. So all desires can be satisfied, every lifestyle is approved. It's a wide-open society, and its chaotic ethical pluralism is far removed from the adamantine laws of Socrates' ideal city. These are in fact some of the things we appreciate in democracy, and Plato agrees that democracy is attractive, despite being defective. He has Socrates say that this is the most beautiful constitution, like a many-colored garment in its variety (557c).

Also disturbing is his suggestion that tyrannies naturally arise from democracies. Here Plato may again have been thinking of the experience of Athens, and the seizure of the city by the Thirty Tyrants in the wake of the Peloponnesian War. His reflections on the relation between democracy and tyranny stand as a warning to all of us who live in democracies today, even if we don't agree that democracy is already about as bad as it gets. Suppose, though, that we did agree that there is a better way to go than democracy. Suppose we liked the sound of Plato's ideal city, and wanted to create one. What would be our first step? What kind of people would we need to select for our true guardians? Without giving anything away, let's just say that those of us who do philosophy for a living are going to like Plato's answer.

AIN'T NO SUNSHINE
THE CAVE ALLEGORY OF
PLATO'S *REPUBLIC*

Midway through the *Republic* Socrates has finished describing the city of perfect justice. In this city there would be three classes of citizens: the true guardians, the auxiliary soldiers, and the craftsmen. The guardians would rule, just as reason rules in the best soul. The other parties to the discussion, Glaucon and Adiemantus, have accepted not only this but some revolutionary proposals, such as the communal sharing of property and children amongst the guardians, and the acceptance that women too can be guardians. Now Socrates promises a final, yet more astonishing claim. He wants to show how the ideal city could, at least in principle, actually come into existence. It could only happen, says Socrates, if the rulers of the city were philosophers (473c–d).

It's fitting that this, the most notorious idea in the *Republic*, is illustrated with some of the most famous passages in the Platonic dialogues. These include what must be the most popular image in all of ancient philosophy: the allegory of the cave. Also found in this stretch of the *Republic* are two more well-known images, the divided line and the comparison between the sun and the Form of the Good. Clearly this part of the *Republic* would feature heavily in any compilation of Plato's greatest hits. And it's no surprise that he's reaching for his best material here, since the view Socrates is presenting is both crucial and, let's face it, hard to swallow. Socrates himself draws attention to this, saying that he expects to be drowned by a wave of objections or plain old ridicule when he says that philosophers should rule (473c). After all, philosophers—then as now—were hardly seen as potential politicians. Admittedly, we've seen that philosophers did occasionally come into contact with political power, for instance Anaxagoras associating with Pericles, or Plato himself going to Syracuse. But more typically philosophers were seen as amusing, detached intellectuals, as they are today. Just think of Thales falling down the well, or Aristophanes' portrayal of Socrates in the *Clouds*.

Thus, when Socrates produces the cave allegory and these other famous images, he is trying to explain why the philosopher should rule the city. But he's also trying to explain why, in our own far-from-ideal societies, the proposal seems absurd. To understand his argument, we should remember that Socrates is thinking of a *successful* philosopher. This will be a man or woman who has achieved knowledge—not someone who, like Socrates himself, knows only that he knows nothing. Indeed, Socrates tells us who the philosopher is by telling us what knowledge is, and how it compares to belief and ignorance. Knowledge and belief, he says, are both powers, and powers are distinguished by their objects (477d). For instance, sight is the power that concerns visible things, whereas hearing is the power that concerns audible things. So if knowledge and belief are powers, what are their objects? According to Socrates, knowledge is the power that concerns what is, whereas belief is the power that concerns both what is and what is not. Ignorance, meanwhile, only concerns itself with what is not (478a–d).

What is all of that supposed to mean? Knowledge concerns what is, and belief what is and is not? It's apt to remind us of the beginning of Parmenides' poem. And like the poem, this bit of the *Republic* has provoked puzzlement and comment in equal measure. The most common way of understanding the passage, and one which became popular among Platonists in later antiquity, is that the objects of knowledge are a completely different level or realm of reality, the Forms.[1] The Forms are separate from physical things in the world around us. These physical items are in turn the things that "are and are not," the objects of belief. But why should I admit that a physical thing, like a giraffe, both is and is not? In fact, what would that even mean? It's not easy to say, though the later ancient Platonists had a few suggestions. For instance, they connected this idea to the Heraclitean flux theory. Since physical objects are constantly changing, always going from being one thing to being something else, they both are and are not. If you don't like that, you might prefer a more recent interpretation: Socrates means to say that knowledge only "is" in the sense that it is always *true*, whereas belief can be either true or false, and thus concerns both what is and what is not. And ignorance, of course, concerns only "what is not" because it is always false.

However we should understand Socrates here, it's clear that the philosophers are a very unusual group. Whereas many people love beautiful "sights and sounds," only the philosophers concern themselves with, and love, beauty itself (480a). But does this really sound like a qualification for the job of political ruler? If anything, it seems like the philosopher would have nothing to say about the messy world of politics, with its conflicts and compromises—the philosopher's head will be squarely in the clouds, as Aristophanes said. For Socrates, though, nothing could be further from the truth. After all, the whole point of the *Republic* is to establish a city governed by perfect justice. So the ruler will have to be the person who grasps the nature of justice. In the first of the series of famous images which now come thick and fast, Socrates describes the situation of a typical Greek city as being like the situation on board a ship (488a). There is a rather stupid shipowner, who represents the people of the city. A crowd of sailors, representing typical politicians, tries to persuade the shipowner to let them steer the ship, using persuasion, drugs, and wine, or whatever else comes to hand (488c). But the one person on the ship who actually understands navigation— who can steer by the stars, understand the weather, and so on—is disdained by everyone else on board as useless (488d–489a). This is the man who should by rights be the captain, just as the philosopher should by rights be the ruler in the city.

So what exactly does the philosopher know, which qualifies him or her for political rule, the way the art of navigation qualifies the true captain to steer the ship? Well, clearly justice itself, and apparently beauty itself too. In short, the philosopher knows about the Forms, as we know and love them from an earlier Platonic dialogue, the *Phaedo*. But now Plato has Socrates say something he didn't say in the *Phaedo*. Yes, there are Forms of Justice, Beauty, and so on, but there is something even more important: the Form of the Good. Knowledge of the Good will be a kind of capstone to the philosopher's wisdom, because without knowing the nature of goodness the philosopher will not understand what is good about all the other Forms (505a–b). And here comes another famous image: Socrates compares the Form of the Good to the sun (508a–509b). Just as the sun makes the visible objects around us visible to sight, so the Form of the Good renders the other Forms intelligible to the soul. Indeed, just as the sun gives growth and nourishment to the things in nature, so the Form of the Good gives being itself to the things known by the soul. In a phrase which will reverberate in centuries to come, the Form of the Good is "beyond being in dignity and power," a kind of super-Form which gives other Forms their goodness and intelligibility (509b).

One of the nice things about the dialogue form is that Plato can have his characters complain that they have no idea what Socrates is talking about, thus voicing the puzzlement the reader is feeling. In this case, it's Glaucon who presses Socrates to explain this image of the sun more fully (509c). Socrates is happy to do so, and in his explanation he provides the two final images in this middle part of the *Republic*: the divided line and the allegory of the cave. The image of the line is supposed to help us understand this idea that the sun, and the Form of the Good, are first causes or principles. The sun, as I said, both makes things visible and helps make the things exist in the first place. In the same way, the Good is a kind of first principle for Forms. The Form of Justice could not be what it is without being good, and neither could the Form of Beauty. So grasping the Good will be a kind of key that unlocks for us the understanding of all the Forms. It seems to stand as the highest principle in a kind of hierarchy, presiding over the Forms. The physical things around us in the visible world partake of these Forms, and thus can be thought of as images of the Forms. Then, at the very bottom of the scale of reality, there are images of these images—for instance, shadows or reflections of physical things.

To illustrate, Socrates asks us to imagine a line cut into two unequal parts, with each part subdivided in the same ratio into two unequal segments (509d). So we have a line with four segments:

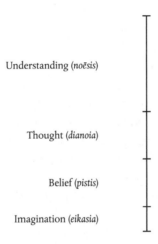

The lowest segment represents those mere images of physical objects, the shadows and reflections (510a). The next represents the physical objects themselves—the things that non-philosophers take to be really real, like giraffes, rocks, and the Eiffel Tower. These two segments together symbolize the whole visible realm. The second, longer part of the line represents what we can know rather than what we can see (510b). It likewise is divided into two segments. Here we are expecting Socrates to say the two higher segments are supposed to stand for the Forms and then, at the very top, the Form of the Good. This isn't quite what he says, though. Instead, he says that the first segment represents the use of hypotheses. Hypothesis could be confirmed only on the basis of some other, more fundamental principle. Then the final, longest segment of the line represents the grasp of those fundamental principles, the truths on which all other truths are founded (510b). Socrates gives the example of geometry, but we might be more comfortable with something like a logical or arithmetical system: you have your fundamental axioms, and from these follows the truth of the whole system. But that way of putting it is somewhat misleading, because for Socrates the basic principle will not be something we simply postulate, like an axiom in mathematics. It will be something certainly and unshakably true. This, then, is the role played by the Form of the Good. An object of completely certain knowledge in its own right, it grounds all our knowledge and makes that knowledge come out true.

And that, finally, brings us to the cave. Unlike the rather abstract image of the line, the allegory of the cave is extremely concrete. We are to imagine a group of prisoners chained at the bottom of a cave. Behind and above them is a low wall, and beyond that a fire (514a–b). There are more people just behind the wall, carrying statues. Thanks to the firelight, these statues cast shadows on the wall in front of the prisoners (514b). The unfortunate prisoners can see nothing but these shadows, and hear nothing but the echoing noises made by the people walking along carrying the statues. They are radically removed from reality, because they see nothing but shadows of things that aren't even real, namely the statues. They engage in pointless games which, in their ignorance, they take to be deathly serious—but all they are in fact doing is competing to predict and identify shadows. Of course, the disturbing message is that we are like the chained prisoners, and that the apparently crucial political debates and public affairs of our societies are like the meaningless shadow-games played by the prisoners.

Now Socrates asks us to imagine what would happen if a prisoner were set free (515c). Wrenched away from their familiar reality of shadows, they would only go kicking and screaming if someone dragged them out into the sunlight. But once they were pulled from the cave, after recovering from their dazzlement, they would finally see reality for what it is (516a). As you've already guessed, this freed prisoner represents the philosopher. Just as the philosopher grasps the Forms, using the Form of the Good as a principle, so the freed prisoner sees the real things outside the cave by the light of the sun. This explains why philosophers seem useless and otherworldly in our corrupt societies. The philosopher has no interest in the shadow-games and second-hand images of normal folk. Meanwhile those normal folk have no hope of understanding the true reality the philosopher has witnessed.

The prospects for achieving justice in the real world would seem to be bleak. We prisoners, duped in our world of images, will never welcome the philosopher as a ruler. Indeed, Socrates admits that just about the only way a philosopher could get to rule a city would be by a stroke of good fortune whereby a philosophically-minded person is born to a king and inherits his throne. This isn't very likely, of course. Interestingly though, Socrates is happy if he can just suggest a way that the ideal city could come about in principle. This has important implications for our reading of the *Republic* as a whole—to what extent is it a serious proposal for political reform, and to what extent just a kind of abstract consideration of the nature of justice that could never be put into practice? The passage about the lucky chance of getting a royal philosopher seems to indicate that the answer lies somewhere in the middle. Plato is not exactly setting forth a set of proposals that would be feasible in the here and now, but he wants to ensure that his proposals could be realized at least in some circumstances, however unlikely.

But there's another problem: why would the true philosophers agree to rule? It's clear they would have no interest in descending back into the darkness of the cave. Why plunge again into the cave of shadows, when they could stay out in the sunlight? Socrates tackles this problem squarely, admitting that it is not really in the philosophers' interest to take charge of the city, to go back down into the cave. But they are not selfish, and they must see that the demand of justice is for them to take command of the city if at all possible (520c). The philosophers of the *Republic*, the true guardians, would then consent to take turns becoming philosopher-kings, but only with a heavy heart. Ironically, it is precisely those who would prefer not to rule who must be made to do so.[2] In fact, Socrates points out that the surest way to avoid conflict within a city is to give power to those who are reluctant to wield it (520d). (Is it me, or does Plato have a point here?)

The allegory of the cave is one of the most powerful passages in the Platonic dialogues, and at the political level its meaning is reasonably clear. It tells us that the philosopher should rule, and also explains the apparent cluelessness of philosophers in defective societies. As I've admitted, I myself am a philosopher who tends to appear clueless, so I can only agree wholeheartedly with that last bit. (By the way, I also declare myself extremely reluctant to be given absolute political power, just in case anyone is thinking of offering it to me.) But what about the other philosophical implications of the allegory? Two misconceptions frequently arise here. The first is that the cave allegory commits Plato to some kind of radical separation between our world and the world of Forms. This is a widespread assumption about Plato, that he believes in a kind of separate heaven of Forms, and urges us to ignore the physical world entirely in favor of that other immaterial world. Aristotle, in fact, often criticized Plato for holding that the Forms are radically separate from the things around us.[3]

But if the shadowy cave world is separate from the sunny world outside, it isn't *radically* separate. You can go from one to the other, after all, as the philosopher does. Also, remember that the shadows that the prisoners see are shadows of statues; and the statues are representations of the things outside the cave. That shows that there is some kind of connection between the shadows and the real things outside. The shadows are second-hand images of reality, but they are still images of reality. Perhaps, then, Plato's point is not so much to stress that there are two utterly different realms of objects—physical, pseudo-realities on the one hand, and real Forms on the other. Instead, the point might be to describe two different ways of seeing one and the same reality. We can grasp that reality by means of transitory, ill-considered beliefs, or with solid, certified knowledge. Usually we make do with truths that are mixed generously with falsehoods; but the philosopher's approach demands truth, and nothing but the truth. So the radical contrast or separation Plato is making is not so much between two realms—one heavenly and immaterial, one shadowy and physical—as between knowledge and mere belief.

A second misconception about the cave allegory is that Plato is endorsing some kind of mysticism. On this interpretation, the philosopher would grasp truth and reality in a kind of flash of insight upon leaving the cave. The result will be an understanding so deep, so otherworldly, that the philosopher cannot explain it to the benighted prisoners down in the cave—it is a knowledge which cannot be put into words. Now admittedly, the idea of turning the eye of the soul from ignorance towards some kind of luminous knowledge does appear in the later Platonic tradition, which we'll be looking at in the next volume of this series. But when Plato himself talks about turning away from the shadows, he describes an arduous process of education, not a divine flash of revelation. First the freed prisoner must climb the steep path out of the cave. And even when he escapes, it is not so much the sun that he sees as the things in the world illuminated by the light of the sun. Seeing can be an active, analytical process—more like examining or looking than a flash of insight.[4]

There are good reasons to think that this is what happens when the philosopher escapes from the cave. Think back to the divided line. As we saw, this image tells us that knowledge has a specific kind of structure, according to which first principles guarantee the truth of the rest of the things we know. This is what Plato calls "dialectic." Dialectic means the process of making hypotheses and then discovering the principles that would support those hypotheses, as they do in geometry. This doesn't sound particularly mystical. Plato presents knowledge as a complex analytical process. It also seems that the fruits of such a process could be put into words. When the philosopher goes back into the cave, he's not able to convert the prisoners to the truth just by talking to them. But this isn't because the philosopher's knowledge is inexpressible or mystical. It's simply because the prisoners would never be able to understand or be convinced by the philosopher's account, until they themselves engage in dialectic.

Some listeners might be suspicious of the points I've been making in this chapter. They may feel that I'm making Plato less, well, Platonist. Surely the whole point of Platonism is that it is an otherworldly philosophy, that there is a separate realm of Forms which can be grasped only by direct intuition? Well, Karl Marx famously said that he wasn't a Marxist. And if this is what Platonism is, then for my money Plato was no Platonist. If you're not convinced yet, the next chapter may do the trick. Because now we're going to turn to a dialogue in which Plato boldly uses Father Parmenides as a spokesman, in order to present a series of devastating objections to the theory of Forms. As it turns out, what Parmenides will call "the greatest difficulty" for the theory highlights the dangers of making the Forms radically separate from our world. So, at least by the time he wrote the *Parmenides*, Plato saw that there were potentially devastating objections to this kind of Platonism, with its totally separate world of Forms. In this dialogue Plato will reveal himself as the first great critic of Platonism.

23

SECOND THOUGHTS
PLATO'S *PARMENIDES* AND
THE FORMS

In the chapter on Plato's life and works we saw that one of the more contentious issues regarding the Platonic dialogues is their chronology. Most scholars accept a broad division of the dialogues into three periods: early, middle, and late, with the so-called Socratic dialogues falling into the early period, the great masterpiece that is the *Republic* dominating the middle period, and more technical works emerging in the late period. This last group includes the one I am going to be talking about in this chapter, the *Parmenides*. But scholars disagree about the exact order of the dialogues, and about more fundamental issues: how much did Plato's philosophical views change during his career? If his views did change, then in what direction and on what topics?

It's no easy matter to answer these questions. Some think that Plato pretty much never changed his mind or developed new ideas, but was rather setting out a systematic body of ideas and doctrines throughout his career, revealing them bit by bit or examining them from different angles in different dialogues. This is how Plato's corpus was seen by ancient Platonists.[1] But I find this implausible, and would be rather disappointed if it were true. I don't claim to know how geniuses like Plato think, but I'm guessing that they reconsider and develop their ideas quite a lot. In any case, the dialogues themselves provide ample evidence that Plato did reconsider his ideas with a critical eye. This was no simple process, where he set out a doctrine in one dialogue but then rejected it in a later dialogue. Rather, he refined his ideas and subjected himself to the kind of searching criticism Socrates would mete out to his fellow Athenians in the marketplace.

There's no better example than the beginning of Plato's *Parmenides*. In this dialogue we see an aged Parmenides (yes, that Parmenides) at the height of his powers, visiting Athens in the company of Zeno (yes, that Zeno). When the dialogue's action begins, Zeno has just finished reading from his book containing the famous paradoxes (127d). The audience includes a youthful Socrates. This juxtaposition of an aged Parmenides, a younger Zeno, and a much younger Socrates helps us establish the relative chronology of the three philosophers, even if we shouldn't take too seriously the idea that the three of them actually met in Athens. Socrates talks to Zeno about the purpose of his paradoxical arguments, which is of course to defend Parmenides' claim that all things are in fact one, by showing that if things in the world are many then they are riven by contradiction. For instance, they would be both similar to each other and dissimilar to each other (127e–128a).

Socrates says that this isn't particularly surprising—of course the things around us are similar in some respects and dissimilar in others. What would be really surprising would be if Similarity itself were dissimilar, or if Dissimilarity itself were similar (129b). Socrates dismisses the idea that things are one and not many, as Parmenides and Zeno want us to believe. Instead, we should admit that they are both one and many. But we should also hold on to the idea that there are Oneness itself and Manyness itself. As we saw in Plato's *Phaedo*, these separate, absolute Forms would exclude their opposites, so that Oneness itself can never be many, nor can Manyness itself ever be one. Forms are, in other words, immune to the compresence of opposites. But a particular object like a man can partake of opposites at the same time. He is, for instance, both one and many: one man with many body parts (129c–d).

Far from being offended at this demolition of his theory, Parmenides is impressed by the young Socrates and presses him to say more about these absolute entities, like Oneness itself and Similarity itself (130b). Socrates elaborates, and in so doing produces one of the very few clear explanations of the theory of Forms in Plato's dialogues. He posits Forms because they are immune from the compresence of opposites, like I just said, but also because the one Form can explain why many things share in some character. For example, giraffes, elephants, and skyscrapers will all be large by sharing in a Form, namely Largeness itself. The Forms are separate from the things that partake of them. Yet they somehow explain the presence of shared characters in the things that participate in them. The Form of Largeness explains or causes the giraffe's being large, the elephant's being large, and so on.

Even if this is an unusually clear account of the Forms, it's basically the theory as we know it from works like the *Phaedo* and the *Republic*. In fact Socrates even mentions the example of sticks and stones, which ensures that we think of the *Phaedo* (129d). Since we tend to think of the theory of Forms as Plato's signature doctrine, what happens next is a bit of a surprise. Emphasizing throughout that the aged Parmenides is a more seasoned philosopher than Socrates, Plato allows the older thinker to pose a series of problems for the theory of Forms. Still young and inexperienced, Socrates is unable to solve these problems. Not only is the theory of Forms coming in for some rough treatment, but we're seeing Parmenides do to Socrates exactly what Socrates usually does to other people—refuting him by asking him questions. At the end of this chapter I'll come back to the question of why Plato might do this. But first let's look at the problems, which are set out in just a few pages of text.

Parmenides' first series of questions is a kind of warm-up to the main event. He wants Socrates to tell him which things have Forms (130b). Socrates is eager to posit Forms like Similarity itself and Oneness itself, and also Forms for Justice, Beauty, and Goodness. But what about, say, man, or fire? Socrates isn't too sure about this (130c). So it looks like the jury is still out on the Form of Giraffe, which will disappoint those of you who are reading this book mostly to find out about the metaphysics of giraffes. Meanwhile, Socrates is downright reluctant to admit Forms for things like hair and dirt, maybe because they are too degraded to have Forms, or because they are mere parts or by-products of other things (130d). Here Parmenides has touched on a fundamental question about the Forms, if not exactly a challenge to the theory as a whole. If there are Forms, then how could we possibly determine the range of Forms? An obvious question that arises here, though it is not mentioned in the *Parmenides*, is whether man-made things have Forms. Is there a Form for chairs, cars, or space shuttles? Well, maybe not for space shuttles, but in the dialogue *Cratylus*, which we'll look at soon, Socrates seems to talk about a Form for the kind of shuttle that is used in weaving (389b). And the *Republic* speaks about a Form of Bed (597a–d). So Plato was certainly open to the idea that there could be Forms for man-made things. Here, though, Socrates is treating even natural things like man and fire as doubtful cases. Presumably man-made artefacts would be still more doubtful.

But as I say, this is just a prelude to more trenchant criticisms. Parmenides chastises Socrates for being particularly worried about cases like hair and dirt, suggesting that this is just a sign of youthful embarrassment (130e). Then he throws down his first fundamental challenge to the theory as a whole. Socrates has talked about things "sharing in" or "partaking of" the Forms. But how should we understand this? Would each large thing have a piece of the Large itself, so that the Large itself is split up into many pieces (131b)? This would give us a bunch of Larges which (in violation of the rule that Forms are not beset by compresence of opposites) would be small compared to the Large itself. Or would the Large itself be in each large thing, and thus be separated from itself—because the Large that is the giraffe is not in the same place as the Large that is in the skyscraper? Socrates makes a nifty suggestion, which is that the Form could be present in its participants the way that the same day is present in many places at the same time (131b). Parmenides changes the example: would it be like a sail spread out over many people? In that case only one part of the sail would be over each person, so we're back to the same problem (131c). Here the reader may be intended to think about how Socrates could have answered more effectively. Parmenides seems to have cheated by using the analogy of a sail rather than a day, and Socrates might have insisted that Forms are more like the day than the sail. A day is not a material object like a sail, so it can indeed be wholly in different locations at the same time. If Forms too are immaterial, perhaps they can pull off the same trick. But Socrates doesn't think of this, or any other response to Parmenides' line of argument.

His puzzlement is only beginning. Parmenides next raises an objection which Aristotle refers to as the "third man" argument.[2] Here in Plato, the example is not the Form of Man, but the Form of Largeness again. Here's how it goes. Socrates has said we should posit a Form every time we see many things which share the same character (132a). For instance, we posit the Form of Largeness to explain the largeness of all the large things. But hang on a minute: isn't the Form of Largeness itself large? If so, there's another, slightly more extensive group of large things, namely the large things that partake of the Form plus the Form of Largeness itself. So we should posit another, second Form of Largeness, to explain the fact that all *these* things—the large items plus the first Form of Largeness—are large (132a–b). And we can keep going, because there's yet another distinct set of large things, consisting of the large items, the first Form of Largeness, and the second Form of Largeness. This means we'll need yet another Form of Largeness. And so on: we will need an infinite number of Forms for Largeness, not just one, and the same argument will go for any Form we choose.

This is the most famous criticism Plato poses of his own theory here in the *Parmenides*, but it's not immediately clear why it is so damaging. What if Socrates just said: "Okay, fine with me: there are an infinite number of Forms of Largeness"? It's not like we will run out of places to put them, given that, large or not, they are immaterial (which was perhaps the lesson we were meant to learn from the sail analogy). The problem, I think, is that Socrates has placed so much emphasis on the idea that each Form is *one* thing that explains *many* things. The whole point was to posit one thing which explains a shared, common character—the one Largeness which is set over all the large things. If there turned out to be indefinitely many Forms of Largeness, then that would be the exact opposite of what Socrates set out to accomplish. Far from being one, the Forms of Largeness would be at least as many, if not more, than their participants.

So Socrates needs to answer the criticism. How could he do so? Well, it looks like the damage is done because Socrates admits that the Form of Largeness is itself large. If he just denied this, then he'd be fine. He doesn't need a second Form of Largeness to explain why both the large things and the first Form are large, if the first Form of Largeness isn't large after all. But it is awkward for him to deny that the Form of Largeness is large. He's made a really big deal about the fact that the Form of

Largeness is not small, whereas its participants are both large and small. It would be rather surprising to find out that, by the way, the Form of Largeness is not large either. Worse, he is inclined to think that the things that partake of a Form somehow resemble or imitate that Form. If the Form of Largeness isn't large, then in what sense do other large things resemble it? On the other hand, even without Parmenides' criticism we might have good reasons for rejecting the idea that the Form of Largeness is large. If Forms are indeed immaterial, then how could a Form be large?

Socrates does not explore this avenue of response, at least not explicitly. Instead he seems to change track, proposing a surprising interpretation of his own theory: what if Forms were not separately existing items in their own right, but just "thoughts" (132b)? He doesn't explain how, exactly, this would solve the regress problem Parmenides has posed. But maybe it's a way for him to do what I just suggested: to deny that the Form of Largeness is large. The Form would just be a thought in my mind, and obviously a thought can't be large, so no infinite series would be generated. Unfortunately for Socrates, Parmenides makes short work of the suggestion by pointing out that a thought has to be a thought about something (132b–c). It will be a thought about the single character that is shared by all the things that are, say, large. Clearly that single character, not our thought about it, will be the Form, Largeness itself, and this must be outside our minds. Socrates agrees, and quickly gives up his proposal. He really wants to say that Forms are, as he puts it, "paradigms that exist in nature, while other things resemble them and are likenesses of them." Oh dear: we're back to the same conception of Forms which triggered the "third man" argument, where we say that they are independent of our minds, separate from the things that partake of them, and somehow similar to the things that partake of them.

So Socrates has it coming to him when Parmenides produces another argument to show that we'll wind up with an infinite regress of Forms. This second version has an important twist. Parmenides focuses on Socrates' claim that the Form will be similar to the things that partake of it. For instance, large things are like the Form of Largeness. Doesn't this mean that we need to invoke a second Form—the Form of Similarity—to explain the fact that the large things are similar to the Form of Largeness (132e)? Well, that seems harmless enough. But now a new regress is looming: we're admitting that each Form has its own character. For instance, the Form of Largeness is large, and the Form of Similarity is similar. But if the large things and the Form of Largeness are all similar to one another, and if the Form of Similarity is also similar, then all these items—the large things, the Form of Largeness, and the Form of Similarity—share in being similar. Of course we will need a second Form of Similarity to explain this. And so on: this time we get an infinite series of Forms, but the Forms are Forms of Similarity rather than Largeness. This clever argument is aimed at the core difficulty of Socrates' theory: he has failed to explain in any detail how the Form is related to the things that partake of it.

But if that's the frying-pan, here comes the fire: Parmenides next poses what he describes as "the greatest difficulty" for the theory of Forms. In this final objection he points out that if the Forms are separate, then although they might relate to one another, they won't relate to us or the things around us (133b–d). Parmenides' example is that a human master is the master of a human slave, not of the Form of Slavery (133e). Meanwhile the Form of Mastery itself is not master of some particular slave; if it has mastery over anything, it must be another Form, the Form of Slavery. So we have two completely disconnected realms: the Forms and the things that were supposed to participate in them. The consequences are disastrous, as Parmenides points out. Socrates wanted the Forms to be objects of our knowledge, but knowledge is a connection or a relation, just like mastery or slavery. So if nothing in our world, including us, can relate to the world of the Forms, we can't know the Forms (134b).

This ends the battery of objections against the theory of Forms. Socrates is unable to fend them off, which might make us think that Plato sees the objections as decisive, and is giving up on his theory of Forms. Yet Parmenides immediately tells Socrates that the objections *must* be overcome (135a–135c). We need somehow to explain how things can share features like largeness. If we don't, it will be impossible even to carry on talking to one another, presumably because we won't be able to say things like "the giraffe and the elephant are both large." On our next trip to the zoo we will be reduced to awkward silence. Now of course, the fact that Plato thinks the objections must be answerable doesn't mean he has already figured out the answers. A famous scholar of Plato's dialogues, Gregory Vlastos, called this part of the *Parmenides* a "record of honest perplexity."[3]

But there are, I think, signs that Plato is optimistic that the objections can be defeated, and perhaps even that sufficiently careful readers can manage this by themselves. Parmenides suggests several times that a more experienced defender of the theory than the youthful Socrates could, with difficulty, answer the objections. And there are a few fairly obvious mis-steps by Socrates, for instance, the one we noted with the sail and the day. Notice also how the series of objections seems to be carefully structured: Parmenides starts by asking what sorts of Forms exist, and then moves on to progressively more crucial issues. The first and second objections focus on how a Form can be one, the third on its real, separate existence outside our minds, the fourth and fifth on the question of how the Forms relate to their participants. So the objections form an implicit road-map, laying out the requirements for a successful theory of Forms: each Form must be one and immaterial, it must be independent of our minds, it must be enough unlike its participants that it is separate, but not so unlike them that the Forms become another world unconnected to ours. All of this suggests that Plato is not rejecting the theory of Forms, but inviting the reader to consider how it might be refined.

UNTYING THE NOT
PLATO'S *SOPHIST*

S ome readers believe that Plato undertook the refinement of his theory in the *Parmenides* itself, in the difficult and puzzling second part of the dialogue.[1] They might be right, but for our purposes I think it will be better to turn to a different dialogue entirely: the *Sophist*. Not that this dialogue is anything other than difficult and puzzling. How could it be, when it deals with that most difficult and puzzling of characters, the sophist? Having taken the measure of men like Protagoras and Gorgias in other works, Plato here wants to provide a more general account of what it means to be a sophist. This is the first part of a threefold project envisioned at the start of the dialogue: to explain the sophist, the statesman, and the philosopher (217a). Are they one and the same, or different kinds? If the latter, then what makes each of them what they are? The second part of the project is carried out in a further dialogue, which Americans call the *Statesman* but British people, for some reason, tend to call the *Politicus*. (Probably because they are so polite.)

There is no dialogue called the *Philosopher* to finish a potential trilogy, and for good reason. For one thing, we're going to find out who the philosopher might be, already here in the *Sophist*. For another thing, the *Sophist* and *Statesman* can already be considered the second and third entries in a trilogy that began with the *Theaetetus*. That dialogue ended with Socrates promising to meet Theodorus and Theaetetus again the following day. At the beginning of the *Sophist* we see them fulfilling that promise, and being joined by a new guest. We never learn his name, only that he is a visitor from Elea, the home of Parmenides and Zeno. In fact he's identified as a member of the group of philosophers gathered around Parmenides (216a). In case that hasn't made us sufficiently eager to hear what he has to say, Plato has Socrates speculate about whether this Stranger from Elea might be more than just a visitor. Perhaps he is divine, come to check on Socrates and the others and see whether their philosophical conversations are up to snuff—a "god of refutation" (216b).

But who needs foreign gods of refutation, when Athens has Socrates? Plato, apparently. He pointedly drops Socrates as the main interlocutor for both the *Sophist* and *Statesman*, allowing him to speak only at the beginning of both dialogues.[2] This is the most ostentatious example of something we find in several dialogues by Plato which seem to date from his later career: the replacement of Socrates with other leading characters. We already saw it happening in the *Parmenides*. There, Socrates is depicted as a young beginner, very much in the shadow of the great Eleatic philosopher. He then drops out of the discussion for the second part of the dialogue, in which Parmenides questions a cooperative youth (named Aristotle!). Similarly, here in the *Sophist* the Stranger says he would be happy to present his ideas in the form of a lengthy speech, or by means of question and answer. In the latter case, he'd like to question someone who won't give him much trouble (217d).[3] Theaetetus is chosen for this role, and is invited to do far less in the way of proposing his own ideas than he did in the *Theaetetus* (though he is too clever to be only a yes-man for the Stranger, and does make important suggestions along the way). The Stranger is very unlike the Socrates of earlier dialogues, who claimed to know nothing, who pretended to be unable to speak at length, and who demanded that his companions speak up fearlessly with their own opinions (which is why he prized the opportunity to talk to the shameless Callicles: *Gorgias* 487a–b).

Why is Socrates being ushered out of the limelight in this way? As usual with Plato, we have to speculate.[4] One possibility might be that the theory of Forms, as criticized in the first part of the *Parmenides*, is about to be substantially rethought here in the *Sophist*. Perhaps Plato associated the original version of the theory with Socrates—either the historical one or the fictional one of his other dialogues—and wanted a new speaker for his new ideas about the Forms. This could be right. But I suspect it has more to do with philosophical method. The idea of inquiry through questioning and refutation is, after all, distinctively Socratic. And the Stranger is introduced here in a way that highlights his approach to the conversation. Not only is he called a "god of refutation," but Plato draws attention to his un-Socratic lack of a strong preference for discussion over speech-making, and his attitude that the ideal interlocutor is one who will not get in his way. This is a man with a new method. Unlike the Socratic method, which always led to the impasse of *aporia*, the Stranger's method will produce results. Both the *Sophist* and *Statesman* end with (if you'll pardon the expression) unapologetic declarations that the inquiry has been a success.

What, then, is this new method? It is mentioned more briefly in a dialogue which does feature Socrates as its main character, the *Phaedrus* (265d–266b; more on this dialogue later). There it is called the method of "collection and division." It's going to be used extensively here in the *Sophist*, and again in the *Statesman*. It works like this. First, you need to gather a lot of things together that share a single kind or character—that's the "collection" part. Then you find distinctions that allow you to "divide" this single class into sub-classes. Shall we have an example? Let's try Australian Rules Football. This clearly falls under a general category, class, or kind that also includes such activities as basketball, poker, and chess. We can call this class "games." Having "collected" all the games into a single class, now we can divide. For instance, by saying there are two kinds of game: those that involve physical exertion and those that don't. Australian Rules Football most definitely falls into the first class. Among these exertion-involving games, some involve balls while others do not. Again, we want the first class: ball-games. Of these, some involve an oblong ball, some do not. Within oblong-ball sports, we can make a division on the basis of protective gear: it might be outlawed or allowed. We can further subdivide the first of these two sub-classes on the basis that at least one such game involves a scrum (rugby), while others do not. In fact, as far as I know there is only one that doesn't, namely our quarry. So we have our account of Australian Rules Football: it is a game which involves physical exertion, uses a ball which is oblong, forbids protective gear, and has no scrums.

I can imagine that you have already been formulating objections as I went through that division. Are ball-games really best divided into oblong-ball games and round-ball games? There could be other ways to divide up that sub-class. For instance, some-ball games involve a hand-held instrument (tennis, cricket, lacrosse), others don't (soccer, handball). Or how about this division: some ball-games are played at Wimbledon (lawn tennis), others aren't (the rest). Clearly there are lots of ways to cut at each stage, so how do we know which is the right division? Plato is sensitive to this objection. In the *Phaedrus* he warns us not to divide "like a bad butcher," but to cut along the "natural joints" of whatever class we are considering (265e). He gives an example in the *Statesman*, imagining someone who thinks it makes sense to divide humanity into two groups: the barbarians and the Greeks (262d). In the *Sophist* he underscores the same difficulty by having the characters go through a whole series of alternate divisions, which to all appearances have an equal claim to validity.

The limitations of the collection-and-division method were also noted by Aristotle. As we'll see later, he wrote a treatise called the *Posterior Analytics* which tries to explain what is involved in demonstrating something. Plato's method, complains Aristotle, could never yield demonstration, because at each step we simply divide and choose the left- or right-hand path. We don't give any explanation of why we have gone left or right (*Posterior Analytics* 91b). The accumulated characteristics at the end of the division—game, physically exerting, ball-involving, etc.—are each of them mere assumptions, and nothing is being proven or explained. In this case, though, Aristotle is like an Australian watching the Dallas Cowboys take on the

New England Patriots: rather than entering into the spirit of things, he complains that the wrong game is being played. Plato's method does not need to be taken as a method of *demonstration*, but rather as an inquiry into the interrelation of classes or, we might go so far as to say, of Forms. With this method we are learning how different kinds are "woven together," some falling under others, some including others, some excluding others. This is what Plato means by "dialectic" at this stage of his career. The person who can collect well and then divide along natural joints, always true to the character of the things in question, has a good claim to be the dialectician, and hence the philosopher (*Sophist* 253c–d).

So that's what a philosopher is. But what is a sophist? Well, let's first note the case used by the Stranger to illustrate his method. Inexplicably, he goes not for Australian Rules Football but for the angler—that is, a fisherman who uses line and hook as opposed to a net. To be honest, it's not really inexplicable, because the angler has much in common with the sophist. He is someone with a kind of expertise that helps him to acquire things, by means of hunting (he hunts living things rather than the unliving, in water rather than on land, etc.: see 221b–c for the full division). The sophist is a hunter too. He preys on rich young men by enticing them with flattery, in order to earn money (223a). That is the upshot of the Stranger's first attempt to chase down the sophist: the hunter has become the hunted. Yet, without explaining what if anything might be wrong with this account, the Stranger proceeds to several alternative attempts. One of these is particularly noteworthy. It describes a type of sophist who removes ignorance from the soul by means of refutation. This so-called "noble sophist" (231b) is clearly supposed to remind us of Socrates. It's another indication that this dialogue is asking us to reflect on Socrates and his method. The noble sophist does good, but only by removing ignorance. He cannot lead us to knowledge we do not have, but only help us eliminate false belief. Again, we may here be seeing why Socrates is replaced with the more didactic Stranger as Plato's main speaker.

The multiple classifications of the sophist, which seem to reveal different aspects of his nature, are only to be expected given the shifty and elusive nature of sophistry itself. But that's nothing compared to the problem which comes to occupy the Stranger and Theaetetus once they have proposed identifying the sophist as a producer of appearances (236a–c). On the one hand, this seems a promising way to think about the sophist. He is, after all, someone who can produce persuasion by making the false appear to be true. On the other hand, the sophist can now escape us using one of his favorite tricks. It's one we've seen in the *Theaetetus* and the *Euthydemus*: he will just say that false statements or beliefs are impossible. They would involve saying or believing "that which is not"; but obviously there's no such thing as "that which is not." Plato is keen for us to notice that this challenge has something in common with the philosophy of Parmenides. Not content with giving us a main character from Elea, he twice has the Stranger quote the passage of Parmenides' poem in which we are cautioned to avoid the path of non-being (237a, 258d).

The *Sophist* now sets out to solve this problem once and for all. The pages that follow are among the most difficult in Plato's writings, and have been much debated.[5] But no one said this history-of-philosophy business was going to be easy. So, as Socrates or the Stranger might say, let's not give up hope but press on with the inquiry. We may immediately be discouraged, because the Stranger begins by pointing out just how intractable the problem of non-being is. After making the familiar point that speaking falsely is saying "what is not," which would mean not speaking at all (237e), he adds that non-being is therefore "unsayable" (238c). Then he raises the stakes, pointing out that we can't even say that non-being is unsayable (238e–239a), since this would be to say something about it! Clearly the Stranger has been paying close attention to Parmenides' teachings back in Elea. Now, though, he dares to contemplate patricide, by criticizing the position of his intellectual father (241d), and showing how it is after all possible to speak and think of non-being.

Our best strategy would be first to look at "what is"—at "being"—given that non-being will have to be understood in opposition to it if it is going to be understood at all. What, then, is being? The Stranger refers back to various Pre-Socratic theories here, which claimed, for instance, that all of being is reducible to some small number of things—like hot and cold—or even to just one thing, as Parmenides and his followers proposed (242c–243a). But, with apologies to Thales, these theories just don't hold water. For instance, being can't simply be identified with the hot and the cold: if the hot is being, and the cold is being, then hot and cold will be identical, which is absurd (243e–244a). And—look away now if you're squeamish, because here comes the patricidal part—the Parmenidean view that being is one is also unsustainable. He wants to say things like "being is one." Thus he applies a name ("one") to being. But then we actually have two things, being and its name, rather than the absolute unity promised in the theory (244d). Furthermore, Parmenides understands being as a kind of sphere, as we saw when we looked at his poem. But in that case it would have numerous parts, for instance, the middle and edges of the sphere, in which case it would after all display some kind of plurality (244e). (Of course, this is precisely the reason why some take Parmenides' talk of a "sphere" to be metaphorical.)

It's now looking as though "being" is no easier to understand than non-being—which doesn't exactly seem to constitute progress. But the Stranger isn't done yet.

He considers two other groups with views about being. We would probably call them materialists and Platonists; he compares them to the "giants" and "gods" who battle in Hesiod's *Theogony* (246a) The "giants" are those who believe only in what they can grasp and perceive with their senses. The "gods" believe in invisible beings, and are hence also dubbed the "friends of the Forms" (248a). Again, considerations can be aimed against both groups. The giants, if they were unusually gentle ones, should be willing to admit that the hallmark of being is the capacity to act on other things, or be acted upon by something else (247d–e). In other words, whatever "is" can enter into causal relationships of some kind. Turning this around, we can say that anything that has causal influence, or can be influenced, deserves to be included in the realm of being. But obviously, there are invisible, immaterial things that have causal influence. For instance, the soul. Or, even if you believe that the soul is a material thing, justice and knowledge in the soul, which are not material but clearly do have an influence on things (247a–b). Thus, being does include some immaterial, invisible things.

The friends of the Forms take the opposite view from these materialist giants. They think that *only* the invisible is properly said to be, and that material things are all constantly changing—in a realm of "becoming" rather than "being." I've said that these "gods" seem to be a kind of Platonist, and indeed in other dialogues (like the *Timaeus*) Plato draws a contrast between being and becoming along these lines.[6] But again, Plato is an acute critic of Platonism. Invoking the same idea that whatever "is" can be acted upon or can act on other things, the Stranger points out that if the invisible Forms are ever known by us, then they are acted upon. After all, if I know something I am doing something to it, namely knowing it. Thus the Forms undergo "change," as they are made the subjects of knowledge (248e). This is, obviously, a rather strange and minimal kind of change. We might think it is no more a real "change" than the change that happens when you go around me while I am standing still, so that I "change" from being on your left to being on your right. But since the "gods" wanted to exclude all change of any kind from the Forms, this will still be enough to refute them.[7] Of course, the Forms will be in other respects "at rest" and not changing (249b), because they will always retain their character. Plato is himself retaining an idea expressed in other dialogues: that a suitable object of knowledge would be one that is stable or "unchanging." Thus, paradoxically, the fact that Forms can be known means both that they change *and* that they are unchanging.

This argument marks a crucial step in the Stranger's account, one that will soon put him in a position to explain non-being (which, you'll remember, was supposedly the point of all this). He's just managed to show that there is a kind of interrelation or "weaving together" of three Forms: Being, Change, and Rest. We've just seen that Being changes, and conversely, Change is something that is—it partakes of Being. We can now see that Plato is dealing with issues raised in the first part of the *Parmenides*, especially the so-called "greatest difficulty." That is, he is exploring the question of how Forms enter into relationships (notice that he uses the same example of a Form being known). And he's showing that Forms relate to one another, when, for instance, Being changes or Change has a share of being. But Forms don't enter indiscriminately into every possible combination. Change, for example, is not going to partake of Rest. That would be like the Form of Large being small. So the realm of Forms involves both partaking and exclusion, both blending and separation. The Stranger compares this to the letters of the alphabet (253a), which are able to combine in certain ways, while other ways are ruled out (except in Wales).

Finally the Stranger identifies two more Forms: the Same and the Different. Every Form will partake of both. For instance, Change will be the same as itself but different from Rest (254d). More generally, the five Forms we have now considered—Being, Change, Rest, Sameness, and Difference—are the "greatest kinds" (254d), because they pervade all the other Forms. And now we can finally see how non-being is woven into being, even if being is conceived as immaterial, unchanging, and intelligible, as proposed by the friends of the Forms. For it has now become clear that Being is pervaded by Difference. And being different is, of course, a way of not-being. Australian Rules Football and American football are things that are, and they partake in Sameness, being games that involve an oblong ball. Yet the two are different (if only in that one forbids protective gear while the other is played by wimps from North America). Thus we can say that Australian Rules Football "is not" American football. This shows us that the section of the *Sophist* on being and not-being is intimately related to the Stranger's method of collection and division.[8] When we collect, we are bringing together things that partake of Sameness in some respect—all games are the same as each other, in that they are games. And each division marks a kind of difference—the oblong-ball games are different from the round-ball games.

The analysis of not-being as a partaking of Difference helps us to understand not just collection and division, but more ordinary uses of language. Remember the worry that false belief and speech are impossible, since they involve the false—and the false is "what is not." Well, yes. But the false is not absolute non-being. Falsehood occurs when terms are combined, either in language or in thought, in a way different from how things are. Of course, just as letters don't combine in any way you like to build words, so words only combine to make statements in certain ways. A string of nouns like "football cricket baseball" is not going to be a statement, something that can be either true or false (philosophers would now say that such a string of words has no "truth value"). To get a meaningful statement, and thus truth or falsehood, the Stranger suggests that we need at a minimum to have a noun and a verb. Like Forms, nouns and verbs can be "woven together" in various ways (262d)—speaking is just weaving words together to produce a meaningful statement. Thinking, meanwhile, works much the same way, since it can be understood as a kind of inward speaking, in which the soul "converses with itself" (263e).[9] A false statement or belief, like "Theaetetus flies" or "Australian Rules Football players can do without health insurance," does not express outright non-being. Rather, it weaves together terms so as to say "something different from what is" (263b).

Having dealt with the sophist's puzzle about non-being, the Stranger and Theaetetus can finally turn back to their collecting and dividing. They are now able to offer a final analysis of the sophist in terms of his production of false images or copies (268c–d), his imitation of wisdom—hence his name (as we saw in the chapter on the sophists, "sophist" comes from *sophia*, "wisdom"). Given the uncharacteristic note of total success struck at the end of the dialogue, you get the sense that Plato is rather pleased with himself. And why shouldn't he be? He's exhibited a cunning method for tracking down conceptual quarry, and managed to catch the most elusive of prey. He's finally laid to rest the formidable problem of non-being, which tripped up even Parmenides, whom he seems to regard as his most outstanding predecessor. And in the process he's revamped the theory of Forms and given the first ever account of what makes language true and false. Not bad for a dialogue's work. But as philosophers and admirers of Socrates, we can't help but pose more questions. Take those remarks about language here in the *Sophist*. Sure, they are clever and groundbreaking, and will still be quoted in philosophical discussions of grammar in late antiquity as if they were cutting-edge stuff.[10] But they don't by any stretch of the imagination answer all the philosophical puzzles posed by language. Fortunately, the *Sophist* gives us only a tantalizing first sample of what Plato has to say on the subject.

WHAT'S IN A NAME?
PLATO'S *CRATYLUS*

In this book I've been emphasizing that Plato dealt with nearly all the topics philosophers have thought about ever since. I suppose even sympathetic readers will have the suspicion, though, that there are some significant issues in contemporary philosophy that don't arise in Plato. What might these be? Here's an obvious thought: since the work of the great logician and philosopher Gottlob Frege in the nineteenth century, philosophers in the analytic tradition have been extremely interested in language. This seems, in fact, to be a distinctive feature of twentieth-century philosophy in general: a fascination with language and problems about language. So how about philosophy of language, then? Is this an area where Plato has little to tell us, apart from his brief musings in the *Sophist*? Or is it yet another area where Plato is a pioneering genius, blah blah blah?

You may not be surprised to hear that it's the latter. Plato may have been the first person to do philosophy of language, and he certainly authored the earliest work specifically devoted to the topic, a dialogue called the *Cratylus*. Of course this dialogue doesn't tackle all, or even most, of the problems dealt with in contemporary philosophy of language. But it does tackle one of the most central problems: how do words have meaning? I'll explain what the problem is, before looking at how Plato deals with it. If I utter a random string of syllables, like "gibbledobtank-furter," that doesn't mean anything. In some sense I haven't even said anything—I haven't produced a piece of language, so I haven't managed to communicate. But if I say a word like "Frege" or "philosophy," then I do communicate, at least to people who know what these words mean. So what exactly is the difference? How do some strings of noises, or symbols in the case of written language, come to have meaning, while others don't? To answer this question is to explain how words get their power to communicate, and thus to establish something fundamental about what language is.

Nowadays, one popular theory about how words come to have meaning is that someone has to stipulate that a given sound or set of symbols will, from now on, represent some particular item. The most obvious example is naming: when a baby is on the way the parents confer with one another, and after overcoming bitter disagreement of the sort which makes each of them wonder if the other is going to be mature enough to raise a child, an agreement is reached. The baby gets a name. Mother and Father Frege dubbed their child "Gottlob" (maybe they should have thought about that one a bit more), and thus stipulated that this word would refer to the infant logician. So here's a theory about how names, and words in general, get their meaning: it happens through an act of arbitrary dubbing, a "baptism," if you will. As it turns out, this is one of the theories that Plato considers in the *Cratylus*.

The name Cratylus may sound familiar. To save you the trouble of flipping back through the pages, I'll remind you that he has been mentioned as a radical follower of Heraclitus. He's the one who said you can't even step into the same river once, and that you can't talk about things because they keep changing: you can only point at them with your finger. And he's one of the three main characters in the dialogue which shares his name. The others are Socrates and a man named Hermogenes. When the dialogue begins, Hermogenes and Cratylus have already been arguing about words and how they get their meanings. Hermogenes adopts the theory of arbitrary dubbing: for him, people can use whatever sound they want and associate any meaning with it, and then it's a matter of usage and convention as to whether that association sticks (384d). Cratylus disagrees. He has been arguing that words have their meaning by nature (383a–b). So what we have here is a nice example of the opposition we saw the sophists making, between convention and nature. And the question of the dialogue is simply: do words have their meanings by convention or by nature?

It's clear to us why words might have their meaning by convention, but what about nature? Cratylus' position becomes clearer as the dialogue goes along—and we also start to understand how his ideas about language might relate to his notorious Heracliteanism. Cratylus thinks that everything has a correct or true name. If you don't use the right word for something you haven't named it at all, so it turns out that you haven't even said anything (430a). This suits Cratylus perfectly, because he wants it to turn out that you can't say anything false. He agrees with the Protagorean relativists and Heracliteans of Plato's *Theaetetus*. At least, he agrees with them to the extent that he thinks there is no such thing as falsehood. But he's giving a reason different from the reasons we get in the *Theaetetus*. His reason is that to use language is nothing but uttering the right word or expression for what you are talking about. Cratylus goes so far as to say that if you use the wrong "word" for something, you haven't actually used a word at all (429b). A word in the proper sense is just the expression which means what you want to say. So, on his view there is no such thing as using language falsely.

That, then, is the dispute Socrates enters into at the beginning of the dialogue: does each thing have a word for it which is correct by nature, or can anything be called by whatever word we want, just by convention? Socrates starts by arguing against Hermogenes, who defends the conventionalist view. Socrates says that words are man-made items, like tools. And like tools, they have a function: just as a hammer is for banging in nails, so a word is for meaning a certain thing (387c–d). This seems plausible, but it suggests that you can't use just any sound to mean anything you want—just as you can't bang in nails using tapioca pudding. But if it's clear what makes hammers suitable for banging nails, and tapioca pudding not so suitable, it's not so clear what could make the sound "hammer" an appropriate word for hammers, and what could make other sounds inappropriate.

Socrates has an answer ready. He says that the right word for something should somehow reveal its nature. This, he says, is what the great poet Homer must have thought (391d). He quotes passages where Homer says that a river, for instance, has one name used by the gods and another name used by humans (391e). Presumably Homer believed that the gods use a true name, one might say the "real" name, which expresses an insight that mere humans lack. But can Socrates provide any examples? Why, he's glad you asked! He now launches into a long series of etymologies of Greek words, trying to show in each case that the word in question perfectly expresses the thing to which it refers. He gives etymologies for the names of the gods, features of the natural world like the moon, ethical virtues, and so on. To give you just a flavor of this, he suggests that the hero in Homer's *Iliad*, Hector, is called that because in Greek *hektor* can mean "one who holds," and Hector is the protector and ruler, thus the holder or possessor, of Troy (393a). Or take the word *theos*, which means "god" (as I've mentioned, this is where we get the word "theology"). Socrates says this relates to the Greek verb *thein*, which means "to run," because those who devised the name thought that the heavens were divine and the heavens are always running their course above us (397d). Speaking of which, one of my favorite etymologies is of the Greek word for "heaven," also the name of a god, *Ouranos*. Socrates suggests that this comes from the phrase *horo ta ano*, which means "looking at things above" (396c).

Socrates' etymologies are ingenious but rather fanciful, not to say extremely far-fetched. Some readers have wondered how seriously we are meant to take the whole exercise.[1] Socrates says several times that he is in the grip of a divine inspiration, which is why he's able to produce all these brilliant etymologies. Could that be Plato signaling us to take this with a grain of salt, since he elsewhere contrasts divine inspiration with the possession of true knowledge? Or maybe the whole thing is a kind of joke, a parody of something the sophists did? The sophists are indeed mentioned several times in a rather teasing way. But it's not very plausible to say that the whole thing is just a joke. For one thing, Plato has clearly put a lot of effort into this—the etymologies go on for pages and pages. For another, he has Socrates designate a few selected etymologies as being less serious, which suggests that the others mentioned are *more* serious. More plausible, I think, would be to say that Plato is competing with other authors who offered etymologies. Perhaps he's displaying his ingenuity and ability to suggest clever derivations for Greek terms. But even so, he may think there could be serious philosophical reasons for producing such derivations.

And in fact there is potentially a big philosophical payoff here. If Socrates is right that the correct words reveal the natures of things, then we could discover the natures of things by producing etymologies of their correct names. The analysis of names would turn out to be a way of doing philosophy. But there are several problems. Firstly, Socrates admits that some words have crept into Greek from foreign languages, so no etymology is possible in these cases (409e). More worrying, he assumes that the Greek of his own day is corrupted. In the Greek spoken in the fifth century BC the original, correct word may have been altered significantly. Letters or even whole syllables may have been added or subtracted, as when pronunciation changes to make a word easier to say (399a–b, 414c). So in some cases he suggests that we need to eliminate letters from a Greek word to discover its correct etymology. This obviously makes it even easier to let one's etymological fancy run wild.

But before we run wild, an even worse problem might give us pause: if I etymologize the word for "god" by saying that it's based on the word for "run," then why is the word for "run" necessarily a correct word? It looks like each word's meaning is simply a function of the meanings of the words on which it is based. So what makes any of these words natural, or revelatory of the natures of things? To stop this regress (421d–422b), Socrates suggests that there is a way that words could be real, natural representations or likenesses of the things they refer to. This is, basically, onomatopoeia (423b–e). If I may indulge in a little etymology of my own, this word "onomatopoeia" comes from ancient Greek, and the first part, *onoma*, is the Greek term I've been translating in this chapter as "word," Sometimes people translate *onoma* as "name" rather than "word," but that might be misleading since Socrates is happy to refer to a common noun or even a verb as an *onoma*. At any rate, onomatopoeia is, of course, when a word literally sounds like what it means. For example, words like "bang," "splash," or "tweet." Socrates' suggestion, then, is that all real or natural words are onomatopoeic. This seems hard to believe. But Socrates argues that if we take the idea seriously, we'll see that when words were originally bestowed upon things the people who bestowed them were expressing certain ideas about the natures of things and crafting words to match.

These ancestors of ours, it would seem, were Heracliteans. They used certain letters to suggest that things are constantly changing (401d, 439c). For instance, Socrates says, the Greek letter *rho* is supposed to signify rapid change because the tongue vibrates when pronouncing it. The letter *lambda* is supposed to represent gliding or flowing. Socrates gives examples of how this onomatopoeic code was used to build words expressing Heraclitean theory. To give a basic example, the very word for "flow" or "flux" in Greek begins with a *rho*, which signifies change (426d). Then, after using onomatopeia as a starting-point, these Heraclitean ancestors built further words etymologically. For instance, the Greek word for wisdom itself, *phronesis*, is supposed to relate to a Greek word for motion, *phora*. Thus Greek, or rather the carefully designed ancestor language of Greek, contained within it a kind of secret philosophical theory, namely that it is the nature of things to be in constant change.

Does all this show that Plato is actually a Heraclitean? Is he really having Socrates claim that the wise ancestors who devised the original, true version of Greek were flux theorists, like the ones he attacks in the *Theaetetus*? Well, yes and no. Socrates does seem convinced that these ancestors had Heraclitean ideas. But he also points out that it is one thing to discover a philosophical theory encoded in our language, and another thing to decide whether that theory is true (436c–e). Perhaps the ancestors were Heracliteans, but then, perhaps they were wrong. And that brings us to Socrates' refutation of the Heraclitean in the room: Cratylus. So far, Socrates has been refuting Hermogenes' theory that language is entirely conventional. Now he points out against Cratylus that language cannot be entirely natural either. The account he's just presented was very much to Cratylus' taste, but it allows for things like the corruption of words. As we saw, sometimes a letter might be added to, or removed from, a word to make it easier to say. When this happens, people are still able to use the word to communicate, to express meaning. So it can't be the case that only the true, natural words function as words. There must also be a role for convention (435b).

Socrates thus takes a sort of middle view between Hermogenes and Cratylus: words have their meanings by both nature *and* convention. So it's no surprise that he also rejects the most radical idea of Cratylus, namely that it's impossible to speak falsely because a real word or string of words must successfully mean the thing it is about. Socrates has already suggested, with his idea about onomatopoeia, that words are likenesses of the things they mean. So they are a bit like paintings: they are representations (430a–b). But if I hold up a painting of, say, Buster Keaton and apply it to Charlie Chaplin, then there is a mismatch between the painting and the thing that is supposedly represented. I've got the wrong silent-movie comedian. Similarly, it must be possible for me to apply a word to the wrong thing. The falsehood occurs because of a mismatch between the representation and what it is meant to represent (431a–b). Notice how Socrates here uses the idea that words are likenesses of things—which fits perfectly into Cratylus' own theory that words are by nature—to undermine Cratylus' more radical claim that falsehood is impossible. Notice also that Plato is here returning to the question, familiar from the *Theaetetus*, of how falsehood is possible, and coming up with an answer a lot like the one we saw there. Just as, in the *Theaetetus*, Socrates talked about imprints in wax which are mismatched with objects of perception, so here he treats words as representations mismatched with the things they are supposed to represent.

In taking a middle view between the naturalism of Cratylus and the conventionalism of Hermogenes, Socrates tries to preserve two possible functions of language. On the one hand, we use language simply to communicate our intentions. For this purpose, convention seems to be enough: if a mother stipulates that this baby with the logical twinkle in his eye is to be called "Gottlob Frege," and the right people get the message, then that will be his name. But on the other hand, Socrates is sympathetic to the hope that words can do something more ambitious: they can reveal the natures of things. This takes us back to the flux theory of the ancestors who devised the original words for things. As I said earlier, even if this does turn out to be the theory encoded in our language, that wouldn't show that the theory is *true*. To discover whether the theory is true, we need to do something other than analyzing the words that have been assigned to the things around us. We need to decide whether the principles that guided that process were the right ones.

As it turns out, Heracliteanism is rejected: the dialogue ends with a reassertion of what I'm tempted to call good old-fashioned Platonism. Perhaps the ancestors were flux theorists, but if so, then our language is devised on false principles. For the right philosophical theory, which we can use to correct the assumptions built into our language, is not a theory of radical change but a theory of stability. I have a dream, Socrates says: in my dream, it seems to me that there may be beauty itself, goodness itself, and so on (439c–440e). Surely beauty itself is always the way it is, and not constantly changing? And won't such things be the objects of true knowledge? Here Plato does what he notoriously fails to do in the *Theaetetus*: he affirms the theory of Forms, or something like it, as a preferable alternative to the flux theory of Heraclitus and his followers. At the end of the *Cratylus* Plato seems for a change to actually talk like a Platonist. If we read the whole dialogue again with this ending in mind, we might even convince ourselves that there is room for a true language—perhaps not ancient Greek—whose words express Platonic Forms rather than a world of change and flux. If philosophy could be done by linguistic analysis, it would have to analyze just such a language.

But if this was Plato's dream, he never tried to turn it into a reality. He did write a dialogue about the world around us, how it came to be, and how it relates to the Forms. But this dialogue does not proceed by analyzing the Greek language, or any other language. And it admits that the theory it presents is a tentative one—only a "likely story," as its main character says. In this story, the world is revealed as the work of a divine craftsman, made as an image of the Forms. As in the closing pages of the *Cratylus*, Platonism is alive and well in this next dialogue we'll be looking at: the *Timaeus*. But the Platonism in the *Timaeus* is combined with some new and rather unexpected ideas. For instance, have you ever looked at yourself in the mirror and wondered if you might be made of triangles? If so, then the next chapter of this book is for you.

26

A LIKELY STORY
PLATO'S *TIMAEUS*

Imagine, if you will, that you're a medieval monk in a well-stocked library. It's the eleventh century AD. One day you go to the shelf where Plato's writings are kept, and find there a single volume. You open it, and begin to read. You aren't going to be reading the *Republic*, because it hasn't been translated into Latin. Nor will you be reading the *Phaedo* or the *Meno*, neither of which will be available in Latin until the middle of the twelfth century. The Platonic corpus has fortunately been preserved and studied in the Greek-speaking medieval Byzantine empire. Its rediscovery in Western Europe, where Latin is still the language of scholars, will help spark the Renaissance. But that's still centuries away. So what you hold in your hands represents the complete works of Plato as they are known in your time and place: an incomplete Latin translation of a single dialogue, the *Timaeus*. Although Plato is hardly more than a name to you, the themes of this work will interest you greatly as you leaf through its pages. For it is in the *Timaeus* that Plato presents his thoughts on the creation of the world and the providential order of the universe—topics that are close to your heart, since you are a medieval monk. In the *Timaeus*, you discover what Plato has to say about god.

Plato's god is, however, rather different from the God of medieval monks. We can tell this already from the way Plato refers to him. Although it is made clear that we are dealing with a god (30a), Plato also calls him a craftsman—in Greek, *demiourgos*. This so-called "Demiurge" has two things in common with human craftsmen which make him unlike God as He is usually understood in Christianity, Judaism, and Islam. Firstly, the Demiurge is working from a set of plans. Just as a house-builder might follow architectural drawings, so the Demiurge looks to the Forms. He seeks to create an imitation of these Forms, and this imitation is the physical universe. Secondly, the Demiurge does not create from absolute nothingness. Instead, he fashions the universe in a kind of receptacle, without which he would have nowhere to put anything. Thus the Demiurge, unlike the God of the revealed religions, cooperates with two further, apparently distinct principles in fashioning the universe: the Forms he uses as patterns, and the receptacle in which the world is born. As Plato puts it, if the Demiurge is the father of the universe, then the receptacle is its mother.

The *Timaeus* is a dialogue, of course, so in addition to these cosmic characters there is also a small cast of dramatic characters. These consist of Socrates and three others. In fact, Socrates counts the others in the very first sentence of the dialogue, which literally begins: "One, two, three." Plato is, as he sometimes likes to do, alluding to a major theme of a dialogue in its opening words. As we'll see, this dialogue is going to have a great deal to say about mathematics, and Plato marks this by putting numbers quite literally at the front of the *Timaeus*. By the way, the best example of this Platonic trick is the *Republic*, which begins with Socrates saying: "I went down to the Piraeus," that is, to the port near Athens. It can't be unintentional that the dialogue with the cave allegory in it begins with someone saying "I went down."

When our action begins in the *Timaeus*, it turns out that the *Republic* is very much on our minds. Socrates begins the dialogue by summarizing a discussion he and his colleagues have had on the previous day (17a–19b). What he says sounds suspiciously like the content of the *Republic*. So this little group has already heard a depiction of the ideal city. This dialogue will fill out the picture, but will paint on an even larger canvas. In the *Republic* we had an extended parallel between the soul and the city. Now a further parallel is drawn between the city and the universe. We will be shown the ideal order that reigns in the universe as a whole, and not just in one city. First, though, we are shown a picture of the ideal city in action. Socrates' associate Critias—our friend from the *Charmides*, if you remember him—tells a story that the great Athenian statesman Solon supposedly heard in Egypt (21a–25d). Once upon a time, Solon was told, Athens faced down an invasion from a mighty foreign land. No, it's not the story about Persia again. This ancient invasion came from a land which lay in the other direction from Persia, out in the Atlantic Ocean, beyond the Straits of Gibraltar—the continent of Atlantis. This myth is taken up again in a second dialogue, the *Critias*, a companion-piece to the *Timaeus* which is very rarely read nowadays, never mind in the Middle Ages.

After this prefatory material we arrive at the account of Timaeus. He is introduced as a philosopher and astronomer, and once he starts talking he is hardly interrupted. In fact this Platonic dialogue consists mostly of a monologue, delivered by Timaeus. One might suspect that Plato has gotten tired of dialogues and decided to sit down and write a didactic theoretical treatise for a change. He's finally going to stop playing dramatic games and tell it like it is. But that impression is undermined to some extent by Timaeus' own description of his speech. Because of the very nature of the topic, he announces that he will only be able to present, as he puts it, a "likely story" or "plausible account" (*eikos logos*, 29c). The reason for his limited ambition is that he will be dealing with the physical cosmos. It is, he says, a realm of change and becoming, and thus is susceptible only to opinion. Certainty and knowledge apply only to the world of true being: the Forms. As I said at the end of the previous chapter, old-fashioned Platonism seems to be alive and well in the *Timaeus*.

Something else that is alive and well is the physical universe itself. Timaeus begins his account by saying that the Demiurge, being good, wanted to create the best universe possible. He thus decided that the universe should itself be a living being with a soul, and should imitate insofar as is possible the Form of living being (30b–d). To put it another way, the universe is an animal that is designed as a copy of the Form of Animal.[1] Timaeus assumes that the universe is a sphere, because the sphere is the most perfect shape (33b). He says it is made of the four elements we know from Empedocles: fire, air, water, and earth. He gives an argument for this: if the universe is to be visible there must be fire, and if it is to be tangible there must be earth (31b). But the universe would not be perfectly bonded together if it did not contain proportions between these two extremes, fire and earth (31c–32a). So for the sake of mathematical completeness, the Demiurge includes air and water in between these first two elements.

Plato is here assuming something that will become familiar in Aristotle and most other ancient thinkers: the four elements mix together but tend towards being arranged in layers, with heavy, solid earth settling at the midpoint of the spherical universe, light, subtle fire dominating at the periphery, and water and air in between. What we now think of as the planet Earth is located at the center of the universe, with the heavens rotating around it. All of this, of course, is in keeping with everyday experience—which is just what we would expect from Timaeus' "likely story." We see that flame flickers upwards in air, that clods of earth and stones sink in water and fall down through air. As for the heavenly bodies, they cannot be observed up close, but Timaeus says that they too are compounded out of the elements (32c). He adds that their regular motions create time, like a cosmic clock (37d–38e). The heavens are the most divine parts of the universe, but the universe as a whole is divine, a god made by the greater god who is the Demiurge (34b).

Timaeus' reasoning throughout this section may itself strike us as an odd mixture that moves in different directions. On the one hand, he appeals to empirical observation—as I said, the ideas about the elements are supposed to explain what we see around us. On the other hand, he invokes mathematical symbolism such as we might expect from a Pythagorean. One example is his idea that air and water must exist in order that there be some proportion bonding together fire and earth. The mathematics becomes even more dominant as Timaeus goes along, particularly in a complicated passage about the creation of soul by the Demiurge. This is explained by means of a detailed analysis of geometrical ratios, with the Demiurge seeking to create an ideally proportionate mixture which will constitute the soul (35b–36b). The Demiurge then weaves this well-proportioned soul with the body of the cosmos, to create a living sphere—as perfect an animal as can exist in the physical realm. This animal is the universe in which we live.

But how do we come to live in the universe? Did the Demiurge create us? No, he did what all good executives do: he delegated. In a characteristically inscrutable little passage, Plato has Timaeus endorse the ancient myths about the generation of the gods, more or less as we know them from Homer and Hesiod. We should, he says, simply take at face value the accounts of the gods that have been handed down to us, even without proof (40d–e). Thus we can go ahead and believe that there is a family of gods on hand to help the Demiurge, who include Kronos, Zeus, Hera, and so on. Unlike the Demiurge, these gods are actually born from one another, just as Hesiod says (40e–41a). If this passage could be read by Xenophanes, the Pre-Socratic who reveled in criticizing the epic poets, we might imagine him sighing in frustration here. Alternatively, he might indulge in a conspiratorial smile, if he assumed that Plato is not serious, and that this ratification of the traditional Greek gods is laced with irony. It's hard to know which would be the right reaction: as usual, Plato is keeping his cards close to his chest.

It is, in any event, these lesser gods who do the dirty work of fashioning the human body. The Demiurge takes care of separating out portions of soul, but his helper gods design our bodies and produce them out of the four elements (42e–43a), making our heads roughly spherical in imitation of the sphere of the universe (44d). The only reason we need our bodies from the neck down, as it turns out, is so that our heads don't roll around and get stuck in ditches. (Again, you have to wonder whether Plato is kidding, but the whole account is delivered with an apparently straight face.) Timaeus also explains how human eyesight works, and at some length. Without getting into these details too much, Plato upholds the view that our vision goes out to the objects we see: the eyes emit rays, which coalesce with light to make seeing happen (45b–d). Thus vision is comparable to using a stick to reach out and touch the visual objects. Yet again, Plato's account will strike us as rather strange. But by assimilating vision to a kind of touch, it explains how we can interact with things at a distance by seeing them. The stipulation that the visual ray must coalesce with light further explains why we can't see in the dark. So this visual ray theory has its advantages, and after Plato it was one of the dominant ways of understanding vision for many centuries.[2] At any rate, Timaeus praises eyesight as the most important of the senses, because it allows us to see the regular motions of the heavenly bodies—we should aspire to imitate these revolutions in the motions of our own souls (47a).

This, then, is Timaeus' description of how the Demiurge and his helper gods fashion the universe and the humans living within it. But Timaeus isn't done. He has so far left out an important part of the story: the receptacle (48e–52d). The receptacle is none of the objects that surround us, but is rather what contains those things. We cannot observe it directly. We know it exists only because there must be some matrix or spatial arena in which things move and change into one another. And things certainly do change; for instance, when water evaporates and turns into air. Not for the first time, Plato sounds a bit like a Heraclitean here, as he has Timaeus describe the physical world as a realm of constant change and flux. Without the receptacle there would be no stability at all in the region here around us, below the orderly and unchanging heavens. The receptacle itself is unchanging, but feature-less—Timaeus compares it to the odorless fluid to which people add further smells when they are making perfume (50e). So it can only be grasped indirectly, by what Timaeus calls "bastard reasoning."

Thus Plato has added a third rung to his metaphysical ladder. In dialogues like the *Phaedo* and the *Republic* we were acquainted with two kinds of metaphysical items: the unchanging Forms and the changing things that participate in them. Now we are given what Timaeus calls "a third kind," namely the receptacle in which these participating things can exist. Timaeus brings in the receptacle in order to illustrate how the universe is the product of not only divine intellect but also what he calls "necessity" (*anangke*) (47e–48a). The Demiurge and helper gods are constrained in certain ways as they fashion the universe. For instance, objects in the universe must take up space, since they are made in the spatial realm of the receptacle. This means that they can collide and interfere with one another. There are other, more subtle limitations too. Timaeus gives the example of the human skull, which turns out to be a kind of compromise. If it were thinner, our brains could be larger and we would be more intelligent, but if it were thicker it would provide better protection (75a–c). Its present thickness is thus the product of necessity: the gods do the best they can with the materials that are physically possible.

The example of the skull comes quite a bit later in the dialogue, towards the end of Timaeus' attempt to analyze the physical world, taking into account not only the Demiurge's wisdom but also the constraints imposed by necessity. As this part of the likely account takes shape, it's one shape in particular that dominates the discussion: triangles. Of course Plato loved geometry—remember the legend that a sign on the Academy said only those who had studied geometry should enter. And his passion for the subject is never more evident than here in the *Timaeus*. We are told that the four elements are not strictly speaking elements, in the sense of being the most basic constituents of bodies. Instead, just as our bodies are made up of fire, air, water, and earth, so those elemental bodies are made of triangles (53c–d). To be precise, the four elements are made out of two kinds of triangles. Earth is made of one kind (55d–e): triangles with one right angle and two further equal angles (we'd say that the angles are 90, 45, and 45 degrees). If you fuse two such triangles, you get a square, and if you fuse six squares along their edges, you get a cube. This explains the solidity of earth: at what we might call the molecular level, it is made of microscopic cubes that are packed together. All the other elements are made of little triangles, each of which is half of an equilateral triangle. Once they join as equilateral triangles, these can in turn be combined to form the surfaces of various three-dimensional shapes (56a–c).

If you were paying attention in geometry class when you were a kid, you will know that these shapes are called polyhedra. And if you've ever wondered why five such polyhedra, the cube, pyramid, octahedron, dodecahedron, and icosahedron, are called the "Platonic solids," then now you know: these are the five solids mentioned in this part of the *Timaeus*.[3] Next, Plato invokes the geometrical features of the solids to explain physical phenomena. We already saw that the solidity of cubes explains the solidity of earth. Likewise, fire consists of tiny pyramids, and the sharp points of these pyramids accounts for the cutting and destructive nature of fire. Another advantage of this account is in explaining how fire, air, and water turn into one another: the three-dimensional molecules are broken up into their triangular atoms, and these triangles then re-form, so that one Platonic solid arises from another (56e–57a). Incidentally, earth, being made of that other kind of triangle, cannot change into the other elements (56d)—a view which Aristotle will go on to reject.

Taking off from this likely account of the elements in terms of geometrical atomism, Timaeus goes on to discuss why some things are hard and others soft, some heavy and others light, some rough and others smooth; why things have color and taste; and why the human body is put together the way it is. In one significant passage he assigns the three parts of the soul familiar from the *Republic* to parts of the body (69c–71e). Reason is located in the brain, spirit in the heart, and appetite in the liver. This too is something that Aristotle will go on to reject. Indeed, a debate will rage for centuries as to whether the rational and perceiving part of our soul is associated with the brain or the heart, with Plato being the standard-bearer for the brain and Aristotle and the Stoics insisting that the heart is, in every sense, central. Only in the second century AD would the doctor Galen put this debate to rest. He performed anatomical experiments—often as a public display—which proved that animal motion is controlled via nerves that stem from the brain. One powerful demonstration was to snip the nerves in the neck of a live animal, rendering the animal lame.

But let's step back from these anatomical details and look one last time at the bigger picture: the cosmology of the *Timaeus*. Plato's cosmic recipe might remind us of the Pre-Socratics. The ingredients of his physical universe include four elements (borrowed from Empedocles), and a divine mind (that's a healthy portion of Anaxagoras), who produces a world in constant change (a dash of Heraclitus), which is fundamentally mathematical (a full measure of Pythagoreanism). But as always, it would be a mistake to reduce Plato to his sources. The *Timaeus* provides us with an ambitious and novel account of the universe and its making. It shows a deep commitment to the idea that the universe is providentially ordered. Though Plato doesn't use any phrase like "the best of all possible worlds," he does stress that the Demiurge is not envious, and wants to make this world as good and beautiful as possible. On the other hand, there are limitations on that possibility. The triangles out of which the elements arise are, Timaeus tells us, the most beautiful and perfect shapes (54a). But the very fact that the elements are made of shapes has to do with the nature of the receptacle, and in general the Demiurge's choices are limited by physical necessity.

This is not the untrammeled creative activity of the Christian God worshipped by medieval monks. Rather, the universe is the work of a divine craftsman who has no choice about which blueprints to use, and who is restricted as regards his materials. Another, equally profound difference is this: the God of Christianity, Judaism, and Islam is a personal diety. He rewards and punishes, He grows angry, He loves his creatures. The Demiurge does none of these things. He may be providential and even generous, but in making the universe his attitude is more like aesthetic taste than love. Indeed, there is a good Platonic reason why the Demiurge cannot love us. The Demiurge is divine and perfect, and needs nothing. And in other dialogues, Plato shows us that love is always bound up with need, with unfulfilled desire, with a longing for a beauty which we strive to possess.

WINGS OF DESIRE
PLATO'S EROTIC DIALOGUES

The past, as they say, is a foreign country. And ancient Greece can often seem to be a very foreign country indeed. Some aspects of Greek culture do find echoes in our own, even if the echoes are distant ones. There aren't really any sophists nowadays, but there are spin-doctors; the Pre-Socratics did philosophy of nature, and we do science; Euripidean tragedy and Aristophanic comedy are very distant ancestors of modern theater; and so on. But there were Greek cultural practices that have no parallel in modern society. One obvious example is pederasty. Nowadays, sexual liaisons between adults and children are not merely illegal, but among the most repugnant moral crimes that can be committed. But in ancient Greece liaisons between grown men and boys played an accepted role in civic life. Ideally the younger partner would be in the "bloom of youth," before the first growth of their beard. This boy was called the "beloved," while the "lover" was the older man.

Notice the implication that the attraction was not necessarily mutual. It was assumed that the older lover would take physical pleasure in their partnering, whereas the boy would not. Boys who showed signs of enjoying their side of the relationship were considered shameless, and a beloved youngster was supposed to demonstrate his decency by playing hard to get, before finally giving in to the blandishments of the lover. So what's in it for the boy, if he isn't expected to get any physical pleasure out of all this? Of course, at the stage of courtship there's the pleasure of being flattered and pursued, something Plato exploits for humorous effect in several dialogues (remember the guy falling off the end of the bench in the *Charmides*). But the main benefit for the beloved was that the lover would provide a special kind of education. For the boy, pederasty was an introduction into the ways of grown-up society, along with political connections and experience. Thus pederasty was linked to political life and, for the young man, the erotic relationship could be a step on the political ladder. He had to put up at least a show of resistance to mask this underlying exchange of benefits which could, to an uncharitable observer, look like prostitution.

Plato was just such an uncharitable observer. He allows his characters to speak in very blunt terms about the benefits the beloved and the lover expect when they embark on an erotic relationship. Nor is he above exploiting these relationships for humorous effect, as I've just mentioned. So it's easy to assume that Plato's attitude towards this practice was one of stern disapproval. We now talk of Platonic relationships and Platonic love, meaning loving relationships that don't involve sex. This gives the impression that Plato was the Nancy Reagan of the erotic: his advice to us is: "Just say no." But in fact Plato's interest in the erotic impulse, and in these pederastic relationships in particular, was complex and multifaceted. A number of his dialogues feature erotic themes, sometimes in the form of the dramatic setting, as in the *Charmides*, and sometimes in passing, as when Socrates teases Meno, saying that as a good-looking young man Meno is always fishing for compliments.

There are two dialogues that are especially important when it comes to his treatment of *eros*—the Greek word for sexual or passionate love. These happen to be two of his greatest works: the *Symposium* and the *Phaedrus*. The *Symposium* is, naturally enough, set at a drinking-party (the word "symposium" means "drinking together"), an occasion where Greek men would gather in the evenings to lie down, imbibe wine, and entertain one another with song or conversation. Further entertainment would be provided by flute-girls, who were often available for the men's physical enjoyment. In Plato's dialogue the *Symposium* the atmosphere is at first quite sedate, since many of those present have already been drinking heavily the night before (176a–e). Instead of getting drunk, they opt to give speeches in praise of love, or *eros* (177a–d). At the end of the dialogue the party gets a lot wilder, with the entrance of Alcibiades, the beautiful young man who grew up to be a notorious political figure.[1]

Plato's masterstroke here is to have a series of characters give a series of speeches about love. This allows him to look at *eros* from a variety of viewpoints, while showing off his ability to mimic a variety of voices. The two most famous voices are given the two best speeches: these are the voices of Aristophanes and Socrates. But even before we get to them, we are presented with a range of ideas about love. Phaedrus—the namesake of the dialogue I'll be discussing below—describes love as a god who brings great blessings (178a–180b). Another character, called Pausanias, goes one better, insisting that there are two gods called love, one of whom is preferable to the other (180c–185c). The man who is in thrall to the lower, "common" love is indiscriminate and jumps at any chance for sexual gratification (181b), whereas the higher, "heavenly" love leads its possessor to show loyalty to his beloved. This idea, that love can manifest itself as crass desire-fulfillment or as an exalted pursuit, also appears in the *Phaedrus*, as we'll see shortly. After Pausanias things are brought down to earth by Erixymachus, who is a doctor. Like Empedocles, he sees love as a force that pervades the cosmos (186a–b). He's particularly interested in its effects on the human body, where love is manifested as the body's harmony and health (186d–e). This is a reminder for us that in Plato's time medical ideas had already penetrated into philosophy—and vice-versa.

But as I say, things really get going with the speech of Aristophanes, a brilliant and funny explanation of erotic attraction by way of a myth. Aristophanes explains that originally humans were joined in pairs, some with two male halves, some with two female halves, some literally "androgynous"—that is, combining a male and a female half (189d–e). These creatures had eight legs and two heads, and could move by somersaulting along the ground (190a). Their speed and strength allowed them to challenge the gods. Mighty Zeus put a stop to this by splitting each of them in half, dividing them into the humans we now see (190c–e). This explains our desperation for sexual union: we are, literally, trying to reunite with our missing half (191a–b). It also explains why, to put it in modern terms, some people are homosexual and others heterosexual: men who love men are split from a man–man pairing, whereas those who love women are split from an androgynous pairing. Aristophanes adds that men who love men are more manly, since they derive from a composite creature which was entirely male (192a).

This amusing myth befits the comic poet Plato has chosen to deliver it. Aristophanes concludes by threatening that, if we do not respect love and the other gods, Zeus may split us again, dividing the left side of our bodies from the right side, sawn in half between the nostrils like relief figures on gravestones (193a). Plato also has Aristophanes constantly protest that he's being serious—which gives us to understand that the rest of the company is laughing at the images he conjures up. Yet the myth makes a serious point too, namely that erotic love is a desire for union in the strongest possible sense. We are, according to the myth, incomplete, and we desire to possess our other halves again. As Aristophanes says, if a god were to appear to two lovers and offer to rivet them together so that they could never be parted, they would say that this is their heart's desire (192d–e). Again, the way this is put has comic overtones. But one shouldn't underestimate the idea that love is really a desire to possess, and in some sense even become identical with, the beloved. Even in the Book of Genesis, it says that man and wife become "one flesh" when they are united in marriage.

Socrates, though, is having none of this. In typical fashion, he sets out not just to give a speech in praise of love but to disprove the ideas of love that have come before him. A beautiful young poet named Agathon has spoken, following

Aristophanes, and praised Eros again as a beautiful and wondrous god (194e–197d). Socrates refutes him, first in a short discussion with Agathon and then by means of his own speech. Of course Socrates doesn't really like to give speeches, as he says at the beginning of the *Apology*.[2] Instead, he claims to be recounting a discussion he had with a wise female philosopher named Diotima. Diotima's speech casts doubt on Agathon's idea that love is a beautiful god, and on Aristophanes' idea that love is a yearning for possession and union.

Diotima admits that love is a divine being—a demigod, if not a god (202d–e). But she objects to the sort of effusive praise of Eros found in Agathon's speech. After all, what is love but desire for what is beautiful? And if I desire something, then obviously I don't have it. So even if Eros is a divine being, he can't be beautiful and wondrous. Rather, he is poor, rough, and barefoot, seeking desperately after a beauty and wisdom that he can never attain (203c–d). Sound like anyone we know? It seems Socrates is, through Diotima, engaging in a little bit of self-portraiture. But if love is a longing for what one doesn't have, then why doesn't Socrates, or Diotima, agree with Aristophanes that it is a yearning for union with our missing half? Diotima alludes to this central idea of Aristophanes' speech and disagrees with it too: she says that if I desire something, that can't be simply because it is part of me, but because I consider it to be good (205e). After all, she points out, I'm happy to amputate a limb if it is infected.

Love, then, is not about possession: it is about seeking what is beautiful, what is good. No prizes for guessing where this is going: if I am after what is beautiful, then it will be a mistake to satisfy myself with beautiful bodies. Rather, I should seek after beauty itself—the Form of Beauty. This is just what Diotima goes on to say. Our desire for beauty is a desire to, as she says, "give birth in the beautiful," to transcend our limitations and finitude by seeking immortality (206b–207a). This is why people seek to produce children, as a way of living on after their deaths (207a–208b). But this is a poor sort of immortality, just as the beauty of body is a poor sort of beauty. So it is a rather debased expression of love if the lover contents himself with the beauty of boys' bodies. A true seeker of beauty will realize that it is not just this one boy's body that is beautiful, but other bodies too, and from there will rise to admire the beauty of souls (210a–e). This kind of lover will wish to educate his beloved, and not just to sleep with him. In praising this sort of impulse, Diotima seems to give qualified approval to the pederastic practices of Greek culture, at least insofar as they revolved around education of the young and not physical consummation.

But this is not yet the highest rung on the ladder of love. Ultimately, the lover's interest in the education of souls will lead him to pursue beautiful laws, in order to improve as many souls as possible (209a–e). Thus a figure like Solon, the lawmaker of Athens, is revealed to be an advanced practitioner of the erotic arts. Even Solon, though, has not ascended the ladder to the top. The lover who graduates to the highest step is the one who seeks after, and arrives at, beauty itself—what Diotima calls the "great sea of beauty." This lover achieves immortality not by giving birth to children, or by writing laws for a city, but by grasping unchanging, immortal truths: the nature of beauty itself (210e–211a). According to Diotima, then, all the other loves she has described are merely defective versions of philosophy. For the true love is love of wisdom, and this is, of course, nothing other than philosophy.

Once it reaches this exalted height, the dialogue is brought crashing back down to the context of a drinking-party by the arrival of Alcibiades (212c). Garlanded with flowers and more than a little drunk, he gives a speech in praise of Socrates rather than Eros—or are they the same thing? This speech is the most powerful evocation of Socrates in the dialogues, and a raucous tale of unrequited love. Alcibiades is Socrates' biggest fan: he tells us of Socrates' toughness, fighting without fear and going without food and barefoot in the snow while on military campaign (219e–220b). He even saved Alcibiades' life in a battle (220e). But it is not Socrates' military exploits that make Alcibiades feel inadequate in comparison. Rather, it is with his probing questions and critique of political ambition that Socrates has made him feel slavish and ashamed (215d–216b). We know that Alcibiades went on to have a political career (to put it mildly), but Plato presents him as powerfully drawn to Socrates' philosophy and his person. Alcibiades has tried to seduce him, perhaps to gain the upper hand in this unequal relationship, but Socrates' powers of self-control are so great that he can withstand the attractions even of the lovely Alcibiades. His interest in boys is not for their physical beauty, but their souls.

This fits reasonably well with the portrayal of Socrates in Plato's other great dialogue about *eros*: the *Phaedrus*. Like the *Symposium*, the *Phaedrus* matches an erotic setting to its erotic themes. Here we encounter Socrates in nature, outside the city walls of Athens—a rarity for Socrates, who normally prefers to stay in the city where he can discuss philosophy. But Socrates does not hesitate to discuss in any setting, and here his interlocutor is another beautiful young man, Phaedrus. The two flirt in this bucolic setting and, in a dramatic device similar to that of the *Symposium*, trade speeches on the subject of love. More specifically, the speeches concern the question of what kind of older man a boy should agree to gratify. Should he prefer a lover who is really in love with him, or one who is not?

One way to phrase this central question of the *Phaedrus* is this: is a lover also a friend? Does love really make a man provide benefits for his beloved, or does it rather give him reason to harm the beloved? Socrates suggests it may be the latter. After all, the lover doesn't want to encounter resistance, he wants the boy to give in.

So it's in his interest for the boy to be weak (238e–239c). He wants the boy to be dependent on him—any advantage the boy has, for instance, wealth, will make the boy more independent (240a). Thus he will scheme to harm, not benefit, the young object of his desires. To this one can add that the lover will abandon the boy as soon as he loses interest, leaving the boy bewildered by the sudden change from fawning pursuit to disdain (240e–241d). A non-lover, by contrast, will be motivated not by physical lust but by good-will and friendship. So the boy should give his body not to the besotted lover, but to an older man who is merely a friend.

At this point, Socrates' divine sign speaks up—the supernatural voice that warns him when he is about to do something wrong. Socrates recants what he has just said, and gives a speech arguing in the other direction. The boy should, after all, gratify the lover, not the non-lover (243d). To explain why, Socrates offers one of the most famous images in Plato. Our souls are, he says, like a team of winged horses being steered by a charioteer. There are two horses, one noble and obedient, the other vicious and wild (246a–b). The charioteer must try to steer a straight path with these flying steeds, keeping the bad horse under control. If he succeeds he may be able to stick just his head up into the realm beyond the heavens, where the gods process in their own chariots (246d–247a). There the soul may behold justice, temperance, and knowledge—in short, it is able to see the Forms (247d). But sometimes the bad horse drags the soul down to earth (247b). Such a soul loses its wings as it is joined to an earthly body. It seems obvious that this image reflects the psychological theory we already met in the *Republic*. The wild horse represents the desiring soul, which tries to defy reason, while the good horse stands for the honor-loving spirit, which can help the soul to subdue desire. The charioteer, of course, symbolizes our rational soul. The theory of recollection also seems to be making an appearance, since Socrates talks about the fallen souls as having forgotten what they beheld up above in the heavens.

It's fun to see familiar Platonic themes turning up in this evocative setting. But what does any of it have to do with love? Well, Socrates explains that when we see beauty—for instance, the beauty of a boy—our soul is reminded of the beauty it saw above (249c). Some souls yield to the seduction of physical beauty and seek physical gratification. But the better souls are prompted to grow their wings again. This is a painful process, and the soul does not understand what is happening to it, which is why falling in love is so agonizing and traumatic (251c–252b). The boy is, then, used as a kind of prompt for the recollection of beauty—a more emotionally intense version of the kind of prompting we were told about in the *Phaedo*, where equal sticks and stones lead us to recollect the Form of Equal. The boy too is eventually drawn into this erotic yearning. Like the lover, the boy's passionate side, represented by the bad horse of his soul's chariot, may lead him to give in to crude physical union. But if the good horses prevail, the two will remain chaste and engage in what turns out to be a truer and more lasting union: the shared pleasures of philosophy (256a–c).

It isn't surprising that Plato sees philosophy as a manifestation of love. After all, the Greek word *philosophia* does literally mean the "love of wisdom." This etymology has nothing to do with *eros*. It is, rather, related to the word *philia*. It's a word with a broad application—for instance, the relation between parents and their children is one of *philia*, and sexual love or *eros* is compatible with *philia* too. I'll follow common practice and use the English word "friendship" as a translation. Which might make us realize that there's something rather unsatisfying about the account of love we find in Plato. Some have complained that in the *Symposium* and the *Phaedrus* Plato gives an account of love which is completely divorced from friendship. The scholar Gregory Vlastos accused Plato of a failure of moral imagination here, insofar as the *Symposium* in particular doesn't give a successful account of interpersonal love.[3] Instead, Plato presents erotic relationships as mere occasions for ascending to Beauty itself and the other forms. If this is right, then one beautiful person will do just as well as any other—just as any two equal sticks will serve equally well to remind me of the Form of Equal.

But this is to assume that Plato was in fact trying to give an account of interpersonal love in Diotima's speech. Perhaps this issue just wasn't on Plato's agenda in the *Symposium*. That needn't mean he had nothing to say on the subject.[4] That he did have something to say is clear from a less famous work, called the *Lysis*. The *Lysis* is a more typical Socratic dialogue: Socrates and some young interlocutors try to define something and fail in their attempt. In this case, the term to be defined is *philia*, or friendship. The dialogue is shorter than the *Symposium* and lacks its mythic and literary power, but it is worth reading nonetheless. Talking to yet another beautiful boy—the Lysis of the title—Socrates wonders whether it's true that birds of a feather really flock together (214a–b). That is, do friendships spring up between people who are alike, or unalike? After presenting objections against both options, Socrates decides that all friendship is based on a love for some kind of good (216c–217a). If I am your friend, it must be because of your goodness—and it must be for your sake that I am your friend. This is an idea about friendship that we'll be seeing again when we get to Aristotle's *Nicomachean Ethics*. As usual, Plato is ahead of the game, and he does seem to be showing an interest in interpersonal love. It is my *friend's* goodness, not goodness in general or the Form of Goodness, that serves as the basis for our friendship, and the friendly feeling I bear towards my friend is for his sake (219b).

Even here, though, Plato integrates philosophy into his account of love. If I am a philosopher, it is because I bear this relation of *philia* towards wisdom, seeking after this great good which I am so far lacking. So Plato seems deeply committed to the idea that philosophy is really a kind of love, a longing and passion for wisdom. It's easy to miss this passionate aspect of philosophy when we are in the midst of some technical argument about metaphysics or epistemology. But Plato makes sure we don't miss the point by using the powerful mythic imagery of the *Phaedrus* and the *Symposium*—all those heavenly chariots, souls sprouting feathers, gods and demigods. These are only two of the dialogues in which Plato uses myth as a vehicle for expressing and reinforcing philosophical ideas. In fact, many of the dialogues we've looked at—including the *Phaedo, Gorgias,* and *Republic*—feature elaborate myths, and it would be doing Plato a disservice if we passed over them before moving on to Aristotle.

28

LAST JUDGMENTS
PLATO, POETRY, AND MYTH

In this book I've dealt at least in passing with three bodies of ancient Greek literature. Obviously, there is the philosophical and scientific literature which has been the main focus. There is history, as written by Xenophon, Thucydides, and others—figures I've had cause to mention a few times. And then there is poetry. At the beginning of our story I discussed how Xenophanes attacked the poets Homer and Hesiod for their inadequately reverential treatment of the gods. We also saw that other Pre-Socratics, like the great Parmenides, wrote their philosophy in poetic form, and that the comic poet Aristophanes is an important source for the historical Socrates. But the poets, whether epic, tragic, or comic, haven't come up much since I reached Plato. You may have been thinking that this was something of an omission, even, dare I say, a gap. After all, Plato is famous for attacking the poets in his greatest work, the *Republic*. Like Xenophanes, he criticized the way that the gods are represented in Homer and Hesiod. But Plato's diatribe against the poets goes far beyond anything we find in the fragments of Xenophanes. He proposes a program of censorship for his ideal republic, mentioning specific verses which should be banned. Later in the *Republic* he attacks the poets of ancient tragedy and comedy, and warns that unless the poets or their adherents can show us that poetry is beneficial to society, they too will be excluded (607d–608a).

Plato's notoriously hostile attitude towards the poets is puzzling, when you think about it. No Greek author could write without being in the shadow of the poets, and Plato was far from an exception to this rule. Throughout his dialogues, including the *Republic*, he frequently alludes to both Homer and Hesiod. He quotes other poets too, like Simonides and Pindar. Those are only the explicit quotations—there are plenty of other, more implicit references that Plato's readers would certainly have noticed, given the immense importance of poetry in aristocratic Greek society. Indeed, a whole book was recently published studying Plato's use of Hesiod.[1] Plato's use of this material was, like everything with Plato, complicated: sometimes disapproving, sometimes approving, more often appropriating poetic remarks for his own purposes. Then, too, there is the fact that Plato was himself producing great literature in the *Republic* and his other dialogues. Of course the dialogues aren't poems. But as we'll see, some of his objections against poetry would seem equally applicable to his own dialogues.

Perhaps the most striking puzzle is this: Plato's objections to the mythic, epic poetry of Homer and Hesiod didn't stop him from composing some epic myths of his own. Several of the dialogues I've discussed include long myths of Plato's own invention. The *Phaedo*, the *Gorgias*, and the *Republic* all include such a myth at or near their conclusion. In the *Republic*, the Myth of Er comes close on the heels of Plato's attack on imitative poetry in the tenth and final book (614a–621b). We've seen myths or mythic elements in other dialogues too, like the story of the winged horses and chariot from the *Phaedrus* (246a–256e) which I discussed in the previous chapter, or the cosmic story of the *Timaeus* which is designated by Plato several times as a *muthos*. The word *muthos* is the origin of our word "myth," and though it can mean something like a story or tale, the *Timaeus* has more than a little in common with the myths we find in other dialogues.

So what was Plato up to here? Why excoriate the myths of others even as he devised replacements of his own? Was this some sort of cynical gamesmanship on his part, an attempt to eliminate the competition, rubbishing other literary artists to make space for a new, Platonic, philosophical artistry? There may be some truth in that: just think of the way he handles Aristophanes as a character in the *Symposium*, putting a brilliantly funny speech into his mouth to show that anything Aristophanes can do, Plato can do too (189c–193d). He does something similar with the sophists, by writing highly rhetorical speeches voiced by characters like Protagoras. But there's more going on here than just artistic competition. To see why, we need to consider Plato's objections to the poets, and then look at what he tries to achieve in his own myths.

Plato criticizes the poets twice in the *Republic*, first in Books Two and Three, where his complaints are mostly about the epic poets Homer and Hesiod, then again in Book Ten, where he takes aim at the tragedy and comedy of the Greek theater. From our point of view these two bodies of literature don't seem to have much in common, apart from the fact that they were written in verse. So you might worry that I'm playing fast and loose by treating the two things together. But I'm in good company. Plato does the same thing, going freely from a discussion of epic poetry to mention theater, and vice-versa. He even calls Homer a tragedian at one point (598d). Furthermore, his most fundamental complaint applies to both genres. The complaint is that the poets are engaging in *mimesis*, or "imitation" (597e). For instance, in the *Iliad* Homer not only speaks in his own voice when narrating events, but also in the voices of his many characters, from Agamemnon to Achilles, from Helen to Priam.

There are a couple of reasons why Plato doesn't like this imitative dimension of poetry. For one thing, the poet is able to slip false teachings into the minds of his listeners. He can have Achilles insult the gods, as Homer does, and describe the gods themselves acting and saying things that are unworthy of divinity. Many of the objectionable verses mentioned in the *Republic* are banned because they instill false beliefs about the gods—Xenophanes would be proud. Plato is particularly emphatic on this point because he's describing the educational arrangements in the ideal city. He has Socrates argue that such teachings about the gods are especially dangerous for the young, since they are impressionable and will be corrupted easily (378d–e). Hence the proposal that the poets be censored, one of the points which has led some modern readers to detect totalitarian tendencies in the *Republic*. It isn't only false beliefs about the gods that need to be expurgated, but also passages where the poets depict heroes as being overly emotional or dishonest. Our young citizens are going to admire these characters, so they must never be shown as being anything other than completely noble. When people nowadays complain about athletes failing to set a good example for young fans, they have something like this in mind.

Plato extends his censorship program to music, and for good reason. Greek epic poetry and theater were performed with music, so that Plato thinks of poetry and music as two sides of a single phenomenon. He eliminates certain musical modes, rhythms, and even instruments from the ideal city, because they induce emotions that are corruptive for society—for instance, sorrow or uncontrolled passion (398d–e). It's not just epic poetry and flutes that incite the wrong emotions in us, though. In Book Ten Plato has Socrates criticize Greek theater for giving its audiences licence to express emotions in a way they would normally find shameful (605d–e). It was common for audiences at a Greek tragedy to wail and weep at the sight of the pitiable events on the stage. Plato finds this repugnant, and no less so the uncouth laughter provoked by Aristophanes and the other comic poets.

To these complaints about the educational effects of poetry, Plato adds another objection. We saw in earlier chapters that he accuses the sophists of inducing persuasion without knowledge: Gorgias can convince someone to take their medicine better than a doctor can, but Gorgias doesn't know which medicine it would be good to take. Similarly, the poets are aiming at pleasure and not knowledge. Their expertise is solely in imitation, and an expert in imitation is precisely someone who can reproduce the appearance of something without needing to understand its true nature. He compares this to painting: a painter can paint a convincing picture of a bed, but to build one you need to go to the man who actually knows what he's doing, namely a carpenter (597d). As Plato points out, images and imitations are easy to have. Just carry around a mirror and you can make reproductions of anything you want. But the mirror-images will be mere imitations, like those we find in poetry (596d–e).

Yet isn't Plato himself liable to all these accusations he's laying at the door of the poets? After all, Plato never writes in anything *other* than imitation. Even Homer, as Plato admits, sometimes gives us straight narration. Plato doesn't even do that—if there is narration in the dialogues it's because a character is narrating and hence imitating a previous conversation. Indeed, Socrates narrates the whole *Republic* in this way. In dialogue after dialogue Plato imitates specific historical people by making them characters, and he certainly shows us people behaving badly—just think of Callicles in the *Gorgias* or Thrasymachus in the *Republic* itself. Why isn't he practicing what he preaches? This is a difficult question, but here are two thoughts.

First, remember that Plato isn't writing literature for an audience in the ideal society, or for children. He's aiming his dialogues at readers who are intimately familiar with the poetry that he is attacking. Shielding these readers from the insidious influence of the poets is no longer an option. Rather, Plato must try to counteract that influence, and he is not above fighting fire with fire. Thus he imitates vicious characters as well as good ones, giving voice to Callicles as well as Socrates. A second, related point is this: because we are not children, Plato wants and expects us to reflect on what we are reading. We are not just going to imitate any of these characters mindlessly, because the dialogues so obviously demand that we think about which characters are really worth emulating. Will we adopt the virtuous life recommended by Socrates or the vicious one praised by Callicles? No one can read the *Gorgias* without being forced to reflect on this choice. In writing the dialogues, then, Plato was writing literature that would have an effect opposite to that of Greek theater, at least as he saw it. The dialogues demand active engagement rather than passivity, rational reflection rather than unleashed emotion.

But if that's how we should explain Plato's use of imitation, how will we explain his use of myth? To decide, we'll obviously need to look at what he actually says in these myths. It's conspicious that three of the most prominent—the myths in the *Phaedo, Gorgias,* and *Republic*—all have to do with our fate in the afterlife. In each case we are told that, after the death of their bodies, souls are sorted out into two groups. One group is rewarded for virtue by going to a higher, more beautiful realm, while the other group is sent down into the depths and experiences torment commensurate with their vice. Take the *Phaedo* first. At the end of this dialogue Plato has Socrates spend his last minutes of life telling his friends that they are in fact living in a kind of hollow space, clustered around the Mediterranean Sea like frogs around the edge of a pond (109a–b). In fact all humans in this life live in lower realms, below the blessed altitudes reached by those who are rewarded in the afterlife. That's where you want to wind up after you die, but it isn't the only possible destination. Below the quite literally depressed region where we live our bodily existence, there is an underworld which is described in some detail, full of underground rivers and lakes. This is where all but the most virtuous souls wind up. The run-of-the-mill wrong-doers are punished on the banks of a lake fed by the river Acheron, but the more evil souls are thrown into Tartarus, and some never escape (112e–114c).

For a more detailed vision of the frightening prospects that await vicious souls in the afterlife we can turn to the closing myth of the *Gorgias*. As in the *Phaedo*, souls are dispatched to different fates depending on their behavior in their earthly life (523a–b). Each soul stands before a judge, and stands naked—more than naked, in fact, since the soul has been stripped even of the body (523e). Socrates, who relates the myth, points out that in our earthly life people can mislead their judges with fine appearance, fancy clothes, and beautiful bodies. In the afterlife, though, the judges will see us as we really are, with our souls bearing the marks of every evil we have committed (523c–d). As you might remember, this dialogue, the *Gorgias*, offers a sustained criticism of Gorgias and other sophists who used rhetoric in the law-courts, and it seems clear that this is a final put-down being woven into the myth. As in the *Phaedo*, the *Gorgias* myth envisions two possibilities in the afterlife. Those of us who have lived well will go to a kind of paradise, the so-called "Isles of the Blessed," while sinners are again dispatched to Tartarus to experience appropriate punishments (523b).

The myths of the *Phaedo* and *Gorgias* are powerfully written and provide a climax for their respective dialogues. But some philosophically-minded readers—the ones who don't just skip the myths entirely—might find the myths disturbing. Not because of the message being delivered, which is the same message as Socrates' philosophical arguments, that we should devote our lives to virtue. The disturbing thing is that the myths give us the wrong kind of reason to devote our lives to virtue. Should we really be virtuous just to avoid being tortured in Tartarus? In the *Gorgias* Socrates has been arguing strenuously that virtue is its own reward, and vice its own punishment. He's shown that it is *bad for us* to engage in vice, whether or not we are punished for our vice in the conventional sense. Even if he gets away with his crimes, the tyrant is already the most miserable creature on this earth. Isn't it a failure of nerve on Plato's part to insist that the tyrant must be the most miserable creature in the afterlife as well? It's almost as if he doesn't have the courage of his convictions, or expects his readers to fail in *their* courage.

This problem appears again, and more explicitly, in the *Republic*. As you'll remember, this masterpiece of Plato is devoted to showing that justice is advantageous and hence choiceworthy. Justice is the harmony of the soul, thanks to its parts working together as they should. So, like the *Gorgias*, the *Republic* contends that the virtuous man is happiest of all men, even if he lacks honor and pleasure, whereas the vicious tyrant is the unhappiest of all men, because his soul is wicked and imbalanced. After nine books' worth of argument to this effect, Plato again concludes the dialogue with a myth of the afterlife, the most detailed yet. It's called the Myth of Er, because the main character in the myth is a man named Er—I guess his family was known for hesitating. Er was killed in a war and, when he was just about to be buried, miraculously woke up, telling of the afterlife as he had just been able to see it.

According to Socrates, Er saw two sets of gates, each with an exit and entrance. One set leads to the heavens, the others to the underworld (614c–d). As in the other myths, those who are virtuous are allowed to go up into a kind of paradise, while the vicious are damned to many years of captivity below. The worst miscreants never return to this world, but are tormented forever (615c–d). But all other souls return back through the exits from heaven and the underworld. They then go on a journey and are granted a vision of the entire cosmos, a set of nested balls rotating on an axis, like the spindle of a spinning-wheel (616c–617d). The three divine Fates are present, and enforce a kind of lottery for choosing the souls' next lives on earth. Each soul is randomly assigned a lot, like the number you get when you're waiting for service at a store. This determines the order in which the souls will choose their next lives.

The choice is a momentous one. Er sees the first soul eagerly snatch up the life of a powerful tyrant, only to discover that this tyrant will wind up eating his children (619b–c). He sees certain mythical figures choose more carefully. Odysseus, the hero of the *Odyssey*, draws the lot which means he will choose last, but is content with the life he finds available, a quiet life with no trouble (620c–d). Some souls choose to return as animals, others as men. Alarmingly, it would seem that the broad outlines of your life—for instance, whether you will eat your own kids—are already settled by this choice of lives. Thus one reason to pursue philosophy in this present life is that we will choose wisely when the next opportunity comes. It's stressed that, since our fates stem from this original choice of lives, the gods are not to blame if our lives are poorly selected (617e). As it says in the myth, "virtue has no master," and the virtuous soul will make the right choice.

So that's the Myth of Er—my favorite Platonic myth, actually. But it does potentially raise the same objection as the *Gorgias* myth. Why is Plato suddenly telling us to be good ... or else? Instead of telling us that we should be good, quite literally, for goodness' sake—because it is better, more advantageous, for us to be good than to be bad? Such worries were already expressed in the ancient world. An Epicurean philosopher named Colotes accused Plato of hypocrisy, on the basis that in the *Republic*, after having criticized the poets for their use of myths, Plato went on to offer his own myth for the sake of frightening the reader into adopting more virtuous ways.[2] Can this sort of objection be overcome?

Well, remember that in all these dialogues the myth comes at the end. In the *Republic*, Socrates explicitly says that virtue is its own reward, but that *in addition to this* we should expect things to go well for the virtuous man, usually even in this life and certainly in the next. So the myths add something, even for someone convinced of Socrates' philosophical arguments. They reassure us that even if virtue is its own reward, it's not the only reward we can expect. It's also worth dwelling on the insistence, in the Myth of Er, that the gods are not to blame for whatever happens to the souls when they are born again. The same could be said of the punishments undergone in the afterlife, which are just requital for sins committed in the souls' previous lives. It may be that all three myths of the afterlife are intended not so much to frighten us into virtue as to show that the universe is not so unjust as it may seem. Divine justice ensures that everyone gets what they deserve, above and beyond the fact that vice is already a kind of punishment.

This takes us back to more general charge of hypocrisy—that Plato criticizes the use of myth and then writes myths of his own. If the message of the myths is in part that the gods are just, then their lesson is the opposite of that found in the poetry banned in the ideal city. Plato attacks the poets not just for using myth, but for using myth as a vehicle for falsehood rather than truth. By writing his own myths, which teach true beliefs about how to live and about the gods, Plato would in effect be saying to Homer and Hesiod: "This, my friends, is how you do it." I should hasten to add, though, that the various myths may have various purposes, just as Plato exploits the dialogue form differently in different dialogues. For instance, some of the myths—like those of the *Phaedo* and *Republic*—combine a vision of how the earth or cosmos is constructed with a vision of how the gods have arranged things to encourage virtue. Here we should recall the *Timaeus*, which as we saw compares the rightly-ordered city to the rightly-ordered universe, described in the long speech of Timaeus which is explicitly labeled as a myth.

That may be a good note on which to leave Plato, as we see him at the height of his ambition. In the Myth of Er and the *Timaeus* he combines an interest in justice and virtue with an interest in the cosmos and in science; he combines philosophical teaching and argument with the literary power of myth; in short, he does it all. It's not for nothing that Whitehead described the entire history of philosophy as a set of footnotes to Plato. After him, what else remained to be done? Well, according to at least one student of Plato's, there was still room for improvement. This student would turn out to be a philosopher who can rival Plato's claim to be the greatest thinker of antiquity, if not of all time. His ideas will be not merely influential, but the basis of all philosophy and science for most of the next two millenia. Let the footnotes begin.

PART III
ARISTOTLE

29

MR KNOW IT ALL
ARISTOTLE'S LIFE AND WORKS

In 2005 the BBC conducted a poll in which people were invited to vote for the greatest philosopher of all time. About 30,000 people voted, and the eventual winner was Karl Marx. (Yeah, I know.) Anyway, while this was going on I mentioned it to a colleague of mine, who is also a historian of philosophy. He said, "What a strange idea!" I asked him why he thought it was strange and, after a moment's consideration, he said, "Well, to begin with, the answer is so obviously Aristotle.' I pointed out that the poll wasn't to name the most *influential* philosopher of all time, but the *greatest* philosopher of all time. He said, "Oh, I see. But ... still, the answer is so obviously Aristotle!"

That conversation is a telling one, I think. It's not so much that my colleague was a partisan of Aristotle—who, in case you're wondering, only came ninth in the poll. It's more my initial reaction to his puzzlement. Greatest philosopher of all time? That's a matter of taste. But most influential philosopher of all time? At least in the Western tradition, there's a clear victor in the race for this title: Aristotle. Although his works did not dominate the philosophical scene in the centuries immediately following his death, once they caught on, they caught on in a big way. For well over a thousand years Aristotle was not just the most widely read and significant philosopher. He *was* philosophy, in the sense that the study of philosophy was often simply the study of Aristotle's works. In medieval times it was possible simply to say "the Philosopher," and everyone would know who you meant. Only after the Renaissance would Aristotle's total dominance of philosophy and science be questioned, and even since then Aristotle has never gone away. Current views in contemporary metaphysics and, especially, ethics, are explicitly presented as expansions on Aristotle's ideas.

Because Aristotle's works were seen as definitive of philosophy, the areas he saw fit to explore became the chief philosophical disciplines in Western thought. And he saw fit to explore an amazingly wide range of areas. Until quite recently, people used the word "philosophy" to cover a much broader range of disciplines and topics than we nowadays have in mind when we say "philosophy." Study of the world we see around us could be called "natural philosophy" well into the modern period. So for Aristotle and his heirs, "philosophy" would include topics like cosmology, chemistry, and biology, just as much as it includes ethics, epistemology, and metaphysics. And here's the thing: Aristotle was, more often than not, the very first person to write a work explicitly dedicated to each of these areas. The Pre-Socratics and Plato certainly touched on many of the topics taken up by Aristotle. But Aristotle dominated the Western tradition in part because he produced works that focused explicitly on separate, more or less well-defined disciplines. What Aristotle left to his successors was not just a bunch of ideas and arguments, but a curriculum of study. Even today, many departments at a typical university will have names which correspond to titles or topics of books by Aristotle: "Physics," "Psychology," "Zoology," "Literature," "Politics."

But what about that remark of Whitehead, that the history of philosophy is a set of footnotes to Plato? Certainly, Plato is the one thinker who could rival Aristotle for the claim of most influential philosopher. But Plato's claim would depend heavily on the indirect influence he exercised through his greatest student. Aristotle came to study at Plato's Academy as a young man. Born in 384 BC, he hailed from a town called Stagira, which is situated in north-eastern Greece in an area called Chalkidike. (This is why you may sometimes see Aristotle called "the Stagirite.") His father, Nicomachus, was a doctor at the royal court of Macedon. Although Aristotle is not thought of as a medical thinker, he certainly inherited his father's scientific turn of mind, and contributed greatly to the history of medicine as well as the history of philosophy. Aristotle eventually had a son who was also named Nicomachus—hence the title of one of Aristotle's best-known works, the *Nicomachean Ethics*.

He came to Athens at the age of seventeen, where he had the chance to study with Plato. I'll be talking a bit more about the Academy at the end of this book, when we reach Plato's and Aristotle's students. For now, suffice to say that Aristotle would have had a rigorous training in dialectical analysis and argument at Plato's feet, training which he would in due course use against the master. Diogenes Laertius, as always a source of entertaining but presumably fallacious details, tells us that Plato said of Aristotle: "He kicked us away, the way ponies do to their mothers upon being born."[1] In one of Aristotle's own works, he excuses himself for attacking Platonic theories with the famous remark that we must honor truth above our friends (*Nicomachean Ethics* 1096a). But as we'll be seeing in some detail, the relationship between Aristotelian and Platonic philosophy is a complicated and subtle one. Certainly Aristotle was no more a slavish follower of Plato than Plato had been a slavish follower of his own teacher, Socrates. But he was at the Academy for some twenty years, so that there was more than enough opportunity for him to ingest and consider the ideas of Plato and other colleagues in Athens. It would be better to think of him as self-consciously and critically engaging with Plato, rather than simply setting out to reject or attack him.

After Plato's death in 347, Aristotle traveled with one of those colleagues, Xenocrates, as the guest of a ruler in Asia Minor named Hermias. He later traveled to the island of Lesbos, where he encountered another philosopher and colleague, Theophrastus. With all due respect to Theophrastus, he was not Aristotle's greatest student. Any BBC poll would award that prize to a young man who was educated by Aristotle soon after the stay in Lesbos: a young man who would later be known as Alexander the Great. Alexander is to the history of conquering what Aristotle is to the history of philosophy. His armies not only swept through mainland Greece, but also eastwards through Persia and ultimately as far as India. Alexander subjugated the entire known world, and then kept going. He was revered as a god and set the standard for imperial rulers of the future, so that no less a figure than Augustus Caesar was eager to invite comparison with Alexander. And he managed all that despite living only until the age of thirty-two. This just goes to show you what you can accomplish if you have the right philosophy teacher. Of course, I'm no Aristotle, so reading this book will not necessarily enable you to conquer the known world and beyond. But if you read the book cover to cover, you might be ready to tackle a small town.

In any case, Aristotle finally came back to Athens in 335 BC, at which point he set up a rival school, the Lyceum. Diogenes preserves an ancient account that Aristotle was annoyed to be passed over as head of the Academy, in favor of his old traveling companion Xenocrates.[2] But whatever his reasons, the Lyceum became a second center of learning. Supposedly philosophical discussions would take place while walking back and forth, which gave rise to the nickname of Aristotle's school: the "Peripatetics," that is, those who walk around. If you read about the history of ancient and medieval thought you'll come across this expression, "Peripatetic." It simply means whatever has to do with Aristotle's teaching and the tradition of his followers. After all that walking around, Aristotle had a chance to do some running, when feelings of anger flared up against Macedon in Athens, subsequent to Alexander's death in 323 BC. Another famous story claims that Aristotle said he was leaving to stop Athens from once again sinning against philosophy—referring, of course, to the execution of Socrates.[3] After this flight from Athens he relocated to the island of Euboia, where he died in 322 BC. Ancient sources fancifully suggest that he may have killed himself by poison—thus imitating Socrates' swan-song after all. I quite like one wildly implausible variation on this story found in the ancient sources, namely that his suicide was prompted by despair after he was unable to understand why the tide rises and falls.

So much for Aristotle's life. Now for his works. Diogenes and several other authors preserve lists of his books, and these show that a great deal has been lost. To give only one example, Aristotle and his students compiled no fewer than 158 political constitutions, in order to study all the ways that cities can be run. Of these only the *Constitution of Athens* has survived. So Aristotle's surviving corpus—despite its considerable size—represents only a fraction of what he originally wrote. Indeed, it would seem that our remaining corpus is one-sided. Aristotle apparently wrote two kinds of works. On the one hand, there were so-called "exoteric" writings. Aristotle refers to these himself (for instance at *Politics* 1278b), so there is no doubt that they existed. What they were like and what they contained is a bit more mysterious. Ancient authors remark that Aristotle wrote very stylishly, and this, as you will know if you've read them, doesn't exactly seem an apt description of the existing writings. The lost exoteric writings, which were for a wider circulation, apparently imitated Plato by fusing literary art with philosophical insight.

But apart from fragments, what remains to us are the so-called "esoteric" writings. These are not esoteric in the sense that they contain some kind of obscure or secret teaching—Aristotle can be obscure, but it's not because he's trying to hide the truth from the reader (despite later ancient claims to the contrary[4]). Rather, the esoteric works were apparently intended to be read in a school setting instead of being for public distribution. The obscurity of the texts may be partially explained by this fact. If these works were for Aristotle's students, he may have been able to take a good deal for granted. It's even been suggested that the works as we have them now are actually nothing more than lecture notes, which Aristotle would expand into proper discourses when he taught. Although this is a fairly common assumption about Aristotle's writings, I don't find it satisfactory. For all their density and allusiveness, Aristotle's writings are often carefully constructed. This is true not only of the structure of whole works or individual books within a work, but also at the level of individual paragraphs and sentences. Furthermore, some of Aristotle's writings are much more clipped and concise than others. Whereas parts of his *Metaphysics* are so dense that they can scarcely be understood at all, a work like the *Nicomachean Ethics* is a comparatively good read. I find the "lecture note" theory insufficient to capture the variation and craft of Aristotle's extant writings, although the works must have been tied to a pedagogical setting.

I've just mentioned two of Aristotle's more famous works: the *Ethics* and the *Metaphysics*. Alongside his treatise *On the Soul*, his *Physics*, his *Politics*, and his logical treatises, these would constitute the Aristotelian writings that are most commonly studied in philosophy courses around the world. They will form the main focus of my treatment of Aristotle in this book. But I will also be looking at some other treatises of Aristotle that aren't usually included in philosophical overviews: for instance, I'll tackle Aristotle's biological works, by which I mean the several texts he devoted to the subject of animals. I'll look beyond Aristotle's *Physics* in considering his understanding of the natural world, and this will take us to treatises like *On the Heavens*. And I'll even touch on Aristotle's literary theory, as expressed in another of his most influential writings, the *Poetics*.

Again, it's worth emphasizing that most of these works are the very first treatises devoted to whatever subject they take up. The exception is his *Physics*: the Pre-Socratics tended to call their books *Peri Phuseos*: "On Nature," and Aristotle's work follows in this tradition.[5] But even here, Aristotle was the first to say explicitly what it means to do physics or natural philosophy, and the first explicitly to distinguish this discipline from other branches of philosophy. We can say the same about other disciplines: *On the Soul* is the first systematic discussion of the soul's nature, the *Politics* the first systematic discussion of political philosophy, the animal works the first systematic discussion of zoology, and so on. Of course Plato too had dealt with such topics—the *Republic* covers the soul, politics, and literature for instance. But Plato wove those various themes together in his dialogues. The later tradition found Aristotle's explicitly thematic treatises—with the topic conveniently identified in the titles—a more useful basis for formulating a philosophical curriculum.

Because Aristotle likes to identify his subject matter and deal with it systematically, it's easy to assume that reading him will be fairly straightforward. Whereas Plato gives us the interplay of characters, Aristotle speaks to us in his own voice. And in these esoteric works, at least, literary flair seldom gets in the way of the relentless march of distinctions and arguments. In this sense Aristotle can seem to be the first person to write philosophy as it is now frequently written: a methodical investigation into the topic at hand, prizing clarity and precision. But as it turns out, Aristotle's works call for delicate exegesis no less than Plato's dialogues do. Part of the reason is that, as I have mentioned, his exposition can be compressed and dense. But there is a deeper and more interesting reason, which can be summed up in a single word: dialectic.

As so often, this word comes to us from ancient Greek. Plato uses the term *dialektike* as having a rather exalted meaning. In his dialogue the *Sophist* he uses "dialectic" for the study of how the Forms interrelate (253d–e). And in the *Republic* it is associated with the higher segments of the divided line (511b). One might, without too much oversimplification, suggest that for Plato "dialectic" is simply the process by which philosophers achieve knowledge. Aristotle gives the term "dialectic" a different sense. For him, dialectic is simply argument that proceeds from agreed premises. For instance, suppose you and I are arguing about who was the greatest silent-film comedian. I ask you to agree that Buster Keaton's *The General* is the greatest ever silent comedy. You concede the point, and on the strength of this, I lead you to see that, as the maker of this film, Keaton must be the greatest silent comedian. But my argument is only as strong as its initial premise. If you disagree about *The General*, and insist that Chaplin's *The Kid* is even better, my argument will be ineffective.

If you think about it, nearly all argumentative discussion works like this: a topic for debate is identified, and the parties to the discussion try to find some point of agreement as a basis for further argument. If no point of agreement is found, then no argument is possible. Arguing without agreed premises isn't rational disputation, it's just posturing and shouting—I refer you to the political debating shows one sees on television nowadays. Because he had a deep interest in the practice of rational debate, Aristotle tried to formalize the rules and strategies of such debate in a work we call the *Topics*. He calls the practice "dialectic." In the *Topics*, Aristotle explains that dialectic can be of immense use in philosophy. Just like any other rational discussion, philosophical inquiry needs to proceed on the basis of some agreed initial premises. Aristotle suggests that the premises we should adopt as starting points in philosophy are the views that are either widely accepted or accepted by "the wise"—by which he means earlier philosophical thinkers, poets, and other authorities. He calls these views *endoxa*—which we might translate as "reputable opinions" (*Topics* 100a–b).

True to his word, Aristotle usually writes dialectically. Especially characteristic is his habit of starting out a work by appealing to a range of *endoxa*. For instance, the first book of his work *On the Soul* begins by surveying previous opinions about the soul; the first book of the *Physics* begins by surveying previous opinions about nature and its principles. This is why, as I mentioned at the start of this book, Aristotle is such a rich source of information about the Pre-Socratics. It is disconcerting to notice that Aristotle lumps Plato in together with the Pre-Socratics, as if he was just one more earlier philosopher, without giving him due credit for making a quantum leap ahead in the history of philosophy. It's clear from these endoxic surveys that for Aristotle, the history of Greek philosophy looks like this: there are the Pre-Aristotelians, who include Plato, and then there is Aristotle. Aristotle presents himself as the man to sort out all the issues the Pre-Aristotelians spoke about.

Towards this end, he finds it especially useful to discover *endoxa* that clash with one another, so that he can weigh up their relative merits and see in what sense they might be true. He doesn't necessarily assume that the *endoxa* are true—when he mentions Parmenides in the *Physics* (186a–187a), he doesn't go on to say that in a sense Parmenides was right to deny the existence of motion. But usually he finds that reputable opinions are a good stab at the truth. They are true in a way, or from a certain point of view, but they don't capture the truth in a rigorous and perspicuous fashion. All this can make it a complex business to read Aristotle. He is usually contrasting various opinions and considering their merits, speaking first on one side of a question, then on another side, and sometimes on yet another side. Aristotle's own answer to any question tends to be "in a way yes, in a way no." He loves to present his own ideas as compromises between more extreme views. Thus Aristotle's works, despite their lack of dramatic setting and literary style, do retain something of the flavor of Platonic dialogues. We are shown a clash of views, with Aristotle remaining tantalizingly out of sight, a referee who may get involved at any moment to decide the issue, but who wants to let each side have its chance to speak.

Among the things Aristotle learned from Plato, then, was a fascination with philosophical method. But he went beyond Plato in one respect, by making philosophical argumentation an object of explicit study in its own right. I've just mentioned the *Topics*, where Aristotle does not just show us dialectical discussions, as Plato did, but actually explores the nature of dialectic. This is only one of numerous works that Aristotle devoted to the rules of engagement in philosophical, and non-philosophical, argument. It was in the context of these works that he made one of his many lasting contributions to the history of philosophy, which we'll be looking at in the next chapter. To put it bluntly: Aristotle invented logic. We now take it for granted that philosophy involves, and even presupposes, logic. On the strength of this invention alone, Aristotle really deserves to finish higher than ninth place in the list of all-time greats.

30

THE PHILOSOPHER'S TOOLKIT
ARISTOTLE'S LOGICAL WORKS

A few chapters back, I asked you to imagine that you were a medieval monk, reading Plato's *Timaeus*. That was good practice for what I'd like you to do now: imagine instead that you're a fifth-century AD student of philosophy. You have come to the great center of learning that is the city of Alexandria in Egypt. (Don't forget to visit the lighthouse, I hear it's wonderful.) You already have a good education under your belt—you are literate, and have studied some rhetoric—and now you are going to try to master philosophy. What's the first thing you will study? Of course it will be Aristotle. In late antiquity even Platonists introduced their students to philosophy through Aristotle, saving Plato's texts for more advanced research. But which book will you begin with? Nowadays a course on Aristotle might start with his ethics, or his physics. But as a late ancient student, you will be taught that there is only one place to begin doing philosophy: logic. In fact, you will spend quite a while digesting Aristotle's logical works—many students will never progress any further into more advanced topics.

The designers of the late ancient curriculum were onto something when they prescribed a foundation in logic for their students. Logic deals with the rules of rational argument, and obviously philosophy is nothing if not a kind of rational argument. So there is good reason to think that the study of logic is fundamental to the study of philosophy as a whole. But your late antique philosophy professor will also be teaching you that logic is not, strictly speaking, a "part" of philosophy. Only the foolish Stoics would call it that. As well-trained Aristotelians, you will be considering logic instead as an "instrument" for philosophy, a tool which is deployed in the various disciplines that really are parts of philosophy, like physics, ethics, and metaphysics. For this reason, you refer to Aristotle's works on logic collectively as the *Organon*—a Greek word which means "tool" or "instrument."

In late antiquity the *Organon* was seen as including no fewer than eight works, namely *Categories, On Interpretation, Prior Analytics, Posterior Analytics, Topics, Sophistical*

Refutations, and to top it off the *Rhetoric* and the *Poetics*. Nowadays we find it strange to think of the *Rhetoric* or *Poetics* as works on logic—they seem to have been tossed in for lack of anywhere better to place them in the Aristotelian system. So for us Aristotle's logical writings—still sometimes called the *Organon*—would at most be the other six works. But thinking of all these works as "logical" would mean taking a very broad view of logic. Take the *Topics*, which I just discussed in the last chapter. It doesn't deal with logic as we understand it, but rather with the rules of dialectical debate, where premises are assumed for the sake of argument or because they are acceptable for some other reason. As for the *Sophistical Refutations*, you might guess from its title what goes on there: Aristotle uncovers the tricks and ambiguities used by the sophists to produce misleading arguments. This is, one might say, the study of anti-logic—the study of intentionally bad arguments, like the ones displayed in Plato's *Euthydemus*.

That leaves us with four "more logical" works by Aristotle, the ones I will be discussing in this and the next chapter: the *Categories*, *On Interpretation*, *Prior Analytics*, and *Posterior Analytics*. So are these the works where he actually discusses logic? Well, not really. It is only the *Prior Analytics* that deals with logic in something like our sense, by analyzing the forms of arguments separate from their content. For instance, it's in this work that Aristotle will discuss the fact that it is legitimate to argue from "Every A is B" and "Every B is C" to the conclusion "Every A is C." Yet ancient students of logic did not plunge right into the argumentative analysis of the *Prior Analytics*; they started with the *Categories*. What is it about? That turns out to be a difficult and much-discussed question. Let's start with the title. It relates to the Greek verb *kategorein*, which can mean "to blame" or "to accuse," but which Aristotle uses with the meaning "to predicate," that is, "to say one thing about another thing." So on the face of it it looks like the *Categories* might be about things that can be said about, or ascribed to, other things. That's still a bit vague, but does seem to fit the content of this work reasonably well. What we get first is a few short chapters making points about words that are predicated—for instance, the difference between synonyms and homonyms. The second chapter makes a fundamental distinction between two kinds of predicates, one of the most important distinctions in Aristotle in fact. The distinction is between what is "said of" something and what is present "in" it (1a–1b). That's how Aristotle puts the point here, but the usual way of putting the contrast is to say that some features of things are essential, and others accidental.

A feature or predicate is "said of" something, or essential to that thing, if it has to do with the very nature of the thing in question. For instance, it is essential to a giraffe to be an animal, to be a ruminant, and to have any other features that are required for membership in the exclusive club that is the species of giraffe. All other features are accidental, or present "in" things. So, for instance, if the giraffe is painted blue, blueness is accidental to it or present in it. If the giraffe is a particularly fine example of its species, then its glossy coat and unusually erect posture will also be accidental to it, because it could get sick, lose the gloss and the good posture, but still be a giraffe. In fact, this is a test you can use to decide whether Aristotle would count a given feature or predicate as being essential or accidental: if you can change a feature of something without destroying that thing, then the feature must be accidental.

After these preliminaries, the Categories gets on to the task it is most famous for: it gives a list of ten so-called "categories," which here means "types of things that can be predicated." There are ten: substance, quality, quantity, relation, place, time, position, state, action, and being-acted-on (1b–2a). What exactly is this list listing? Maybe something like this: if you think about all the features that can be predicated of something, you'll see that they will fall into these ten types. Consider our friend the silent-film comedian Buster Keaton. Firstly, he is a human; that's a predication in the category of substance, because it tells you what sort of thing he is. All his essential features will arise from his being this sort of substance, and the only way he can lose these essential features is to stop being a human, in other words, to die— which, I'm sad to report, Buster Keaton did do in 1966. It was only then that he stopped being, for instance, alive, rational, embodied, and so on—these were the features that were essential to him. But Buster had lots of features that are not essential. For instance his feet were big, and that's an accidental feature which falls under the category of quantity. He was silent, which falls under quality. He lived in California, which falls under place. He made films—that's the category of action. In these films he got smacked in the face and thrown out of windows—that would very much be in the category of being-acted-on.

This whole project of classifying predicates into ten classes is not necessarily something Aristotle thought up on his own. Scholars believe that it originated in the context of Plato's Academy, where Aristotle studied for many years. You can imagine how this might have gone—they'd send a student to the front of the class, tell him to stop fidgeting, and everyone else would call out words that described him, which would be divided up into classes. They wanted to make sure that they had a category for every predicate they could think of. Obviously I'm pretty much making this up, except that we do know that the Academy was mad about classification and logical exercises of this sort. I can't resist mentioning here the famous anecdote about another philosopher, Diogenes the Cynic. Upon hearing the Academy's definition of man as "two legged animal without feathers," Diogenes showed up with a plucked chicken and said, "Here is Plato's man."

I'm tempted to make a joke of my own here, maybe something about this leaving Plato in a fowl mood. But I think it would be better to go back to Aristotle's logical works. I will leave the *Categories* for now, and return to it when I come to talk about Aristotle's metaphysics, because when he is talking about the category of substance Aristotle makes a number of points that bear on metaphysics. Indeed, even some ancient readers found it problematic to label the *Categories* as dealing only with logic or language, since it does have this metaphysical content as well.[1] Of course, it's no surprise that Aristotle would make some metaphysical remarks while discussing substance, and in general he seems happy to make wide-ranging points about each of the categories. He says especially interesting things about the category of relation, and we will return to that subject down the line—for instance, when we talk in a future volume about the innovative theories of relation developed in medieval philosophy.

For now, though, we've got three more logical works to cover. Next we'll tackle *On Interpretation*. Again, this does not quite seem to be a work on "logic" in our sense. Rather, it looks more like a contribution to the philosophy of language. As we saw, this is an area Plato explored in his dialogue the *Cratylus*, which considered whether words have significance by nature or convention. Aristotle flatly declares at the beginning of *On Interpretation* that the conventionalist answer is correct (16a). Names are conventional symbols, and Aristotle says something interesting about what they symbolize. You might think the sound "Buster Keaton" would simply represent Buster Keaton, and it does; but in the first instance Aristotle thinks it represents a thought in my soul. He says that this thought is one link in a chain of representation: if I write down a word, that represents the word as spoken, so that verbal language is more fundamental than written language. The spoken name in turn represents the thought. And it is the thought which represents the thing out in the world (16a). All this will, again, inspire some innovative philosophy in the medieval period.[2]

But Aristotle is only warming up to his main theme, which is the study of sentences that assert or deny something. For instance, I might assert that Buster Keaton is human, or deny that Buster Keaton is a giraffe. This is a point that does have clear relevance for logic, especially Aristotle's logic—his logic is sometimes called "categorial" because he is always focusing on statements that relate a predicate to a subject (remember the verb *kategorein* means "to predicate"). He makes another distinction that will be crucial down the line, when he states that some predications are universal, and others are particular (17a). So I could say, "*all* humans are rational," or I could focus on only one particular human and say, "Buster Keaton is rational." Aristotle uses this distinction to look at the question of which sentences are directly opposed to which. He says that one statement is contradictory of another if it is an exact negation of it. As he points out, it's a matter of some subtlety to determine the exact contradictory of a statement. For instance, the contradictory of "all humans are white" is not "all humans are not white," but rather "some human is not white" (17b).

The reason this is important and useful is that for every pair of contradictories, one and only one can be true. So in the example I just gave, either there is at least one non-white human, or all humans are white—it *has* to be one or another. (Perhaps you might worry, "What if there are no humans?" I'll be dealing with that question in the next chapter, so in the meantime I have to ask you to be patient and assume for now that there are in fact humans. To be honest, if all of a sudden there are no humans, then the logical issue will be the least of our problems.) Aristotle's point about contradictory statements leads him to the most famous part of *On Interpretation*: chapter 9. He's told us that for any pair of contradictory statements, one will be true and the other false (18a). But this raises a problem: what if the statements we're considering are about the future? To take Aristotle's example, what if I say, "There will be a sea battle tomorrow"? This has a contradictory, namely "There will not be a sea battle tomorrow." According to Aristotle's rule, one of these is true and the other false (18a).

Suppose, then, that it's true that there will be a sea battle tomorrow. In that case, worries Aristotle, it is already fixed or settled that the sea battle will occur. It looks like it is too late for anyone to do anything about it. The admirals may confer about strategy, consult the weather forecasts, and so on, all the while thinking it is not yet decided. But in fact it must already be *inevitable* that there will be a sea battle, because the statement that "there will be a sea battle" is already true! Meanwhile, if the statement is now false, then there will be no sea battle, regardless of what preparations or arguments are made. Aristotle finds this troubling, warning that if the argument is right, there will be no point in deliberating about any course of action. The future is already written, as it were—everything that happens, happens necessarily (18b). The good news is that Aristotle offers a solution to the problem (19a–b). The bad news is that it's rather unclear what his solution is meant to be.[3] On the most popular interpretation (sometimes called the "traditional interpretation"), he says that these statements about the future are in fact neither true nor false, so he makes an exception to his rule about contradictories in this one case. But there is reason to find that unsatisfying. If we're surveying the wrecked ships in the Thames Estuary tomorrow and you turn to me and say, "See, I told you there'd be a sea battle," it would be implausible for me to say, "No, you weren't right, because when you said that it wasn't true, at least, not yet."

That is the most famous part of *On Interpretation*, and it clearly relates to what we think of as logic. But as I've said, the core of Aristotle's logic is presented in the *Prior*

Analytics. The ancient interpreters saw these texts as forming a sequence: the *Categories* would talk about individual terms, the words that would fall into the ten categories; then *On Interpretation* talks about words put together into statements; now the *Prior Analytics* will talk about sentences put together into arguments. This story is too simple, especially when it comes to the *Categories.* But it's true enough that the *Prior Analytics* studies conjunctions of sentences that form arguments. In particular, what it studies is the arguments Aristotle calls by the Greek word *sullogismos*—this, of course, is where we get our word "syllogism."

For Aristotle, a syllogism is an argument with two premises and a conclusion (24b). Of course, there has to be one term which appears in both premises, since otherwise you can't conclude anything. So a typical syllogism might go like this: all mammals are animals, some mammals are giraffes, therefore some animals are giraffes. When Aristotle tells us in the *Prior Analytics* that this kind of argument is successful, he doesn't simply use an example like the one I just gave. Instead, he uses variables. For the argument I just gave, it will go like this: All A is B, some A is C, therefore some B is C (25b). It's easy to underestimate the importance of this. For us nothing could be more natural than using letters or symbols as variables when discussing the logical form of an argument. But someone had to invent this, and the someone who invented it was Aristotle. This deceptively simple little device is arguably what enabled Aristotle to invent logic, because it allowed him to consider various argument forms abstractly, and to state rigorously how one argument can relate to another.[4]

That is just what he goes on to do in the *Prior Analytics.* But at first glance he's only handling a rather small range of arguments. He only considers these two-premise arguments he calls syllogisms, and in fact he only looks at syllogisms where one thing is being asserted or denied of another thing—again, his logic is "categorial," all about predication. So the types of premises he considers are: A is true of all B, A is true of some B, A is true of no B, and A is not true of some B. Putting in examples instead of variables: every animal is a giraffe, some animal is a giraffe, no animal is a giraffe, and some animal is not a giraffe. Aristotle then exhaustively considers all the possible ways that such premises can be combined, and proves that some will immediately produce a conclusion—these syllogisms he calls "complete" (24b). Others need further argument to show that they do produce a conclusion, while still others are unproductive.

Furthermore, Aristotle shows us that incomplete syllogisms can always be made complete by reducing them to valid cases of the "first figure syllogism" which can produce all conclusions (26b, 29a). First figure syllogisms are those where the predicate of the first premise becomes the subject of the second premise, like this:

First figure
A B
B C

And as we just saw, the As, Bs, and Cs can be linked in different ways, such as "all A is B" and "some A is not B," so that there are numerous permutations of this first figure. Here are two examples of complete first figure syllogisms:[5]

A is true of every B	A is true of no B
B is true of every C	B is true of all C
So A is true of every C	So A is true of no C

Or, with added giraffes:

"Alive" is true of every animal (i.e. Every animal is alive)
"Animal" is true of every giraffe (i.e. Every giraffe is an animal)
So "Alive" is true of every giraffe (i.e. Every giraffe is alive)

"Blue" is true of no animal (i.e. No animal is blue)
"Animal" is true of every giraffe (i.e. Every giraffe is an animal)
So "Blue" is true of no giraffe (i.e. No giraffe is blue)

Of course you can devise a first figure syllogism that is not only incomplete, but also invalid, like this:

A is true of no B
B is true of some C
So A is true of all C

Putting terms into this bad argument form we would get, for instance:

"Blue" is true of no animal (No animal is blue)
"Animal" is true of some giraffe (At least one giraffe is an animal)
So "Blue" is true of every giraffe (Every giraffe is blue)

Don't argue like that at home. Now, there are two further possible figures of the syllogism (26b, 28a):

Second figure	*Third figure*
A B	A B
A C	C B

Syllogisms in these figures can, again, be valid or invalid. But when they produce conclusions validly they do so "incompletely," which means that we need to do some reasoning to show, on the basis of the first figure syllogisms, that valid syllogisms of the second and third figures are indeed valid.

To sum all this up for those whose eyes started to glaze over about a paragraph ago: Aristotle identifies some basic, immediately productive syllogisms (the "complete" ones in the "first figure"). He then finds other cases of syllogisms that are also productive, but not immediately so ("incomplete" ones, where work needs to be done to show that they succeed). He shows how to reduce the incomplete cases to the complete cases, to prove that they do actually work. Finally, he declares all the others invalid. Aristotle's meticulous discussion of these syllogisms is one of his greatest achievements. It set the stage for more than two thousand years of logic, which would be done largely within the framework envisioned in the *Prior Analytics*. In fact it was only with Frege in the nineteenth century that logic finally departed from this Aristotelian paradigm.

Amazingly, though, that isn't the only thing Aristotle tries to do in the *Prior Analytics*. For one thing, he's conscious of something I've mentioned, which is that he seems to be looking at a rather restricted range of argument types. So he attempts to show that all productive arguments can be reduced to his syllogisms—he's not right about this, as will be pointed out by the Stoics, themselves great contributors to the history of logic. He also spends a good deal of the *Prior Analytics* discussing the fact that the premises and conclusion of an argument can be either possible or necessary. Suppose I say, "Giraffes are necessarily mammals, and all mammals nurse their young." Does that show me that giraffes *necessarily* nurse their young? Is the necessity transferred from the premises to the conclusion? This is an area where Aristotle's ideas about logic are rather different from the ideas that philosophers have today. For instance, he thought that if a statement is necessarily true, it must always be true—which seems fair enough. But he also thought that you can go the other way: if something is always true, you can infer that it is necessarily true. This isn't nearly so obvious. For instance, I don't have a sister, and in the absence of some startling news from my parents I am never going to have a sister. But is it necessarily true that I don't have a sister? It doesn't seem so. Clearly, this whole issue of necessity needs some further sorting out. And Aristotle does have more to say on the issue, as we'll see now by turning from the *Prior Analytics* to its sequel, the predictably titled *Posterior Analytics*.

31

A PRINCIPLED STAND
ARISTOTLE'S EPISTEMOLOGY

"**A**ll men by nature desire to know." This is the opening line of Aristotle's *Metaphysics*. It expresses his conviction that the thirst for knowledge is not something limited to full-time thinkers like himself. It's something we all share. But the fact that everybody wants something doesn't mean that everybody gets it. After all, most of us would like to live forever, but no one has managed that yet. (I myself hope to achieve immortality. In fact I may need to, if I'm going to cover the whole history of philosophy in these books.) Surely in the case of knowledge, though, everyone does get what they want, at least to some extent. Everybody knows quite a few things. You, for instance, know that you are reading a book right now. You know that the book is about ancient philosophy. Probably you know what you had for breakfast—and I do hope you had a good breakfast, since, as you also know, it's the most important meal of the day.

But what allows you to say that you know any of these things? What, in fact, is knowledge? As I've mentioned before, this is the core question of the area of philosophy called epistemology, the study of knowledge. Epistemology recognizes a basic distinction between knowledge and mere belief. Clearly these are different. If I know something, then it seems I must also believe it—to know you're reading a book, you must at least believe you're reading a book. But the reverse is not true. I optimistically believe that Arsenal will win the English football league next year, but sadly, I do not *know* this. If we can believe things without knowing them, then what's the difference? Well, it can't just be that knowledge involves truth, whereas belief doesn't. Admittedly, there are false beliefs—but there are also true beliefs that don't count as knowledge. If Arsenal does turn out to win the league, that won't mean that my belief was in fact knowledge. It was more like a lucky guess, or wishful thinking, or perhaps even a well-informed prediction—but not knowledge.

As we've seen, Plato was the first philosopher to distinguish clearly between knowledge and true belief. He does so in the *Meno*, the *Theaetetus*, and other dialogues, and his characters have little trouble showing that there is indeed a distinction to be made here. But it is more difficult to say what turns a belief into knowledge. The *Meno* suggests that some kind of causal account might do the trick, but fails to provide details. Some interpreters think that Plato gave up on the project in the *Republic*—that in this dialogue knowledge is seen not as true belief plus something, but instead as the grasp of a completely separate kind of object, namely the Forms. Earlier, I suggested some reasons to doubt this interpretation. But on any reading of the *Republic*, it looks as though knowledge—and in particular, knowledge of really important things like justice, the good, and so on—is reserved for a small elite. The rest of us make do with belief, while the philosophers use dialectic to achieve true knowledge.

On this issue, as on many others, Aristotle has paid close attention to Plato. In his treatment of knowledge he reacts to Plato, and finds quite a lot to agree with, even if he also openly disagrees with his master on occasion. Aristotle not only accepts the fundamental distinction between knowledge and belief. He also, like Plato, sees knowledge as a formidable accomplishment—one achieved by the elite, and only with great difficulty. His view on this matter is set out in the rather un-enticingly named *Posterior Analytics*. As you might expect, it seems to be a kind of follow-up to that pioneering work of logic, the *Prior Analytics*. Both works are complicated, and undertake a variety of projects. But if you wanted a one-sentence summary of both *Analytics*, you could do worse than to say the following. First, in the *Prior Analytics*, Aristotle explains the rules governing valid arguments. Then, in the *Posterior Analytics*, he explains which valid arguments are sufficient to provide knowledge. Okay, that was two sentences.

So the *Posterior Analytics* is, among other things, the closest thing to an Aristotelian treatise on epistemology. It asks, what are the conditions that have to be satisfied if we are to take ourselves as knowing something? The short version of Aristotle's answer is that you know something when you have demonstrated it. This immediately helps us to see what the *Posterior Analytics* has to do with the *Prior Analytics*: demonstrations are valid arguments, so we need to know the rules of argument before we can say what a demonstration is. In fact a good way to think about demonstrations, as Aristotle conceives them, is that they are the *best* kind of valid arguments. But this brings us to the long version of Aristotle's answer. Not just any old valid argument will be demonstrative, and thus provide knowledge. Aristotle thinks that a whole series of criteria need to be satisfied to achieve demonstration—like a series of boxes that need to be ticked. Looking at these criteria will take us through the rest of this chapter, and expose just how demanding Aristotle's epistemology turns out to be.

Let's first remind ourselves of what a valid argument looks like, according to Aristotle. It's going to be an argument with two premises, which have a term in common. These premises will, together, yield a conclusion. Such an argument is called a syllogism; and Aristotle thinks that all productive arguments can be reduced to certain types of syllogism. So demonstrations will definitely be syllogisms. But which ones? Aristotle's fundamental idea here is that if you are going to demonstrate something, then you need to *explain* it. Thus the syllogisms that are demonstrative will need to be explanatory. For instance, I might notice that giraffes have long necks. As a giraffe-ologist I now ask myself, "Gosh, why do giraffes have long necks?" What I'm looking for is an argument that will explain this feature of the noble animal that is the giraffe.

Obviously, what Aristotle is after is not the kind of knowledge we have when we simply notice that giraffes have long necks. He is thinking, rather, of some kind of systematic, well-founded—we might even say "scientific"—understanding of giraffes' having long necks. Indeed, it's been proposed that "understanding" would be a better translation of the Greek *episteme* than "knowledge," at least in this context.[1] This leads us, then, to the first important box that needs to be ticked: a demonstrative syllogism needs to be not only a valid argument, but also genuinely explanatory. It has to show me not just *that* the conclusion is the case, but *why* the conclusion is the case. In our example, an appropriate syllogism might be something like this: giraffes are land animals that eat leaves off tall trees. Land animals that eat leaves off tall trees have long necks. Therefore giraffes have long necks. Aristotle will point to the feature that links the two premises—he calls this the "middle term"—and say that in a demonstration, the middle term helps to explain the conclusion. Giraffes have long necks *because* they are land animals that eat leaves off tall trees.

So are we done? Will any valid argument that explains something count as a demonstration? Well, no. Aristotle adds several more criteria, and the next one I want to mention is a bit more surprising. His idea is that if we are really going to have understanding, what we are after is an explanation not of just one particular thing but of a whole class of things. Knowledge or understanding must be *universal* (85a–86a, 88b). It will have to do with general features of the world around me. This means that if I'm looking at a particular giraffe—let's say her name is Hiawatha—then it doesn't count as a demonstration if I say that Hiawatha has a long neck because she eats leaves off tall trees. This is true all right, but it isn't an example of *episteme*, that is, knowledge or understanding. Rather, if I really understand Hiawatha's having a long neck, it's because I realize that she's a giraffe, and understand that her long neck is just one instance of a universal feature that belongs to all giraffes.

This relates to something I mentioned in the previous chapter: the distinction between accidental and essential features. To remind you how this works, the essential features of something are the features the thing has by its very nature. I can't be human without being rational, so rationality is essential to me, whereas my baldness is accidental to me, because I don't need to be bald to be human. (In fact, I used to be human without being bald; but let's not get any further into that painful subject.) So a giraffe, we're supposing, can't be a giraffe without having a long neck and without eating leaves off trees; these features are essential to it. Obviously the universality criterion is relevant here: the essential features of a thing will be shared with all other members of its kind. If it is essential to Hiawatha that she has a long neck, then all other giraffes must have long necks too. So here's another box to be ticked: the premises of a demonstrative argument must mention essential features of the things that they are explaining (75a).

This point is worth dwelling on for a moment. Aristotle is claiming that there simply isn't any such thing as knowledge or understanding, in the proper sense, of accidental features, meaning features that are exceptional among a given class. If Hiawatha has a broken toe, for instance, this will not interest the Aristotelian giraffe-ologist, because in general giraffes don't have broken toes. Aristotle accordingly has a strong tendency to relegate accidental or unusual things to his list of things not to worry about very much. Insofar as we're doing science, we aren't going to concern ourselves with the accidental features of things. This makes Aristotle very different from modern-day scientists. Of course, they do look for regular laws or patterns in nature, as Aristotle recommends. But they are also interested in surprising exceptions, in events or features that threaten to falsify their general theories. By contrast, Aristotle encourages us to ignore such exceptions, and to study only the generalities of nature. If a giraffe is born without ossicones (those things like horns on its head), or with only three legs, that won't be worthy of study, it will just be ignored as unnatural.

Nonetheless, what Aristotle calls "knowledge" or "understanding" is closely related to what we call "science." (Indeed, our word "science" comes from the Latin *scientia*, which was used to translate Aristotle's term *episteme*.) Some even say that the *Posterior Analytics* is Aristotle's treatise on the philosophy of science. This makes sense given his criteria for demonstration, which focus on generality and systematicity. I have called it a work on "epistemology" more generally, but really there's not much difference between Aristotelian epistemology and Aristotelian philosophy of science. One should bear in mind, though, that he uses the word *episteme* not just for biology and so on, but also for disciplines like mathematics and even metaphysics. For him, all of these are "sciences," that is, types of knowledge. It is in this broader sense that the *Posterior Analytics* sets out a scientific program. According to the program, science gets hold of explanations, which are universal and are based on the essential features of things. If Aristotle's criteria are demanding, it is because he is telling us how to achieve full understanding of the world around us—how to become scientists, if you will.

But he's still not done. Go back to the fact that you can only know something if it is true. Aristotle draws a rather surprising conclusion from this simple observation. He says that if the things I know cannot be false, then they are *necessarily true* (88b–89a). When I demonstrate something, not only will I have premises and a conclusion which deal with universal and essential features of things, but I will have premises and conclusions that are guaranteed always to be true. Thus I can know, or understand, why giraffes have long necks, because giraffes must necessarily have long necks—a giraffe with a short neck is impossible—and because it's always the case that giraffes have long necks. The first part there stands to reason: if long necks are an essential feature of giraffes, then of course a giraffe can't have a short neck, because if it does it won't be a giraffe anymore. But we're not likely to agree with the "always" part, because we don't think that giraffes have always existed. We think they evolved, so that once upon a time the world had to struggle along without giraffes. Even more depressingly, we anticipate that one day giraffes will be extinct. Aristotle will have none of this. For him, all species are eternal. They'd better be, because all knowledge is of eternal truths, so if giraffes didn't always exist there could be no demonstrative knowledge of them.

Couldn't we try saying something slightly different here? We could say: "Bad news, Aristotle, you're wrong about giraffes always existing. But here's something that's always true: *if* something is a giraffe, then it has a long neck." That could be true even when there are no giraffes. Aristotle might be grateful for the suggestion, but it isn't how he thinks about the situation. In his logic, it seems to be assumed that "B is true of A" can only be true if there is at least one A. So a statement like "giraffes have long necks" will, for him, be false if there are no giraffes.[2] He doesn't explore the strategy I just suggested, which might be more to the taste of a modern logician. This issue came up in the last chapter. There, I said that for Aristotle either all humans are white or there is at least one non-white human. I promised to come back to the question of what happens if there are no humans. Excitingly, I've now come back to the question: for Aristotle the answer is that there are always humans, and if there were no humans, then there would be no true propositions about humans being white or non-white.

Let's take stock. We started by saying that Aristotle believes that knowledge or understanding is produced through demonstration, and that demonstration is going to be a kind of valid argument. We then looked at the boxes that need to be ticked to turn a valid argument into a demonstrative argument, and discovered that to be demonstrative an argument has to be explanatory, universal, and eternally necessary, dealing with the essential features of the things concerned. Surely we're finally done, right? Well, yes and no. These do pretty well exhaust the special features of demonstrations, but there is still another worry we might have. Aristotle is keenly aware that my knowledge of a conclusion will only be as good as my knowledge of the premises I used to generate it (71b). For instance, go back to the giraffe example one more time. Suppose I demonstrate that giraffes have long necks on the basis that they eat leaves off tall trees, but I don't understand why they eat leaves off tall trees. Now it looks like I don't understand why they have long necks either. My understanding of the conclusion in the demonstration can only be as good as my understanding of the premises. So those too stand in need of demonstration.

Perhaps you can already spot the problem that is looming here. If each demonstration depends on further demonstrations of its premises, then won't I be sucked into a regress of explanation (72b)? If I understand giraffes' necks because I understand their eating habits, then I must understand their eating habits on the basis of something else, like maybe the structure of their stomachs. But then there must be something else that makes me understand their stomachs…and so on. There will be no stop to the chain of demonstrations. Aristotle raises this problem explicitly, and declares that, like all good things, the demonstrative chain must come to an end (73a). It can't just go on in an endless regress, and neither can it be circular (if I wind up explaining giraffes' necks via their eating habits and their eating habits via their stomachs, I'd better not explain their stomachs on the basis of the kind of necks they have). So the regress must end—but how?

Aristotle answers the question at the very end of the *Posterior Analytics*. He says that any demonstrative argument will derive ultimately from what he calls a "first principle," and that our grasp of first principles must be even more certain and solid than our grasp of the things we demonstrate via those principles. Aristotle is what we nowadays call a "foundationalist": he grounds all knowledge on some fundamental, certain truths. These are, of course, not demonstrated. So how do we know them? Aristotle raises, but dismisses as absurd, the idea that we know these things already but are unaware of them—obviously an allusion to Plato's theory of recollection (99b). Instead, we get hold of fundamental principles through the most modest of means, using a faculty possessed even by animals: sensation.

It is through sensation, says Aristotle, that we arrive at a grasp of the universal features of things, but only after repeated experiences (100a). In a striking analogy, he suggests that this is like a group of retreating soldiers who turn again to fight, so that their formation is restored. Each soldier that turns seems to represent an individual experience, and when everything clicks, as it were—their phalanx snapping back into line, the shields in a neat row again—that is like getting the universal into our minds. Here Aristotle seems to reveal himself as some kind of empiricist, since he traces our knowledge back to sense experience.[3] He even uses a term which is often translated as "induction": *epagoge*. But Aristotle is no David Hume. His brand of empiricism is not tinged by skepticism. He has a serene confidence that our minds are perfectly fitted to receive universal, necessary truths just by examining the world around us.

There's a further difference between Aristotle and modern empiricists like Hume. Even though Aristotle appeals to sense experience to stop the regress of demonstration, he isn't relentlessly committed to the idea that all our knowledge somehow depends on sensation. That term I just mentioned, *epagoge*, also appears in Aristotle to describe the careful consideration of commonly held or reputable opinions.[4] This goes back to something I have mentioned already: his practice as a philosopher is to begin from what already seems plausible, even if these appearances may ultimately be overthrown. For Aristotle, all search for knowledge begins from what is "prior to us," even if it is not "prior in itself," that is, really fundamental in the causal structure of things. So, what is fundamental in the causal structure of things? To divine the answer to that question, we'll need to turn next to Aristotle's views on metaphysics, beginning with his views on the most fundamental metaphysical question: what is it that is? Or to put the same question the way Aristotle does: what is substance?

32

DOWN TO EARTH
ARISTOTLE ON SUBSTANCE

A few years ago I had the chance to visit the Vatican Museum. Apparently being Pope gives you good opportunities to collect art, because the Vatican houses a number of very impressive objects. The thing I most wanted to see was Raphael's painting *The School of Athens*, which depicts several of the thinkers we have looked at in this book. In the center, of course, are Plato and Aristotle—the most famous image of these two philosophers. I was very excited at the prospect of seeing this work in person, so you can imagine how I felt when we came into the room to find it walled off from view as it was undergoing restoration. I'm a trained philosopher, so my reason should be in charge of my soul, making me immune to such disappointments. But sadly, this would be one of the areas where my philosophical training has been inadequate. So I glared petulantly at the plywood blocking my view, until finally my companions dragged me off to see some chapel with a decorated ceiling, which I'm sorry to say did not feature either Plato or Aristotle.

In the painting that I didn't get to see, Raphael depicts Plato pointing up towards the heavens, an apparent allusion to his theory of Forms. Aristotle, meanwhile, is painted holding his hand flat to the ground. Usually this is seen as representing a traditional contrast drawn between Plato and Aristotle. Whereas Plato seems to encourage us to turn away from the world towards an ideal realm, Aristotle is interested in the here and now. He's the sort of man who devotes many hours to biological pursuits—he delights in dissecting fish to see how their organs are arranged. His natural philosophy looks carefully at the mechanisms of moving bodies, developing theories that will remain dominant until Galileo. In his ethics, he praises a life of virtuous practical action, rather than seeing political engagement as something one would rather avoid, as Plato did in the *Republic*.

You have probably noticed that whenever I mention one of these traditional ideas about the history of philosophy, I go on to say that it's too simple and that the standard view is at best an oversimplification. The contrast between Plato and Aristotle represented by Raphael is no exception. We've already seen that Plato was very interested in the natural world too, as we can see especially from his dialogue the *Timaeus*. And as we'll see later, Aristotle's ethics present a life of pure contemplation as superior even to the life of practical virtue. Yet, when it comes to the question of substances, we might seem to be on firmer ground in contrasting Plato and Aristotle. I didn't use the word "substance" in discussing Plato, because it isn't a technical term he uses. In fact, Plato in general is much less fond of technical terminology than Aristotle, and frequently has his characters say that terminology is not important so long as the philosophical ideas are clear. For Aristotle, though, "substance" is a technical term: the Greek word is *ousia*, which is simply a form of the Greek verb "to be." So "substance," in this context, means something rather straight-forward: it is simply that which is. And of course, this is a topic on which Plato does have plenty to say. You may remember that in both the *Republic* and the *Timaeus* Plato describes Forms as the objects of knowledge and as things that truly are, whereas things that participate in Forms are objects of opinion—they both are and are not.

Aristotle thinks that Plato is deeply wrong about this. There are two mistakes being made, in fact. For one thing, Aristotle denies that there are Forms as Plato conceived them. For another, he believes that concrete, sensible objects around us— things like me, a giraffe, or the Eiffel Tower—are good candidates for being the most real beings that there are. These points appear in a variety of Aristotelian works. It's in his *Nicomachean Ethics* that Aristotle makes that famous remark that truth is to be honored above our friends, as a prelude to his strenuous rejection of Plato's idea that there is a Form of the Good.[1] But the two texts that are most important for setting out Aristotle's views on substance are the *Categories*, which we've already looked at a bit in the chapter on his logic, and, unsurprisingly, the *Metaphysics*. When we try to piece together an account of substance on the basis of these two works, we quickly discover that Aristotle's ideas on this score seem to have changed. The *Categories'* account of substance is much simpler than the one we find in the *Metaphysics*, though they are not necessarily inconsistent. And when we turn to the *Metaphysics*, we find Aristotle rehabilitating the idea of separate, immaterial substances. It turns out that, on Aristotle's view, Plato was dealing with the right question—how should we understand immaterial things to be the principles of all else that exist? It's just that the theory of Forms was not the right answer to this question.

Let's begin, though, with the *Categories*. The reason substance even arises here is that substance, *ousia*, is the first of the ten categories. As you might remember, the categories seem to be the most general classes of predicate—in other words, if you list terms that can be ascribed to things, you discover that they fall into ten types. Or at least, that's what the *Categories* asks us to believe. The reason that substance is the first category to be mentioned is that it is so basic. Here we would be dealing with ascriptions like "Socrates is a man" or "Hiawatha is a giraffe." Predications of substance tell you what kind of being you are dealing with, so that these predications are more fundamental than the others. Before something can be white, or tall, or walking, or in a room, it must first be some kind of being, like a man, for instance. Here we have already arrived at a difference between Aristotle and Plato. From Aristotle's point of view, things like individual men and giraffes are basic, because they are the subjects of predication. If I want to ascribe humanity or whiteness or tallness to something, then I need something to which I can ascribe it. And this will be a substance, like the individual man Socrates, or the individual giraffe Hiawatha. Thus individual items in the world around us are, as Aristotle puts it, *primary* beings, rather than derivative beings as Plato suggests. Where Plato thinks of beautiful things as caused by Beauty Itself, Aristotle holds that without beautiful things, there is no such thing as beauty.

Here Plato might appeal to his point about the compresence of opposites, insisting that individual substances can be both equal and unequal, or both beautiful and ugly, in relation to other things. So how can they be primary? Aristotle will say: "Actually that proves my point: substances are indeed primary, because they are the bearers of predication. And if you check my list of categories, you'll see that one type of predicate is relation." (This response would be all the more telling given that the list of ten categories was, as we saw, probably developed within Plato's own Academy.) He also subverts Plato's idea that true beings are unchanging, by insisting that one reason individual substances are primary is precisely that they undergo change. When there is a change from short to tall, it is some individual substance that is first short and then tall, like our giraffe Hiawatha growing from childhood up to her full, majestic, adult height. The capacity for change goes hand-in-hand with being a subject of predication.

So these particular beings that we can actually see around us are what Aristotle, here in the *Categories*, calls "primary substances." He also recognizes what he calls "secondary substances" (*Categories* 2a). These are things like species and genera. A species is a basic class of entity, like human or giraffe. A genus is a wider class which includes numerous species, like, for instance, animal, which embraces both human and giraffe. Aristotle sometimes calls his secondary substances "universals" (*ta katholou*), because they apply generally to a whole class of primary substances. The reason these universal things are secondary is that they are predicated of individuals: the species human is predicated of particular humans (*Categories* 2b). Again, the particulars are doing all the metaphysical work here. Just as it is beautiful things that guarantee and explain the presence of beauty in the world, so it is the fact that there are individual humans that ensures there is a species of human. Thus the

Categories, at least at first glance, seems to present a metaphysical picture that is more or less faithful to our experience. Forget the radically revisionary ideas of Heraclitus with his unity of opposites, Parmenides with his One Being, and Plato with his Forms. Aristotle says that the basic bits of reality are particular things you can touch and interact with. Admittedly, the universals are still being recognized as "substances" or "beings" of a kind. But they are dependent entities, which could not exist without primary, particular substances.

Is this just a matter of taste, or does Aristotle have good arguments for why his metaphysical picture is the right one? We've just seen that Aristotle believes that being a subject of predication, and being capable of change, will make things good candidates for being genuine substances. But Plato isn't likely to accept these criteria. So what can Aristotle say that might convince Plato? Well, he says several things that look a little familiar from Plato's own self-criticism in the dialogue *Parmenides*. For instance, he complains that if Forms are really separate from things, then they won't be able to causally influence them—this is reminiscent of the argument Plato calls "the greatest difficulty" in the *Parmenides*. Aristotle also takes advantage of some of his own technical distinctions to force unappealing choices on Plato. For instance, he's invented this contrast between particular things, like Socrates, and universal things, like the species human. And as we saw in the last chapter, he's managed to capture Plato's intuition that knowledge deals with general features of the world, by agreeing that knowledge must be universal in scope. But since universals are dependent on particulars, it is still going to be things like Socrates that make our knowledge of humanity possible.[2] Now, Aristotle can ask Plato: are these Forms of yours supposed to be universal, or particular? They seem in fact to be an uneasy compromise between the two: for they are each supposed to be one substance, like a particular (*Metaphysics* 1040a), yet they are also supposed to explain general features of the world, like goodness, beauty, equality, and so on.

Aristotle also produces more specific criticisms. For instance, in his *Ethics* he argues that Plato's doctrine of the Form of the Good is incoherent (1096a–b). There are too many ways that things can be good—as Aristotle says, "good is said in many ways." So there is no one, common idea of good for the Form to embody. That locution, "said in many ways," appears elsewhere too, and never more prominently than in the *Metaphysics*. The *Metaphysics* is perhaps Aristotle's most complex and difficult work. It encompasses a number of different topics and problems, and in fact it is far from clear whether it was intended as a single work or was rather assembled after Aristotle's death as a collection of originally separate texts. But to the extent that the *Metaphysics* is a unity, it is because it envisions a single science devoted to nothing less than being. Aristotle never calls this science "metaphysics," speaking instead of "first philosophy." One fundamental thesis of this science of first philosophy is that being, like goodness, is "said in many ways."

We've already seen an example of this in the *Categories'* discussion of substance. Remember, the word "substance" is in Greek just a form of the verb "to be." So when Aristotle talks about primary and secondary substance, really what he is saying is that there are two kinds of being, one of which is more fundamental than the other. Hiawatha is primary and giraffe is secondary, because particulars are more fundamental than species. Similarly, Hiawatha is a more fundamental being than the accidental properties she has, like her skin-color, height, or that twinkle she gets in her eye when she sees a good-looking male giraffe. Accidents are beings, and the substances in which they inhere are beings, but the latter beings are more primary. By the time we get to the *Metaphysics*, Aristotle has made a further distinction which complicates his understanding of substance. This is the distinction between matter and form. To understand this, we need to return to the question of change. I mentioned earlier that he sees individuals as primary because they can undergo change, as when Hiawatha gets taller. In such a case a substance goes from having one predicate to having another predicate. But what about when a change is substantial, rather than accidental? What do we say, that is, when the change in question is that a giraffe is born, or, tragically, dies? Giving a complete answer to this question would mean wading into some rather deep waters, since it would involve dealing with Aristotle's theory of soul.

We'll dive into that topic soon. For now, though, we can say this: Aristotle is sympathetic to Parmenides' rule that there can be no generation from nothing, and no destruction into nothing. On the other hand, he thinks it is obvious that Parmenides' ultimate conclusions are wrong. Things clearly do change, whether accidentally or in respect of their substance. We can explain this if we assume that every change involves two components. On the one hand, there is something that changes, and this will always be some nature or property. This Aristotle calls form. On the other hand, there is something that undergoes the change and takes on the new property. This Aristotle calls matter. The clearest illustrations are man-made artefacts. A table, for instance, is made by taking some pre-existing matter, for instance wood, and imposing the form of a table upon it. The wood persists through the change but acquires a new shape. The centrality of this sort of example is suggested by the fact that Aristotle's word for "matter" is simply the Greek word for "wood," namely *hule*. But the same analysis goes for other kinds of change, whether or not they involve wood, and whether they are substantial or accidental changes. When Hiawatha was born, form was imposed on some pre-existing matter, namely blood or whatever stuff was in the mother's womb that took on the new form of giraffe. Then, when Hiawatha grows, she takes on the new form of being tall, and she is like matter for this new form.

We'll look at these ideas in more detail in the next chapter. For now, I just want to consider a problem they pose for Aristotle's theory of substance. In the *Categories* things looked relatively simple. The most fundamental sort of being was a particular substance, like Socrates or Hiawatha. These substances have and take on various features, which are the predicates that fall under the ten categories. But now, with our new distinction between matter and form, we can analyze the situation further. There is still the substance with its features—for instance, Socrates who is a man and who is in the marketplace, badgering hapless Athenians. But the substance itself is further divided into matter and form. Socrates is, as Aristotle will now say, a "composite" of matter and form, just as a table is a composite of wood and the shape of a table. Hence the problem: in light of this further analysis, should we still say that Socrates, the composite, is a being of the most fundamental kind—primary substance? Or should we instead say that his matter is the primary substance? Or, perhaps, that form is primary substance?

This is one of the questions considered by Aristotle in the difficult middle section of his *Metaphysics* (especially Book Seven). He's still convinced that primary substance will be something of this world—he is no closer to accepting Plato's theory of separate Forms. But he now needs to reconsider the *Categories*' theory of substance in light of the matter–form distinction. He could stick to his guns and insist that it is the whole particular that is primary substance. This answer has much to recommend it. A particular man or giraffe can exist independently of other things, for instance—and it's still going to be the case that universal generalities about men are made true by individual men. (For instance, it is because each particular man is necessarily an animal that we can universally affirm that man is a species falling under the genus animal.) Also, the particular is still a subject of predication: Socrates has a snub-nose, Hiawatha is tall.

But hang on, Aristotle now thinks. Maybe snub-nosedness is predicated of Socrates, and tallness of Hiawatha: but within Socrates and Hiawatha don't we have predication of another kind? In each case a form—whether human or giraffe—is predicated of matter. And this seems to be more basic than accidental features that can be lost, for instance, if Socrates goes to a plastic surgeon and has his nose de-snubbed. By contrast, the only way to remove the human form from Socrates' matter is to do what the Athenians in fact did do: kill him. Thus, if we're looking for a fundamental subject of predication, it seems that we should say matter is primary substance. On the other hand, form has its own claims to be the most fundamental kind of being. Aristotle shares with Plato the intuition that being should be intelligible, and it is through having determination of a certain kind—that is, form—that things are intelligible.

This puts Aristotle in a bind, which he attempts to resolve in a formidably complicated discussion in the *Metaphysics*. This discussion is difficult, so I'm only going to gesture towards his answer here. Aristotle declares that if we are looking for the being of something, what we are after might be called its "essence." It is this that we are grasping when we grasp what a thing is. This will certainly not be its matter: there's a lot more to being human than having flesh and bones. Rather, the essence of Socrates will be in a sense the same as Socrates, because each thing must be the same as its own being (*Metaphysics* 1031a–1032b). Yet Aristotle also finds it plausible—and in the end, more compelling—to associate substance with form alone (1041b). Some readers (for instance, among medieval philosophers, though the interpretation still has its adherents) have thought that Aristotle was emphasizing the priority of form here to set up a discussion that comes later in the *Metaphysics*.

In the twelfth book he argues that although Plato was right to accept immaterial substances, those substances should not be conceived as Platonic Forms. Rather, they are separate intellects, responsible for the motion of the heavenly bodies. As pure intellects, these can apparently be understood as forms that are not predicated of matter. Among primary substances, these intellects would be the *most* primary, especially the first mover of all: God. We will be returning to Aristotle's discussion of God in a later chapter. To understand his philosophical theology, though, we'll need to know more about change, which means taking a closer look at form and matter. As we'll now discover by turning to the *Physics*, these turn out to be only two of four types of cause recognized by Aristotle.

FORM AND FUNCTION
ARISTOTLE'S FOUR CAUSES

I'm not a technically proficient person, but I did manage to write this book on a computer. Probably you have one too. In fact, you might even be reading this book on a computer or other electronic device, now that paper books are an endangered species. But if you're anything like me, there is a lot that you don't understand about computers. To be honest, for me a computer might as well be a magical device: I turn it on and it starts to glow, giving me powers I do not possess by nature, like the ability to surf the internet, or watch amusing videos about cats. But of course, some people do understand computers: the ones who design, study, build, and repair them. These people are in a good position to answer all kinds of questions about computers. We might describe them as "computer scientists"—some of them indeed describe themselves this way. The more that someone understands about computers, the more claim they would have to possess the science of computers.

For all his achievements, Aristotle was of course not a computer scientist. This was a man whose prodigious accomplishments were achieved without the benefit of the internet or amusing videos about cats. (Actually, that may have been an advantage.) But if Aristotle were shown a computer, he would agree that there must be some kind of science or knowledge for computers—what he would call the *episteme* of computers. For him, this would amount to being able to give causal explanations of computers and the things they can do. As we saw, his theory of knowledge assumes that having *episteme* means being able to give such explanations by means of a demonstration. The goal is to understand, not just *that* something is the case, but *why* something is the case. Aristotle is thus very interested in what sorts of causal account we can give. Is there any systematic way of dividing up the kinds of explanation that can feature in demonstrations? To put this in a less technical way, Aristotle wants to know: How many different kinds of answer are there to "why" questions?

Given the title of this chapter, it's a bit late for me to leave you in suspense. So I'll just say right off that, according to Aristotle, there are four kinds of cause (or explanation), namely material, formal, efficient, and final. These English terms are drawn not from Greek, but from Latin translations of Aristotle's Greek. For instance, "efficient" relates to the Latin verb *efficio*, which means "do" or "bring about." Thus, the efficient cause is the one that brings something about—for instance, the carpenter who builds a table is the efficient cause of the table. Similarly, the word "final" relates to the Latin word for "end" or "purpose," a final cause being a purpose or goal. Aristotle often uses less technical expressions for his four causes, as when he refers to the category of final cause as "that for the sake of which."

Aristotle sets out his four kinds of cause in his *Physics* (194b–195a). Perhaps the easiest of the four to understand is the material cause. This is just whatever something is made of; Aristotle gives the example of a statue's being made of bronze. The next kind of cause is formal: the form will be whatever gives something its definition or determination. Aristotle's example is that the form of the octave is the ratio of 2 to 1. What he has in mind is the strings on a musical instrument: if you have two strings at the same tension, one of which is exactly half as long as the other, the notes they give when struck will be one octave apart. Third is the efficient cause, which brings something to be by imposing form on matter. Aristotle provides the example of the father being the cause for his child.[1] The final type of cause is, appropriately enough, the final type of cause. Final causes are purposes: Aristotle's example is that health is the final cause of taking a walk or of administering medicine.

With all due respect to Aristotle, these examples are less helpful than they might be. In particular, it isn't so enlightening when he illustrates formal cause with the example of the octave. And it would be nice to have him enumerate causes of all four types for one and the same thing. So let's try to do that, using the example I started with: a computer. If we can apply the four causes to a computer, that would testify to the perennial utility of Aristotle's scheme. Unfortunately, what I know about computers could fit onto a 1980s floppy disc, but I'll do my best. Let's warm up with the material cause, which is easy enough: the matter of a computer is whatever it is made of, like plastic and silicon. The formal cause will be the structure of the computer—roughly speaking, the way that the matter is arranged in order to yield a computer. So this might include things like being a certain shape, having the circuits set out in a certain order, the pattern of keys on the keyboard, and so on. But the true form of the computer is going to consist only of the structural elements it needs to be a computer. The fact that the G key is right in the middle of a keyboard will only be incidental, because the G key could be moved elsewhere on the keyboard without rendering the device non-functional. To use terminology I introduced earlier, the formal cause of a computer is what gives the computer its essential properties: the features it must have if it is to be a computer. So the placement of the G key is not vital (it is accidental to the computer), but the computer must be able to process information. Its ability to do this will derive from its arrangement or form.

As for the efficient cause, this too is easy to name: it is the person who built the computer, just as the father is the efficient cause of the child. In general, it looks like an efficient cause is whatever comes along and does something, so that something comes to be. This immediately raises the prospect that eternal things—things that have always existed—cannot have efficient causes. It may not seem that important a point, but philosophers will wrestle with this implication of Aristotle's theory for many centuries in the late ancient and medieval periods. More on that in future volumes of this series. For now, you might worry about the more basic fact that your computer probably wasn't put together by just one mechanic with a screw-driver. Won't the efficient cause be a whole team of people, or perhaps machines in a factory? Well, why not? Aristotle will be happy to admit that many entities sometimes come together to form an efficient cause—imagine, for instance, a battalion of soldiers pushing their boat out to sea, perhaps one of the ships launched by Helen's beautiful face. They are jointly the efficient cause of the boat's movement into the water.

As for the final cause, in the example I just gave, the purpose of launching the ship would be to retrieve Helen from Troy. The purpose of the computer, of course, is to watch amusing videos about cats. Okay, not really. Rather, it is something more general, like processing and storing information (and what could be more inform-ative than an amusing video about a cat?). Notice that the final cause is intimately related to the formal cause: the form of a computer allows it to achieve its purpose. This is exactly what we would expect, of course: it amounts to saying that the design of the computer enables it to do what it was designed for. For a full explanation, we can add in the efficient and final cause. An efficient cause, for instance a human, comes along and formulates a purpose to be achieved—that's the final cause. This agent then selects some appropriate materials—the material cause—and imposes upon them the form suitable to the task. To give a more Aristotelian example than the computer, a carpenter might impose the form of a table on some wood in order to have something to eat off. The carpenter is the efficient cause, the shape and structure of the table is the formal cause, the wood is the material cause, and having something to eat off is the final cause.

But are these all really *causes*? Of the four types Aristotle has named, there is really only one we'd normally describe as a cause, namely the efficient cause. For us, causes are pushers and pullers. They are whatever makes something happen, whatever introduces a change in the world. That mention of change already leads us closer to Aristotle's point of view, though. In the last chapter, we saw that to explain change we need both matter and form. The matter is whatever persists through the change, and the form is whatever is added to, or subtracted from, the matter. For instance, when a rock is heated, the rock is the matter and heat is the new form. When wood becomes a table, the wood is the matter that remains and the form of table is added. So if it's change you're interested in, you will need to agree that matter and form are vital. Moreover, Aristotle can point out that matter and form remain on the scene even after the efficient cause has done its job: the carpenter leaves the workshop and goes to sleep or perhaps even dies, but the wood is still shaped as a table.

You might retort: okay Aristotle, I grant that it is useful to invoke matter and form when discussing change. But that doesn't make matter and form *causes*. The cause is the carpenter, or more generally, the efficient cause: the thing which brought about the change. We don't need to talk about "causes" for a table that is standing still in a quiet workshop. But Aristotle will remind you what we started out trying to do. We were trying to learn how many kinds of answer there are for "why?" questions. Efficient causes do fit the bill: why is there a table here? Because the carpenter built it. But how about, "Why does this have right-angled corners?" Because the top is square; an answer in terms of formal cause. Or, "Why is this flammable?" Because it's made of wood; an answer that invokes material cause. Aristotle wants us to see that we can't understand or explain things without invoking their form and matter as well as their efficient causes. Talking about pushers and pullers will only get us so far.

Since you have struggled against Aristotle for this long, you're clearly not easy to please. So even now you will probably want to draw a line in the sand (you're the efficient cause, the sand is the material cause, line is the formal cause... sorry, I'll stop). You will want to say, fine then Aristotle, I'll grant you three of your four causes. The carpenter, the wood, the shape of the table—those are all real things out in the world. They have, so to speak, metaphysical respectability. So it's fine to point to them as kinds of cause. But what about the fourth type, the final cause? There are no purposes or goals floating around free in the world. The carpenter might have a goal *in mind* when he builds the table, like to eat off it, or to make money by selling the table. But if this is a cause, it's a cause in a very different sense. You might press your point home by asking Aristotle to think about the difference between a table or a computer on the one hand, and something like a giraffe on the other hand.

Giraffes too have efficient causes, namely their giraffe fathers. And they have form and matter, as we saw in the last chapter. But they don't have final causes. There is no goal or purpose to a giraffe, lovely though she may be. This, you might insist, is a big difference between man-made things and natural things. The reason for the difference is that the goal of a man-made thing is imposed by the human who makes it. So we don't need to take final causes seriously in the same way as the other three kinds. Even if it is useful to talk about them when discussing carpentry and the like, final causes just aren't *real*.

Here we've arrived at a notorious aspect of Aristotle's conception of nature: when you say that giraffes don't have purposes, have no final causes, he will firmly disagree. How can you say that a giraffe has no final cause, he will say, when even the *parts* of giraffes clearly do have final causes? He needs only to mention its famous neck, which has the purpose of allowing the giraffe to eat leaves off tall trees. (Or maybe not: I've seen it claimed that the long necks are actually for fighting other giraffes. But I'm a philosopher, so I'm not going to let a few silly facts get in the way of a good example.) In fact, if we look through the animal kingdom we see example after example of animals that are amazingly fit for purpose: the frog with eyes that can look around while the rest of it stays underwater, the lizard whose skin is the same color as its environment, and so on. How can we explain this, Aristotle will ask, without saying that there really are final causes in nature? The parts of animals perform certain functions, such as camouflage, reaching leaves, and watching for enemies. These functions contribute to the overall function of each animal, which is simply to flourish and reproduce so that its species is preserved through the generations. The same goes for plants and, of course, for humans, who likewise have bewilderingly complex bodies that can only be explained by admitting the presence of final causation. If I may introduce a technical term, we can therefore say that Aristotle's conception of nature is *teleological*—this word comes from the Greek *telos*, which means "end" or "purpose." To say that nature is teleological is simply to claim that nature involves final causation.

Here you will be tempted to smile indulgently and say that Aristotle's teleology was plausible in its day, but has ultimately been shown to be wrong by the theory of evolution. Since Darwin, we know that functional aspects of animals have nothing to do with some kind of natural final causation. They are rather the result of a long process whereby certain features are selected for inheritance, depending on whether or not they are conducive to survival. The apparent design we see in nature *is* merely apparent: it is actually nothing but randomness constrained by the mechanisms of survival pressure and genetic inheritance. Poor Aristotle, of course, knew nothing of this, so his teleological theory is quite literally antiquated. But things are a bit more complicated. Aristotle did know of an attempt to explain natural phenomena by an appeal to chance rather than teleology. This is something we've seen already, in the chapter on the Pre-Socratic philosopher Empedocles. To remind you, Empedocles believed that separate parts of animals arose first by chance, and then came together randomly to produce whole animals, with the suitable animals managing to reproduce. No one today can read Aristotle's report of this theory without thinking of evolution. And as it happens, the ancient report is found in this very same book of the *Physics*. Aristotle presents Empedocles' theory as a challenge to his own; so he is well aware that one could try to explain nature through randomness rather than final causation (198b).

Aristotle rejects the theory, for the following reason. For Empedocles, everything in the natural world is to be explained by chance. For instance, teeth would just happen to spring up in such a way that they are suitably arranged for grinding and tearing food. But this is simply a misunderstanding of what chance is. When I say that something is a chance or lucky event, this means that it is unusual, precisely because it might have been intentional but is not. Aristotle gives an example, which I'll fill out a bit. Suppose I am looking for someone because I am collecting money to throw a party, and need to get his contribution. I go to the market to do my shopping, and just happen to run into him. Lucky me: I didn't go to the market to find him, but I found him anyway—the result is *as if intended*, but not intended (196b–197a). Another example would be if a rock just happens to fall off a cliff at the right time to kill my enemy (197b). Again, lucky for me. But if this is what chance or luck means, it is only intelligible against a background of things that really are intentional. What happens for the most part is that purposes are pursued and achieved: final causes do their work. Occasionally, but only occasionally, a desirable result is achieved without being pursued, without any final cause being involved. And that is what we call chance or luck. How, then, could everything in nature be like this, since the whole point of luck is to be exceptional, whereas nature is just what almost always happens (199a)?[2]

Aristotle's response to Empedocles is, I think, a reasonably effective one, if only because Empedocles has not spelled out the mechanisms by which random processes could yield uniform and predictable processes. At least on Aristotle's telling, Empedocles has said nothing about genetic inheritance and next to nothing about survival pressures. So, oddly, Aristotle may have the better of this particular argument, even if Empedocles was closer to being right. But once we add the machinery of modern genetics and evolutionary theory, it seems that we really can dispense with final causes. Here some scholars still attempt a last-ditch defense of Aristotle, by adopting a less metaphysically loaded reading of his teleology. On this reading, Aristotle would not insist that final causes are metaphysically real. Rather, he would say that they are required for us in making sense of nature. Whereas matter, form, and efficient causes are actually out there in the world, final causes would have a merely heuristic function. They would help us to explain what we see, without being a real part of what we see.

This brings us back to where we started, which was Aristotle's quest to find explanations, to answer "why?" questions, to produce demonstrative syllogisms and hence knowledge. On the less metaphysical reading, Aristotle wants to say only that we can't avoid talking of function and purpose when we investigate nature. This makes his account rather plausible: while accepting evolutionary theory, we still happily speak of giraffes needing long necks in order to reach trees, and chameleons changing color in order to avoid being eaten. Perhaps that phrase "in order to" simply cannot be eliminated from our scientific language. And perhaps this is all Aristotle needs: the claim that final causes would appear in proper scientific explanations. This strikes me as a clever defense of Aristotle, though I suspect that he did have a more metaphysically committed understanding of final causes. We can reserve final judgment for a few chapters, since I will be soon be discussing Aristotle's views about animals. But animals are only one part of the natural world around us, and Aristotle has plenty to tell us about the natural world as a whole, not least in this work we've been discussing, the *Physics*. Thus far, like a carpenter trying to give a table that old-fashioned look, we've only scratched its surface.

34

LET'S GET PHYSICAL
ARISTOTLE'S NATURAL
PHILOSOPHY

Simplicity, they say, is a virtue. But is it really? I suppose it depends what you're trying to accomplish. Producing a piece of minimalist art? Then simplicity should be your watchword. But designing a baroque church? Not so much. Scientists seem to side with the minimalist artists and not the baroque architects. As we can see from modern attempts to produce a unified theory of physics, scientists often seek to provide the simplest possible explanations of the world around us. If you can reduce the number of principles or concepts needed to account for what you see around you, that seems to count as a scientific advance, even if the simpler explanation doesn't, for instance, allow you to predict things with any greater accuracy. We seem instinctively to feel that explanations of nature *should* be simple, and that if we can restrict ourselves to a smaller number of explanatory factors, we must be getting closer to the underlying reality.

Whatever you make of this feature of science, it has clearly been around for a long time, indeed, for as long as there has been anything we can plausibly call science. As we saw, the first Pre-Socratics sought to explain all natural phenomena in terms of a single principle, which might be water, according to Thales, air, according to Anaximenes, or the more obscure "infinite" of Anaximander. These Milesian thinkers are often called "material monists" because of their attempt to derive the whole natural world from a single original matter. The search for simplicity reached its climax with Parmenides, for whom everything is one and complexity is not just a theoretical blemish, but an illusion. When Aristotle sets out to do natural philosophy in his work the *Physics*, he adopts his characteristic method of surveying previous views. And what he finds is that nearly all his predecessors sought to explain the natural world in terms of a small number of principles. The Milesians and Parmenides, as we just saw, get the number of principles all the way down to one. Empedocles doesn't get quite that far, since he invokes two opposed principles, love and strife (actually one could argue that he has six, since there are also the four elements). Those who don't go for a small number of principles tend to go all the way in the other direction, and say that there is an infinity of principles—which might be an infinity of atoms, or the infinite seeds in the mixture of Anaxagoras.

In discussing this material, Aristotle does us the favor of preserving a lot of information about the Pre-Socratics—later commentaries on the *Physics* preserve further information. But Aristotle is not telling us all this out of mere historical interest. In fact, he risks distorting the views of his predecessors, because he forces those views into a scheme which will allow his own ideas to emerge more clearly. In this case, the scheme pivots around this question of how many principles there are for nature. This is bound to be a misleading question to put to the Pre-Socratics. Is Parmenides' one really a principle in the same sense as air according to Anaximenes, or the infinite atoms of Democritus? Surely not. The principles Aristotle himself will invoke are principles in yet another sense. Yet Aristotle has put his finger on something: his scheme reveals that the drive towards simplification was already a leitmotif of early Greek thought.

Although Aristotle has no quarrel with the urge towards simplicity, he would caution us not to *over*-simplify. This is, after all, the man who builds a whole ethical theory around the golden mean. He will want to pursue the project of identifying basic principles of nature, but within moderation. He argues that theories based on only a single principle are too, well, simple. If you have only one thing, it cannot interact with anything else, so it will remain inert. This, of course, is exactly what Parmenides had in mind: that reality consists of an unchanging, single being. Aristotle pauses to refute this idea, but remarks that the discussion doesn't really belong to natural philosophy as such (184b–185a). Parmenides' theory says that the natural world is an illusion, whereas natural philosophy should assume that the natural world does exist, and then attempt to understand it. We are, then, going to need at least two principles to explain the changes and features of the natural world. Even that won't be enough, though. If we posit two opposed principles, as Empedocles did, then why wouldn't they just cancel each other out (189a)? Yet the two principles would need to be opposed in order to account for variety and change.

No, what we need, says Aristotle, is three principles: a principle to be worked on, and then two other contrary principles to work on the first one (189a–189b). Putting it this way makes his idea seem rather abstract, but we've already seen in the last two chapters how he would spell it out. The key notion is going to be change. Parmenides and his followers claimed that change would mean that being emerges from non-being, which cannot happen. Aristotle agrees that this sort of absolute coming-to-be from nothing is impossible. But this isn't the right way of understanding change. Rather, there is change when something that already exists gains a new feature, or loses a feature it already had. Aristotle illustrates with the example of a man becoming musical (189b–190a).[1] Here the man undergoes the change; he is the subject of the change. He first lacks a form, when he is not musical, and then gains a form, by becoming musical. So we have three principles: the subject of change, the absence of form, and form. Just the right number of principles—simple enough, but not too simple.

This brings us to another key piece of Aristotelian terminology. You'll be reading it a lot from now on, so I hope you like it. Aristotle is going to say that if a man can acquire the form musical, then he is "potentially" musical. Once he acquires the form and is musical, the man is "actually" musical. The Greek word for "potentiality" is *dunamis*, which is where we get our word "dynamic": it means power or capacity. "Actuality," meanwhile, translates *entelecheia*, which roughly means completeness, or alternatively *energeia*, which is of course where we get our word "energy." Aristotle wields this pair of concepts, potentiality and actuality, as a basic weapon in his philosophical arsenal. He finds that perennial (and not-so-perennial) philosophical problems can be answered by distinguishing the potential from the actual. In this case, the distinction allows him to solve Parmenides' challenge against the possibility of change. He can say that change does not require that nothing becomes something, or that something becomes nothing. Rather, one thing that is *potentially* something else becomes *actually* that other thing. When a cold rock that was potentially hot is heated, it becomes actually hot; and only things that start by being potentially hot can be heated so as to become actually hot. Simple, right?

But what does any of this have to do with natural philosophy? That is, after all, supposedly the subject of the *Physics*. Indeed, seeing as we're in an etymological mood, I'll remind you that the word "physics" comes from the Greek word for nature, *phusis*. Why, then, does Aristotle start out a general investigation of nature by talking about change? The answer is revealed when we get to Book Two of the *Physics*, where Aristotle attempts to give a definition of nature. According to his definition, nature is a principle of change, so we cannot understand nature or the natural world without understanding change (193a). To see why, consider the difference between a man-made object and a natural object. In honor of those heroes of simplicity, the minimalist artists of the 1960s, let's take as our example of a man-made thing a steel cube, and contrast it to a giraffe. They're clearly very different; about the only thing they have in common is that they are sometimes put on public display, and greet their audiences with cool indifference. Steel cubes don't, for instance, eat leaves off trees. In fact, to be honest, they don't do much of anything. Even their shape is imposed upon them from the outside, by a minimalist artist, or more likely the artist's team of assistants. If the cube changes, the change is forced upon it. For instance, it will move when people pick it up and bring it to a museum, perhaps wondering why minimalist artwork has to be maximally heavy. How different is the giraffe, which begins as a foetus in its mother and naturally transforms into a baby giraffe, then moves itself around to get at plants, which nourish it, enabling it to grow into an adult.

Aristotle, pondering this sort of contrast, decides that the key difference between the man-made and the natural is that the natural things have an *innate* capacity for movement and change. Even when they are at rest, without changing or moving—for instance, when giraffes go to sleep—it is their nature which explains this and not some force from outside. Aristotle gives us a vivid example to push the point home: if you take a wooden bed and bury it, and it sprouts up as a plant, what you'll see growing is a sapling, not another bed (193a). The nature of the wood or the tree remains, even though it is forced into the shape of a bed. Similarly, the minimalist steel cube may have some natural tendencies—as we'll see in a moment, Aristotle thinks it does—but it is not natural for it to be cube-shaped or to be in a museum, since these features are imposed from outside. Hence, Aristotle understands *phusis*, or nature, as an internal principle of motion and rest.

Aristotle's conception of nature means that his physics is in one way strikingly like modern physics and in another way strikingly different. It is strikingly similar because he thinks that physics, or natural philosophy, should investigate motion. Motion is, of course, one of the things we all studied as teenagers in physics class: rolling balls down ramps, learning about acceleration, and so on. Of course, spatial motion is only one kind of change, albeit an important kind, and Aristotle understands it as just one of the kinds of change that natural philosophy can investigate. The physicist must also investigate processes like heating and cooling, changing color, and so on. Really, any change that things do naturally will come under the heading of Aristotelian natural philosophy. All this seems reasonably relevant to physics as we conceive it today.

Yet Aristotle's physics is also unlike modern physics, because it puts so much emphasis on innate tendencies towards motion and rest. Now that we can build machines that seem able to move themselves, Aristotle's distinction between the artificial and the natural might seem in danger of breaking down. And anyway, do all natural things really have an innate tendency to change? This may seem plausible when it comes to giraffes and the like, since they do have an internal principle of motion—they can stand up and gallop across the savannah in search of succulent acacia leaves. But what about things like rocks and clouds? These are not alive, but surely they are natural. And they don't have an internal principle of motion and rest. Here Aristotle definitely parts ways with our modern physicist. For him, a rock does indeed have an internal principle of motion: just drop one to see it in action. First get your foot out of the way, because that rock is going to go straight down. Whereas we would think of this as the rock's falling due to gravity, Aristotle, who lived about two millennia too early to discuss the fine points of falling bodies with Isaac Newton, thought that the rock falls due to its natural tendency to move down.

To explain this, we need to glance at how Aristotle believes the natural world as a whole is structured. I'll be looking more at his cosmology later in this book, but here are the basics.[2] For Aristotle, as for Plato before him, the earth is at the center of a spherical universe, and is tiny in comparison to the heavenly bodies that surround it. The realm below the heavens, where we live, is made of the four elements familiar from Empedocles: fire, air, water, and earth. Unlike Plato, Aristotle thinks that the heavens are made not from particularly pure versions of the four elements, but rather from a fifth element, sometimes called *aither*. The fifth element is not, as a science-fiction movie from the 1990s would have you believe, a young lady with bright red hair, but rather a transparent, indestructible material. This material makes up the spheres carrying the visible heavenly bodies in their circular orbits around the earth.

As for the four lower elements, they move not in circles but rather in straight lines—down in the case of earth and water, towards the midpoint of the universe, and up, away from the midpoint, in the case of air and fire. This is why rocks and raindrops fall, but bubbles of air move upwards in water and flames flicker upwards in air. These motions are natural to the four elements. So Aristotle can say that the falling rock does indeed have an internal principle of motion. Due to its earthy nature, it has a tendency to move towards the center of the universe if nothing gets in its way. That minimalist steel cube is the same in this respect. It's made of metal, and metal is obviously an earthy kind of material. As you'll discover if you drop the steel cube while carrying it, it has a very powerful tendency to move downwards. (Like I said, mind your foot.) Even though the steel cube is man-made, it retains natural tendencies, as do all man-made items, like the bed that sends up shoots when it is buried.

Thus, motion and change are central notions in Aristotle's natural philosophy, indeed definitive of what it is for something to have a nature. So Aristotle has good reason to provide a careful analysis of motion and change, which is exactly what he goes on to do in the *Physics*. He relies heavily on his distinction between potentiality and actuality. For Aristotle, any change is going to be a transition from potentiality to actuality. This will be true of both spatial motion and change more generally. If I go from London to Paris, then on the way I gradually actualize my potentiality for going to Paris. If the summer sun is blazing so that Paris heats up and, as it is wont to do, sizzles, then its potentiality for heat is actualized.

A striking feature about change, which becomes obvious once we start thinking in terms of potentiality and actuality, is that changing inherently involves a degree of incompleteness. When I'm on the way from London to Paris, I have partially, but not completely, actualized my potential for moving towards Paris. At the very moment where I reach Paris, my potentiality is fully actualized—because I *am* *actually* in Paris. As soon as that happens, the change is over, it is complete. Likewise, something that is potentially hot is partially actualized as it is heated, and fully actual once it is hot. This is one reason why Aristotle uses that word *entelecheia*, or "completeness," for the form or actuality that is reached in change. Another resonance of *entelecheia* would be with the related word *telos*, which we just met in the last chapter when I mentioned the term "teleology," As we saw, *telos* means purpose or end. We can think of the end state of a change as the completion, fulfillment, and purpose of the process of change. Every change is identified by the end state towards which it is directed. Hence, if I am on my way from London to Rome by way of Paris, my journey is incomplete when I reach Paris—I am still in a state of potentiality—whereas my goal is reached if I intended only to get as far as Paris.

A side benefit of this analysis is that it allows Aristotle to understand something which has remained central in the study of physics: time. Here he engages in the simplifying tactic so popular among scientists. He defines time in terms of change, so that he reduces the question of time's reality to the less contentious reality of change. Plato too connects time to motion—he says in the *Timaeus* that time is produced by the movement of the heavens (37d–40d). It's no surprise that both philosophers see motion and time as having an intimate connection. If you try to envision time passing, you will likely imagine some change or motion, such as a clock's hand sweeping around its face. Aristotle endorses this way of understanding time, and in fact proposes that time is simply the measure of motion and rest (*Physics* 219b–221a). So for him, our conception of time is entirely dependent on our awareness of change and potential change. Most obviously, as Plato emphasizes, we measure days via the motion of the sun around the Earth.

But Aristotle doesn't link time exclusively to heavenly motion. Any motion can be measured by time, for instance, when a sprinter moves 100 meters in ten seconds. As you might recall, this was the basis for Aristotle's response to Zeno's dichotomy paradox, according to which we can never move because we'd first need to move half of the distance. Aristotle answers that it does not take an infinite time to move a finite distance (233a). Zeno is right that the distance is infinitely divisible, but time is infinitely divisible in the same way. Rather than moving through an infinite number of divisions, we move over the whole distance, which can be divided up however we like. The time is divided along with the motion, which only stands to reason, since it measures the motion. No matter how we divide the distance and the time, we will still have a finite total amount of time and of distance.

We saw when we looked at Aristotle's views on substance that he considers particular beings, like Socrates and Hiawatha the giraffe, to be "primary" substances, the basic building-blocks of reality. So it isn't surprising that he makes time ultimately dependent on these substances. Time exists because it is a measure of the changes that primary substances undergo—whether these substances are the massive spheres of the heavens as they rotate, or tiny fleas as they leap. Aristotle has something similar to say about place. Rather than setting forth a concept of absolute space, as Newton will do, Aristotle contents himself with the notion of place as the limit surrounding a particular body (212a). My place is simply the border where the air around me is touching me. Like Aristotelian time, Aristotelian place is entirely dependent on the particular objects that he calls substances.

This feature of Aristotle's physics is comforting, in a way. He does not postulate metaphysically mysterious things like absolute time and space, but contents himself with the familiar substances that surround us. Time and place emerge only as phenomena dependent on these substances. But I do not want to leave you with the impression that Aristotelian natural philosophy concerns itself only with bodies in motion, in time and in place. This is fundamental to his understanding of "physics," but he would include other disciplines under the rubric of natural philosophy. In particular, Aristotle shows a keen interest in the study of living things. He even dissected animals to discern their inner workings. Just as the *Physics* is his foundational work on natural philosophy in general, so the part of his natural philosophy devoted to living beings has a foundational work: *On the Soul*. For Aristotle believes that anything that is alive has a soul. Thus, as we now turn our attention to his views on the soul, we will be remaining squarely within the domain of the philosophy of nature.

35

SOUL POWER
ARISTOTLE'S *ON THE SOUL*

Are you comfortable on that sofa? I want you to relax—this is a safe space. Nothing that's said within these walls will leave the room. You aren't being judged. I'm here to help. So, shall we start at the beginning? Tell me a little bit about your mother.

Yes, in this chapter, we're doing psychology. But actually, don't start to unburden yourself—especially if you're reading this while on public transport. Because we're actually going to be doing Aristotelian psychology, which has less to do with uncovering your true character and the traumatic experiences of your childhood, and more to do with uncovering the true nature and experiences of the soul. As you won't be surprised to learn, the word "psychology" comes from ancient Greek; the Greek word *psyche* means "soul." Psychology, then, is simply the study of the soul. And the very first work devoted to psychology is of course Aristotle's *On the Soul* (frequently known by its Latin title, *De Anima*). With all due respect to James Brown, it is really Aristotle who deserves the title "godfather of soul."

But what about Plato? He did write the *Phaedo*, which proves the soul's immortality not just once but numerous times. Surely that counts as an earlier work on psychology? Well, yes. What I mean is not that *On the Soul* is the first work to focus on the soul, but that it is the first work to attempt a general, systematic discussion of soul. As we saw when we looked at the *Phaedo*, Plato simply assumes the distinction between soul and body. He examines the capacities and properties of the human soul only in passing, since the main topic of the dialogue is to prove the soul's immortality. By contrast, Aristotle mentions the soul's immortality only in passing. But he discusses just about every other possible question regarding the soul, starting with the question of just what we mean by *psyche*, or "soul." As in the *Physics*, the work we looked at over the last couple of chapters, Aristotle begins his discussion here in *On the Soul* by surveying previous views on the topic at hand. In this case, one of his objectives is to determine just what topic *is* at hand. He looks to his predecessors to formulate a kind of checklist of questions that a theory of soul should answer. The Pre-Aristotelians, including Plato, generally presume that soul is somehow distinct from body. So this is one question: how does soul relate to body? Then there is the question of why we are positing soul in the first place. What is the soul supposed to do? What does it even mean to say that something has a soul?

Perhaps most obviously, soul is meant to explain life. Aristotle is comfortable ascribing soul to anything that is alive, which means that for him not only humans but also animals, and even plants, have souls. This is going to be important for Aristotle, because if there are plant souls, animal souls, and human souls, then souls can be very different from one another—my soul is going to have something in common with the soul of a sunflower, because both are souls. But equally, my soul and the sunflower's soul will be different. They will differ in terms of the abilities they confer on the living being. Sunflowers take in nutrition, they turn towards the sun, they grow. And, with all due respect to sunflowers, that pretty much exhausts their repertoire. I, by contrast, can do all these things. Taking in nutrition, turning towards the sun—I do these things on an almost daily basis, and when I was young growing was a more or less constant pursuit. But I can do many other things in addition, such as see, talk, move from place to place, and on good days, think about Aristotle.

Considering his predecessors, Aristotle finds that soul has indeed been associated with just this sort of range of capacities. In particular, he finds that soul is associated with motion or change (*kinesis*) and with perception (*aisthesis*) (403b27). He takes both of these in a rather broad sense. When the sunflower takes in nutrition, it is displaying its internal principle of change, which is its nature, as we saw above. But plants do not perceive, at least according to Aristotle. For that, we need to look up the food-chain to animals, who are capable not only of sense perception, but also of motion from one place to another. These are linked, Aristotle believes, because the animal needs perception to find its food, and needs the capacity for motion to go towards that food. Again, we see his commitment to the idea that change or motion can be explained with reference to the natures of things, and of course also his commitment to teleology, the idea that everything that is natural to a plant or an animal will serve the purpose of its flourishing. If it is natural to sunflowers to turn towards the sun, and for giraffes to trot towards acacia trees, this must be because these behaviors contribute to their well-being (415b).

Aristotle also uses his survey of previous views to indicate that there are two extremes to be avoided in thinking about how soul relates to the body. At one extreme are strongly dualist theories of soul. According to these theories, the soul is an entirely different entity from the body—the two just happen to coexist, as it were. This would apply to Plato's immaterialist theory of soul, but also materialist views like those espoused by the atomists, where soul is made up of particularly round, fast-flowing atoms located within the atomic compound that is the animal (403b–404a). It is, as it were, a body within the body. The problem with these dualist views is that they dissolve the unity of the living being, making it hard to see why the soul's relation to body is intimate rather than casual. As Aristotle says when criticizing such views, we must explain why not just any soul can join to any body (407b). At the other extreme, there is the view that soul is nothing more than a certain harmony or arrangement of the body (407b–408b). This idea is criticized also in Plato's *Phaedo*, and Aristotle agrees with the criticisms: the soul must be able to exert causal influence on the body, for instance, by initiating motion. It's hard to see how this could happen if the soul were a harmony, any more than the tuning of the strings on a guitar can make the guitar play by itself.

This leaves Aristotle right where he likes to be: occupying the middle ground. On his view, the soul will not be just another body, as the atomists proposed, but neither will it be some separate entity with a merely accidental connection to the body, as Plato seems to hold in the *Phaedo*. To arrive at a compromise position, Aristotle reaches for his favorite distinction between actuality and potentiality (412a–b). As we saw, he uses this distinction to account for change and motion. When James Brown slides across the stage doing his signature dance-move, he actualizes his potentiality for dancing. But this distinction isn't yet refined enough to provide the basis for Aristotle's psychology. We need to make a further distinction between two kinds of potentiality (412a). On the one hand, there is the kind of potentiality exercised when James Brown suddenly starts to dance. On the other hand, there is the kind of potentiality he possessed as a child, before he even knew how to dance (in his case, I think we can assume he learned to dance and to walk at about the same time). As a child, what James Brown had was the ability to acquire an ability. Or to put it in Aristotle's terms, the potentiality for acquiring a potentiality.

Aristotle thus distinguishes between what he calls "first potentiality" and what he calls "second potentiality." First potentiality is the ability to gain an ability; second potentiality is the ability you actually have (412a, 417b–418a). The insight here is that second potentiality is itself a kind of actuality, even though it isn't necessarily active at any given moment. When James Brown is backstage getting ready for the show, he's actually able to dance, but he isn't actually dancing. So we can also call second potentiality—the actual ability—"first actuality," to contrast it to the second, or full actuality that occurs when we actually exercise our abilities. Aristotle gives a similar example (417a), which suffers from its failure to involve James Brown but makes the same point. You have someone who can learn his letters, who is in first potentiality; or someone who is literate but is not using his literacy (for instance, because he is asleep, see 412a). This is second potentiality, which is the same thing as first actuality.

Then there is the person who is actually deploying their literacy, as you are right now. This person has reached second or complete actuality.

You may already be able to guess what this all has to do with the soul. We already saw that plants, animals, and humans all have souls, but of different kinds. The difference in kind is bound up with a difference in abilities: plant souls enable plants to engage in nutrition and reproduction, but nothing else; animal souls bestow upon their possessors the power to perceive and to move around; and human souls bring the capacity for thought. In his survey of previous views on the soul, Aristotle has already given us to understand that soul is defined in terms of such capacities. That was in Book One of *On the Soul*, and it has carefully prepared the way for his definition of soul in Book Two. The soul, he says, is the first actuality of a living body (412a). It is first actuality—or, if you prefer, second potentiality—because having a soul is simply having a range of actual capacities or abilities. Which abilities are at stake depend on which kind of soul is involved.[1] If you are a sunflower, your soul will help you to live and produce more sunflowers, but if you are James Brown, you have the most complex and multifacted kind of soul there is: you can live, perceive, think, and, of course, dance. No wonder they called him Soul Brother Number One.

Let's pause for a moment to compare Aristotle's idea here to the ideas put forward by contemporary philosophers of mind. Philosophy of mind is devoted in part to discussing the question of how mental phenomena relate to physical phenomena. Like Aristotle, most contemporary philosophers are suspicious of extreme answers to this question. Only a few would say that we could entirely abolish talk of the mental, so that proper science would need no concepts of desires, thoughts, or intentions. Equally, very few want to say, with Plato and Descartes, that the mind is a separate substance which is only casually related to the body. So today's philosophers of mind tend to occupy the middle ground, along with Aristotle. There are almost as many ways of doing that as there are philosophers of mind. However, we should note a major difference between these philosophers and Aristotle which is easy to overlook. What Aristotle gives us is not a theory of mind, but a theory of soul. For him, the soul explains mental events like seeing, desiring, and thinking; yet it also explains functions like digestion, reproduction, and growth. It is obvious to him that plants have souls, whereas it is equally obvious to us that plants do not have minds. In short, what Aristotle talks about in *On the Soul* is a principle of life, not a principle of *mental* life, which we usually call consciousness. This complicates any attempt to situate him relative to the contemporary debate.

Having defined soul as a kind of actual capacity or set of capacities, it is clear what Aristotle needs to do next: examine the various kinds of psychological capacities in turn, giving a philosophical account of them in ascending order of nobility. This is exactly what he does, more or less covering nutrition and sense perception in the rest of Book Two, and the higher cognitive powers of thinking and imagination in Book Three. It's really in that context that Aristotle tells us his views on mind (or intellect: in Greek, *nous*). His remarks about thinking are among the most influential, but also controversial, passages Aristotle wrote, and I am going to return to them in a later chapter. For now, I want to concentrate on nutrition and sense perception.

Here Aristotle refers us back to another issue he has covered in the survey of his predecessors. He told us that there was a dispute among the Pre-Socratic thinkers regarding the question of how one thing can affect another thing (409b–410a). Some philosophers, Aristotle says, believed that in order for causal interaction to occur between two things they must be dissimilar. For instance, if something cold is going to be acted on so that it changes, it will need to be acted on by something hot. Other thinkers insisted that two things must share some nature if they are to interact. For instance, Empedocles thought that the sense organs need to be made of all four elements, so that they can sense all four elements (410a). Thus we have a classic dialectical opposition, the sort of opposition Aristotle delights in dissolving by showing that there is a third way. In this case, the third way is provided by the increasingly familiar contrast between potentiality and actuality. Thanks to Aristotle, we know that when one thing heats another, this can occur because something potentially hot encounters something else that is actually hot. For instance, a cold rock is brought near to a fire. The actually hot fire actualizes the rock's potential to be hot. This solves the Pre-Socratic puzzle, because the rock is in a way like the fire and in a way unlike it. It is like the fire because it is hot in a way (that is, potentially hot), and unlike the fire because it is not hot in another way (that is, it is actually cold). This simple point turns out to be the key to understanding both nutrition and sensation.

With regard to nutrition, Aristotle can explain that food nourishes us, not because it is simply like us or unlike us, but because it is potentially what our bodies are actually (416a–b). You may remember that Anaxagoras thought there must be flesh and bone in cheese, because when we eat it our flesh and bone are restored and even increased. Aristotle could respond that there is no flesh and bone *actually* in the cheese, but the cheese is *potentially* flesh and bone. Anything that is alive, whether plant, animal, or human, will have a nutritive power, which simply is the power to actualize that potentiality. Just as the fire heats the rock, so the cheese-eating animal turns the cheese into flesh and restores itself. The same kind of story can be told regarding sense perception. Consider what happens when you see. When you are not seeing—as when you're asleep or your eyes are closed—you are of course potentially seeing (417a). You just need to wake up, to open your eyes, and if those eyes are in good working order you'll see whatever is in front of you. Again, you might be able to guess what Aristotle will say here. Just as the actually hot fire actualizes the potentially hot rock, so the actual colors and shapes of the objects in front of your eyes will actualize the potential of your vision. If you see, for example, a red apple, your vision goes from being potentially red to being actually red (423b–424a). The redness of the apple simply activates the potential redness of sight.

What exactly does this mean? Some scholars, most prominently Richard Sorabji, have proposed that the physical organ, the eye itself, literally turns red. This is encouraged by the fact that Aristotle says that the eye must in itself be colorless, since otherwise it would not be able to take on all the colors that we see (424a). Other interpreters, sometimes called "spiritualists," think that the eye, or vision, becomes red when we see red, but not in a literal, physical sense. Rather, for vision to become red is simply for us to have the experience of seeing red.[2] This has interesting consequences for lining up Aristotle with contemporary philosophy of mind, since on Sorabji's reading the eye's turning red would be identical with seeing red. That is, "my eye fluid turned red" and "I saw red" would be two different descriptions of the same event—this sort of account is prominent among philosophers of mind, many of whom also want to identify mental and physical events.

But however literally we take Aristotle's theory, it is clear that sensation is for him nothing but the actualization of a capacity on the part of the animal or human that engages in perception. If we go back to Aristotle's definition of soul, this makes perfect sense. What you get by having a soul is, as we said, a whole range of capacities, which will be actualized or not depending on your circumstances. Some functions will be actual pretty much all the time, for instance, the power to breathe and produce the warmth needed to keep you at body temperature. These things go on even while you sleep. But most other functions shut down while you sleep—in terms of actual activity, sleeping people who aren't dreaming are much like plants. But even sleeping people have the *capacity* to do a wide range of things, from moving, to seeing and hearing, to thinking. Just shake them so they wake up, and they will manifest some or all of these capacities almost immediately, for instance, the capacity to be annoyed that they have just been woken up for no good reason.

Part of what Aristotle's *On the Soul* has done, then, is to sketch out the principles for a much larger project, which we could call "biology." Aristotelian biology would study all living organisms, whether plant, animal, or human. In this project, Aristotle's ideas about nature and psychology would come together. He would explore in detail his idea that all natural beings have purposes which they naturally pursue, and his idea that each living thing has a different kind of soul, which brings with it a specific range of capacities. After all, it isn't only the case that plants, animals, and humans have different capacities—so do different kinds of plants, like sunflowers as opposed to venus flytraps; and different kinds of animals, like giraffes as opposed to gorillas. From this point of view, *On the Soul* can be seen as simply the first step in the direction of a systematic biology, in which the full range of living organisms would be explored and explained on Aristotelian principles. Did Aristotle undertake such a project? You bet your life he did, as we'll see in the next chapter.

CLASSIFIED INFORMATION
ARISTOTLE'S BIOLOGY

A short story by the Argentine writer Jorge Luis Borges imagines a Chinese encyclopedia, entitled the *Celestial Emporium of Benevolent Knowledge*. This fictional work suggests a division of animals into fourteen kinds, namely:

1. those that belong to the Emperor,
2. embalmed ones,
3. those that are trained,
4. suckling pigs,
5. mermaids,
6. fabulous ones,
7. stray dogs,
8. those that are included in this classification,
9. those that tremble as if they were mad,
10. innumerable ones,
11. those drawn with a very fine camel-hair brush,
12. et cetera,
13. those that have just broken the flower vase,
14. those that at a distance resemble flies.[1]

I don't know if this joke is partially meant to be at Aristotle's expense. But if not, it could have been.

Aristotle is the father of animal classification. When we talk about the animal kingdoms being divided by genus and species, we are not only engaging in an Aristotelian project, but using Aristotelian terminology to pursue that project. (The word "genus" comes from the Greek *genos*.) Animals were not the only thing Aristotle classified. As I mentioned in the chapter on his life and works, he and his students collected and categorized political constitutions of city-states. Even when he presents Pre-Socratic views, Aristotle shows his classifying instincts: we saw how, in the *Physics*, he divides up his predecessors in terms of how many principles they postulate to explain nature. He learned the practice of division from his master, Plato. In several dialogues Plato has his characters try to reach definitions by dividing larger kinds into smaller kinds. We saw that the divisions need to be made "at the natural joints," rather than chopping at random like a bad butcher (*Phaedrus* 265e). This is the idea Borges is playing with: his imaginary *Celestial Emporium* reminds us just how many ways there are of dividing things up, and so invites us to ask whether classification is always arbitrary.

But if you do think there is a right way to divide, as Plato and Aristotle did, then a philosophical task awaits.[2] We can understand the world by classifying the things in that world. We will sort out the frogs from the toads, and also the bullfrogs from the tree-frogs. If we do the dividing right, and do it completely, we will get a comprehensive and accurate inventory of things in the world. Furthermore, we will understand how those things relate to one another: we will see that bullfrogs are closely related to tree-frogs, since both are frogs; that frogs in general are related to salamanders, since both are amphibians; and that frogs are loosely related to giraffes, since both are animals. Aristotle already outlines a project of this kind in his logical works, suggesting that a definition will set out a general kind—a genus, like *animal*—and then divide off a more specific kind or species, like *man*, by saying what makes this type of animal special. Man will be the kind of animal that is rational, for instance.

But there is more to philosophical understanding than mere classification. For Aristotle, as for Plato, true understanding or knowledge will require giving a causal account. In the animal world the relevant causes will frequently be final causes, that is, the purposes of things. For instance, we may distinguish between two species of bird on the basis of the shape of their beaks. This isn't yet an *explanation*: each type of bird has been isolated, but we don't yet have understanding. We understand when we come to see that, for instance, some beaks are designed to strain food out of pondwater, while others are designed to pluck insects out of trees. This will be at least part of what it is to understand the difference between a duck and a woodpecker. A more detailed analysis might help explain the difference between different types of duck, or different types of woodpecker—again, understanding would come when we see what purposes the distinguishing features would serve. Aristotle's motto here is, "nature does nothing in vain" (*On the Heavens* 291b). Whatever makes each species special must serve a purpose and help the members of that species to flourish.

This whole train of thought is reflected in Aristotle's writings about animals—his zoological works. Along with a few smaller treatises, the main three texts are the *History of Animals*, the *Parts of Animals*, and the *Generation of Animals*. These are sizeable treatises. All together, zoology takes up more than a quarter of Aristotle's extant writings. The *History of Animals* in particular is a massive, sprawling survey of information. In the title, the word *History* reflects the Greek *historia*, which just means an account laying out the results of an inquiry. Though Aristotle has included a good deal of hearsay, some of which he would have done better to ignore, the inquiry was undertaken largely by himself. After Plato's death and his departure from the Academy, but before he founded his own school, the Lyceum, Aristotle traveled in the eastern Mediterranean. He had an especially productive time on the island of Lesbos, where he undertook extensive scientific investigations. He studied marine animals with particular intensity, and made some genuinely impressive discoveries. For instance, he was the first to note that whales and dolphins are not kinds of fish.[3]

Aristotle didn't just look at animals, though; he actually dissected them. He is able to talk in detail about the internal organs of animals, comparing different species and talking about the variation in their reproductive systems, digestive organs, and so on. He urges us not to spurn the task of close observation and dissection, but to get our hands dirty. This, just as much as the study of the divine heavenly bodies, provides an insight into the astonishingly well-designed world around us. Aristotle in fact says that astronomy and biology provide equal pleasure: the stars are nobler than terrestrial animals, but we have little access to them, something he compares to catching only a glimpse of one's beloved (*Parts of Animals* 644b).

The *History of Animals*, all ten books of it, can seem a barely organized miscellany of facts. In a single chapter (9.6), it tells us that tortoises eat marjoram to avoid being poisoned after eating vipers (612a); speaks of a man who could predict the weather by closely observing hedgehogs (612b); and mentions that the marten likes honey and has genital organs that can be turned into a powder for medicine (612b). One hopes the marten is given some honey first, in compensation. But a more sensitive reading, one Aristotle suggests himself, would see it as a preparatory work for the *Parts of Animals*. On this reading, the *History* presents the observations that allow us to divide up the animal world into its types. Aristotle's fascination with certain details betrays this. By picking out the distinctive features of, say, the marten or tortoise, Aristotle prepares the way for scientific understanding.

The *Parts of Animals* then supplies that understanding, by explaining the purposes of these distinctive features which serve to distinguish one species from another. Since nature does nothing in vain, any feature natural to a species will contribute to the proper functioning of the animals in that species. The eating of the marjoram, the shape of the birds' beaks, and so on will all be "hypothetically necessary," as Aristotle puts it (639b). If the tortoise is to avoid being poisoned, it must eat marjoram; if the duck is to strain food from pondwater, it needs a mouth that acts like a sieve; and so on. Aristotle's careful dissection of animals and their parts was motivated by this quest to understand these functions, like someone taking apart a car and trying to decide what each part is designed to do.

Aristotle also records observations about plants, which seem to have been a speciality of his associate Theophrastus, who sojourned with him in Lesbos and wrote a work dedicated to plants. (More on him later.) But Aristotle had a particular interest in animals. And no wonder; animals are the most highly functional entities in Aristotle's functional and hierarchical world. At the bottom of his hierarchy are the familiar four elements, air, earth, fire, and water. These can all transform into one another in a cycle, as Aristotle argues in another work, *On Generation and Corruption*; here he is disagreeing with Plato, who believed that earth could not become any of the other elements. When they combine they form basic constituents, which are the same through and through: things like blood and other bodily humors. These combine again to form the more complicated parts of animals (*Parts of Animals* 640b). It is really here that biological purposiveness enters into the equation. An organ like a liver or hand can only be understood within the context of the animal's functioning. As Aristotle says, an eye removed from its socket is an eye in name only (*On the Soul* 412b).

Of course, for all his careful observation Aristotle did not always arrive at the right answers. He got things badly wrong when it came to the major organs of the body. For him, one of the most important principles in biology is what he calls "vital heat." This isn't so crazy: after all, living animals tend to be warm, and to cool down fast when they die. Relying on this idea, Aristotle believed that the heart's function was to spread vital heat through the body, and to serve as the center of motion and sensation (*Parts of Animals* 670a). For him, the brain was little more than a refrigeration device for regulating vital heat, and breathing in air plays the same kind of role: to balance out the heat generated in the heart. You might believe that you can tell you are thinking with your brain, and that it is just obvious that your thoughts and sensory experiences are, as it were, happening in your head. But it is clearly not obvious: Aristotle, and the Stoics after him, thought that the heart was the controlling organ of the body, the seat of motion and sensation. As for thinking, Aristotle denied that this is done with any bodily organ, as we'll see a few chapters below.

Just as vital to Aristotle's biology (pun, as always, intended) is the question of how new animals are formed. Here too he was a keen observer, even keeping a careful record of the development of chicks by looking inside eggs at different stages of incubation. (If you're curious about which came first, the chicken or the egg, I direct you to *History of Animals* 6.3.) The preservation of species is of tremendous importance for Aristotle, because he believes that when we are dividing up animals and understanding their functions, we are learning about eternal, necessary features of the world. The celestial bodies rotate around the earth eternally. But chickens, tortoises, and humans cannot live forever, as the celestial bodies do—they are not made of the indestructible fifth element that exists out there in the heavens. So the only way that species can be eternal is through reproduction (*On the Soul* 415b). Thanks to reproduction and the permanence of species it makes possible, zoology is a fit subject for the Aristotelian scientist, who is interested only in necessary and eternal truths.

This brings us to the third major zoological work, the *Generation of Animals*. As in *Parts of Animals*, Aristotle here deals with purposiveness. As it develops, a chick embryo is relentlessly pursuing its final cause, which is to be born as a chick which can grow into a mature chicken. But to explain the mechanics of reproduction Aristotle has recourse to two other kinds of cause: form and matter. His basic idea is that the female human or animal provides the material for the fetus, namely menstrual fluid, while the male provides form through his seed. The seed contains certain "motions" which transmit the form to the blood, and set up a chain of developments in the matter that lead to the formation of a fetus (*Generation of Animals* 729b). Again, heat is the chief physical mechanism here. Human seed causes the matter to be heated in just the right way so that the blood is concocted into a human embryo, and not the embryo of, say, a giraffe. Mechanics aside, it's worth noticing how Aristotle here diverges from Plato. Forget the single, transcendent Form of Man. A man is caused by nothing more or less exalted than another man, namely his father, in cooperation with the cosmos which provides the context in which nature unfolds. As Aristotle famously puts it, "man is generated by man and the sun" (*Physics* 194b).

Of course, things cannot be quite this simple. After all, humans resemble their parents and grandparents more than they resemble other members of the species. So the father must transmit more than the basic form of human or horse; he must also transmit, say, the property of having a snub or acquiline nose. Furthermore, people also resemble their mothers. So the mother cannot, after all, be providing just a substrate of matter, with the male seed doing all the work of transmitting form. Realizing this, Aristotle not only allows that the motions in the father's seed bring along the father's idiosyncratic features, but also admits that there must already be highly specific potentialities in the woman's menstrual fluid (*On Generation of Animals* 768a). These can emerge as the embryo is formed, so that you might inherit your mother's brown eyes despite having a blue-eyed father. Finally, Aristotle seems to allow for new features to arise in the child, to explain features that are apparently possessed by none of the child's immediate forebears.[4]

This raises the intriguing possibility that Aristotle could have allowed for the possibility of something like evolution. After all, if you can be blue-eyed when your parents have brown eyes, then why can't species themselves change from generation to generation? Make enough incremental changes across the generations, and you can turn apes into humans, as Darwin taught us. Aristotle clearly rejects this, but why? I suspect that Aristotle simply didn't consider it physically possible, within the mechanics of reproduction, for variations to arise that would lead to an actual change in species. To explain why, he might point to the cosmic cycle itself: if events here in our lower world are causally connected with the regular, eternal motions of the heavens, then it is no surprise that the events are always more or less the same.

This, in broad outline, is Aristotle's account of how species are propagated. But there's a rather large exception we still haven't considered. Aristotle believed that some animals are generated without parents—that is, *spontaneously* generated (*History of Animals* 538b, with examples throughout Book Five, in chapters 11, 15–16, 19). Usually this is explained by referring to the appearance of maggots and worms in rotting flesh. Failing to notice any insects laying eggs in the flesh, Aristotle and others leapt to the conclusion that such creatures can generate spontaneously. That is part of the story, but Aristotle was also drawing an inference from his dissection work. He looked at a variety of species without finding any reproductive organs, and inferred that these species must arise spontaneously.

This is the sort of mistake that can lead modern readers to regard Aristotle with amused condescension. But in a way, I think we should congratulate him on his intellectual honesty. Within his system, spontaneous generation is clearly a problem. It is a major exception to his theory that form is passed on to offspring by parents. So it's to his credit that he gave serious thought to an apparently unavoidable fact of observation, especially given the lowliness of many apparent products of spontaneous generation. Aristotle wasn't going to let a nice theory, or the fact that maggots are disgusting, distract him from his scientific integrity. Briefly, his account of spontaneous generation is that some external heat-source, like the sun, does the work of setting off motions in suitably prepared matter, the work that would normally be done by generative seed. This happens when a bubble of warm liquid is somehow enclosed so that vital heat cannot escape, and an animal is more or less randomly formed (*On Generation of Animals* 762a).

It's worth emphasizing that many types of animals are *only* generated in this fashion. This is surprising, given Aristotle's insistence against Empedocles, in the *Physics*, that natural things cannot be the result of chance and spontaneity, which we looked at a few chapters back. In light of this, how can Aristotle say that there are eternal species that are propagated by chance? The solution, perhaps, is to say that the particular time and place of spontaneous generation is a matter of chance. This is a striking difference from normal generation, where animals and humans very intentionally set about the process of reproduction, perhaps after dinner and a movie. In the case of a spontaneously generated worm, it just happens that the right kind of bubble is heated in the right way. But in another sense this is anything but random. Whenever such a bubble is so heated, the result will be a worm, and it's entirely predictable that this will happen on a regular basis, even if we cannot predict where or when.

Finally, we should admit a similar tension that arises frequently for Aristotle: he wants to say that nature does nothing in vain, that the world around us is full of form and purpose. Yet we frequently see nature fail. Human and animal babies are born with deformities. Even whole species sometimes seem defective, as for instance moles, which have underdeveloped eyes below their skin, a fact Aristotle observes and discusses with some interest (*History of Animals* 491b, 533a). In general, Aristotle is not too concerned when nature falls short. Nature does nothing in vain, but it also acts only for the most part, and the fact that animals and plants are made of matter means that form can always be thwarted. We care more, of course, when humans are defective. On this point, Aristotle seems to depart from his usual optimism. He thinks the human race is in fact made up largely of defective types, including women and so-called "natural slaves," but also plenty of free male citizens who are vicious when they should be virtuous, boorish when they should be pursuing the pleasures of knowledge. Aristotle needs to account for this, and tell us how to make sure we fall into the relatively small class of those humans who do fulfill their purpose. It is this task that he takes up in what may be his most enduring work, the *Nicomachean Ethics*, and in its sequel, the *Politics*.

37

THE GOLDILOCKS THEORY
ARISTOTLE'S ETHICS

There's this new branch of social science which calls itself "happiness studies." I read about it in a magazine article,[1] which related some of the surprising findings made in this field. For instance, it turns out that people who win the lottery are no happier than people who aren't, and that while being poor doesn't make you unhappy, living amongst people who are richer than you *does* make you unhappy. But how do they figure out how happy these people are? Well, it's simple: they ask. For instance, they've asked lottery-winners and other people to say, on a scale of one to ten, how happy they are, and discover that the average answers are about the same. Lessons from this research are even being applied to government policy. For instance, it's useful to know, if you are running a society, that income equality may make people happier than absolute increases in wealth.

Whenever I read something along these lines, I like to ask myself, "What would Aristotle make of this?" Would he endorse this new and exciting field of happiness studies? I guess Aristotle would say the same thing he always says: "in a way yes, and in a way no." He would certainly agree that happiness is worth studying, and even that it is of paramount importance, and the right goal to have in mind when designing a society. But he would also have a reservation, I think. He would raise a quizzical eyebrow at the suggestion that we can find out how happy people are just by asking them. Not only are people poor judges about what will make them happy, as the happiness scientists have shown by studying lottery-winners. People are even poor judges about whether they are *already* happy. Or so Aristotle thinks.

Here, then, we have a subject of paramount importance, on which people tend to get badly confused. Looks like a job for a philosopher. Aristotle takes up the challenge in one of his best-known works, the *Nicomachean Ethics*. This is actually one of three works he wrote on ethics, along with the *Eudemian Ethics* and another, rarely studied text called the *Magna Moralia*. The *Nicomachean* and *Eudemian Ethics* share a large section in common, and there is a debate about how they relate to one another, which was written first, and so on. I'll focus on the *Nicomachean Ethics*, since that's by far the most commonly studied Aristotelian ethical treatise. It is quite a long work, and takes in not only ethical virtue but also the idea of voluntary action, theoretical virtue, friendship, pleasure, and the superiority of the philosophical life. As with Plato's *Republic*, I will be devoting two chapters to it, without even scratching the surface.

Aristotle begins the *Ethics* with the surprising announcement that we are here embarking on what he calls *political* philosophy (1094b). The *Ethics* is thus explicitly linked to another work, called the *Politics*, which we'll look at later. His idea is that the political theorist's aim is to figure out what will make the whole community happy. To do that, we need first to understand the happiness of individual people. The Greek word for "happiness" is *eudaimonia*, which already gives us a clue as to why Aristotle believes that people can be wrong about how happy they are. The word *eudaimonia* relates to the word *daimon*, a kind of spirit or minor divinity—like the guardian spirit that whispered in Socrates' ear whenever he was about to do something wrong. For this reason, *eudaimonia* has the connotation of blessedness, rather than mere cheerfulness. Thus, for Aristotle, happiness consists in living a life that is blessed, a life that right-thinking people would admire and wish to lead themselves. If someone thinks they are happy simply because they are rich, or famous, then they are wrong: this isn't the sort of life one should rightly admire.

But why not? Couldn't we just say, "to each his or her own," letting everyone decide how happy they are on a scale of one to ten? Aristotle thinks not, because there are good reasons to dismiss certain lifestyles as falling short of happiness. Take the goals just mentioned: being rich, and being famous. If you think wealth will make you happy, Aristotle cautions, then think again. After all, when you pursue wealth what you really want is not wealth, it's what wealth can buy (1096a). As Socrates already pointed out, wealth is no good to you without an understanding of what to do with it. Even without the benefit of empirical happiness studies, Aristotle knew that a lottery win will not make you happy all by itself. To think that it could is indeed a crass conceptual error, confusing the end we strive for with a means towards that end. Happiness, by contrast, could never be the means to anything. As Aristotle points out, it is the most final end we have: there is no further purpose for which we wish to be happy.

Aristotle levels a similar criticism at the life of fame, or to put it in a more Greek way, a life of honor. Many Greeks would probably have endorsed this as the most choiceworthy life: a life centered around political success, military conquest, and lasting reputation. Aristotle's own student, Alexander the Great, was perhaps the happiest person in the ancient world, if happiness and honor are the same thing. And like Plato, who deals with this topic extensively in the *Republic*, Aristotle is well aware of the allure of honor among his readers. But he sets it alongside wealth as a misguided goal, because honor as such is not good enough—we care *why* we are honored. If a gang of lowlife criminals admire and praise me for my successful thievery, that is no reason to think that I am leading a good life. Nor would we wish to be honored falsely for things we didn't actually do. So if I am seeking honor, what I must really be seeking is some kind of life that would be *worth* honoring. In that case, the honor seems to be secondary. What I am really after is the good life that rightfully earns me the admiration of others.

Here again I think we have to admire Aristotle, whether it makes him happy or not. His argument strikes me as persuasive, and seems to get to the heart of, for instance, the problem with contemporary celebrity culture. (There is indeed something empty and absurd about being famous just for being famous.) But a big question is left hanging. If what I want is a life that would rightly be honored, what would such a life look like? Aristotle, adopting an argument found towards the beginning of Plato's *Republic*, suggests that we can discover the answer if we think about what human beings are for (1097b). What is our purpose? What are we, as it were, designed to do? If we do have some purpose, then surely the good life will be the life in which that purpose is fulfilled to the greatest extent possible. Just as being a good flute-player will consist in playing the flute well, so being a good human will consist in doing whatever humans are supposed to do, and performing that function well (1098a).

Is it really obvious, though, that all humans share some purpose or function? Aristotle answers that question with a question of his own: how could it be that the parts of my body, like my eyes, have a function, without *my* having a function (1097b)? This would be as if my car were made of functional parts, yet the car had no overall purpose. Aristotle's train of thought here runs along tracks laid in his philosophy of nature. Remember that, for Aristotle, all animals, plants, even simple things like the four elements, are pursuing some kind of goal. The goal of a plant is to grow to maturity and reproduce. The goal of a stone is to move downwards towards the center of the universe. If Aristotle believes that even these things have purposes, it's no surprise that he should think humans have them too. This is not to say that Aristotle actually invokes any heavy-duty theory of nature or metaphysical considerations here in the *Ethics*. But the considerations would be available, if we pressed him on the point.

For the sake of argument, then, let's grant him that humans do have a purpose. How, then, can we tell what the purpose of humans will be? It can't be merely being alive, or having sensation, because these things are shared in common with plants and animals. If there is a human function, it must be characteristic of humans—it must be the performance of the activity that belongs to us alone. What could this be? For Aristotle, there's only one possible answer: it must be the use of reason (1098a). For it is rationality that distinguishes us from plants and animals. This is Aristotle's so-called "function argument," which provides the foundation for his ethics.[2] Given its importance, we're likely to feel that he should be working harder to convince us. Aristotle seems to think we'll find it immediately plausible, not only that humans do have a function (in Greek *ergon*), but also that our function will reside in whichever activity is unique to us. The upshot is that we cannot disentangle the question of what we humans are from the question of what we ought to be.

For all that this is unsurprising, given Aristotle's conviction that every natural thing has a purpose, it means that he is starting from a very different place from most modern ethicists. Perhaps the most notorious problem in ethics nowadays is the so-called "is/ought gap" pointed out by David Hume.[3] The problem is that we have, on the one hand, a factual description of the world and the things in it, and on the other hand, a set of notions about right and wrong. A description about how things *are* does not by itself give us an account of how things *ought* to be. For instance, we can observe that some actions cause pain and suffering, without thereby showing that those actions are wrong. To do that, we'd need to explain why pain and suffering are bad, why they ought not to happen. And yet, it looks like whatever we can observe about the world just gives us factual description. So where do we get morality from? It's an intractable enough problem to have led some to ethical skepticism. But for Aristotle, it's a problem that never arises. He would reject the basic idea that we can describe and understand things without invoking purpose and function. These concepts are, as philosophers say nowadays, "normative"; in other words, they already imply value-judgments. To put it more plainly, Aristotle thinks that saying what a giraffe is involves saying something about what a good giraffe would be like. And the same goes for humans.

Finally, then, we have a fix on the happy life. It will be a life of reason, because that will be the kind of life that allows humans to achieve their distinctive excellence. We can now see why Aristotle thinks you can be wrong about whether you are happy: your happiness is determined not by how you feel about yourself, but by how well you are using your rationality. Now, though, we're tempted to ask what any of this has to do with ethics. When we imagine ourselves using reason, we're more apt to imagine ourselves, say, doing mathematics than, say, helping old ladies across the street. And if we think about people who are ethically defective, we don't usually think they are failing in respect of *rationality*. In short, Aristotle has to tell us what reason has to do with virtue, and what failures of reason have to do with vice. He has a very good story to tell here, and I'll get to it in just a moment. But first I want to point out that, for Aristotle, the excellent use of reason *would* include things like mathematics. The *Ethics* includes a discussion of excellence in the pursuit of know-ledge for its own sake. He sees understanding, in effect, as a kind of non-practical virtue (1142b–1143a). Indeed, at the risk of giving away Aristotle's punch-line, it will turn out that the life of theoretical inquiry is actually the happiest life of all.

For now, though, Aristotle is trying to build a picture of human life in which rationality is fully exploited, including rationality in the practical sphere. Virtue arises insofar as the practical sphere is an opportunity to use our reason. But the practical sphere is the sphere in which we form preferences and perform actions. So virtue will be using reason to form the right preferences and to perform the right actions. On this point, Aristotle is admirably modest. He concedes that there is no possibility of total "exactness" when we are dealing with the realm of particular situations, as opposed to universal truths (1104a). There is no hard-and-fast set of ethical rules that can be applied to every case that might arise. Rather, practical rationality is, for Aristotle, the ability to confront each situation as it comes, and to choose the right course of action in every case. This could be something as humble as choosing the right amount to eat at each mealtime—the virtue of temperance—or choosing to fight on a battlefield—the virtue of courage.

Of course, it would be disappointing if all we could say is that virtuous action is the action that would be chosen by the virtuous person. So Aristotle adds a more general observation, perhaps the most famous idea in his ethics: that the virtuous action will lie at the mean between two extremes (1104a). This is what a friend of mine likes to call the "Goldilocks theory."[4] Virtue is when you choose and enjoy what is not too much, not too little, but just right. Each kind of virtue is a mean between some excessive tendency and a tendency towards deficiency. For instance, temperance is the mean between gluttony and being overly abstemious. Courage is the mean between recklessness and cowardice. Generosity is the mean between stinginess and prodigality. And so on. Of course, this isn't to say that you should literally engage in *everything* in moderation. You can't do just the right amount of incest or unprovoked murder. These actions shouldn't be done at all—which perhaps poses a problem for Aristotle, unless he can convince us that such actions are excesses in relation to some other type of action which should be done in moderation. For instance, incest might be an excessive use of one's sexual capacities. Sex, unlike incest, is something that should be pursued moderately.

Though that sounds reasonable, this part of the *Ethics* is bound to remind us that we are reading an author from a very different culture. Consider how his definition of virtue as a mean would relate to Judeo-Christian morality. The Christian saints were not engaging in chastity, faith, and humility to a moderate degree, but rather striving towards perfect chastity, faith, and humility. If incest is excessive sexuality, then chastity must be deficient sexuality—so not a virtue at all, on Aristotle's theory. A nice example of Aristotle's cultural otherness here is his discussion of "the man who has greatness of soul." The rather wonderful Greek word for him is *megalopsychos*. The great-souled man is perfectly virtuous, is well aware of his virtue, and acts accordingly, behaving with great dignity and seeing himself as significantly superior to those around him (1123a–1125a). Here we see that Aristotle's ethical exemplar is closer to Achilles than to Mother Teresa. Aristotle would, of course, admit that you can be overly prideful. But the great-souled man has *earned* his massive self-esteem by being massively virtuous. A normal person who behaves like Achilles isn't being virtuous, he's being an arrogant twerp. Neither, though, should Achilles act like a normal person. That would be to rate his own virtue too low.

How, then, do we achieve virtue? This has already been marked as a political question by the aforementioned opening of the *Ethics*. Aristotle thinks that people who do not grow up in healthy societies have effectively no chance of becoming virtuous. So a complete answer would mean looking at Aristotle's political philosophy. But in the *Ethics* he already explains why our social upbringing is so important: virtue is achieved by habituation. The very word "ethics" shows this, as Aristotle points out. It comes from the Greek *ethos*, which means "habit" or "custom" (1103a). Thus, we already develop the virtues when we are children. Parents chastise their kids for being insufficiently bold or truthful, and this inculcates in them a habit towards courage and honesty.

On this point, it's traditional to draw a contrast between Aristotle and Socrates. As you'll remember, Socrates apparently thought that virtue involves some sort of intellectual knowledge, so that virtuous people must be able to give a definition of virtue. For Aristotle, this picture is far too intellectualist. As we've seen, he certainly believes that ethical action requires some kind of cognitive process—it is rational excellence, after all. But Aristotelian virtue is more like a kind of rational discernment or perception, in which I rely on my training to find the right response to any given circumstance. Again, the variation between circumstances means that no abstract definition or account can guarantee that I choose rightly. Ultimately it's down to my ingrained habit, which not only enables me to make the right choice, but also means that I will *want* to make the right choice. I will take pleasure in doing what is right, since it is what I am used to; it is second nature (1099a, 1105a). This means that virtue is not all about beliefs or knowledge, as Socrates thought—it is about feelings and actions (1106b). The difference between the virtuous, excellent man and the vicious, defective man is largely the result of training. The virtuous man enjoys and chooses the mean between extremes as a matter of course, whereas the vicious man enjoys the wrong things and has ingrained habits for making the wrong choices.

Aristotle's picture is rather compelling. He's described virtue as something which brings us enjoyment and allows us to achieve our own personal excellence. My goal, as an ethical agent, is to do what I am meant to do, and do it well. Aristotle compares this to athletic pursuits, observing that we award admiration to those who actually perform virtuous deeds, just as at the Olympics they give prizes to those who compete and win, not just those who are most fit and beautiful (1099a). This makes virtue sound really worth having, and it's obvious why it is in our interest to have it: virtue makes us the best humans we can be. But doesn't this sort of ethical athleticism leave something out, something that is fundamental to ethics? What about treating others well for *their* sake? Should I really be generous, help my friends, have healthy relationships with my loved ones, all in order to pursue my own personal excellence? Aristotle makes it sound like other people are mere tools for me to use in attaining perfection. This is a problem we'll look at next, as we turn to Aristotle's theory of friendship, and consider in greater depth how the Aristotelian virtuous man uses and enjoys both the things and the people around him.

38

THE SECOND SELF
ARISTOTLE ON PLEASURE
AND FRIENDSHIP

When you think of the good things in life, what springs to mind? Perhaps a nice meal, a glass of fine wine? Pleasant conversation with friends? Or maybe you're less high-minded, and will go straight for sex, fast cars, and cold, hard cash. As we saw in the last chapter, Aristotle identifies the good life as the life of reason and virtue. So would he purse his lips in stern disapproval at us as we pursue those pleasant dinners, not to mention the sex, cars, and money? Or does he leave a place for such things in his consideration of happiness?

A modern reader of Aristotle's *Nicomachean Ethics* is apt to come away with the impression that Aristotle is quite grumpy about this whole pleasure thing. Towards the beginning of the *Ethics* he mentions the life devoted to pleasure, and dismisses it with a snort of derision. This is a life for cattle, not humans, he says (1095b). So it's surprising to discover that many ancient readers of the *Ethics* thought of Aristotle as a defender of the comfortable life. He wasn't as objectionable as the crassly hedonist Epicureans, but for these critics he still fell short of the full moral rigor one would expect from a proper philosopher. The critics were comparing Aristotle to Stoic and Platonist ethical thinkers, for whom *only* virtue is valuable, and all else is intrinsically worthless. We've seen a view like this already in the mouth of Socrates, who argued that such things as wealth and power benefit their possessors only if they are joined to wisdom and virtue. We've seen Plato, too, arguing in the *Republic* that a virtuous man is happy even if he is hated by society and subjected to injustices and torments.

Aristotle, as so often, is happy to occupy the middle ground. On the one hand, he rejects hedonism: though pleasure has its place in the good life, it is not the primary goal of the good life. But on the other hand, he adopts the common-sense judgment that someone who is, say, tortured to death after his family has been murdered by an unjust tyrant, is not happy, no matter how virtuous he is. Of course he knew that he was disagreeing with his master Plato here, but as he says in the *Ethics*, we must honor truth above our friends. And as we saw last time, the truth about the good life is that it must be admirable and enviable for right-minded men. Unless we're Stoics or Platonists, we will probably agree with Aristotle that virtue is no guarantee of happiness, even if it is the best route to happiness. But this forces Aristotle to admit that our happiness is to some extent out of our own control. A tyrant can always come along and destroy our lives. In fact, Aristotle even wonders whether our happiness might retroactively be destroyed after our deaths, if our close friends and descendants have horrors visited upon them (1101a–b). Although he concludes that happiness could not be completely destroyed in this way, the worry is a reminder that, for Aristotle, being happy is more like being blessed than being content.

There's another reason why Aristotle includes so-called "external goods" in the happy life, that is, goods like wealth, health, and family in addition to virtue. He believes that virtues must be exercised to be worth anything. You'll have no opportunity to be generous if you have no money, or to be loyal if you have no friends. So the virtuous man needs a measure of material success just to make use of his virtue (1099a–b). On this point Socrates might agree with Aristotle. Socrates, as portrayed by Plato at least, did allow that wealth and power would be valuable so long as it is in the hands of a wise and virtuous man, who would use them to do good. It's just that wealth and power have no value, and can even be harmful, in the absence of wisdom and virtue. Still, there's no doubt that Socrates and Aristotle differ in their emphasis, with Aristotle happy to accept the importance of external goods and Socrates constantly pointing out their intrinsic uselessness. Those Stoic and Platonist critics sided with Socrates, but again, I suspect we're liable to find Aristotle's view attractive.

Another attractive feature of Aristotle's ideas about happiness is something I already mentioned in the last chapter. For Aristotle, virtue itself is pleasurable to the virtuous man. This is because he is habituated to perform virtuous actions. He's used to them, to the point that they come naturally to him. However fearful it might be for him to stand bravely in battle, it would be even more painful for him to run away—he fears shame more than he fears a noble death (1115a). He is courageous and would find it excruciating to flee from a battle when he should not. He will also find it unpleasant to over-eat at a banquet, whereas a moderate repast will be just what he likes best. I say this view is attractive, but maybe you'll disagree. Maybe you'll say that if virtue is really to be admirable, it should be tough going. We should have to grit our teeth and do the right thing, not because we enjoy it, but because it is the right thing.

It's traditional here to draw a contrast between Aristotle and a much later philosopher, Immanuel Kant. Whereas Aristotle thinks that enjoyment of virtue is a sure sign of a virtuous character, Kant insists that morality really has nothing to do with enjoyment. It's not that Kant necessarily wants you to find moral duty unpleasant; that would be rather perverse. But certainly, for Kant, if you help an old lady across the street just because you get a kick out of it, this doesn't count as a properly moral act. In a way, you're just lucky. You happen to be a person who enjoys helping old ladies, rather than stealing their purses. The right reason for helping the old lady is that it is your duty, and any enjoyment you take in this is morally irrelevant, even if it is a nice bonus.[1] Now, it must be said that Kant has a point. Aristotle's theory of virtue depends heavily on the idea of habituation—you become virtuous by being trained in virtue as you grow up. This means that if you don't get the right upbringing, you will not take enjoyment in the right things and so you will not be virtuous. Thus Aristotle is vulnerable to what is sometimes called the problem of "moral luck."[2] That is, our ethical condition should not be a matter of happenstance; it should be up to us to control.

Aristotle has a reply ready. He will say that there are indeed people who manage to do the right thing against their ingrained habit and inclination. These are people with *enkrateia*, which means something like "self-control" (1145b). If you enjoy being on time and naturally show up when expected, then you have the virtue of punctuality; whereas if you are one of those people who has to set their watch ten minutes ahead to fool yourself into staying on schedule, you are merely self-controlled. Outwardly, the self-controlled man and the virtuous man seem very similar. They both will stand fast in battle, eat moderately at table, help the old lady across the street. The difference is that, whereas the virtuous man enjoys doing these things and does them out of habit, the self-controlled man would rather run away in battle, eat like a pig, and ignore the old lady. Yet he does the right thing because he knows that's what he's supposed to do. Now Aristotle might ask: who would we admire more, and who would we rather be? I guess it's clear that we'd rather *be* the virtuous man, but the question of who we *admire* more is trickier. When I think about this, I find myself changing my mind depending on the example. Someone who has to exert self-control to avoid snatching old ladies' purses seems to me less admirable than someone who would never consider doing such a thing. And certainly, I feel more confident in making appointments with genuinely punctual people. On the other hand, someone who fights bravely in battle, even as every fibre of his being tells him to run, or someone who has to exert willpower to stay on their diet and eat moderately, seems to me more admirable than people who do these same things naturally and with enjoyment. So it's not clear to me who has the better of this dispute between Aristotle and Kant.

Of course, Aristotle recognizes that not everyone does the right thing. So he identifies two other character-types, in addition to the virtuous and self-controlled man. Completely opposed to the virtuous man is the vicious man, who does bad things the way the virtuous man does good things (1145a). He naturally, and out of habit, turns up late to battles and then runs away from them. He snatches purses and gobbles up cakes. As my grandfather likes to remark, "everyone has some use, if only to serve as a bad example," and that's all that this vicious man is good for. More complex is the bad twin of the self-controlled man, the weak-willed man. Aristotle calls this condition of weak will *akrasia*, often translated as "incontinence." Someone with this defect of character knows what he should do, unlike the vicious man. But he is unable to do it, because he is overcome by his desires and the prospect of pleasure or avoiding pain (1147a, 1148a).

Akrasia is precisely the phenomenon that Socrates claimed was impossible when he said that no one does wrong willingly. If you recall, his reasoning went like this: when we make choices, what we are doing is trying to choose what is good, or what is best. So there is something self-defeating, even contradictory, about consciously choosing what is bad. It is tantamount to thinking, "I reckon the best thing to do is this bad thing." Aristotle explicitly refers to Socrates and admits that he has leveled a powerful challenge against the possibility of *akrasia*. But, again defending a more commonsensical position, he says that *akrasia* obviously does exist. The question is how. Aristotle suggests that Socrates is right in a way, because the akratic man is indeed suffering from a failure of reasoning (1147b). He knows, for instance, that this cake is unhealthy and that one shouldn't eat unhealthy things. But the prospect of the delicious cake makes him temporarily unable to make use of this knowledge, so he pops it into his mouth. In this case, I am less persuaded by Aristotle. He must be right that *akrasia* genuinely exists. But I'm not sure he's right that *akrasia* resides in some kind of thoughtlessness, in being swept away by pleasure. No doubt that does happen, but I would say people sometimes consciously, in full awareness, do things they know are bad (philosophers sometimes call this "clear-eyed *akrasia*"). If that really does happen, it is apparently not what Aristotle is trying to explain in his theory of *akrasia*.[3]

We've seen, then, that Aristotle thinks the good life includes quite a lot of pleasure, and for a variety of reasons. For one thing, the total absence of pleasurable goods apart from virtue, like wealth and family, will destroy our happiness. For another, we'll need such things just in order to exercise our virtue. Finally, virtue itself will bring us pleasure as we exercise it. The good life is starting to look pretty pleasant after all. In that case, why can't Aristotle just go ahead and be a hedonist? Why can't he say that the best life is simply the most pleasant life, by insisting that the virtuous man is the one who gets the most pleasure out of his activities? In that case, he was wrong to dismiss the life of pleasure as a life fit for cows. Far from it; it is actually a life fit for the best, most admirable men among us, and in short, a happy life. In fact we should organize our lives around the pursuit of pleasure.

Aristotle does come back to the topic of pleasure later in the *Ethics*, and when he does so he makes it clear why he is not a hedonist. For him, devoting one's life to pleasure is not only a mistake, it is downright incoherent. To see why, we need to think a bit about the nature of pleasure itself. Pleasure always involves enjoying some activity, whether it is eating, driving a fast car, or simply feeling at peace with yourself. So pleasure is a kind of secondary phenomenon, which comes along on top of some primary activity or experience and in a way completes it (1174b). This seemingly innocuous fact spells doom for the hedonist. It means that when we ask whether a certain pleasure is worth pursuing, the answer will always depend on the activity to which the pleasure is attached. If you take pleasure in doing mathematics and in eating cake, then the question of which pleasure is more worthwhile will depend on whether mathematics or cake is intrinsically better. This allows Aristotle to insist that even if pleasure, in itself, is always good, it is to be avoided when it accompanies an activity which is bad.

Again, notice how he has staked out a compromise position: he's not denying that pleasure is good, but neither is he saying that it is *the* good. Rather, it is in itself a good thing and sometimes accompanies other good things; but sometimes it arises from bad things. And this makes all the difference. The hedonist might try responding that we should try to maximize pleasure, that is, choose between pleasures not on the basis of their associated activities but on the basis of what is most pleasant. To this, Aristotle might say that there is no reason to suppose that we are able to compare, say, the pleasure of mathematics and the pleasure of cake. Nonetheless, you might well have to choose, for instance, if you were invited both to a birthday party and a mathematics seminar. And then, Aristotle will insist that the choice should not depend on the quantity of pleasure each activity would provide, but on which activity is more worthwhile: which activity will do more to contribute to my overall well-being and flourishing.

As appealing as all this sounds, there is still a problem lurking, the one I mentioned at the end of the last chapter. Aristotle's ethics seems to be all about my own personal flourishing and excellence. I am trying to achieve happiness, and the way to do it is to engage in the activities distinctive to me as a human: the use of reason, in both the practical and theoretical spheres. It's an ethical theory that is demanding, that calls us to achievement and great deeds, be they political, military, or best of all, philosophical. But isn't it also, well, a little selfish? What if my friends and family get in the way of my excellence? Of course Aristotle has said that no one can be happy without friends and family, and perhaps I need them around to exercise some of my virtues, like generosity and loyalty. But aren't these the wrong reasons to value my loved ones? I shouldn't be keeping them around for my own benefit; if anything, I should be seeking to promote their good above my own.[4]

Aristotle's answer comes in books Eight and Nine of the Ethics, which are devoted to friendship—the Greek term, which I already mentioned when discussing Plato's erotic dialogues, is philia. It's worth emphasizing that two out of the ten books of the Ethics are about this topic. Clearly this is an aspect of our ethical lives that Aristotle took seriously, though I don't think this is necessarily because he felt that ethics needs to be other-regarding rather than self-regarding. His ethical theory is fundamentally "eudaimonist," meaning that it seeks to ground ethics in the eudaimonia, or happiness, of the ethical agent rather than in some kind of responsibilities or duties the agent owes to other people. But Aristotle definitely thought the virtuous person would have friends. In fact, he thought something much stronger than this: he thought that in the strict and proper sense, only the virtuous person can have friends.

According to Aristotle, there are three kinds of relationship that we count as "friendships." Some friends spend time together simply because it is useful to both parties (1156a). These "utility friendships" may be long-lasting and deeply valued—think, for instance, of two business partners, who might work together for their whole career and help to make one another rich and successful. But such relationships are also vulnerable to circumstance. If you and I are friends in this way, I may just drop you like a hot potato as soon as your usefulness ends. Similar are friendships of pleasure, which are predicated on some shared activity the friends enjoy (1156a–b). The drinking buddy is the ultimate example of this. Again, the friendship is based on something incidental to the actual friend, and this makes the friendship vulnerable. Suppose I give up drinking—I'll give up my drinking buddies too. Although these two kinds of friendship are in a sense defective, we can nonetheless call them friendship because of their resemblance to true friendship.

This sort of friendship is grounded not in something incidental to the friend, like their usefulness or shared pleasures, but rather in the character of the friend (1156b). If I am really and truly friends with you, it must be because I admire and value your character, and you admire and value my character. This is why, in a sense, only virtuous people can really be friends, because they are the only ones who really have admirable and valuable characters. In the ideal case, the two friends will be equal in virtue. Inequality, for Aristotle, is inimical to friendship. I regret to report that, on this basis, he says that men can't be perfect friends with women, not even with their wives—because women are intrinsically inferior to men (1158b). It also explains, as he says in a striking passage, why we cannot be friends with God (1159a).

So Aristotle can explain why virtuous people are not selfish egotists. They may not cherish the worth of all other humans equally. But other people who are more or less virtuous will be valued by the virtuous person, and for their own sakes. In the ideal case of virtue friendship, Aristotle even says that the virtuous man considers the friend a "second self," and will consider his deeds to be effectively his own. This again is a noble idea, though one might worry that it collapses back into egotism after all. If, in an ideal virtue friendship, my friend is for all intents and purposes "another me," doesn't that show that virtue is really selfish? It is all about me, me, me, and there are as many "me's as I have virtuous friends. The problem becomes even more pressing when we get to the notorious end of the *Ethics*, in which Aristotle suddenly announces that the best life is not, after all, a matter of political activity, but rather a life devoted to philosophical contemplation (1177a–1178a). Where does this leave interpersonal relationships, or for that matter, virtuous activity?

Here we've arrived at one of the most hotly disputed interpretive questions in the *Ethics*.[5] Some scholars believe that Aristotle sees contemplation as the capstone to a full and complete life, which would include all the other goods—not only political activity, but also so-called "external goods" like health, family, and friends. (This is sometimes called the "inclusivist" reading of Aristotle.) Others read Aristotle as saying that contemplation trumps all other considerations, and that a life devoted to contemplation alone would be the best, with a more politically engaged life being second-best (sometimes called the "exclusivist" or "dominant" interpretation). I won't try to sort out this issue here, but the next two chapters, on Aristotle's views concerning the intellect and political affairs, may help you to make up your own mind.

GOD ONLY KNOWS
ARISTOTLE ON MIND AND GOD

How can you tell if someone is a philosopher? There are a number of potential clues. Does this person like to argue? Do they have a habit of staring off silently into the middle distance? Do their grooming and hygiene leave something to be desired? Chances are you're in luck: you've found yourself a philosopher. But an almost sure-fire test is this. Tell them that you yourself are a philosopher. If you are dealing with a normal person they'll say something like, "Gosh. So, um, what do you do all day?" But if you're talking to a philosopher, they will ask you what area of philosophy you work in. Professionals know that philosophy has many branches, and that no one, these days, is a "philosopher" in the sense Aristotle was: a pursuer of all the knowledge that mankind can hope to possess.

In the English-speaking world, the philosophers you meet at parties will often say, when asked what area of philosophy they do, that they are philosophers of mind. Not that philosophers of mind go to many parties. They are too busy debating issues like the nature of consciousness, the relation of our minds to our bodies, and the philosophical relevance of empirical research in brain science and psychology. This is cutting-edge stuff, but like most, if not all, areas of philosophy, it has ancient roots. Aristotle was arguably the inventor of the philosophy of mind, just as he was the inventor of logic, biology, and numerous other disciplines. Of course, when I was talking about his work *On the Soul*, I did say that it is a mistake to confuse soul, as Aristotle understands it, with the topic considered by today's philosophers of mind. Aristotle's soul is rather the explanation for all our vital functions, including nutrition, motion, and sensation as well as thought. So when Aristotle talks about the relation between soul and body, this is not the same as when Descartes, or a modern-day philosopher, talks of the mind–body relationship.

Yet Aristotle does provide an account of thinking, in the third book of *On the Soul*. Here he takes up the topic of mind, not in the sense of all our experiences, or of consciousness—what philosophers now call "mental" phenomena—but rather mind in the sense of intellect. The Greek word for "intellect" is *nous*. It refers here specifically to the capacity by which we achieve knowledge. Aristotle considers this to be an exalted, even divine, capacity which distinguishes humans from lower animals. When he concludes his *Ethics* by suggesting that a life of contemplation is the best life for humans, he means that our greatest happiness would be achieved through the exercise of intellect. And yet, Aristotle sees close ties between intellect and the lower functions of sensation and imagination. We already saw that, at the end of the *Posterior Analytics*, he claims that sensation is the basis for the first principles of demonstrative knowledge—and he calls the state of grasping those principles by the same word, *nous*, or intellect.

Here in *On the Soul*, meanwhile, Aristotle draws a close parallel between intellect and sensation. As we've seen, he understands sensation as the actualization of a potentiality. If your eyes function properly, then even when you are not seeing anything, you are potentially seeing red; you have the capacity to see red. When you are confronted with a red apple, that capacity is realized. Your sight becomes not just potentially red, but actually red, which is just to say that you see red. The same kind of story can be told for the intellect. Your intellect is a capacity you have, thanks to your possession of a human soul. When it is actualized, what you do is think. But what Aristotle seems to mean by "thinking" here is something rather special. He doesn't mean thinking about what you'll have for dinner, say, or trying to remember where you left your keys. He means having a grasp of essences or forms out in the world. When you think in this way about giraffes, you actually grasp the nature of giraffe, just as vision actually grasps the redness of an apple. So we might think of intellect as relating to natures the way vision relates to colors.

Despite the analogy between thinking and sensation, there are, of course, also differences. One difference is that there is no falsehood in sensation. Sight can provide you with a *misleading* appearance, like the mirage in the desert that looks like an oasis (or indeed the sound made by a tribute band that sounds like Oasis). But according to Aristotle, sight itself is always true, as is any kind of sensation (428a)—the falsehood would appear at the level of a judgment made on the basis of this misleading impression. Falsehood already appears in a faculty Aristotle calls *phantasia* (often translated, rather inadequately, as "imagination").[1] Imagination is distinct from both sensation and thought, but intimately connected to both. Imagination is always based on what we have perceived with the senses, though we may manipulate what we have sensed (like combining the images of a human and a horse to get a centaur), and thinking cannot occur without imagination (427b, 431a). It is perhaps clear enough that sensation isn't the same thing as imagination, but one might be tempted to identify thinking with imagination. This would be a mistake, says Aristotle, since belief only comes in at the level of thinking. When you imagine, you are, as it were, entertaining a picture of how things might be, but you are not convinced that things actually are this way. Imagination is "false" only in the sense that it does not represent reality as it is. But merely imagining things to be a certain way does not mean you believe they actually are that way. False belief arises only in thought, through combinations of terms that don't correspond to reality (430b—we might remember the similar point made by Plato in the *Sophist*, with the example "Theaetetus flies"). Aristotle thinks this marks a dividing-line between us and the non-human animals: they are capable of imagination, but not belief (427a).

Another difference between thinking and sensation is that thinking happens without the use of any bodily organ (429a). It is realized through our souls, but not through any part of our body. It's no surprise that Aristotle fails to identify the brain as the seat of intellect. For him, the brain is basically just a refrigeration unit, designed to balance the heat stemming from our heart.[2] It is the heart that serves as the command center; for instance, it is the ultimate seat of sensation. But we don't use it to think, nor do we use any other part of the body. Aristotle's argument for this begins from the observation that you can think about anything: everything is a possible object of intellection. And intellect thinks by actually taking on the form of what it thinks about. This means that if it were seated in an organ that were, for instance, hot, it would always be thinking about heat, because it would always be actually hot. But this is clearly not the case. Rather, in its basic state intellect is only *potentially* everything. So it cannot have any bodily organ, given that every organ already has many actual features.

This argument probably won't be keeping my colleagues who do philosophy of mind up at nights. They would already be puzzled by the idea that thinking is taking on a form. And even granting this to Aristotle, surely the sense in which the intellect takes on a form could be different from the sense in which a bodily organ has that form. Still, the argument does underscore Aristotle's commitment to an idea that will have a far-reaching historical impact, namely that our minds become identical in form to whatever we think about. He's also being consistent with what he's said about sensation. Regarding vision, for instance, he remarked that the fluid in the eye must have no color, since otherwise we would always be seeing that color. Rather, it must be potentially all colors. In the same way, the intellect is potentially everything.

The idea that we think without using a bodily organ gives us a hint as to why Aristotle believes that intellect is something divine. As he says in the *Ethics*, the life of the mind is not so much the best life for us, but a life which is, if anything, too good for mere humans. Really, it is divine. This isn't just a figure of speech. As we can see if we turn to works other than *On the Soul*, Aristotle in fact portrays God as a pure intellect. To piece together his account, we need to return to his cosmology, as it is laid out in the *Physics* and another treatise called *On the Heavens*. In these writings he describes the cosmos as spherical in form, made up of many nested spheres. At the edge is the outermost sphere, in which are embedded the so-called "fixed stars"—the ones that, when seen from earth, appear to rise and set every night, and to move together. Other stars can be seen to change position from night to night, wandering against the background of these fixed stars. These are the so-called "planets" (the word comes from the Greek verb meaning "to wander"). The planets are embedded in further spheres nested inside the outermost sphere of fixed stars.

Our lower realm is beneath these heavenly spheres, at the center of the cosmos. It is made up of the four elements, which are mixed together to produce the earth, the seas, the sky, and all the plants, animals, and other substances we see around us. It would seem that the celestial motion is somehow responsible for the mixture of these elements. And the celestial motion can be traced back to the motion of the outermost sphere. For it is the daily rotation of this sphere that accounts for most of what we see in the night sky. The wandering of the planets is due to slight changes in their rotation, introduced by the various motions of the spheres upon which they are seated. But basically the planetary spheres likewise go around once per day, carried around by the outermost sphere.

Thus, if we want to ask what ultimately explains all motion, all generation and destruction, in our cosmos, we need to find the cause of the eternal motion of the outermost sphere. It will be this mover that sets in chain the complex series of celestial rotations that mix up the four elements to yield the environment we live in. When giraffes lope across the savannah, that motion can be traced—very indirectly—back to the single, simple rotation of the outermost sphere. I think I'm not giving anything away if I now say that the cause of this rotation is God, an unmoved mover (*Physics* 260a). But why think that this motion, or any celestial motion, has any cause at all? Why not just say that the motion is a brute fact about the cosmos? This question presents itself with particular force in light of Aristotle's belief that the world is eternal, a central claim in both the *Physics* and *On the Heavens*. Aristotle is convinced that the world has not only always existed, but has always looked much as it does now, with the same heavenly rotations, the same animal and plant species. Although Aristotle does want to find a place for God in his cosmology, his God is not a creator. So again: why think that the heavens need any explanatory principle?

Aristotle gives several answers here—though perhaps the basic underlying idea is simply that the eternal heavenly motion cannot just happen to be the way it is, but must have a cause. This would bring the heavens within Aristotle's general conception of nature, where nothing is unexplained and everything has a purpose. But he wants to establish exactly what this cause will be like. So he gives the following argument. The motion of the heaven is eternal, and thus in a sense infinite. But nothing finite can have enough power to perform an infinite motion (*Physics* 266a–b). Imagine trying to run a car forever on a finite amount of fuel. However efficient the car is, it will run out of fuel eventually. Now, the heavens are finite, since they are bodies of enormous, but nonetheless limited, size. So they cannot have the power to move eternally under their own steam. They need an external mover. Obviously this mover cannot have a body, since if it did it too would be limited and finite. So the external mover "has no magnitude"—that is, it is immaterial (267b).

At the risk of complicating matters, I should say that Aristotle's argument will apply to each individual heavenly sphere. There is not only the outermost heaven, but also each of the planetary spheres. Actually it's even worse, since Aristotle, following the astronomical theory produced in Plato's Academy by men like Eudoxus, believed that each planetary motion must be explained as a combination of several simple rotations. This explains why the planet moves in a wandering path across the sky from night to night. Aristotle seems to have improved upon the mathematicians here, by positing several actual physical spheres for each required planetary motion, with further spheres to counteract those motions to prevent them from being passed on to lower planets (*Metaphysics* 1073a–1074a). Eudoxus and others had simply observed that combining enough circular motions would yield the right mathematical calculation for expressing, say, the motion of Venus, but they postulated no physical mechanism. Aristotle instead assumes that there are real physical spheres, and to account for planetary motions we see we will need several dozen of them, each of which needs its own immaterial mover (1074a). So God is, for Aristotle, simply the greatest and most important of the bodiless celestial movers. As Aristotle says, earlier thinkers had a vague intuition of this truth when they spoke of many gods (1074b). There are indeed numerous divine beings, but they are not the squabbling family of Hesiod and Homer. Aristotle follows the lead of Xenophanes and Plato by scrubbing the "gods" clean of almost all human features. They are simply separate, immaterial substances, and they cause the various heavenly spheres to move.

So far, so good, except that it's hard to see how immaterial beings can make spheres rotate. Not, presumably, by getting out and pushing. Aristotle does have an answer to this question, which he gives in the twelfth book of his *Metaphysics*. Here Aristotle presents his theory of the divine as an improvement on Plato. He has captured something of what Plato wanted to do with his theory of Forms, by tracing physical phenomena back to immaterial causes. But whereas the Forms, according to Aristotle at least, can't really explain motion (1070a), Aristotle's celestial movers will give rise to simple, circular motions—which go on to cause everything else.

Aristotle is no doubt right that it is a mystery how the Form of Large causes things to be large. But his story will only count as an improvement if he can tell us how God moves the outermost heaven, and how the other divine movers move their spheres.

When Aristotle answers this question, he winds up admitting that the divine does, after all, have something in common with humans. For the sole activity of the divine movers turns out to be a distinctively human activity: thinking (1072b). These movers are nothing but separate intellects, and the spheres move in imitation of their eternal thinking by performing eternal circular motions. So Aristotle describes God as a kind of final cause, saying that it moves the outermost heaven the way that the beloved moves the lover (1072a). Just as the pretty girl at the dance makes the boys shuffle shyly towards her without doing anything herself, so God can without moving cause other things to move, out of their aspiration to be like the divine. Here again we have an idea that will inspire centuries of philosophers, and it isn't hard to see why. For Jewish, Christian, and Muslim readers, the notion that God is the final object of love and desire in the universe was, if you'll pardon the pun, highly attractive.

Still, though, has Aristotle really given us a story about why God and the other movers are *thinking*? Why couldn't they be doing something else? Granted, he has argued that they are immaterial. And for Aristotle, the activity that we perform without using any part of our body is thinking. This seems to have been enough to make him leap to his conclusion. God is immaterial and he must be doing something; when we do something immaterially we are thinking; therefore God thinks. This simply assumes, rather than arguing, that there is only one kind of immaterial activity. But there are a few things Aristotle could say in his defense. He might insist that it is needlessly complicated to presuppose further immaterial kinds of activity: if we know of one already, namely thinking, why postulate another one? Moreover, he might argue that thinking simply *is* immaterial activity, that the two are one and the same. After all, what is it for us to think, apart from possessing form immaterially? So if God is doing something, and is immaterial, it follows more or less from Aristotle's definition of thinking that God is thinking.

Even if we grant this, we'll want to know at least one more thing: what is God thinking about? Aristotle responds that, since we're talking about God, we need to allow him to think about the best possible object. There are some things that it would be better not to think about at all. God is clearly not thinking about where he left his keys. In fact, if God is going to think about the absolutely best thing, there's only one candidate: himself. God will be, as Aristotle famously puts it, "thought thinking about thought," sometimes paraphrased as "thought thinking itself" (1072b).

This phrase is famous, but also a bit disturbing. Are we being presented with a divine navel-gazer, a God who does nothing day after day, for all eternity, but think about himself? This sounds disappointing. After all, if God is nothing but an intellect who thinks himself, then the only thing he can think about is, what? The fact that he's thinking about himself? Sounds not only self-absorbed, but rather pointless.

Some interpreters assume that, for Aristotle, God thinks about everything, but indirectly. Since he is the cause of the first celestial motion which leads to all the other motions, he could grasp all things as implications of his own causal influence. But Aristotle certainly doesn't say this explicitly, and actually I don't think he was too worried about the *content* of divine thought. I would guess that he just meant to say that whatever God thinks about, God must be permanently self-aware. Just as we, at our best moments, consciously reflect on our own knowledge—and what is philosophy, if not such conscious self-reflection?—so God permanently thinks of Himself as thinking about whatever else it is that he thinks about. The extent of his knowledge regarding other things may be left as an open question.[3]

At any rate, it's clear that Aristotle seriously intends us to regard this first celestial mover—the so-called "prime mover"—as worthy of respect and perhaps even something like worship. I'm not saying that he wants us to go to the temple of Zeus and sacrifice animals to the prime mover. But he does end his discussion of God in the *Metaphysics* with an unusually rhetorical passage, identifying the prime mover as the ultimate source of order in our cosmos (1075b–1076a). It not only causes the motion of the outermost heaven, but also somehow coordinates all the other motions. Quoting a line from Homer, Aristotle finishes with a flourish, saying "the rule of many is not good; let there be one ruler" (1076a). He seems to be hinting that his God is not just perfect, but also providential. Again, authors in future generations will take note, and take advantage, weaving Aristotle's theology together with the teachings of revealed religion.

Aristotle's God is very much a god of the philosophers, in every sense of that phrase. The most appropriate type of worship is no doubt what Aristotle himself does: to contemplate God through reasoned argument. And God is himself a kind of philosopher, but better, a pure intellect who always thinks, always thinks about his thinking, and never has to go to sleep. God thus provides a standard for all other things to imitate. The heavens imitate his thinking by their unending celestial rotations. Even plants and animals imitate the divine through reproduction, which allows them to attain a kind of immortality of their own—their species will live on endlessly, although the individuals die. As for us, we can imitate God by doing philosophy. If this all leads Aristotle's readers to infer that Aristotle is the most godlike man they know, that would probably be okay with him. But there is another way for us to imitate God. God is the ruler of all things, who brings order and harmony. We can do something similar in our practical affairs. By setting up sound systems of governance in our cities, we humans can imitate the order of the universe—an idea already endorsed by Plato in the *Republic* and *Timaeus*. What systems would produce the best possible order? To find out, we'll need to turn to another Aristotelian treatise, which is in no small part a response to the *Republic*, and which handles its political proposals just as roughly as the *Metaphysics* handles Plato's theory of Forms.

40

CONSTITUTIONAL CONVENTIONS ARISTOTLE'S POLITICAL PHILOSOPHY

No one is likely to confuse Aristotle with Oscar Wilde. He is not exactly known for his wit or fine style. If you're looking for snappy aphorisms in Greek philosophy, you're better off with Heraclitus. And yet, Aristotle did produce his fair share of memorable quotations. There is his insistence that "nature does nothing in vain." His observation in the *Metaphysics* that "being is said in many ways." In the *Ethics*, explaining that happiness is a whole life of virtue and not just virtue exercised for a brief time, he observes that "one swallow does not make a summer."[1] But perhaps Aristotle's most famous phrase appears in his work the *Politics*, when he describes man as a "political animal" (1253a). At one level this is simply an empirical observation. Humans have a natural tendency to gather together into groups—not only families, but also smaller communities on the order of villages, and ultimately cities (1252b). As I have mentioned before, the word "politics" relates to the Greek word for city, *polis*. Aristotle, like Plato before him, considers the city-state or *polis* to be the natural, and maximum, size for a political community. Of course both were aware that larger political unions were possible: they knew of the Persian empire and, closer to home, pan-Mediterranean groups like the Delian League, led by Athens. But when Aristotle talks about political arrangements, he has in mind not the modern nation-state, or for that matter empires or leagues of nations. He is thinking about cities.

Of course, if it is *natural* for humans to gather together into cities, then calling man a "political animal" is not merely descriptive. Remember, "nature does nothing in vain." So if humans naturally gather together, there must be a good reason for it. Thus, a central question of Aristotle's *Politics* is, what is the city for? The answer to this question should structure our political philosophy. We should also remember that at the beginning of his *Ethics*, Aristotle claimed to be embarking on political philosophy. His *Ethics* and his *Politics* are explicitly presented as connected works, and that literary connection is based on a philosophical connection: the proper goal of the city is closely related to the proper goal of the individual. In the *Ethics*, Aristotle told us that happiness is pursued through a life of reason and virtue. In the *Politics*, he will tell us how political affairs can be arranged to facilitate such a life.

An appealing consequence is that, for Aristotle, the point of political affairs is to promote the good life of all its citizens. A government does not exist for the benefit of those who govern, but for the whole community. Thus, when he classifies the different possible types of political constitution, he contrasts three legitimate types to their perversions (1279a–b). The legitimate types play the role a political constitution is meant to play. They are kingship, aristocracy, and what Aristotle calls constitutional government (confusingly, he uses the Greek word *politeia* both for this third system and for the general concept of a constitution, which applies to all three types). The difference between the three is basically the number of people involved in governing the city: a king rules by himself, aristocrats as small groups of elites, while in a constitutional government the many rule for the good of the city. But in each case we have a legitimate political constitution, insofar as the purpose in view is the good of the whole community.

These three constitutional types become perverted when the rulers look instead to their own good: kingship becomes tyranny, aristocracy becomes oligarchy, and constitutional government becomes democracy (1279b). As when we discussed Plato's *Republic*, we are apt to be disturbed at seeing democracy classed as a perversion. But what Aristotle means by "democracy" is a situation where the largest group in the city (the *demos*), who are usually the poorer citizens, simply wield power for their own advantage. Unlike tyranny or oligarchy, this involves seeking the benefit of a large number of people. But it is unjust in precisely the way that tyranny or oligarchy is unjust—one group of citizens has simply got power over the others, and is using that power to take what it can get. Aristotle didn't need to read Karl Marx to develop an acute sensitivity to the possibility of class-conflict. In fact, the idea that the rich and the poor are locked in a struggle for power is prominent in his *Politics*, and not unreasonably, because the tension between these two classes had led to internal conflict in many Greek states. This condition was referred to as *stasis*—a kind of debilitating civil struggle in which a city turns against itself, rather than devoting its energies to making its citizens happy.

So far, so good. It sounds as though we would quite like Aristotle advising our own political leaders. Which, in fact, is exactly what he is out to do in the *Politics*. He says many times that he wants this work to be useful for the hands-on task of legislating. On the other hand, as in the *Ethics*, he stresses that practical philosophy must allow for the infinite variety of the situations we face. There can be no universal rules that would allow us to stipulate detailed laws that should apply to all cities. Variations in population, geography, and other factors make this impossible. But still, should we try to arrange a seat in the cabinet for Aristotle, or at least someone who has made a careful study of his *Politics*? (If any presidents or prime ministers happen to be perusing this book and would like some advice, I could probably fit that into my schedule.) Perhaps we should hesitate for a moment, though, because there are aspects of Aristotle's *Politics* that will strike us as a bit less charming.

I've said that he encourages the city to look after the welfare of all its citizens. But I didn't tell you who counts as a citizen. Aristotle devotes some attention to this question, and concludes that a citizen is someone who is actively involved with political affairs (1275a). Not all citizens will necessarily be running the city at any given time, but they may take turns carrying out official duties, and must at least participate in the political process. (Thus, in a tyranny nobody in the city apart from the tyrant is truly a citizen, by Aristotle's definition. Only the tyrant has a say in the running of the city, and the tyrant's welfare is pursued to the exclusion of everybody else.) So men must pass a high standard in order to qualify as citizens. They must be ready to help govern, and they can qualify because of their nobility, their wealth, or their virtue, depending on the constitution. For instance, an aristocracy puts a lot of emphasis on nobility and wealth.

No matter what constitution we are talking about, Aristotle assumes that it will be *men* alone who can pass the standard and be citizens. Plato had argued in the *Republic* that women can perform all the same activities as men, even if not equally, and that there would therefore be women guardians and rulers in the ideal city. We saw Aristotle remarking in his *Ethics* that men and women cannot share perfect friendship, because women are inferior to men. Now, in the *Politics*, he goes further, saying that the rational power in women lacks control or authority. Women need men to tell them what to do, since they are by nature unable to regulate their own affairs properly, never mind the affairs of the city (1259b–1260a). Obviously this is not Aristotle's finest hour, and we haven't even gotten to his notorious discussion of slavery.

As you probably know, slavery was a pervasive phenomenon in the ancient world. It was very common for warfare to involve the enslavement of conquered peoples, and a wealthy Greek or Roman household would typically include slaves, who did menial and even not-so menial tasks. In Aristotle's account of slavery, we see the downside of his fidelity to common opinion and empirical research. He seems to think that, since slavery is such a widespread phenomenon, it must be explained philosophically—and his explanation sounds uncomfortably like a defense of the indefensible. Even this, though, is perhaps letting him off too lightly.

After all, Aristotle is willing to reject received opinion when it suits him. And he is aware that rejecting the naturalness of slavery is an option, because he mentions a view held by others, according to which all slavery is by custom, not nature (1253b). But he has no truck with this, and instead adopts what he no doubt sees as one of his characteristically moderate, middle positions. He argues that some people are what he calls "natural slaves," and that it is not only permissible to enslave such people, but actually the right thing to do (1254a). A natural slave is, as he puts it, a "living tool," and is in an even worse condition than a free woman when it comes to conducting his own life. It is good for the slave to be owned, just as it is good for a woman to be dominated by her husband or father (1254b).

Obviously, I am not going to speak out in support of Aristotle's ideas about slavery. But we should take account of his aims in this discussion.[2] He is not trying to persuade his reader that slavery in general is legitimate—despite the aforementioned abolitionist view, few ancient readers would have needed persuasion on this score. Rather, he is trying to articulate a set of rules or limits to be placed on slavery. It is wrong, on his view, to enslave those who are not natural slaves. So putting whole Greek cities into bondage after victory in war is definitely not acceptable, given that many who live in that city will not be natural slaves (1255a). These are people whose souls make them fit to be citizens participating in a political community, not mere tools of other men. Plato made a similar point in the *Republic*, exhorting the Greeks to stop enslaving one another, but also saying that those outside the fold of Greek society—so-called "barbarians"—were fit for enslavement (471a–b). Aristotle agrees, remarking, for instance, that everyone who lives in Asia is a natural slave. He connects this to climate, in a way familiar from the Hippocratic corpus—there too, it is said that one's character is affected by one's environment. It just so happens, according to Aristotle, that the climate of Greece is perfectly temperate, so that the Greeks tend not to be naturally slavish (1327b). It follows that barbarians cannot really engage in proper political arrangements, since they do not have the souls one would need to engage successfully in such arrangements. And indeed, he says bluntly that among the barbarians no one is a natural ruler: their cities are "communities of slaves" (1252b).

We should also recognize that Aristotle's views on women and slavery hang together with more attractive views he holds on other topics. For instance, in his *Ethics* he has argued that the happy life is a life lived in accordance with reason, a conclusion many find plausible. Aristotle's ideas about women and natural slaves are simply a corollary of this, given his empirical claim that such people are not fully endowed with reason. Such people will be better off if someone who *is* fully rational takes charge of them. When Aristotle comes to discuss his vision of the ideal political arrangement, we find the same ideas in play. He doesn't really get around to this until Book Seven, out of the eight books of the *Politics*. The last two books are almost like a miniature version of the *Republic*, a work that is never far from Aristotle's mind throughout the *Politics*. He agrees with very few of Plato's recommendations, but does take over the *Republic*'s agenda of topics. He not only discusses defective types of city and the situation of women, but also the nature of the ideal city and how education would work in such a city.

On these topics Aristotle again makes clear that he is writing for real legislators. One can imagine him thinking of a reader who is, for instance, charged with drafting a legal code or settling a colony somewhere on the Mediterranean coast. (Here you might recall that, according to legend, Heraclitus was asked to write laws for his home city of Ephesus, and that the great sophist Protagoras was appointed by Pericles to legislate for a new colony.) So Aristotle provides plenty of detail, despite his strictures about universal pronouncements in the practical sphere. For instance, he recommends that the city have easy access to the sea (1327a), and that it should build defensive walls (1330b). Regarding political arrangements, in the ideal case there will be a group of excellent men who serve as citizens and share in governing the city (1328b). They will attempt to create the conditions needed to achieve a happy life. For instance, the citizens should have plenty of leisure, not least to engage in philosophy, though these same citizens may also need to serve as soldiers, much as Plato had recommended (1329a). As in the *Republic*, this ruling class will depend on the presence of many laborers and farmers to keep the city going. And, of course, there will be slaves and women as well, who will be excluded from the benefits provided by the ideal city.

That's the optimal solution, but it isn't how things usually go. Aristotle prides himself on being a realist. One gets the sense that he finds Plato's utopian project faintly ridiculous, however much he also indulges in a description of the best possible city at the end of the *Politics*. Before getting to the ideal case, he's spent a lot of time discussing politics in the real world. If we are interested in understanding the political dynamics that prevail now, perhaps with a view to improving legislation rather than starting from scratch, we will want to study the cities that already exist. I've mentioned before the ancient report that Aristotle and his students collected a large number of real constitutions for cities, and he is clearly drawing on this material as he alludes frequently to how they do things down in Sparta, or Carthage. From this mass of information, Aristotle concludes that the basic types of constitution are the ones already mentioned: kingship, aristocracy, and constitutional government, with the constant threat that these may turn into the perverted versions which look to the interest of the rulers rather than the community.

Since Aristotle assumes that his ideal city is usually going to remain just that—an ideal—he also describes the best arrangement that will be practicable in usual circumstances.

This brings us back to the opposition between rich and poor. In a pure aristocracy or oligarchy, the rich and well-born run the show. In a pure democracy or constitutional government, it is the majority of the free men, who are usually less wealthy, who call the shots. Aristotle sees both arrangements as excessive. He reminds us that, for the individual person, virtue is a mean between extremes, as he showed in the *Ethics*. The same will be true at the level of the city. What we want is an arrangement which serves the interests of both the rich few and the poorer majority. How can we achieve this intermediary solution, which Aristotle calls a "mixed" state? Aristotle's recommendation will sound familiar to anyone who follows British or American politics: empower the middle class. The citizens who are neither rich nor poor, but in the middle, should occupy the most influential roles in the city (1295b–1296a). Of course, one might wonder why the middle class is necessarily going to look to the benefit of all the citizens. Certainly, nowadays, some worry that the middle class might impose heavy taxes on the rich, or withhold much-needed support from the poor. But Aristotle seems to assume that the interests of the middle class will naturally form a kind of compromise between the interests of the rich and poor. Of course, this might not happen in every case, but it's not implausible that the interests of this class would overlap with the interests of both rich and poor.

It's about at this point that a reader of the *Politics* might frown with puzzlement, thinking: "what about Alexander the Great?" Aristotle was the tutor of the greatest conqueror of the ancient world, a man who was revered as a god in his own lifetime and taken as a model of leadership by kings and emperors for centuries to come. How can we reconcile this advice to empower the middle class with Aristotle's association with a single individual who gathered all political authority for himself? Well, if we were hoping Aristotle would allude specifically to the Macedonian royal family, we will go away from the *Politics* disappointed. But he does say something relevant to such a remarkable political animal as Alexander. In the midst of his discussion of the various political arrangements, he pauses to consider a case where a small group or single man possesses excellence that outstrips the rest of the city put together. If such a superhuman ruler were to appear, Aristotle thinks, the right thing would be for everyone simply to submit to him—objecting to the rule of a man like this would be like objecting to the rule of Zeus (1284a–b, 1288a).

Clearly this is, to put it mildly, an exceptional circumstance. But it does highlight an assumption Aristotle has been making throughout: political power is naturally apportioned to those whose gifts make them fit to wield it. At one level this is another neutral, empirical observation. The reason democracies arise is that the majority are formidable when they work together, simply by virtue of being so numerous. The reason oligarchies arise is that wealth is a source of political strength. But Aristotle is also saying that this is how things *ought* to be. If a man is excellent, he should help run the city. And if a whole group brings military or economic strength to the table, it's only right that they should wield a corresponding degree of power. As with Plato, Aristotle's political ideas spring from deep convictions about justice. But he does not have in mind anything like our modern idea of human rights—he's happy to shut women and natural slaves out of political life, because they cannot contribute anything. The justice he has in mind has more to do with reciprocation: those who make the city strong should have a say in the decision-making.

In Aristotle's political philosophy, excellence is both the source of political legitimacy and the fruit of the *polis*. The more excellent men live in a city, the better the city will be run, and the more we can call the city a success. Its purpose was, after all, to produce excellent men, men who are happy according to the standards of his *Nicomachean Ethics*. This is why his ideal city is simply a city of excellent citizens, supported by an underclass of women and laborers who cannot achieve excellence, but whose lives are improved by living under good rulers. This condition serves as the final end of all cities—the ideal towards which real legislators should work. But as I've said, Aristotle thinks of himself as a realist. He wants to provide not only rational argument about political affairs, but also the tools for persuading people to change their beliefs. He recognizes that less-than-perfect reasoning, and also emotion, play a major role in our practical lives and in any real city. And it's emotion that will take centre-stage now, as we turn to two more Aristotelian works: the *Rhetoric* and the *Poetics*.

41

STAGE DIRECTIONS
ARISTOTLE'S *RHETORIC*
AND *POETICS*

You've heard of Aesop, right? The Greek guy with all the fables involving animals? It turns out that Aristotle is one of the earliest sources to mention him. He relates the following anecdote. Aesop was in the island city-state of Samos, home of Pythagoras, pleading the case of a city leader who was accused of exploiting his position for money. Aesop, of course, had a fable ready for just this occasion. It seems there was this fox, who was trapped in a hole by a river. Fleas started sucking his blood, and the poor fox had no defense. Then a hedgehog happened by and offered to scatter the fleas away. No thanks, said the fox. The fleas are all full of my blood; if you chase them away others will just come, and they'll still be hungry. In the same way, concluded Aesop, my client is already rich. So you may as well leave him alone—better than replacing him with a poorer man who would have reason to steal more of your money. Now that, my friends, is rhetoric.

Aristotle tells the story to illustrate the use of fables, just one of many techniques he explains in his work, the *Rhetoric* (1393b–1394a). In the *Rhetoric* Aristotle takes up the themes we saw Plato exploring in dialogues like the *Gorgias*. In the ancient Greek world, and especially in democratic Athens, public speaking was one of the most important skills an educated gentleman could possess. It was a path to political power, and would also come in handy if you were ever involved in a court-case. So, already before Plato, as we saw when we looked at the sophists, numerous authors had turned their attention to the skills and techniques needed to persuade an audience. Gorgias was only one such author—many others are mentioned in Aristotle's *Rhetoric*. So this is one area where Aristotle was no pioneer. He may have been the first to write about logic and zoology, the first to write a systematic treatise on the soul, and so on. But when he turned his attention to rhetoric, he was adding one more volume to a shelf full of treatises on the subject.

Of course, when Aristotle can't claim to be a pioneer he does the next best thing: he complains that all his predecessors got things wrong. In this case he blames previous rhetoricians for covering only part of the subject (1354a). They mostly tell you how to whip up emotion in an audience. This is an important rhetorical technique—as we'll see, Aristotle too discusses it in some depth. But the rhetoricians have missed out something even more important, namely the classification and study of what Aristotle calls "enthymemes" (1355a). These are arguments that are designed not to prove a proposition, but simply to persuade an audience. Aristotle's greatest contribution to the study of rhetoric will be a classification of these enthymemes, or persuasive arguments. Incidentally, I should mention that Aristotle's criticism of his predecessors has led some scholars to worry about the *Rhetoric* as it has come down to us. Can this beginning part, where he chastises authors of rhetorical textbooks for concentrating on emotion, really belong to the same original work as the careful discussion of emotion that comes later on? Another problem is that the third and final book of the *Rhetoric* suddenly adds a long discussion of style and metaphor, which doesn't seem to be part of the plan envisioned in Books One and Two. So, as with works like the *Metaphysics*, there is concern that our *Rhetoric* is not a text composed by Aristotle so much as a later compilation of Aristotelian material. I won't get into this any further, except to say that I don't see the point about emotions as decisive. The criticism of the predecessors is not that they focus on emotions, but that they focus *only* on emotions, which is only one of several topics a good study of rhetoric would include.

Because Aristotle puts enthymemes, not emotion, at the center of his story, he sees rhetoric as a discipline that is closely related to logic. In his logical works Aristotle discussed demonstrative arguments, which prove things with complete certainty, and also dialectical arguments, which argue from agreed premises. Now, in the *Rhetoric*, he tackles another kind of argument: arguments that are persuasive. Along with these enthymemes, the good rhetorician needs to be able to use "examples." The fable used by Aesop is an example, not an enthymeme. Aristotle compares the use of examples to the use of induction in the proper philosophical sciences (1393a). Someone doing zoology might observe common features of pigeons and chickens, and reach a better understanding of birds through induction. Similarly, Aesop asks his audience to think that someone who is already sated is less likely to do us harm, whether that someone is a blood-sucking flea or a blood-sucking politician.

But it's the enthymemes that tend to provoke the most interest among philosophical readers of the *Rhetoric*. What does it mean for an argument to be merely persuasive? Well, it's easy to see why enthymeme differs from demonstration. A demonstrative argument must be based ultimately on first principles, deal with universal necessities, and so on—all the constraints we saw outlined in the *Posterior Analytics*. By contrast, Aristotle actually discourages the rhetorician from building a long chain of inferences to reach his conclusion, since this will just confuse the audience (1395b). Furthermore, a rhetorician is always dealing with some particular decision or case, not with universal necessities. It's harder, though, to see the difference between enthymemes and dialectical arguments. A dialectical argument is one based merely on agreed premises. You might agree the premises just for the sake of argument, but more typically we choose premises that are reputable and widely acceptable—so-called *endoxa*—whether or not they are definitely true. An enthymeme does something very similar, by appealing to premises that the audience will find compelling, whether these are true or not.

Perhaps the right way to think about this is that an enthymeme is just a *type* or *class* of dialectical argument. After all, in rhetoric we do not just choose any old reputable premises, we argue on the basis of what will persuade the specific audience before us. Aristotle tells us, for instance, what young people or old people are apt to find convincing, to help us tailor our arguments to our target audience. Also, dialectical arguments can concern any topic, even abstract ones like metaphysics or the soul. Enthymemes, by contrast, deal with practical questions. Thus, Aristotle says that rhetoric is akin to ethics or political philosophy, as well as logic (1356a). Just as in ethics we use reason to deal with a specific practical situation, so in rhetoric we try to adapt our arguments to the case we are arguing and the audience that confronts us.

Since rhetoric, like ethics, is concerned with the infinitely variable practicalities of individual cases, Aristotle cannot offer us ready-made arguments that will work in every context, any more than he could give us foolproof general instructions for how to be good. Instead, in the *Ethics* he gave us a useful guideline by describing virtues as means between extremes. So, here in the *Rhetoric*, he offers us rules-of-thumb, strategies that tend to be useful in a variety of contexts. He calls these by the Greek word *topoi*, which means "places" (1358a). The word probably comes from a memory trick used to recall all the various rhetorical tropes: you might imagine yourself walking around Athens, and associate each type of enthymeme with a place in the city. (Aristotle discusses this mnemonic device in another work, called *On Memory*.) Dialectic in general uses this same technique of remembering argument types, which can be filled out with detail to be applied to the case at hand. This is why Aristotle's work on dialectic is called the *Topics*—if you've been wondering about that ever since I got to Aristotle, then sorry for leaving you in suspense for so long. In the case of rhetoric, the so-called *topoi* would include things like invoking precedent, itemizing the possible results of a proposed course of action to show that all are unwelcome, using wordplay based on the names of the people involved in a case, or appealing to the audience's base desires if the opponent has appealed to their noble desires, and vice-versa.

ー

So there are many types of rhetorical argument. But overall, there are only three kinds of rhetoric, because there were three contexts in ancient Greek society that called for rhetorical speech. First, you might speak in a court setting, whether in a lawsuit or a criminal case. Second, there were explicitly political contexts—as when you are trying to persuade the Athenian assembly to make some decision. Third and finally, you might speak in praise or blame of a specific person, for instance, in a funeral oration. Aristotle calls the types of rhetoric corresponding to these contexts forensic, deliberative, and epideictic (1358b). In none of the three types would you restrict yourself to enthymemes; audiences get bored with strings of unbroken argument. Rather, you would scatter the enthymemes through your speech, along with examples and other material, for instance, a narrative of how a crime was committed when you are prosecuting a court-case (1416b–1417a).

Whatever the topic, what you're aiming at is not to prove your case beyond all doubt—though that would of course be great if you could do it. Rather, you're just trying to show that your case is the more likely one. Aristotle's discussion of forensic oratory doesn't use the standard of "innocent until proven guilty." It's more like, "he's probably guilty, and that's good enough for us." So you might defend your client by saying: "Would he start a fight with that other man, as he's accused of doing? My client is small, and small men don't usually start fights with bigger men." Or you might say something about a fox and hedgehog, or even a giraffe. In addition to tipping the balance of probability with arguments and examples, you have two other tools at your disposal. It's very important to get the audience to think that you, the speaker, are credible. So Aristotle gives advice on how to make oneself seem virtuous and trustworthy before an audience (1377b–1378a). The other tool is that good old standby, whipping up emotion.

This leads Aristotle to give his most in-depth discussion of the emotions, in the second book of the *Rhetoric*. What he's really interested in here, as so often, is underlying causes: what is it that makes people angry, or induces them to feel pity? He shows himself a keen student of human psychology, observing for instance that we get angry when we are insulted, and we get angrier if the insult comes from a friend than from an enemy (1379b). A knowledge of these causes will help us provoke an audience into pity, fear, anger, and so on, in order to bring that audience onto our side when making speeches. But isn't it pretty underhand to persuade someone by manipulating their emotions? Why is Aristotle encouraging us to use such tactics? Pretty much everything I've described him saying could have been said by a sophist. You can imagine Aristotle's old teacher Plato, sitting in the corner listening in tight-lipped annoyance, as Aristotle teaches us how to argue on both sides of any argument just as Gorgias and Protagoras did, and how to appeal to the audience's emotions as well as their reason.

But of course Aristotle isn't claiming, with Gorgias and Protagoras, that rhetoric is the greatest of human arts. For him, rhetoric is a necessary tool in Greek society and thus one worth understanding. Nor is this a merely sociological project: Aristotle would deny that when you are doing rhetoric truth is irrelevant. Nor does he think that a rhetorician should use any strategem, no matter how base, just so long as it works. As far as truth goes, we have to admit that, unlike demonstration and even dialectic, rhetoric does not help discover the truth. But on the bright side, Aristotle claims that those who argue for the truth tend to be more persuasive, all else being equal. Nonetheless, a rhetorician will argue whatever case it falls to him to defend, and the more skilled he is, the better the chance of his winning. In this respect, it seems Gorgias was right to compare rhetoric to boxing: it is a technique that can be used in both good causes and bad. Yet it is indeed a technique, an art, not just an "anything goes" struggle to win over an audience. Aristotle mentions a number of arguments which seem to be enthymemes, but don't qualify because they are downright fallacious (1400b–1402a). Enthymemes merely persuade rather than proving something to their audience, but that doesn't mean they are allowed to be invalid. Rhetoric may not be philosophy, but like philosophy, and boxing for that matter, it does have rules.

The *Rhetoric* has a number of things in common with one final Aristotelian work I want to look at: the *Poetics*. Like the *Rhetoric*, the *Poetics* seems incomplete, since it famously lacks a discussion of comedy and deals mostly with tragedy. Again like the *Rhetoric*, it discusses the style and structure of a whole type of discourse, and grapples with the topic of human emotion. Finally, it too has a political context. This is less obvious with the *Poetics* than with the *Rhetoric*. But remember that Plato's discussion of poetry came in his political masterwork, the *Republic*. Aristotle himself discusses music, which for the Greeks was closely linked to poetry, in the final book of his *Politics*. His purpose there is to discuss education, and it's interesting to note that along the way he mentions one of the most famous ideas expressed in the *Poetics*: that poetry can give rise to a kind of purging, in Greek, *katharsis* (1449b). In fact, Aristotle doesn't say nearly as much about *katharsis* as you might expect, given how famous the idea is. If anything, he says more, though still not much, while dealing with education in the *Politics*. The political and educational purposes of poetry remain mostly tacit in the *Poetics*. The work falls most neatly into the area of philosophy we now call "aesthetics." What Aristotle is out to do in most of the *Poetics*, or at least the part that has come down to us, is to tell us what makes a beautiful or pleasing poem. He tells us at the outset that there are various types of poetry (1448b–1449b), just as he mentions different types of rhetoric in his work on that topic. Aristotle's habit of providing classifications is on display here, as is his interest in the purposes and structures of things. For most of the surviving *Poetics* he discusses the purposes and structures of tragedy, though a brief discussion of epic poetry features at the end.

If you were to summarize Aristotle's attitude towards tragedy in five words, you could do worse than: he knows what he likes. He has firm views on what makes for good tragedy, and he names names, expressing admiration for Euripides—while in the epic context, he's a big fan of Homer (1459b). He defends both of them against would-be literary critics, while complaining about other authors. Euripides delivers what a good tragedian should: despite other shortcomings, his works have the right kind of plot, the kind that can purge the audience of emotions such as pity and fear (1453a). As it happens, Aristotle also discussed pity in the *Rhetoric*. There he told us that a pitiable story is one that we can imagine happening to ourselves (1385b). He's thinking along these lines in the *Poetics*, when he tells us that the tragic poets should not depict a bad man striking good fortune, or bad fortune befalling a man so excellent that we cannot relate to him (1452b). Nor should they show a bad man getting the bad fortune he deserves, since this won't be met with sympathy. It's comedy that properly deals with bad people; tragedy is a grander enterprise and should depict people who are admirable. So, ideally, a decent but basically normal man—Aristotle's famous "tragic hero"—should have some dramatic turn of fortune for the worse, by means of a reversal or sudden discovery (1453a). This unleashes the torrent of pity and fear in the audience which will purge them of their emotions and, thus, give them pleasure.

This, then, is the purpose of tragedy, what we've learned to call its final cause. And as we've also learned, formal causes are tailored to serve final causes. Just as the form or structure of a giraffe serves its biological purposes, so the form of a tragedy should relentlessly serve the aim of generating pity and fear. For Aristotle, this is achieved not so much by depicting characters or spectacles of such and such a sort—he wouldn't be impressed by method actors or special effects. He instead lays all his emphasis on plot, and insists that a good plot has a unity of action, which proceeds in a plausible and straightforward way towards the moment of reversal or discovery (1451a–1452a). He enumerates the parts of a tragedy and argues that they need to form a unified whole, just as the parts of a giraffe do. This notion was influential much later, when playwrights in modern Europe expanded on it to include the idea that a play should be unified in terms of time and place as well, rather than changing the setting from scene to scene. This idea doesn't arise in Aristotle, but it's not too far from the spirit of his *Poetics*.

The implicit, and occasionally explicit, conversation partner throughout the *Poetics* is (of course) Plato. Aristotle never has the *Republic* far from his thoughts as he writes, and one can read the *Poetics* as a subtle response to the aesthetic theory of that dialogue. One of the most striking differences is also one of the most basic. Where Plato complains that poetry is an imitative art, and thus an art removed from reality, Aristotle observes more cheerfully that imitation, or *mimesis*, is naturally pleasing to all men (1448b). Our delight in imitation goes hand-in-hand with our delight in learning. The reason we enjoy poetry is that "all men desire to know," as Aristotle says at the beginning of his *Metaphysics*. Here Aristotle seems to allude to a challenge made to Socrates in the *Republic*, when Glaucon says that people who enjoy things like the theater—the so-called "lovers of sights and sounds"—are like philosophers in their desire to learn (475d–e). Socrates responds with a rigorous distinction between philosophers, who seek knowledge of what is, and these sight-lovers who are content with what both is and is not. Aristotle is rather more generous to the theatergoer. He's happy to see both impulses—the thirst for philosophical knowledge and the hunger for theatrical imitation—as part of the same natural human drive.

This is only one of innumerable cases in his writings where Aristotle engages closely with Plato. Of course, Aristotle is usually thought of as an anti-Platonist—and we've seen him excuse himself for attacking Plato with the famous remark that truth is dearer than our friends. But this doesn't do justice to the subtlety of Aristotle's relationship to his master. His response to the *Republic* in the *Politics* and *Poetics* is particularly sustained and explicit, but in just about everything Aristotle wrote he has Plato in mind. He apparently expects his reader to know Plato well, since he often responds to the dialogues without bothering to say explicitly that he is doing so—and not just to a generalized "Platonism" either, but specific passages from specific dialogues on a wide range of topics. Occasionally he does engage with "Platonism" as we usually think of it nowadays: a metaphysical view about eternal, immaterial causes. In these contexts it is not only Plato he has in mind. For him, the Platonist theory was associated with a movement, and not just a single master. The most significant proponents of that movement were two fellow students of Plato, who carried on the traditions of the Academy after his death: Speusippus and Xenocrates. We'll be taking a look at them below, and also at the outstanding early representative of Aristotle's school, Theophrastus. First though, I want to consider a kind of ancient philosopher who was apparently more welcome at the Academy than at the Lyceum.

42

ANYTHING YOU CAN DO
WOMEN AND ANCIENT
PHILOSOPHY

The philosophers in this volume have several things in common. They all came from the lands clustered around the Mediterranean Sea. They all spoke Greek. Presumably they all enjoyed olive oil (especially Thales, who got rich off the stuff). But here's something that may not have struck you, at least until you saw the title of this chapter: they were all men. Of course they were, right? When we conjure up an image of an ancient philosopher, don't we think of a man, probably an older one, with a full beard, wearing a toga? Actually the Greeks didn't wear togas, the Romans did, but that's not the myth I'm trying to dispel just at the moment. Rather, I want to banish the notion that there were no women philosophers in antiquity. There were, though we don't know nearly as much about them as we would like to.

Many female philosophers from the ancient world in fact remain nothing more than names. Archeologists have unearthed a number of grave-inscriptions telling us that the person interred there was a woman, and a philosopher. Interesting, for sure, but not of great use for the historian of philosophy. Fortunately, for some female thinkers more detailed evidence survives. In these cases we are admittedly still dealing with mere scraps of second-hand information. But after all, we didn't let that stop us in the case of Thales and other early Pre-Socratics. And it's among the early Pre-Socratics that we find a figure reputed to have been the first woman philosopher: Theano, who was the student or wife (or both) of Pythagoras.[1] We have a supposed quotation from a work she wrote on the subject of piety, which corrects the widespread impression that Pythagoras derived all things from number. Rather, Theano explains, things come to be in a sequence, and hence *in accordance with* number. Other sources emphasize her virtue and modesty. In one anecdote, Theano is praised for the beauty of her arm, and she says, "It's not for the public." In another, she is asked how soon after having sex a woman can attend a religious festival. If the sexual partner is her husband, replied Theano, then right away, "otherwise never."[2]

These stories are more typical than that technical remark about Pythagoreanism. The ideas of women ancient philosophers are, of course, always preserved by men, when they are preserved at all, and the quotations often tell us more about the men doing the quoting than the women being quoted. Repeatedly we find women being cited for their views on sex, the duties of a good wife, the good running of a family or household, and so on. Another Pythagorean, named Phyntis, is cited as having written on the moderation of women. She asserted the appropriateness of philosophy for women, on the basis that, although some activities belong especially to men or to women, philosophy is not one of them. For philosophy is the attempt to make the soul excellent, and women's souls too can be excellent—precisely by being moderate (albeit not courageous or wise, since these are male virtues). This amounts to good behavior towards her husband, her own body, her house, her family, and the gods. Not very feminist, and not particularly Pythagorean either. In fact, the argument that women should pursue philosophy looks suspiciously like a paraphrase of what Plato says in the *Republic* (more on that later in this chapter), which a later source has likely put into Phyntis' mouth.

One of the more interesting texts ascribed to an ancient woman philosopher deals with similar topics. This is *On the Harmony of Women* by Perictione, who was none other than Plato's mother! Having raised Plato and two of the main characters in the *Republic* (Plato's brothers, Glaucon and Adiemantus), Perictione had already rendered significant service to philosophy in the way normally expected by ancient Greek society. But she didn't leave it at that, and wrote down her thoughts on the virtue appropriate to women. Or at least, so we are asked to believe. In fact, the author of this text too seems to be influenced by Plato, even alluding to the three aspects of soul in the *Republic*. As Plato taught, the goal is to subordinate the lower aspects, and that goes for women too. Women should defeat their desires for opulent food, clothing, and wealth. On the other hand, "Perictione" strikes a moderate note when she mentions that wealth and honor are welcome if they do come, though they are not necessary. She is not urging radical asceticism, then, but endorsing the traditional family values of ancient Greek culture. A woman's virtue crucially involves the preservation of her marriage and, by extension, her family as a whole. Perictione may agree with Phyntis and Plato himself that women can be philosophers, but the place of women philosophers is still the home.

We can safely assume that this little text is not really drawn from a treatise by Plato's mother. In fact, there is plenty of reason to be skeptical that it was written by a woman philosopher at all. (If so, perhaps by a different woman named Perictione?) Though it certainly demonstrates philosophical competence on the part of the author, and some familiarity with the writings of Plato, we might even feel that it would almost be less depressing if it were by a man. As so often, excitement at coming across a text by a female thinker is followed by disappointment, as the text uses rather derivative philosophical considerations to endorse the inferior and home-bound role of women. A fragment by a second woman named "Theano" even encourages wives to bear their husbands' adultery with cheerfulness: "If he associates with the courtesan with a view towards pleasure, he associates with his wife with a view towards the beneficial."[3] Here she echoes the frankly misogynistic sentiment found in a speech ascribed to Demosthenes: "We have courtesans for our pleasure, concubines for the requirements of the body, and wives to bear us lawful children and look after the home faithfully."[4]

Obviously one cannot infer from all this that ancient women philosophers rarely, or never, spoke or thought about topics other than such "women's issues." Rather, we should infer that male authors tended to quote, or pretend to quote, women writers on such subjects as sex, female virtue, and the family. Still, it remains significant that women could present themselves as philosophers, and that they were recognized as paragons of virtue—if not usually as masters of metaphysics or experts in epistemology. The image of the first Theano sets the tone, in that her "philosophy" in large part consisted in being virtuous. As we've already been seeing, and will see even more in the next volume of this series, philosophy in the ancient world was not just an academic pursuit. It was a way of living. Indeed, when we read a grave-inscription telling us that a woman was a "philosopher," this could well mean not that she wrote treatises on logic or physics, but that she lived a life of self-restraint and virtue. In late antiquity it will be possible for both male and female Christians to describe themselves as "philosophers," and to mean by it simply that they are ascetics, living a life devoted to virtue and God.[5] That may already be going on with the women philosophers of the time up to Plato and Aristotle. It could help to explain why so many of the references to such women are to Pythagoreans, famous for their rigorous and religious way of life. Iamblichus, our source for the legends concerning Pythagoras himself, refers to no fewer than seventeen female Pythagoreans. There were even ancient comedies written about women who "pythagorize."

On the other hand, being a paragon of virtue is not *incompatible* with setting forth philosophical doctrines. As we saw, Theano was cited for her views on the meta-physics of numbers, not just for her modesty regarding her shapely arm. Did other women do philosophy in a more doctrinal sense? Apparently so. The most famous example from antiquity is certainly Hypatia, who was possibly a Platonist and certainly a highly skilled mathematician, and who taught (male) students. She'll come along quite a bit later, having lived—and then died at the hands of a Christian mob—in the late fourth and early fifth centuries. So we'll be discussing her in the next installment of our history of philosophy. Closer to the time we've been covering, there is Arete of Cyrene. If the accounts of later ancient authors, including good old Diogenes Laertius, are anything close to the truth, Arete was a truly formidable contributor to the Cyrenaic philosophical school. Again, this school is something we'll be looking at in the next volume. For present purposes, the thing to note is that Arete was the head of the school, having taken it over from her father, Aristippus. She was succeeded in the headship of the school by her pupil and son, also named Aristippus.[6] In commemoration of this relationship, the younger Aristippus was known by the sobriquet "mother-taught." Nor did she teach only her son. She is said to have had more than a hundred students, and to have written forty books on topics in ethics and physics.

Then there's Aspasia, the woman philosopher before the time of Aristotle about whom we are best informed.[7] (The just-discussed Arete would have been roughly a contemporary of Aristotle's.) She came from Miletus, the original philosophical city. Her fame, or perhaps we should say the fame she deserves to have, rests on a number of sources which draw a romantic, political, and intellectual connection between her and Pericles. One text regarding her is the Menexenus, a dialogue ascribed to Plato whose authenticity is disputed. The author has Socrates say that Pericles' speech in honor of the war-dead of Athens was actually written by Aspasia—one of numerous ancient allusions to her influence over Pericles. Socrates also claims to have learned the art of rhetoric directly from Aspasia, and to have memorized this funeral speech she wrote for Pericles (235e–236a).[8] Socrates then recites this speech for his younger companion, Menexenus, a recitation that constitutes almost the entirety of the dialogue. Really, this dialogue ought to be called Aspasia rather than Menexenus.

The content of the speech is not, in truth, particularly philosophical. It falls roughly into three parts. In the first part Socrates—in other words, Pericles—in other words, Aspasia—gives an outline of the military deeds of the Athenians. The second part is a speech within the speech (within the dialogue), in which we hear what the Athenians would say to their loved ones before going off on military campaign. This section alludes to the Delphic motto, "Nothing in excess," and applies it to the wise man's attitude towards fortune: when good things come to him he will not be overly glad, nor will he be overly upset when the tide turns against him (247e–248a). Finally, there is a conclusion which touches on the duty of the city towards the dead, and then urges the listeners too to be moderate in respect of their grief for the fallen. As usual with Plato, it is hard to know what the purpose of all this might be, and why he gives a starring role to Aspasia. Is he showing off his ability to compose Periclean rhetoric, while teasing Pericles for his dependence on a female advisor? Or is he perhaps paying tribute to Aspasia, as would be suggested by a non-ironic reading of Socrates' claim to have learned from her?

Either way, the dialogue suggests that Plato (if he indeed wrote the *Menexenus*) saw Aspasia as part of the sophistical movement. We saw that this movement was associated with Pericles, and also that Anaxagoras may have been put on trial for impiety because he too was linked to the great statesman and orator. This is something Aspasia has in common with Anaxagoras, and with Socrates. Presumably because of her political prominence, she too was put on trial, but was acquitted thanks to Pericles. Yet there was more to Aspasia than rhetoric and an association with a famous Athenian leader. She was an important enough presence in Socrates' circle that she is mentioned in Xenophon,[9] and the "Socratic" thinkers Aeschines and Antisthenes wrote dialogues featuring her. In these sources we see Aspasia as something akin to a female Socrates, encouraging virtue and providing a model of wisdom and temperance to others.

Aspasia is bound to put us in mind of another philosophical woman found in Plato: Diotima from the *Symposium*. As we saw, there too Socrates depicts himself as the pupil of a woman, and repeats her ideas in a speech within the dialogue. The question inevitably arises whether Diotima is being described accurately, and indeed, whether she even existed. Somewhat less ink has been spilled seeking the historical Diotima than the historical Socrates, but the issue has certainly provoked its share of discussion.[10] For my part, I'd say that the question of whether Diotima really existed is probably unanswerable, and also somewhat beside the point. While it would be nice to add another name to our growing list of ancient women thinkers, even if she was real we cannot hope to know anything about the historical Diotima. The Diotima of the *Symposium* is a literary construction, like the Protagoras of the *Protagoras* and the *Theaetetus*, and indeed the Platonic Socrates himself. And in the case of Diotima, we have no non-Platonic sources to use as a check on Plato's portrayal, the way we used Xenophon and Aristophanes when looking at Socrates.

As for the reason why Plato chooses a woman for this culminating passage in the dialogue, this too is destined to remain a matter for speculation. So let's speculate! For one thing, as we've seen so far in this chapter, it was common for Greek men to quote "wise women" when they were writing about topics like sex and childbirth, themes that are fundamental in Diotima's speech. In this respect, Plato simply uses a common literary device by letting Socrates repeat the ideas of a woman (this point holds true whether or not the woman in question is fictional). For another thing, Plato may be using a woman speaker in order to give the passage a certain religious, even oracular, character. We see him do this elsewhere, when he refers to certain priests *and priestesses* when introducing the theory of recollection in the *Meno* (81a). For a similar example outside Plato, we might consider Themistoclea, a Delphic priestess who, according to tradition, taught Pythagoras.[11]

What with all these mysterious Pythagoreans and possibly fictitious Platonic characters, our harvest of female thinkers from antiquity may seem rather meagre. It will increase with the next installment of our history, though, when we'll have a chance to look not only at Hypatia, but also female Christian thinkers like Macrina, sister of the Cappadocian Fathers. For now, our look at women and ancient philosophy would be incomplete if we didn't briefly dwell a bit more on the remarks about women found in the male authors who have occupied us throughout this book. Take Hippocrates. The body of writings ascribed to him includes writings about women's medicine, and indeed insists on the need for a specific branch of medicine that studies the treatment of women.[12] For the Hippocratic authors, the humoral theory is crucial in grasping the difference between women and men. Women are by nature more wet and hot than men, which explains their softer, more pliant flesh. The reason they menstruate is that they need to expel excess moisture from their bodies on a regular basis—if the menses fail to occur, a nosebleed is a good plan B. Sex and childbirth are good for women because they help to keep the womb open, so that moisture can be channeled out of the body. Physical activity, by contrast, is bad, since the female body is badly suited to it.

Not for the first time, this ancient material is likely to provoke mixed reactions in us. On the bright side, the Hippocratic authors are at least thinking hard about women, taking their medical needs seriously as an object of study. They also frequently enlist the women in their own treatment. Women can be trusted to make judgments about the health of their own bodies to at least some extent (while of course still consulting a doctor, who does after all need billable hours).[13] On the not-so-bright side, the whole theory assumes that the male body is the ideal—women are by nature *excessively* moist—and of course it rationalizes the traditional roles imposed on women, emphasizing their need to have sex, to bear children, to avoid physical exercise. A healthy woman, it's pretty clear, is liable to be one who stays at home having children, and who confines her ambitions to running the household. Here Aristotle has a lot in common with the Hippocratics. Although he disagreed with them by making women's bodies excessively cold rather than hot, he agreed that women are wetter than men. More importantly, like the Hippocratic authors he sees one half of the human race as being *naturally* defective, physically speaking. In Aristotle's case, of course, it is much more than half, since, as we saw, he also thinks that all non-Greeks are naturally suited to slavery.

We've already touched on Aristotle's lamentable remarks about women in the *Ethics* (they can't be perfect friends with men, since they are inevitably inferior, *Ethics* 1158b) and the question of the role played by women in his reproductive theory. So I don't need to belabor the point that Aristotle was no feminist. In fact, this is so even by the standards set by other ancient philosophers. It's unusual that he made no provision for the study of philosophy by women. Already the Pythagoreans had allowed women to become philosophers, or so our evidence would have us believe. The Stoics, Epicureans, and Cynics, three groups of philosophers we'll be looking at in the next volume, all believed women could and should do philosophy. The Stoic Cleanthes wrote a work called *That Virtue is the Same in Man and Woman*, while a later Roman Stoic, Musonius Rufus, argued explicitly that women should undertake philosophy (since it would help them to carry out their household roles more perfectly!). As for the Epicureans, there were female students in the first generation of the school. Of particular significance was Leontium, supposedly a former courtesan, who took up with Epicurus himself as his student and lover. And then there are the Cynics, the counter-cultural philosophers who flouted convention, embraced poverty, and lambasted their contemporaries for hypocrisy. One of the most famous Cynics was a woman: Hipparchia, partner of Crates.

But, of course, the ancient philosopher most famous for welcoming women into philosophy is Plato. We've already looked briefly at the relevant passage in our discussion of justice in the *Republic*, but let's revisit it now. It's clear that Plato, or Socrates, realizes how scandalous his proposals will seem. The idea that women could be guardians is likely to provoke laughter rather than agreement (452a). Thus Socrates feels the need to argue for allowing women to engage in traditionally male activities. His argument is the one alluded to by Phyntis and "Perictione," as we saw earlier in this chapter. Namely, that while there are certainly spheres of activity proper to women (like weaving and baking, 455c), in general the natures of different men are also possessed by women. Some women, like some men, are better than others at learning, while others are more warlike. Above all, some are more given to philosophy, the love of wisdom (456a). Admittedly, we can expect that men with an aptitude for philosophy or war will be superior to women who have similar natures, since, generally speaking, women are weaker than men. Still, it would be a waste of the better women's nature if they were not assigned a share in guardianship. Plato's message to women is, then: anything we can do, you can do worse. But we'll still let you do it.

There are two ways of looking at this passage—well, more like fifteen ways, but let's keep things simple. The optimistic reading is the one I briefly indicated earlier in this book: Plato is showing himself to be forward-thinking, compared with the rather benighted attitudes of his contemporaries. This take on Plato gains in plausibility if we compare him to (say) Aristotle. On the other hand, as Julia Annas has rightly said, "it is hardly a feminist argument to claim that women do not have a special sphere because men can outdo them at absolutely everything."[14] For Annas, Plato's argument is not really relevant to the concerns of modern-day feminism. He just wants his ideal city to avoid wasting resources. He is as convinced as Aristotle that women are second-best to men. (This is made abundantly clear elsewhere; for instance, Timaeus 90e, which says that cowardly men are punished by being born as women in their next life.) But the good of the city demands that we wring every last bit of usefulness out of the citizens, even out of the inferior ones.

Here we might also recall that it is not really in the interest of the philosophers (both men and women) to rule—they have to "go back into the cave" and assume leadership for the good of the city. Similarly here, Plato has the good of the city in view, not the good of the women who are to serve as guardians. He has no interest in allowing them to attain a sense of self-fulfillment, or in liberating them from social constraints for the sake of their psychological well-being. Furthermore, there is room for a feminist critique of even his most apparently progressive claim, namely that women are like men in their natures. Could we not instead think that women are *different* from men by nature, but different in a way that is valuable? Ancient authors, Plato included, instead tend to think of women merely as worse versions of men, and of the female as a negation or privation of the male. This very tendency has made ancient texts a rich hunting-ground for feminist philosophers, and I'd like to end this chapter by mentioning just one example.

It's a surprising one, in terms of the ancient source-text: Aristotle's theory of place in the *Physics*. We touched on this briefly when we surveyed his physical theory. As we saw, Aristotle sees the place of something not as a kind of three-dimensional extension occupied by something—like our notion of "space"—but as the containing boundary of a thing, for instance, the inside limit of the air surrounding your body. The French philosopher Luce Irigaray wrote a fascinating essay on this text.[15] Unlike Plato's discussion of the Receptacle in his *Timaeus*—the passive spatial or material principle which is compared at one point to a mother—Aristotle makes no attempt to describe place in gendered terms.[16] But Irigaray argues that Aristotelian place is implicitly feminine. In fact, woman *is* place, defined by man in terms of what she contains (as during sex, or while carrying a child) and not allowed to be something in her own right. Thus, Aristotelian worries about place are reconfigured as concerns about femininity. For instance, the question of whether a place can be in a further place becomes the question of whether there is any place for woman, if she is understood in such a negative fashion. And Aristotle's idea that elements have "natural places" is exploited to think about the way that the male is attracted to the female.

Irigaray isn't just engaging in a subversive reinterpretation here, though that is certainly part of her approach. She also criticizes the Aristotelian theory of place on its own terms. She accuses Aristotle of imagining that what occupies a place is always rigid, with well-defined boundaries. Referring to bodily fluids like mucous, she argues that Aristotle's understanding of place will break down in cases where porous or intermingling bodies meet—here, what surrounds is not a container with a rigid inner boundary, but a kind of bridge between one thing and another. Of course, even with this sort of direct criticism, Irigaray is using Aristotle for her own philosophical purposes. In this case, rejecting the dichotomy between a passive, negatively defined place (woman) and a rigid, positively defined thing that has a place (man) allows Irigaray to articulate her own ethical position. For her, the relationship between man and woman (one embodied in physical sex) can be seen not as one thing containing another, but as a "mutual envelopment" where both partners shape and are shaped by the other.

Obviously, this is not standard-issue history of philosophy. As Cynthia Freeland says in discussing Irigaray's piece, "it may seem unclear whether one is reading Aristotle scholarship, a primitive biology text, or an erotic novel."[17] Yet in a sense Irigaray is engaged in one of the most traditional and long-standing ways of doing philosophy: re-reading and re-interpreting the ancients, especially Plato and Aristotle. This way of doing philosophy will come to the fore in late antiquity, but it began already in the lifetimes of Plato and Aristotle, as their students and successors expounded and expanded on their ideas. It turns out that Plato practiced what he preached, and had female philosophy students—the names of Axiothea and Lasthenia are known to us. They apparently continued to study at the Academy under Plato's immediate successor, Speusippus. Aristotle was also true to his word, and had no female students. But he did have students, and at his Lyceum business was carried on after his death. A look at the fortunes of both schools after the death of the two great masters will make a fitting conclusion to this first part of our history of philosophy, and give us a chance to look ahead to the next one.

43

THE NEXT GENERATION
THE FOLLOWERS OF PLATO
AND ARISTOTLE

s I said at the start, my aim in this series of books is to cover the history of
philosophy without any gaps. We've finished Aristotle, and it's right about
here that there would normally be a gap. In an undergraduate philosophy course
you might reasonably expect to jump from Aristotle to, perhaps, Descartes, leaping
over about 2,000 years of history in the process. A more enlightened approach
might include looking at Thomas Aquinas, in the thirteenth century—still omitting
the better part of two millenia. Better still would be to skip only as far as Plotinus or
Augustine in late antiquity. Of course, it's fair enough to be selective in designing a
philosophy curriculum, and to concentrate on the household names. But I'm
allowing myself the luxury of not skipping ahead at all. In the next volume I will
be looking in detail at the philosophical movements which began already in the
lifetime of Aristotle, and which dominated the Hellenistic period. There are some
household names here, too: the Stoics, the Epicureans, the Skeptics. But to move on
directly to these Hellenistic schools would still be to leave something out.

One of the most striking and puzzling features of Hellenistic philosophy is that
Plato and Aristotle play a relatively small role. Though the Stoics and others did
respond to them, it took a few hundred years for their influence to become dominant.
Still, Plato and Aristotle had established schools, with physical property to keep them
going and groups of disciples to carry on their work. It's that immediate legacy that
I want to consider in this chapter, first looking at the so-called "Old Academy": Plato's
two immediate successors, Speusippus and Xenocrates—not to be confused with the
Pre-Socratic thinker Xenophanes. Then I'll be checking in at the Lyceum to see how
Aristotle's school got on without Aristotle. Here the main personality to discuss is
Theophrastus. I know what you've been thinking: sure, Aristotle shows an impressively encyclopedic range, inquiring into everything from logic, to animals, to the
rules of good poetry. But hey, what about *plants*? Well, Theophrastus is just the man to
fill that particular gap.

Before we look at the roots of Aristotelianism with Theophrastus, though, let's look at the brief blossoming of hard-core Platonism in the wake of Plato's death. I've just mentioned that Plato's immediate successors as heads of the Academy, Speusippus and Xenocrates, are often referred to under the rubric of the "Old Academy." This is in contrast to the so-called "New Academy," who came after them. The New Academy took their cue from a rather different Plato from the one who inspired Speusippus and Xenocrates. New Academics were skeptics. They were particularly impressed by Plato's early, "Socratic" dialogues, in which Socrates raises philosophical questions, refutes whatever answers are offered, and draws things to a close with an expression of puzzlement. Speusippus and Xenocrates were instead inspired by the Plato whose mathematical, logical, and metaphysical speculations are on display in dialogues like the *Timaeus* and *Sophist*. This brand of Platonism would go out of fashion for a few centuries, only to return with a vengeance in the Roman empire.

When I say that the Old Academy took its cue from the later, more technical dialogues of Plato, I'm actually leaving something out. But then, Plato left it out too. It would seem that Speusippus and Xenocrates were trying to develop ideas which had been discussed in Plato's Academy, but which either were omitted from the dialogues or were referred to only very obliquely. These ideas are sometimes called by the somewhat histrionic phrase "unwritten doctrines." Since even the most intrepid historian of philosophy can't read unwritten doctrines, we have to rely on indirect sources of information about this aspect of Plato's teaching. This means, above all, relying on Aristotle. He's our main source for some of the ideas Plato apparently didn't see fit to share with us in his dialogues. He's also our main source for the way that Speusippus and Xenocrates carried on those ideas. So it's a bit unfortunate that Aristotle thought the unwritten doctrines were ludicrous and barely worth taking seriously. Imagine Donald Trump trying to explain the principles of Marxism, and you'll get pretty close to Aristotle's reliability as a reporter on this particular topic.

The most famous story about Plato's unwritten doctrines, though, is found not in Aristotle but in later authors, beginning with Aristotle's student Aristoxenus—who nonetheless is just reporting what Aristotle told him. At any rate, the story goes that Plato offered to give a public lecture on the topic of the Good. An audience turned up, expecting to hear about how to acquire happiness, perhaps by way of wealth, health, and other such goods. Instead, they got a long lecture on mathematics, and went away totally bemused.[1] This rather depressing story suggests that even if Plato had written down his unwritten doctrines, we *still* might not be able to figure out what he was talking about. But if it has any basis in truth, it shows that Plato believed mathematics to be at the core of philosophy, including what we would think of as ethics: inquiry into the nature of the Good.

Though we don't find this story about the lecture on the Good in Aristotle's own works, we do find him explaining, or at least making fun of, Plato's ideas about numbers and how they relate to his theory of Forms. The theory as Aristotle tells it is complicated and mysterious. Many Plato scholars are happy to ignore it, preferring the literary riches of the real Plato's dialogues to the off-putting abstractions Aristotle puts in Plato's mouth. Others think they can find traces of the so-called unwritten doctrines in the dialogues. Either way, we can't understand the Old Academy without saying at least a little about this theory. So here goes. Plato seems to have been taking up ideas from the mathematics-obsessed Pythagoreans. He was particularly interested in the production of numbers from two principles, a principle of unity and a principle of multiplicity. Plato apparently called the second principle "the great and small."[2] The idea was that you could get numbers by imposing some limit or unity on a continuum. Imagine a musical scale, for instance—remembering that, for the Greeks, music and mathematics were intimately related. What you have is a range of sounds, which become musical notes only when certain limits or intervals are imposed. Similarly, numbers would emerge from the interaction of unity and multiplicity. In the Old Academy this was sometimes understood in frankly sexual terms: unity is a male principle, multiplicity a female principle, and from their copulation are born the numbers. (And you thought Pythagorean metaphysics was dull!)

Aristotle further tells us that Speusippus and Xenocrates took up these ideas of Plato and tried to work them out in detail. An anecdote about Xenocrates relates that he asked a would-be student whether he knew anything about geometry or astronomy. The aspiring philosopher admitted that he did not. Xenocrates sent him away, saying, "You give me no handles for philosophy."[3] This is to be put in the same box as the legend about the sign posted outside the Academy: "Only those who have studied geometry should enter." Whether or not there's any truth in these stories, the successors of Plato certainly agreed with the sentiment. They put forward their Pythagoreanizing version of Platonism in the setting of Plato's Academy, whose headship Speusippus inherited upon Plato's death in 347 BC. Speusippus was Plato's nephew, so this was keeping the business in the family. Xenocrates took it over next, in 339, supposedly to the annoyance of Aristotle who, in a fit of pique, set up the rival Lyceum.

Here I should remind you that the Academy was in a grove named for the Greek hero Hekademos, outside the walls of Athens. Plato seems to have acquired a house near the grove, which was public property—he and his associates would have pursued philosophy both in the pleasant surroundings of the public grove and in the private household. By all accounts they spent a lot of their time on mathematics. Aristotle is again our source for certain astronomical theories developed in the Academy, for instance, by Plato's associate Eudoxus, who devised mathematical models of the planetary motions we see in the night sky. In the dialogues, Plato recommends astronomy as a stepping-stone towards philosophy, and that was certainly put into practice in the Academy. Another favorite activity was classification and division. I've already mentioned the story about Diogenes the Cynic: mocking the Academy's definition of man as "featherless biped," he turned up with a plucked chicken and said, "Here is Plato's man." He wasn't the only one who was amused. A comic author named Epicrates depicts Academic philosophers sitting around trying to decide whether the pumpkin is a vegetable, a tree, or a kind of grass.[4]

In fact, this is an Academic practice that *is* written in the dialogues, for instance in the *Sophist* with its method of collection and division. Plato's successors too wrote treatises on logical method. Speusippus supposedly said that unless you can enumerate all the ways one thing differs from another, you lack knowledge about both things.[5] But, like everything else they wrote, these treatises on division and classification are lost. This is why we're dependent on Aristotle's rather tendentious testimony. He mostly focuses on their theory of first principles, which was based on Plato's theory about unity and multiplicity. Aristotle tells us that Speusippus derived a series of further principles from these two basic foundations.[6] For Speusippus, the one, or monad, interacts with multiplicity, the so-called "dyad," to generate numbers, and then geometrical figures, like triangles for instance. The soul of the world then builds a physical universe on the basis of the geometrical figures. That sounds pretty weird, but you might remember that Plato's *Timaeus* does talk about a world soul and offers a geometrical analysis of the four elements, saying that fire, air, earth, and water are made up of atomic shapes formed from triangles. So the weirdness, both written and unwritten, already started with Plato.

Aristotle's big complaint about Speusippus is that his system is "episodic."[7] In other words, all these levels—the principles of number, the numbers, the figures, and then bodies—seem to be more or less independent, like the layers in a sandwich that threatens to fall apart when you try to eat it. He also presents Speusippus as if he eliminates Plato's Forms and replaces them with numbers.[8] But this is probably a distortion. Rather, Speusippus was in some way identifying Forms with numbers, or perhaps with the principles that generate numbers. Aristotle isn't much more impressed by Xenocrates, but he does imply that Xenocrates made more of an effort to tie the levels of his system together.[9] Xenocrates again has a monad and dyad as generating first principles. Below this, he envisions three levels of reality:

Forms, mathematical entities, and the bodies you can actually see. He thinks of the mathematical entities as a kind of middle level which can tie together the Forms and the bodies. Again, he puts the soul at this middle level, and even says that soul itself is a "moving number"—it brings the motion of life and the structure associated with number.[10]

This all sounds pretty abstract and, if you're being ungenerous, not even very philosophical. It suggests that the Old Academy was taking a good idea way too far, the good idea being the Pythagorean and Platonic conviction that reality has an underlying mathematical structure. But the Old Academy's ideas had staying-power. In particular, the idea that reality derives from a single principle of unity will become fundamental in the Platonism of late antiquity, and from there it went on to influence religious ideas about God in Judaism, Christianity, and Islam. In those traditions there was constant debate about whether this single first principle is beyond our understanding, or comprehensible as the first of causes. Speusippus and Xenocrates anticipate this debate. Speusippus is reported to have said that the principle of unity is beyond even goodness and being.[11] In the next volume, we will see that later authors make a similar claim, for a variety of reasons. Speusippus' reason is that since the principle is the source of these things, it cannot partake of them. Xenocrates, by contrast, said the monad was a kind of divine mind,[12] like Aristotle's God, perhaps. Maybe he even wanted Plato's Forms to be ideas in this godlike intellect. Here then, at the infancy of Platonism, we have one of the most fundamental tensions that will occupy our attention when we reach late ancient and medieval philosophy. Is God, the first principle, so transcendent that he surpasses our concepts and our language? Or is he sort of like us, but better, a mind that can think about everything instead of only a few things at a time?

It should also be said that Speusippus and Xenocrates did not spend all their time worrying about numbers and gods. They also had things to say on the subject of ethics. There's a great story about Xenocrates going with Plato and Speusippus to the court of the tyrant Dionysius in Syracuse. You might remember from the chapter on Plato's biography that this association turned out badly. On some accounts, Plato barely escaped with his life. Supposedly, Dionysius threatened to execute Plato, and the faithful Xenocrates stepped forward and said, "Only after you cut off my head first." But before these unpleasant scenes everyone had been getting along famously. Clearly, if you invite philosophers to your court you need to host a drinking contest, and this is what Dionysius did. Xenocrates drank everyone else under the table, and was awarded a gold laurel wreath. Displaying his disdain for material wealth, he left the gold wreath on the head of a statue of Hermes in the city.[13]

This disdain for the things valued by most of us is confirmed by the little we know about the ethics of the Old Academy.[14] It seems that they didn't care much for pleasure. Xenocrates encourages us to look after both the soul and the body, but more especially the soul, which he says is our *daimon* or guardian spirit. Before him, Speusippus recommends a life in accordance with nature, which is as free as possible from trouble and disturbance. This means steering clear of pleasure as well as pain. These ideas of living naturally and achieving a quiet, undisturbed existence will be commonplace in Hellenistic philosophy, and it's interesting to see them turning up in Plato's immediate successors. In the next volume we'll see Hellenistic philosophers fighting over the role of pleasure in the good life, and pleasure's relation to virtue. This was already a hot topic in the Academy. It's not only Speusippus and Xenocrates who raised the issue, but also that astronomical whiz-kid Eudoxus. Eudoxus, according to Aristotle's *Ethics*, was willing to accept that pleasure is in fact the good.[15] One argument he gave was that pain is clearly bad; since pleasure is the opposite of pain, it must be good. Speusippus refuted this. He admitted that pain is bad, but that doesn't mean pleasure is good. If happiness lies in a quiet, neutral life, then it could be a golden mean between the two extremes of pain *and* pleasure, both of which would be bad.

Plato's successors, then, tackled a fairly wide range of topics, carrying on the logical, metaphysical, and ethical activities of the Academy. Over at the Lyceum, they were also keeping the flame alive. In this case, we have the advantage that the torch was handed to a man whose writings are partially preserved today. This was Theophrastus, whom we already met as a partner in Aristotle's biological investigations on the island of Lesbos—in fact, Theophrastus hailed from the city of Eresos on Lesbos. Perhaps there was something of a division of labor here, because Theophrastus developed an expertise in plants to rival Aristotle's zoological prowess. His surviving writings about plants are valuable evidence of ancient ideas about botany, classifying plants into their types in true Aristotelian manner.[16] Another work, *On Stones*, does a similar classificatory and descriptive job for the mineral world.

Theophrastus seems to have been concerned to fill out and complete Aristotle's natural philosophy, by explaining features of the inanimate world and minor topics Aristotle had left unexplained. For instance, he wrote about the causes of dizziness and sweat and—perhaps after all the research he'd done on plants and stones—on fatigue.[17] His master had left not only a body of texts, but implicitly a whole research program that could be pursued by his students. Not that those students followed Aristotle slavishly. Theophrastus is known to have raised some challenges to Aristotle's definition of place, for example. His combination of fidelity and creativity is on display in his most important surviving work, usually called the *Metaphysics*.[18] Here Theophrastus creatively fuses together ideas from Aristotle's physics and his metaphysics to explain the principles of the universe—for instance, how God influences our cosmos through heavenly motion. Although he is weaving a tapestry out of Aristotelian threads, Theophrastus introduces a knotty problem here and there. He generally accepts Aristotle's teleology—the view that nature does nothing in vain. But he wonders what the purpose of some natural phenomena might be; for instance, why men have nipples, or why deer lose their antlers.

Aristotelianism did not die with Theophrastus. His successor, Strato, was another specialist, in this case concentrating on physical theories rather than empirical research like Theophrastus. There was also Eudemus, who may have edited Aristotles' *Eudemian Ethics* (hence the name), and whose area of expertise was mathematics. Aristoxenus, the fellow I mentioned who relays the story about Plato's lecture on the Good, wrote about music. But all these figures had died by the first half of the third century BC. We have to wait until the end of the first century, around the time of Cicero and the demise of the Roman Republic, for a resurgence of Aristotelianism. Even then, though, Aristotle's immediate successors were not forgotten. Theophrastus imitated his master by writing down a good deal of information about earlier Greek philosophical ideas. So later reports on the Pre-Socratics frequently draw on lost works by Theophrastus—in fact, he may be the most important conduit for Pre-Socratic philosophy apart from Aristotle himself. Especially important was his critical discussion of pre-Aristotelian theories of sensation, which we know through a later adaptation of the Theophrastean text.

Clearly the Old Academy and the early Peripatetics (as the Aristotelians were called) do not represent anything like a highpoint of ancient thought. These were minor thinkers who carried on the work of the two greats, Plato and Aristotle. History has passed a severe judgment on them, insofar as their texts are mostly lost (even if we know more about them than about Plato's female students, who are nothing but names to us). What we do know suggests what might have happened had ancient philosophy settled immediately into the pattern that would eventually prevail in late antiquity. A few centuries ahead, Platonism will contend with, and ultimately be reconciled with, Aristotelianism. Platonists will write commentaries on Aristotle, sometimes attacking him, but usually just expounding and explaining him. The two traditions will make common cause against shared enemies. In order for all that to happen, perhaps, the Platonists and Aristotelians needed some enemies worth uniting against. And the intervening few centuries will certainly provide that, as several new philosophical schools arise in the period we call the Hellenistic age.

If you liked the atomists, you'll love the physical theories of Epicurus. Or if, like Eudoxus, you think pleasure is the good, then Epicurean and Cyrenaic ethics will be just the thing to satisfy you. And if you enjoyed Eudoxus' taste for astronomy, wait until we get to Ptolemy. Readers of an antisocial temperament (or who like an amusing anecdote) can thrill to the counter-cultural exploits of the Cynics. More ambitious souls might enjoy the Stoic tradition, which set out an ethics and epistemology so demanding it would make even Plato blush, and saw one of its members become an emperor (hint: it wasn't Caligula). Earlier Stoics matched Aristotle for logical rigor and innovation, and faced off against their epistemic enemies the Skeptics—who will be kindred spirits for those of you who still haven't made up your mind what to think about all of this philosophy business. And as if these Hellenistic schools weren't enough, late antiquity has different delights to offer. There is the resurgence of Platonism and Aristotelianism just mentioned, which made possible the writings of greatest philosopher of the ancient Greek tradition apart from Plato and Aristotle: Plotinus. Already in his lifetime, in the third century AD, there was an ongoing saga of tension and influence between Hellenic philosophy and the new faith of Christianity. This became central to the career of another great thinker, Augustine, who will be only the most significant of many Church Fathers I'll be examining. Join me then, for the rest of antiquity—in Volume 2 of the *History of Philosophy Without Any Gaps*.

NOTES

Chapter 2

1. For a good introduction to this genre see the article "Doxography of Ancient Philosophy" by J. Mansfeld, on the online Stanford Encyclopedia of Philosophy <http://plato.stanford.edu/entries/doxography-ancient>.

Chapter 3

1. Quoted from Homer, *Iliad*, trans. M. Hammond (New York, 1987), 15.14–17.
2. Both works available in Hesiod, *Works and Days and Theogony*, trans. S. Lombardo (Indianapolis, 1993).

Chapter 4

1. For Galen see his *My Own Books* 40; an English translation is available in Galen, *Selected Works*, trans. P. N. Singer (Oxford, 1997). For Ptolemy, *Almagest* 1.1; English translation in G. J. Toomer, *Ptolemy's* Almagest (London, 1984).
2. In the anti-vegetarian camp was the Pythagorean Aristoxenus (Diogenes Laertius, *Lives of the Philosophers* 8.20); but most sources claim he never ate meat, an emphatic example being the late ancient Platonist Porphyry. For his fascinating defense of vegetarianism see Porphyry, *On Abstinence from Eating Animals*, trans. G. Clark (London, 2000).
3. For a detailed overview of what is known about various parts of the ancient Greek world see M. Grant, *The Rise of the Greeks* (New York, 1987).
4. English translation in Iamblichus, *On the Pythagorean Way of Life*, trans. J. M. Dillon and J. Hershbell (Atlanta, Ga., 1991).
5. Plato, *Phaedo* 85e–86d; Aristotle, *On the Soul* 407b–408a.
6. In fact it is this theory that Aristotle associates with Pythagoras at 407b.

Chapter 5

1. See e.g. M. M. Mackenzie, "Heraclitus and the Art of Paradox," *Oxford Studies in Ancient Philosophy*, 6 (1988), 1–37 (at 9–10, with further references).
2. On which see L. Tarán, "Heraclitus: The River Fragments and their Implications," *Elenchos*, 20 (1999), 9–52.

Chapter 6

1. Here I'm following the most "literal" reading of Parmenides, sometimes called "strict monism." Several other types of interpretation, which allow for some recognition of

multiplicity, have been offered. For a couple of prominent examples see A. P. D. Mour-
elatos, *The Route of Parmenides: A Study of Word, Image, and Argument in the Fragments*
(New Haven, 1970), and P. K. Curd, *The Legacy of Parmenides: Eleatic Monism and Later Presocratic
Thought* (Princeton, 1998).

2. Again, this is not a universally adopted reading. Some think, for instance, that the two parts
of the poem are complementary and together provide a single account of reality. See e.g.
A. Finkelberg, "Being, Truth and Opinion in Parmenides," *Archiv für Geschichte der Philosophie*,
81 (1999), 233–48.

3. For a classic study of the difficulties concerning this verb in Greek philosophy see
C. H. Kahn, *The Verb "Be" in Ancient Greek* (Dordrecht, 1973, reprinted Indianapolis, 2003).

Chapter 7

1. For modern attempts to apply mathematics to Zeno's paradoxes, see A. Grünbaum, *Modern
Science and Zeno's Paradoxes* (Middletown, Ind., 1967), and somewhat more recently M. White,
The Continuous and the Discrete: Ancient Physical Theories from a Contemporary Perspective (Oxford,
1992).

Chapter 8

1. This sort of option is nowadays sometimes called "reductionist," because the theory would
"reduce" apparent reality to a more fundamental, underlying genuine reality.

Chapter 9

1. For instance, B. Inwood, "Anaxagoras and Infinite Divisibility," *Illinois Classical Studies*, 11
(1986), 17–33; D. Sedley, *Creationism and its Critics* (Berkeley, 2007).

2. For views along these lines see e.g. D. W. Graham, "Was Anaxagoras a Reductionist?,"
Ancient Philosophy, 24 (2004), 1–18; E. Lewis, "Anaxagoras and the Seeds of a Physical
Theory," *Apeiron*, 33 (2000), 1–23; and P. Curd, "Anaxagoras and the Theory of Everything,"
in P. Curd and D. W. Graham (eds.), *The Legacy of Parmenides: Eleatic Monism and Later
Presocratic Thought* (Las Vegas, 2008), 230–49.

Chapter 10

1. The fragments have been edited and studied by Martin and my colleague in Munich, Oliver
Primavesi, in *L'Empédocle de Strasbourg* (Berlin, 1999).

2. Diogenes Laertius 8.69. For a Greek text with facing-page English translation, see in the
Loeb series R. D. Hicks, *Diogenes Laertius: Lives of Eminent Philosophers*, 2 vols. (London and
Cambridge, Mass., 1925).

3. Translation taken from G. S. Kirk, J. E. Raven, and M. Schofield, *The Presocratic Philosophers*
(Cambridge, 1983).

4. This increase in unity must mean that Empedocles is describing the generation of animals
in the part of the cosmic cycle that goes from total Strife towards total Love.

5. On the question see O. Primavesi, "Empedocles: Physical and Mythical Divinity," in P. Curd
and D. W. Graham (eds.), *The Oxford Handbook of Presocratic Philosophy* (Oxford, 2005),
250–83.

Chapter 11

1. English translations of numerous Hippocratic treatises, with facing-page Greek, are available in the Loeb series (ten volumes). *The Sacred Disease* is in volume 2, ed. and trans. W. H. S. Jones (London and Cambridge, Mass., 1923).
2. *Regimen* 4.87, in volume 4 of the Loeb series (London and Cambridge, Mass., 1931).
3. In volume 1 of the Loeb series (Lonson and Cambridge, Mass., 1923).
4. Hippocrates, *Aphorisms* 1.1, in volume 4 of the Loeb series.
5. The *Oath* is included in volume 1 of the Loeb series.

Chapter 12

1. Reports and quotations of the sophists are collected in J. M. Dillon and T. Gergel, *The Greek Sophists* (London, 2003); for this passage in Plato see p. 104.
2. *The Greek Sophists*, 126.
3. Excerpted in *The Greek Sophists*, 22–32.
4. *The Greek Sophists*, 5.
5. *The Greek Sophists*, 10, quoted from Plato, *Theaetetus* 152a. I discuss the remark further in the chapter on the *Theaetetus* later in this book.
6. *The Greek Sophists*, 318–33.
7. *The Greek Sophists*, 61–2.
8. *The Greek Sophists*, 62.
9. *The Greek Sophists*, 76–84.
10. *The Greek Sophists*, 67–75.

Chapter 13

1. The most famous example is *The Death of Socrates* by Jacques-Louis David, which pointedly depicts Socrates calmly declaiming while his associates are giving in to despair.
2. A convenient translation is in Plato and Aristophanes, *Four Texts on Socrates*, trans. T. G. West and G. S. West (Ithaca, NY, 1984).
3. Xenophon, *Memoirs* 1.1; Plato, *Phaedo* 96a–c.
4. For an overview of literature on his Socratic writings see D. R. Morrison, *Bibliography of Editions, Translations and Commentary on Xenophon's Socratic Writings, 1600–Present* (Pittsburgh, 1988). For translations see Xenophon, *Memorabilia*, trans. A. L. Bonette (Ithaca, NY, 1994); Xenophon, *Conversations of Socrates*, trans. H. Treddenick and R. Waterfield (London, 1990).
5. See e.g. *Memoirs* 1.4.
6. Xenophon *Apology* 12–13; *Memoirs* 1.1, 4.3, 4.8.
7. See the opening of Xenophon's *Apology*.
8. *Apology* 16–19.
9. *Memoirs* 1.2.
10. *Memoirs* 3.6. The young man is in fact Plato's brother Glaucon, one of Socrates' interlocutors in the *Republic*. The themes I am emphasizing here have been explored by D. K. O'Connor, "Socrates and Political Ambition: The Dangerous Game," in *Proceedings of the Boston Area Colloquium in Ancient Philosophy*, 14 (1998), 31–52.
11. *Apology* 15.
12. These three examples are from *Memoirs* 2.2, 1.3, 3.13.

Chapter 14

1. A much-discussed subject in scholarly literature. See e.g. A. Nehamas, *Virtues of Authenticity: Essays on Plato and Socrates* (Princeton, 1999); G. R. F. Ferrari, "Socratic Irony as Pretence," *Oxford Studies in Ancient Philosophy*, 34 (2008), 1–33; M. Lane, "The Evolution of *Eirôneia* in Classical Greek Texts: Why Socratic *Eirôneia* is not Socratic Irony," *Oxford Studies in Ancient Philosophy*, 31 (2006), 49–83.

2. The demands made by Socrates in his search for definition were criticized in an influential article by P. Geach, "Plato's *Euthyphro*: An Analysis and Commentary," *The Monist*, 50 (1966), 369–82, at 371. On the issue see W. J. Prior, "Plato and the 'Socratic Fallacy'," *Phronesis*, 43 (1998), 97–113.

Chapter 15

1. This is a theme that has been explored extensively by Pierre Hadot. See his *What is Ancient Philosophy?*, trans. M. Chase (Cambridge, Mass., 2002), and *Philosophy as a Way of Life: Spiritual Exercises from Socrates to Foucault*, ed. A. I. Davidson, trans. M. Chase (Oxford, 1995).

2. In *Process and Reality* (New York, 1929), 39.

3. The legend originated in late antiquity. As far as I could find out, the earliest reference is a note written in the margin of a manuscript of a work by Aelius Aristides, a rhetorician of the second century AD.

4. For his report see R. D. Hicks, *Diogenes Laertius: Lives of Eminent Philosophers*, 2 vols (London and Cambridge, Mass., 1925). All of Book Three is dedicated to Plato.

5. These letters are included in Plato, *Complete Works*, ed. J. M. Cooper (Indianapolis, 1997). This also includes Plato's dialogues and a number of doubtful and spurious works (i.e. things he supposedly wrote but probably or certainly did not in fact write).

6. There are perhaps as many answers to this question as readers of Plato, but here are some studies of the issue from the past couple of decades, in chronological order: M. Frede, "Plato's Arguments and the Dialogue Form," *Oxford Studies in Ancient Philosophy*, supplementary vol. (1992), 201–20; K. Sayre, *Plato's Literary Garden: How to Read a Platonic Dialogue* (Notre Dame, Ind., 1995); C. H. Kahn, *Plato and the Socratic Dialogue: The Philosophical Use of a Literary Form* (Cambridge, 1996); D. Clay, *Platonic Questions: Dialogues with the Silent Philosopher* (University Park, Pa., 2000); C. L. Griswold (ed.), *Platonic Writings, Platonic Readings* (University Park, Pa., 2002); G. A. Scott (ed.), *Philosophy in Dialogue: Plato's Many Devices* (Evanston, Ill., 2007).

7. Diogenes Laertius, *Lives of the Philosophers* 3.37, seems to be saying that Plato's student Philip of Opus was tasked with copying the dialogue, which existed only as a working copy (on wax tablets) when Plato died.

8. For an assessment of such analysis see C. M. Young, "Plato and Computer Dating," *Oxford Studies in Ancient Philosophy*, 12 (1994), 227–50.

Chapter 16

1. J. M. Cooper (ed.), *Plato: Complete Works* (Indianapolis, 1997). As mentioned in the Note on References at the start of the book, citations of Plato are to the Stephanus pages which are printed in nearly all translations of the dialogues, usually in the margins as in this collection.

Chapter 17

1. A further counter-intuitive claim made by Socrates is that someone who is actually guilty of misconduct should want to be punished, rather than wanting to escape without paying any penalty. For punishment is correction, and correction makes us better. Socrates compares this process to receiving medicine, which may be unpleasant but leads to beneficial results (478b–e).

Chapter 18

1. On this see e.g. L.M. Antony and N. Hornstein (eds.), *Chomsky and His Critics* (Oxford, 2003).
2. Indeed Plato's *Meno* has been seen as the first work in the history of philosophy to introduce the still-influential idea that knowledge is justified true belief. Impressively, Plato is also the first to see the potential flaw with this definition, with the jury example in his *Theaetetus*. See the end of the next chapter on that dialogue, and for issues concerning belief and knowledge in Plato the papers collected in G. Fine, *Plato on Knowledge and Forms* (Oxford, 2003).

Chapter 19

1. Despite anecdotal evidence to the contrary, I am convinced that this title is amusing. It is a play on the title of a novel by Maya Angelou, *I Know Why the Caged Bird Sings*.
2. A further move might be for Socrates to say that it is *true for him* that Protagoras' doctrine is *absolutely* false, that is, *false for everyone* including Protagoras. The question here is whether Protagoras would allow us to infer "it is true for everyone that the doctrine is false' from 'it is true for Socrates that it is true for everyone that the doctrine is false." Presumably not, since in general, he won't allow us to assert X on the basis that "it is true for Socrates that X."
3. I will here pass over a final, difficult section of the dialogue in which Socrates and Theaetetus discuss the possibility that some kind of "rational account"—a *logos*, that favorite word of Heraclitus—is what you'd need to add to true belief to render it into knowledge. As we expect by now, they don't manage to make this work, and yet we do learn a bit more about knowledge, in particular how it does and does not relate to giving an account of yourself when you believe something.

Chapter 20

1. This seems to be an application of the more general "like is known by like" principle ascribed by Aristotle and Theophrastus to some Pre-Socratics, for example, Empedocles, at *Metaphysics* 1000b.
2. Support for this reading is provided by an analogous argument at *Republic* 523c–e, which seems to be saying that one's ring-finger is long compared to one's little finger, but short compared to one's middle finger. Thus it is both short and long, albeit in different respects.
3. The two examples are from *Hippias Major* 289b (though it mentions a generic beautiful woman, not Helen specifically) and *Republic*, Book I, 331e–332a.
4. The debate on this in modern scholarship goes back a long way. See e.g. F. C. White, "The Compresence of Opposites in *Phaedo* 102," *Classical Quarterly*, 27 (1977), 303–11, taking up a debate that goes back to F. Cornford's *Plato and Parmenides*, published in 1939! Since then see e.g. A. Nehamas, "Plato on the Imperfection of the Sensible World," *American Philosophical*

Quarterly, 12 (1975), 105–17; N. P. White, "Forms and Sensibles: Phaedo 74B–C," *Philosophical Topics*, 15 (1987), 197–214.

Chapter 21

1. 5.89. For an English translation see e.g. Thucydides, *History of the Peloponnesian War*, trans. R. Warner (New York, 1954).
2. Closer to the Greek would be "the powerful exact what they can, and the weak have to comply," as pointed out by Mary Beard in the *New York Review of Books*, 30 Sept. 2010.
3. T. Hobbes, *Leviathan*, ed. J. C. A. Gaskin (Oxford, 2008).
4. K. Popper, *The Open Society and its Enemies* (London, 1945), vol. 1.
5. On this notorious argument see J. M. Cooper, "Plato's Theory of Human Motivation," *History of Philosophy Quarterly*, 1 (1984), 2–31; D. Jacquette, "Plato on the Parts of Soul," *Epoche*, 8 (2003), 43–68; H. Lorenz, *The Brute Within: Appetitive Desire in Plato and Aristotle* (Oxford, 2006); R. F. Stalley, "Persuasion and the Tripartite Soul in Plato's *Republic*," *Oxford Studies in Ancient Philosophy*, 32 (2007), 63–89; J. Moss, "Appearances and Calculations: Plato's Division of the Soul," *Oxford Studies in Ancient Philosophy*, 34 (2008), 35–68; R. Barney, T. Brennan, and C. Brittain (eds.), *Plato and the Divided Self* (Cambridge, 2012).

Chapter 22

1. For a challenge to this reading see G. Fine, "Knowledge and Belief in *Republic* V," *Archiv für Geschichte der Philosophie*, 60 (1978), 121–39. Prominent proponents of the "two world" view, as mentioned by Fine, are e.g. G. Vlastos, "Degrees of Reality in Plato," in R. Bambrough (ed.), *New Essays on Plato and Aristotle* (London, 1965), 1–20, and J. Hintikka, "Knowledge and its Objects in Plato," in J. M. E. Moravscik (ed.), *Patterns in Plato's Thought* (Dordrecht, 1973), 1–30. The proposal about truth that I mention later in this paragraph is based on Fine.
2. On the oft-discussed question of why the philosopher would go back into the cave, see recently A. Silverman, "Ascent and Descent: The Philosopher's Regret," *Social Philosophy and Policy*, 24 (2007), 40–69.
3. For instance at *Metaphysics* 1039b.
4. My thanks to M. M. McCabe for many discussions of this point.

Chapter 23

1. In fact, as we'll see in the next volume, they went further and held that Plato's ideas can be reconciled with those of Aristotle. On the development of this idea see G. Karamanolis, *Plato and Aristotle in Agreement?* (Oxford, 2006).
2. For instance at Aristotle, *Metaphysics* 990b. The discussion of this argument practically constitutes a whole branch of the study of ancient philosophy over the last decades. See e.g. G. Vlastos, "The Third Man Argument in the *Parmenides*," *Philosophical Review*, 63 (1954), 319–49; P. Geach, "The Third Man Again," *Philosophical Review*, 65 (1956), 72–82; C. Strang, "Plato and the Third Man," *Proceedings of the Aristotelian Society*, supplementary volume, 37 (1963), 147–64; S. Waterlow, "The Third Man's Contribution to Plato's Paradigmatism," *Mind*, 91 (1982), 339–57; C. C. Meinwald, "Good-bye to the Third Man," in R. Kraut (ed.), *The Cambridge Companion to Plato* (Cambridge, 1992), 365–96; T. Scaltsas, "A Necessary Falsehood in the Third Man Argument," *Phronesis*, 37 (1992), 216–32; P. Schweizer, "Self-Predication and the

Third Man," *Erkenntnis*, 40 (1994), 21–42; D. Hunt, "How (Not) to Exempt Platonic Forms from *Parmenides*'s Third Man," *Phronesis*, 42 (1997), 1–20; F. J. Pelletier and E. N. Zalta, "How to Say Goodbye to the Third Man," *Noûs*, 34 (2000), 165–202; D. T. J. Bailey, "The Third Man Argument," *Philosophy Compass*, 4 (2009), 666–81. You get the idea.
3. G. Vlastos, "The Third Man Argument in the *Parmenides*," 328.

Chapter 24

1. For instance C. C. Meinwald, "Good-bye to the Third Man," in R. Kraut (ed.), *The Cambridge Companion to Plato* (Cambridge, 1992), 365–96.
2. The last sentence of the *Statesman* may also be spoken by Socrates—it's hard to tell since, in another provocative move, the *Statesman* has the Eleatic Stranger talking to a youth who is also named Socrates.
3. As we'll see, the 'lengthy speech' option is used by Plato in the *Timaeus*, another dialogue where Socrates appears but is demoted to the grade of audience member. Plato flags the fact that the *Sophist* is reprising the method of question-and-answer with a young, pliable interlocutor by having Socrates refer back to the conversation of the *Parmenides* (217c).
4. For discussion see M. Frede, "The Literary Form of the *Sophist*," and C. Gill, "Afterward: Dialectic and the Dialogue Form in Late Plato," in C. Gill and M. M. McCabe (eds.), *Form and Argument in Late Plato* (Oxford, 1996), 135–51 and 283–311.
5. If you can read German, it's worth checking out the classic study by Michael Frede, *Prädikation und Existenzaussage: Platons Gebrauch Von "Ist" und "Ist Nicht" im Sophistes* (Gottingen, 1967). If not, then go learn German! It's a great language. In the meantime, see also G. E. L. Owen, "Plato on Not-Being," in G. Vlastos (ed.), *Plato I: Metaphysics and Epistemology* (Garden City, 1970), 223–67; L. Brown, "Being in the *Sophist*: A Syntactic Inquiry," *Oxford Studies in Ancient Philosophy*, 4 (1986), 49–70; M. Frede, "Plato's *Sophist* on False Statements," in R. Kraut (ed.), *The Cambridge Companion to Plato* (Cambridge, 1992), 397–424; J. van Eck, 'Not Being and Difference: On Plato's *Sophist* 256d5–258e3,' *Oxford Studies in Ancient Philosophy*, 23 (2002), 63–84; P. Crivelli, *Plato's Account of Falsehood: A Study of the Sophist* (Cambridge, 2011); F. Leigh, "Modes of Being at *Sophist* 255c–e," *Phronesis*, 57 (2012), 1–28.
6. See M. Frede, "Being and Becoming," *Oxford Studies in Ancient Philosophy*, supplementary volume (1988), 37–52.
7. See further F. Leigh, "Restless Forms, Changeless Causes," *Proceedings of the Aristotelian Society*, 112 (2012), 239–61.
8. And, just as an example of how carefully Plato constructs his dialogues: we now can read with new eyes the opening question about whether the sophist, statesman, and philosopher are the same or different in kind.
9. A similar characterization of thinking is offered at *Theaetetus* 189e.
10. For instance, the Latin translator Boethius, in his commentary on Aristotle's *On Interpretation*, tries to explain why Plato only deals with two parts of speech, the noun and verb.

Chapter 25

1. The case for taking them seriously is put by R. Barney, *Names and Nature in Plato's Cratylus* (London, 2001) and D. Sedley, *Plato's Cratylus* (Cambridge, 2003). The point I go on to make in this paragraph about Plato being in competition with other authors is inspired by Barney.

Chapter 26

1. The word for "animal" in Greek, *zoon*, derives from the verb "to live" and thus could also mean simply "living thing."
2. The other main contender is Aristotle's account, according to which a visual form is transmitted to the eye through an illuminated medium (like air). Not until Ibn al-Haytham, a scientist of medieval Islam, will it be (correctly) argued that we see thanks to light-rays bouncing off objects and into our eyes.
3. Why five solids for only four elements? Because the dodecahedron is associated with the cosmos as a whole, probably because it is nearly spherical (55c).

Chapter 27

1. See Chapter 13, on Socrates in Xenophon and Aristophanes.
2. Plato not infrequently has Socrates give long speeches, while also having him say that he doesn't really go in for speeches. For a good example see *Protagoras* 335c (disavowal of being able to give speeches) followed by 342a–347a (a lengthy disquisition on the poet Simonides).
3. G. Vlastos, "The Individual as an Object of Love in Plato," in G. Vlastos, *Platonic Studies* (Princeton, 1981), 1–34.
4. For this sort of reading see F. C. C. Sheffield, *Plato's* Symposium: *The Ethics of Desire* (Oxford, 2006).

Chapter 28

1. G. R. Boys-Stones and J. H. Haubold (eds), *Plato and Hesiod* (Oxford, 2010).
2. We learn about this in Plutarch's *Against Colotes*, on which see E. Kechagia, *Plutarch Against Colotes: A Lesson in the History of Philosophy* (Oxford, 2011).

Chapter 29

1. Diogenes Laertius, *Lives of the Philosophers* 5.2.
2. *Lives of the Philosophers* 5.2.
3. This story is related in *Vita Aristotelis Marciana*, ed. O. Gigon (Berlin, 1962), 42.
4. Atticus (quoted by Eusebius) said that Aristotle "uses darkness, like a squid, to make himself hard to catch." Cited by J. Barnes, *Method and Metaphysics: Essays in Ancient Philosophy I* (Oxford, 2011), 195.
5. The ancient commentators in fact divided it into two halves with their own titles, "On Physical Principles" and "On Motion." There was disagreement about whether Book Five belonged to the first or second half.

Chapter 30

1. For the late ancient views on the *Categories* see section 3 of R. Sorabji, *The Philosophy of the Commentators 200–600 AD*, 3 vols. (London, 2004), vol. 3: *Logic and Metaphysics*.
2. The medieval discussion is mediated by the ancient Platonist philosopher Porphyry, whose work on Aristotle's logic was transmitted to the Latin world by Boethius. For a useful

collection of texts see N. Kretzmann and E. Stump, *The Cambridge Translations of Medieval Philosophical Texts*. Volume 1: *Logic and the Philosophy of Language* (Cambridge, 1988).

3. On this see G. E. M. Anscombe, "Aristotle and the Sea Battle," *Mind*, 65 (1956), 1–15; J. Hintikka, "The Once and Future Sea Fight: Aristotle's Discussion of Future Contingents in *de Interpretatione* 9," *Philosophical Review*, 73 (1964), 461–92; D. Frede, "The Sea-Battle Reconsidered: A Defence of the Traditional Interpretation," *Oxford Studies in Ancient Philosophy*, 3 (1985), 31–83; R. Gaskin, *The Sea Battle and the Master Argument* (Berlin, 1995).

4. An anonymous reader who made many useful comments on this book's manuscript has asked me to emphasize how 'utterly, mind-blowingly fantastic' Aristotle's innovation is. Consider it emphasized.

5. In the Middle Ages the argument forms received nicknames used as mnemonic devices, based on the use of vowels to indicate the kind of predication used. For instance, the kind of predication in 'all X is true of Y' is symbolized with the letter *a* (you can abbreviate it like this: X*a*Y). So the first example here is called a 'Barbara' syllogism. This is not because it was invented by someone named Barbara, but because the predications in the two premises and the conclusion are all *a* predications: A*a*B, B*a*C, A*a*C, hence B*a*rb*a*r*a* (the consonants in the nickname don't mean anything, they are just to help you remember it). The second example is named 'Celarent' because *e* is used to represent predications of the form "X is true of no Y." So the first premise and conclusion are *e* predications and the second predication an *a* predication: A*e*B, A*a*C, A*e*C, hence C*e*l*a*r*e*nt. For a helpful overview of all this see R. Smith, "Logic," in J. Barnes (ed.), *The Cambridge Companion to Aristotle* (Cambridge, 1995), 27–65.

Chapter 31

1. M. Burnyeat, "Aristotle on Understanding Knowledge," in E. Berti (ed.), *Aristotle on Science: The* Posterior Analytics (Padua, 1981), 97–139.

2. Note that he would also tend to think about it in these "categorial" terms, asking whether long-necked is predicated of giraffes (all A is B), rather than in the hypothetical way I suggested: if something is a giraffe then it has a long neck (if A then B). The Stoics will pioneer in the analysis of such "hypotheses," meaning 'if–then' statements.

3. There is a debate about how 'empiricist' he is. On this question, see T. Irwin, *Aristotle's First Principles* (Oxford, 1988), ch. 7; J. Barnes, *Aristotle's* Posterior Analytics (Oxford, 1994), 259; M. Frede, "Aristotle's Rationalism," in M. Frede and G. Striker (eds.), *Rationality in Greek Thought* (Oxford, 1996), 157–73.

4. For the meaning of *epagoge* in Aristotle see D. Hamlyn, "Aristotelian *Epagoge*," *Phronesis*, 21 (1976), 167–80 and T. Engberg-Pedersen, "More on Aristotelian *Epagoge*," *Phronesis*, 24 (1979), 301–17.

Chapter 32

1. I.6, 1096a, mentioned in Chapter 29, on Aristotle's life and works.

2. Here it's worth repeating the point that, for Aristotle, there must always be individual men so that there will be something for universal truths about men to be true *about*.

Chapter 33

1. As we'll see in a later chapter, Aristotle associates the mother more with the material cause, since she provides the matter out of which the embryo will be formed.
2. On the argument see e.g. J. G. Lennox, "Aristotle on Chance," *Archiv für Geschichte der Philosophie*, 66 (1984), 52–60; D. J. Furley, "The Rainfall Example in *Physics* II 8," in A. Gotthelf (ed.), *Aristotle on Nature and Living Things* (Pittsburgh, 1985), 177–82; D. Sedley, "Is Aristotle's Teleology Anthropocentric?," *Phronesis*, 36 (1991), 179–96; R. Wardy, "Aristotelian Rainfall or the Lore of Averages," *Phronesis*, 38 (1993), 18–30.

Chapter 34

1. The word *mousikos* ("musical") in Greek actually means something more like "educated" or "cultured," but the example works just as well if you imagine someone learning to play piano.
2. For all this see e.g. Aristotle, *On the Heavens* 268b–270b.

Chapter 35

1. This helps explain Aristotle's point that not just any soul can inhabit just any body (sunflowers cannot be made of flesh and bone). Rather, each body has just the right potentiality to take on the soul it has. For this reason, Aristotle believes that the successful biologist needs to take account of both soul and body—both matter and form.
2. For Sorabji's view see his "Body and Soul in Aristotle," *Philosophy*, 49 (1979), 63–89, and for further discussion, including Burnyeat's contrary spiritualist account, see M. Nussbaum and A. Rorty, *Essays on Aristotle's De Anima* (Oxford, 1992). See also the assessment in V. Caston, "The Spirit and the Letter: Aristotle on Perception," in R. Salles (ed.), *Metaphysics, Soul, and Ethics: Themes from the Work of Richard Sorabji* (Oxford, 2005), 245–320.

Chapter 36

1. Quoted from J. L. Borges, "John Wilkins' Analytical Language," in *Selected Non-Fictions*, ed. E. Weinberger (London, 1999), 231.
2. This is not to say that they agreed about the right way to divide. Aristotle criticizes Plato's theory of division, and expectations about what division can accomplish, at *Posterior Analytics* 2.5–6.
3. He classifies them as cetaceans, at e.g. *History of Animals* 1.5.
4. Here I am following D. Henry, "Aristotle on the Mechanism of Inheritance," *Journal of the History of Biology*, 39 (2006), 425–55.

Chapter 37

1. E. Kolbert, "Everybody Have Fun: What Can Policymakers Learn from Happiness Research?," *New Yorker*, 22 Mar. 2010.
2. On which see e.g. J. E. Whiting, "Aristotle's Function Argument: A Defence," *Ancient Philosophy*, 8 (1988), 33–48.
3. David Hume, *A Treatise of Human Nature*, book 3, part 1, section 1.

4. I owe the phrase to David Vessey. On the theory see R. Hursthouse, "A False Doctrine of the Mean," *Proceedings of the Aristotelian Society*, 81 (1980), 57–72; C. Young, "The Doctrine of the Mean," *Topoi*, 15 (1996), 89–99; and L. Brown, "What Is the "mean relative to us" in Aristotle's Ethics?," *Phronesis*, 42 (1997), 77–93.

Chapter 38

1. See Immanuel Kant, *Grounding for the Metaphysics of Morals*, trans. J. W. Ellington (Indianapolis, 1981), 11 (p. 398 in the standard German edition). He does, however, immediately go on to argue that one has a duty to secure one's own happiness.
2. See e.g. A. Kenny, *Aristotle on the Perfect Life* (Oxford: 1992), ch. 6.
3. There is no general agreement about Aristotle's position here, or the sense in which the weak-willed person is "ignorant" according to him. For some recent views of the question see P. Destree, "Aristotle on the Causes of *Akrasia*," in C. Bobonich and P. Destree (eds.), *Akrasia in Greek Philosophy: From Socrates to Plotinus* (Leiden, 2007), 139–66; D. Charles, "*NE* VII.3: Varieties of *Acrasia*," in C. Natali (ed.), *Aristotle's* Nicomachean Ethics Book VII (Oxford, 2009), 41–71; M. Pickavé and J. Whiting, "*Nicomachean Ethics* VII.3 on Akratic 'Ignorance'," *Oxford Studies in Ancient Philosophy*, 34 (2008), 323–71; J. Moss, "*Akrasia* and Perceptual Illusion," *Archiv für Geschichte der Philosophie*, 91 (2009), 119–56.
4. On this problem see C. H. Kahn, "Aristotle and Altruism," *Mind*, 90 (1981), 20–40, and R. Kraut, *Aristotle on the Human Good* (Princeton, 1989).
5. A classic contribution to the debate is J. L. Ackrill, "Aristotle on *Eudaimonia*," *Proceedings of the British Academy*, 60 (1974), 339–59. See subsequently e.g. Kraut, *Aristotle on the Human Good*; A. J. P. Kenny, *Aristotle on the Perfect Life* (Oxford, 1992); D. Charles, "Aristotle on Well-Being and Intellectual Contemplation," *Proceedings of the Aristotelian Society*, supplementary volume, 73 (1999), 205–23; G. R. Lear, *Happy Lives and the Highest Good* (Princeton, 2004).

Chapter 39

1. On this topic and its applications in practical action, see J. Moss, *Aristotle on the Apparent Good: Perception, Phantasia, Thought, and Desire* (Oxford, 2012). The reason 'imagination' is inadequate is that *phantasia* is involved in a very wide range of functions, including memory and dreams.
2. For this see his *On Sleep* 458a.
3. On this topic see R. Norman, "Aristotle's Philosopher-God," *Phronesis*, 14 (1969), 63–74; L. Elders, *Aristotle's Theology: A Commentary on Book Lambda of the* Metaphysics (Assen, 1972); T. De Koninck, "Aristotle on God as Thought Thinking Itself," *Review of Metaphysics*, 47 (1994), 471–515; A. Kosman, "*Metaphysics* Lambda 9: Divine Thought," in M. Frede and D. Charles (eds.), *Aristotle's* Metaphyiscs Lambda (Oxford, 2000), 307–26.

Chapter 40

1. See respectively *On the Heavens* 271a, *Metaphysics* 1028a, and *Nicomachean Ethics* 1098a.
2. For more on his views on slavery see e.g. W. W. Fortenbaugh, "Aristotle on Slaves and Women," in J. Barnes, J. Schofield, and R. Sorabji (eds.), *Articles on Aristotle. Volume 2: Ethics and Politics* (London, 1977); M. Schofield, "Ideology and Philosophy in Aristotle's Theory of Slavery," in G. Patzig (ed.), *Aristoteles Politik* (Göttingen, 1990), 1–21; N. D. Smith, "Aristotle's

Theory of Natural Slavery," in D. Keyt and F. D. Miller, Jr. (eds.), *A Companion to Aristotle's Politics* (Oxford, 1991), 142–55; P. A. Brunt, "Aristotle and Slavery," *Studies in Greek History and Thought* (Oxford, 1993), 434–88; P. Garnsey, *Ideas of Slavery from Aristotle to Augustine* (Cambridge, 1996).

Chapter 42

1. The 'first woman philosopher' tag is assigned by the Church Father Clement of Alexandria, as reported by R. Hawley in "The Problem of Women Philosophers in Ancient Greece," in L. J. Archer, S. Fischler, and M. Wyke (eds.), *Women in Ancient Societies* (London, 1994), 70–87, at p. 77. This article is a good introduction to the subject, but for more detail see M. E. Waith, *A History of Women Philosophers*. Volume 1: *600 BC–500 AD* (Dordrecht, 1987). I draw quite a bit on both in what follows here.
2. Hawley, "The Problem of Women Philosophers," 77–8.
3. Quoted from Waith, *A History of Women Philosophers*, 44.
4. Cited by J. Annas, "Plato's *Republic* and Feminism," in J. K. Ward (ed.), *Feminism and Ancient Philosophy* (New York, 1996), 3–12, at 7.
5. See J. Barnes, "Ancient Philosophers," in G. Clark and T. Rajak (eds.), *Philosophy and Power in the Graeco-Roman World* (Oxford, 2002), 293–306, which mentions the phenomenon of women philosophers being memorialized in inscriptions.
6. See Diogenes Laertius, *Lives of Eminent Philosophers* 2.86.
7. My thanks to George Boys-Stones for help with research on her.
8. On the dialogue see further P. M Huby, "The *Menexenus* Reconsidered," *Phronesis*, 2 (1957), 104–14.
9. *Memorabilia* 2.6.
10. For a useful list of contributions on both sides of the question see Ward (ed.), *Feminism and Ancient Philosophy*, 226–7, n. 59. One tempting possibility is that Diotima is a fictionalized version of Aspasia, since we know that Socrates associated with her, whereas no other source aside from Plato discusses Diotima.
11. For the comparison between Themistoclea and Diotima, I am indebted to Hawley, "The Problem of Women Philosophers," 72.
12. For this see H. King, "Producing Woman: Hippocratic Gynecology," in Archer, Fischler, and Wyke (eds.), *Women in Ancient Societies*, 102–14.
13. King, "Producing Woman," 110.
14. In Ward (ed.), *Feminism and Ancient Philosophy*, 7.
15. "Place, Interval: a Reading of Aristotle, *Physics* IV," English translation in C. A. Freeland (ed.), *Feminist Interpretations of Aristotle* (University Park, Pa., 1998), 41–58. In what follows I also draw on Freeland's essay on Irigiray in this volume.
16. Julia Kristeva, another contemporary thinker who has engaged seriously with ancient philosophy, has drawn on the idea of the Receptacle as space (*chora*) in Plato. For an introduction to Kristeva's work see N. McAfee, *Julia Kristeva* (London, 2004).
17. Freeland, *Feminist Interpretations of Aristotle*, 60.

Chapter 43

1. On this see K. Gaiser, "Plato's Enigmatic Lecture 'On the Good'," *Phronesis*, 25 (1980), 5–37.
2. Aristotle, *Metaphysics* A.6, 987a.

3. For discussion and quotation of our information on the Old Academy see J. Dillon, *The Heirs of Plato: A Study of the Old Academy (347–274 BC)* (Oxford, 2003). I will cite from this frequently in what follows. The anecdote about Xenocrates is cited by Dillon at p. 95. Xenocrates may have had in mind passages in Plato which give a central role to astronomy in progress towards philosophy: *Republic* 528e–530c and *Timaeus* 46e–47c.

4. Dillon, *The Heirs of Plato*, 7–8.

5. Dillon, *The Heirs of Plato*, 79.

6. Dillon, *The Heirs of Plato*, 49–50, 56–7.

7. Aristotle, *Metaphysics* Z.2, 1028b.

8. Aristotle, *Metaphysics* M.1 1076a, and see Dillon, *The Heirs of Plato*, 108.

9. Aristotle, *Metaphysics* N.3 1090b, and see Dillon, *The Heirs of Plato*, 111.

10. Aristotle, *On the Soul* I.2, 404b, and see Dillon, *The Heirs of Plato*, 121.

11. Dillon, *The Heirs of Plato*, 56–7, 63. Here Speusippus is extrapolating from the oft-quoted passage in the *Republic* which says that the Form of the Good is "beyond being in dignity and power" (509b), discussed in Chapter 22, on the cave allegory.

12. Dillon, *The Heirs of Plato*, 101.

13. For anecdotes on Speusippus and Xenocrates see Diogenes Laertius, *Lives of the Philosophers* 4.

14. Dillon, *The Heirs of Plato*, 64–77, 136–50.

15. Aristotle, *Nicomachean Ethics* X.2 1172b.

16. The Loeb series from Harvard University Press has a Greek–English edition of *On Plants* in several volumes.

17. Theophrastus, *On Sweat, on Dizziness and on Fatigue*, ed. and trans. W. W. Fortenbaugh, R. W. Sharples, and M. G. Sollenberger (Leiden, 2003).

18. Theophrastus, *On First Principles*, ed. and trans. D. Gutas (Leiden, 2010).

FURTHER READING

Further reading is suggested here for each of the main sections of the book, along with recommendations for the topics of specific chapters.

Early Greek Philosophy

J. Barnes, *The Presocratic Philosophers* (London, 1982).

V. Caston and D. W. Graham (eds.), *Presocratic Philosophy: Essays in Honour of Alexander Mourelatos* (Aldershot, 2002).

P. Curd and D. W. Graham (eds.), *The Oxford Handbook of Presocratic Philosophy* (Oxford, 2008).

D. J. Furley, *Cosmic Problems* (Cambridge, 1989).

D. J. Furley and R. E. Allen (eds.), *Studies in Presocratic Philosophy*, 2 vols. (London, 1970, 1975).

G. S. Kirk, J. E. Raven, and M. Schofield (eds.), *The Presocratic Philosophers: A Critical History with a Selection of Texts* (Cambridge, 1983).

A. A. Long (ed.), *The Cambridge Companion to Early Greek Philosophy* (Cambridge, 1999).

A. Mourelatos, *The Pre-Socratics* (Garden City, 1974).

J. Warren, *The Presocratics* (Stocksfield, 2007).

Thales, Anaximander, Anaximenes, and Xenophanes

K. Algra, "The Beginnings of Cosmology," in A. A. Long (ed.), *The Cambridge Companion to Early Greek Philosophy* (Cambridge, 1999), 45–65.

J. Engman, "Cosmic Justice in Anaximander," *Phronesis*, 36 (1991), 1–25.

G. Freudenthal, "The Theory of the Opposites and an Ordered Universe: Physics and Metaphysics in Anaximander," *Phronesis*, 31 (1986), 197–228.

D. W. Graham, "A New Look at Anaximenes," *History of Philosophy Quarterly*, 20 (2003), 1–20.

D. W. Graham, *Explaining the Cosmos: The Ionian Tradition of Scientific Philosophy* (Princeton, 2006).

D. W. Graham, *The Texts of Early Greek Philosophy, Part I* (Cambridge, 2010).

U. Hölscher, "Anaximander and the Beginnings of Greek Philosophy," in D. J. Furley and R. E. Allen (eds.), *Studies in Presocratic Philosophy*, vol. 1 (1970), 281–322.

E. Hussey, "The Beginnings of Epistemology: From Homer to Philolaus," in S. Everson (ed.), *Epistemology* (Cambridge, 1990), 11–38.

J. H. Lesher, *Xenophanes of Colophon: Fragments: A Text and Translation with Commentary* (Toronto, 1992).

E. Mogyoródi, "Xenophanes as Philosopher: Theology and Theodicy," in A. Laks and C. Louguet (eds), *Que-est-ce que la philosophie présocratique?* (Lille, 2002), 253–86.

M. Schofield, "The Ionians" in C. C. W. Taylor (ed.), *The Routledge History of Philosophy*, vol. 1 (London, 1997), 47–87.

Pythagoras

W. Burkert, *Lore and Science in Ancient Pythagoreanism*, trans. E. L. Minar (Cambridge, Mass., 1972).

J. M. Dillon and J. Hershbell, *Iamblichus: On the Pythagorean Way of Life* (Atlanta, Ga., 1991).

C. A. Huffman, "The Pythagorean Conception of the Soul from Pythagoras to Philolaus," in D. Frede and B. Reis (eds.), *Body and Soul in Ancient Philosophy* (Berlin, 2009), 21–44.

C. H. Kahn, *Pythagoras and the Pythagoreans: A Brief History* (Indianapolis, 2001).

J. A. Philip, *Pythagoras and Early Pythagoreanism* (Toronto, 1966).

Heraclitus

R. Dilcher, *Studies in Heraclitus* (Hildesheim, 1995).

H. Granger, "Argumentation and Heraclitus' Book," *Oxford Studies in Ancient Philosophy*, 26 (2006), 1–17.

C. H. Kahn, *The Art and Thought of Heraclitus* (Cambridge, 1979).

M. M. MacKenzie, "Heraclitus and the Art of Paradox," *Oxford Studies in Ancient Philosophy*, 6 (1988), 1–37.

M. Schofield, "Heraclitus' Theory of Soul and its Antecedents," in S. Everson (ed.), *Psychology* (Cambridge, 1991), 13–34.

L. Tarán, "Heraclitus: The River Fragments and Their Implications," *Elenchos*, 20 (1999), 9–52.

Parmenides

P. K. Curd, "Parmenidean Monism," in *Phronesis*, 36 (1991), 241–64.

P. K. Curd, *The Legacy of Parmenides: Eleatic Monism and Later Presocratic Thought* (Princeton, 1998).

A. A. Long, "Parmenides on Thinking Being," *Proceedings of the Boston Area Colloquium in Ancient Philosophy*, 12 (1996), 125–51.

M. M. MacKenzie, "Parmenides' Dilemma," *Phronesis*, 27 (1982), 1–12.

A. P. D. Mourelatos, *The Route of Parmenides: A Study of Word, Image, and Argument in the Fragments* (New Haven, 1970).

G. E. L. Owen, "Eleatic Questions," *Classical Quarterly*, NS 10 (1960), 84–102, reprinted with additions in R. E. Allen and D. J. Furley (eds.), *Studies in Presocratic Philosophy*, vol. 2: *Eleatics and Pluralists* (London, 1975), 48–81.

Zeno and Melissus

D. Bostock, "Zeno and the Potential Infinite," *Proceedings of the Aristotelian Society*, 73 (1972), 37–51.

J. Faris, *The Paradoxes of Zeno* (Aldershot, 1996).

P. S. Hasper, "Zeno Unlimited," *Oxford Studies in Ancient Philosophy*, 30 (2006), 49–85.

J. Lear, "A Note on Zeno's Arrow," in *Phronesis*, (1981), 91–104.

R. McKirahan, "Zeno's Dichotomy in Aristotle," *Philosophical Inquiry*, 23 (2001), 1–24.

G. E. L. Owen, "Zeno and the Mathematicians," *Proceedings of the Aristotelian Society*, 58 (1958), 199–222.

J. Palmer, "Melissus and Parmenides," *Oxford Studies in Ancient Philosophy*, 26 (2004), 19–54.

The Atomists

D. Furley, *Two Studies in the Greek Atomists* (Princeton, 1967).
P. S. Hasper, "The Foundations of Presocratic Atomism," *Oxford Studies in Ancient Philosophy*, 17 (1999), 1–14.
D. Konstan, "Atomism and its Heritage: Minimal Parts," *Ancient Philosophy*, 2 (1982), 60–75.
T. O'Keefe, "The Ontological Status of Sensible Qualities for Democritus and Epicurus," *Ancient Philosophy*, 17 (1997), 119–34.

Anaxagoras

D. W. Graham, "The Postulates of Anaxagoras," *Apeiron*, 27 (1994), 77–121.
W. Mann, "Anaxagoras and the *Homoiomere*," *Phronesis*, 25 (1980), 228–49.
M. Schofield, *An Essay on Anaxagoras* (Cambridge, 1980).
G. Vlastos, "The Physical Theory of Anaxagoras," *Philosophical Review*, 59 (1950), 31–57.

Empedocles

P. Curd, "A New Empedocles? Implications of the Strasburg Fragments for Presocratic Philosophy," *Proceedings of the Boston Area Colloquium in Ancient Philosophy*, 17 (2001), 27–50.
D. W. Graham, "Symmetry in the Empedoclean Cycle," *Classical Quarterly* 38 (1988), 297–312.
D. O'Brien, *Empedocles' Cosmic Cycle* (Cambridge, 1969).
D. O'Brien, "Empedocles Revisited," *Ancient Philosophy*, 15 (1995), 403–70.
O. Primavesi, "The Structure of Empedocles' Cosmic Cycle: Aristotle and the Byzantine Anonymous," in A. L. Pierris (ed.), *The Empedoclean Kosmos: Structure, Process and the Question of Cyclicity* (Patras, 2005), 245–64.

The Hippocratics

G. E. R. Lloyd, *Hippocratic Writings* (Harmondsworth, 1978).
J. Longrigg, *Greek Medicine: From the Heroic to the Hellenistic Age* (London, 1998).
V. Nutton, *Ancient Medicine* (London, 2004).
W. D. Smith, *The Hippocratic Tradition* (Ithaca, NY, 1979).
P. van der Eijk, *Medicine and Philosophy in Classical Antiquity: Doctors and Philosophers on Nature, Soul, Health and Disease* (Cambridge, 2005).

The Sophists

R. Bett, "The Sophists and Relativism," *Phronesis*, 34 (1989), 139–69.
S. Broadie, "The Sophists and Socrates," in D. Sedley (ed.), *The Cambridge Companion to Greek and Roman Philosophy* (Cambridge, 2003), 73–97.
J. M. Dillon and T. Gergel, *The Greek Sophists* (London, 2003).
D. W. Graham, *The Texts of Early Greek Philosophy*, part 2 (Cambridge, 2010).
W. G. K. Guthrie, *The Sophists* (Cambridge, 1971).
G. B. Kerferd, *The Sophistic Movement* (Cambridge, 1981).
R. Wardy, *The Birth of Rhetoric: Gorgias, Plato and their Successors* (London, 1996).
U. Zilioli, *Protagoras and the Challenge of Relativism* (Aldershot, 2007).

Socrates

S. Ahbel-Rappe and R. Kamtekar (eds.), *A Companion to Socrates* (Oxford, 2005).

H. H. Benson (ed.), *Essays on the Philosophy of Socrates* (New York, 1992).

T. C. Brickhouse and N. D. Smith (eds.), *Plato's Socrates* (Oxford, 1994).

T. C. Brickhouse and N. D. Smith (eds.), *The Trial and Execution of Socrates: Sources and Controversies* (Oxford, 2002).

L. Judson and V. Karasmanis (eds.), *Remembering Socrates* (Oxford, 2006).

D. R. Morrison (ed.), *The Cambridge Companion to Socrates* (Cambridge, 2011).

A. Nehamas, "Socratic Intellectualism," *Proceedings of the Boston Area Colloquium in Ancient Philosophy*, 2 (1987), 275–316.

W. Prior (ed.), *Socrates: Critical Assessments of Leading Philosophers*, 4 vols. (London, 1996).

D. K. O'Connor, "Socrates and Political Ambition: The Dangerous Game," *Proceedings of the Boston Area Colloquium in Ancient Philosophy*, 14 (1998), 31–52.

M. Trapp, *Socrates from Antiquity to the Enlightenment* (Aldershot, 2007).

P. A. Vander Waerdt (ed.), *The Socratic Movement* (Ithaca, NY, 1994).

G. Vlastos (ed.), *The Philosophy of Socrates: A Collection of Critical Essays* (New York, 1971).

G. Vlastos, *Socrates: Ironist and Moral Philosopher* (Cambridge, 1991).

G. Vlastos, *Socratic Studies* (Cambridge, 1994).

R. Woolf, "The Practice of a Philosopher," *Oxford Studies in Ancient Philosophy*, 26 (2004), 97–129.

R. Woolf, "Socratic Authority," *Archiv für Geschichte der Philosophie*, 90 (2008), 1–38.

Xenophon, *Conversations of Socrates*, trans. H. Treddenick and R. Waterfield (London, 1990).

Plato

H. Benson (ed.), *A Companion to Plato* (Oxford, 2006).

J. M. Cooper and D. S. Hutchinson (eds.), *Plato: Complete Works* (Indianapolis, 1997).

G. Fine (ed.), *Plato 1: Metaphysics and Epistemology* (Oxford, 1999).

G. Fine (ed.), *Plato 2: Ethics, Politics, Religion, and the Soul* (Oxford, 1999).

G. Fine, *Plato on Knowledge and Forms* (Oxford, 2003).

G. Fine (ed.), *The Oxford Handbook of Plato* (Oxford, 2008).

T. Irwin, *Plato's Ethics* (Oxford, 1995).

R. Kraut (ed.), *The Cambridge Companion to Plato* (Cambridge, 1992).

A. S. Mason, *Plato* (Durham, NC, 2010).

A. Nehamas, *Virtues of Authenticity: Essays on Plato and Socrates* (Princeton, 1999).

C. Rowe, *Plato and the Art of Philosophical Writing* (Cambridge, 2007).

G. Vlastos, *Platonic Studies* (Princeton, 1981).

Plato: *Apology* and *Euthyphro*

R. E. Allen, *Plato's Euthyphro and the Earlier Theory of Forms* (London, 1970).

T. C. Brickhouse and N. D. Smith, *Socrates on Trial* (Oxford, 1990).

M. F. Burnyeat, "The Impiety of Socrates," *Ancient Philosophy*, 17 (1997), 1–12.

P. Dimas, "Euthyphro's Thesis Revisited," *Phronesis*, 51 (2006), 1–28.

R. Kamtekar, *Plato's* Euthyphro, Apology *and* Crito: *Critical Essays* (Lanham, Md., 2005).

C. D. C. Reeve, *Socrates in the Apology* (Indianapolis, 1989).

Plato: *Charmides* and *Euthydemus*

M. Dyson, "Some Problems Concerning Knowledge in Plato's *Charmides*," *Phronesis*, 19 (1974), 102–11.

M. M. McCabe, "Silencing the Sophists: The Drama of Plato's *Euthydemus*," *Proceedings of the Boston Area Colloquium in Ancient Philosophy*, 14 (1998), 139–68.

M. M. McCabe, "Looking Inside Charmides' Cloak," in D. Scott (ed.), *Maieusis: Essays for Myles Burnyeat* (Oxford, 2007), 1–19.

T. Robinson (ed.) *Plato: Euthydemus, Lysis, Charmides: Proceedings of the Fifth Symposium Platonicum* (Sankt Augustin, 2000).

M. Tuozzo, *Plato's* Charmides: *Positive Elenchus in a "Socratic" Dialogue* (New York, 2011).

Plato: *Gorgias*

E. R. Dodds, *Plato: Gorgias* (Oxford: 1959).

J. Doyle, "The Fundamental Opposition in Plato's *Gorgias*," *Oxford Studies in Ancient Philosophy*, 30 (2006), 87–100.

J. Doyle, "Socrates and Gorgias," *Phronesis*, 55 (2010), 1–25.

T. Irwin (trans.), *Plato: Gorgias* (Oxford, 1979).

C. H. Kahn, "Drama and Dialectic in Plato's *Gorgias*," *Oxford Studies in Ancient Philosophy*, 1 (1983), 75–121.

Plato: *Meno*

H. Benson, "The Priority of Definition and the Socratic Elenchus," *Oxford Studies in Ancient Philosophy*, 8 (1990), 19–65.

J. M. Day, *Plato's* Meno *in Focus* (London, 1994).

D. Scott, *Recollection and Experience: Plato's Theory of Learning and its Successors* (Cambridge, 1995).

D. Scott, *Plato's* Meno (Cambridge, 2006).

H. Tarrant, *Recollecting Plato's* Meno (London, 2005).

R. Weiss, *Virtue in the Cave: Moral Inquiry in the* Meno (Oxford, 2001).

Plato: *Theaetetus*

D. Bostock, *Plato's* Theaetetus (Oxford, 1988).

M. F. Burnyeat, *The Theaetetus of Plato* (Indianapolis, 1990).

M. F. Burnyeat, "Protagoras and Self-refutation in Plato's *Theaetetus*," in S. Everson (ed.), *Epistemology* (Cambridge, 1989), 39–59.

T. Chappell, *Reading Plato's* Theaetetus (Indianapolis, 2005).

G. Fine, "False Belief in the *Theaetetus*," *Phronesis*, 24 (1979), 70–80.

G. Fine, "Protagorean Relativisms," *Boston Area Colloquium in Ancient Philosophy*, 19 (1996), 211–43.

J. McDowell, *Plato: Theaetetus* (Oxford, 1973).

R. Woolf, "A Shaggy Soul Story: How Not to Read the Wax Tablet Model in Plato's *Theaetetus*," *Philosophy and Phenomenological Research*, 69 (2004), 573–604.

Plato: *Phaedo*

D. Bostock, *Plato's* Phaedo (Oxford, 1986).

R. Dancy, *Plato's Introduction of Forms* (Cambridge, 2004).

D. Devereux, "Separation and Immanence in Plato's Theory of Forms," *Oxford Studies in Ancient Philosophy*, 12 (1994), 63–90.

D. Gallop, *Plato's* Phaedo (Oxford, 1975).

A. Nehamas, *Virtues of Authenticity* (Princeton, 1999).

D. Scott, *Recollection and Experience* (Cambridge, 1995).

D. Sedley, "Platonic Causes," *Phronesis*, 43 (1998), 114–32.

G. Vlastos, "Reasons and Causes in the *Phaedo*," *Philosophical Review*, 78 (1969), 291–325.

Plato: *Republic*

J. Annas, *An Introduction to Plato's* Republic (Oxford, 1981).

J. M. Cooper, "Plato's Theory of Human Motivation," *History of Philosophy Quarterly*, 1 (1984), 3–21.

G. R. F. Ferrari (ed.), *The Cambridge Companion to Plato's* Republic (Cambridge, 2007).

S. Menn, "On Plato's *Politeia*," *Proceedings of the Boston Area Colloquium in Ancient Philosophy*, 21 (2006), 1–55.

C. D. C. Reeve, *Philosopher-Kings: The Argument of Plato's* Republic (Princeton, 1988).

G. Santas, "Two Theories of Good in Plato's Republic," *Archiv für Geschichte der Philosophie*, 57 (1980), 223–45.

M. Schofield, *Plato: Political Philosophy* (Oxford, 2006).

P. Shorey, "The Idea of Good in Plato's *Republic*," in P. Shorey, *Selected Papers* (New York, 1980), 28–81.

N. P. White, *A Companion to Plato's* Republic (Indianapolis, 1979).

J. Wilberding, "Plato's Two Forms of Second-Best Morality," *Philosophical Review*, 118 (2009), 351–74.

Plato: *Parmenides*

J. Malcolm, *Plato on the Self-Predication of the Forms* (Oxford, 1991).

M. M. McCabe, *Plato's Individuals* (Princeton, 1994).

C. C. Meinwald, *Plato's Parmenides* (New York, 1991).

S. Panagiotou, "The Day and Sail Analogies in Plato's *Parmenides*," *Phoenix*, 41 (1987), 10–24.

K. Sayre, *Parmenides' Lesson: Translation and Explication of Plato's* Parmenides (South Bend Ind., 1996).

Plato: *Sophist*

R. S. Bluck, *Plato's Sophist: A Philosophical Commentary* (Manchester, 1975).

L. Brown, "Innovation and Continuity: The Battle of Gods and Giants in Plato's *Sophist* 245–249," in J. Gentzler (ed.), *Method in Ancient Philosophy* (Oxford, 1998), 181–207.

D. Charles (ed.), *Definition in Greek Philosophy* (Oxford, 2010).

L. M. de Rijk, *Plato's Sophist: A Philosophical Commentary* (Amsterdam, 1986).

F. Leigh, "Being and Power in Plato's *Sophist*," *Apeiron*, 43 (2010), 1–23.

J. McDowell, "Falsehood and Not-Being in Plato's *Sophist*," in M. Schofield and M. C. Nussbaum (eds.), *Language and Logos* (Cambridge, 1982), 115–34.

N. Notomi, *The Unity of Plato's Sophist: Between the Sophist and the Philosopher* (Cambridge, 1999).

Plato: *Cratylus*

F. Ademollo, *The* Cratylus *of Plato: A Commentary* (Cambridge, 2011).

R. Barney, *Names and Nature in Plato's* Cratylus (London, 2001).

M. M. Mackenzie, "Putting the *Cratylus* in Its Place," *Classical Quarterly*, 36 (1986), 124–50.

M. Schofield and M. Nussbaum (eds.), *Language and Logos* (Cambridge, 1982).

D. Sedley, *Plato's* Cratylus (Cambridge, 2003).

Plato: *Timaeus*

M. F. Burnyeat, "*Eikôs Mythos*," *Rhizai*, 2 (2005), 143–65.

A. Gregory, *Plato's Philosophy of Science* (London, 2000).

T. K. Johansen, *Plato's Natural Philosophy* (Cambridge, 2004).

S. Menn, *Plato on God as Nous* (Carbondale, Ill., 1995).

G. Reydams-Schils, *Plato's Timaeus as Cultural Icon* (Notre Dame, Ind., 2003).

A. Silverman, "Timaean Particulars," *Classical Quarterly*, 42 (1992), 87–113.

Plato: *Lysis, Phaedrus, Symposium*

J. Lesher, D. Nails, and F. C. C. Sheffield (eds.), *Plato's* Symposium: *Issues in Interpretation and Reception* (Cambridge, Mass., 2006).

A. Nehamas and P. Woodruff, *Plato:* Symposium (Indianapolis, 1989).

A. Nehamas and P. Woodruff, *Plato:* Phaedrus (Indianapolis, 1995).

T. Penner and C. Rowe, *Plato's* Lysis (Cambridge, 2005).

A. Price, *Love and Friendship in Plato and Aristotle* (Oxford, 1989).

C. D. C. Reeve, "Telling the Truth about Love: Plato's *Symposium*," *Proceedings of the Boston Area Colloquium in Ancient Philosophy*, 8 (1992), 89–114.

C. J. Rowe, *Plato:* Phaedrus (Warminster, 1986).

F. C. C. Sheffield, *Plato's* Symposium: *The Ethics of Desire* (Oxford, 2006).

G. Vlastos, "The Individual as Object of Love in Plato," in G. Vlastos, *Platonic Studies* (Princeton, 1981), 3–34.

Plato on Myth

J. Annas, "Plato's Myths of Judgement," *Phronesis*, 27 (1982), 119–43.

G. R. Boys-Stones and J. H. Haubold (eds.), *Plato and Hesiod* (Oxford, 2010).

D. K. O'Connor, "Rewriting the Poets in Plato's Characters," in G. R. F. Ferrari (ed.), *The Cambridge Companion to the* Republic (Cambridge, 2007), 55–89.

C. Partenie (ed.), *Plato: Selected Myths* (Oxford, 2004).

C. Partenie (ed.), *Plato's Myths* (Cambridge, 2009).

Aristotle

J. Ackrill, *Aristotle the Philosopher* (London, 1981).

J. Ackrill (ed.), *A New Aristotle Reader* (Oxford, 1987).

G. Anagnostopoulos (ed.), *A Companion to Aristotle* (Oxford, 2009).

J. Barnes, *Aristotle* (Oxford, 1982).

J. Barnes (ed.), *Aristotle: The Complete Works*, 2 vols. (Princeton, 1984).

J. Barnes (ed.), *The Cambridge Companion to Aristotle* (Cambridge, 1995).

J. Barnes, M. Schofield, and R. Sorabji (eds.), *Essays on Aristotle*, 4 vols. (London, 1975–9).

T. H. Irwin, *Aristotle's First Principles* (Oxford, 1988).

T. H. Irwin (ed.), *Aristotle: Metaphysics, Epistemology, Natural Philosophy* (New York, 1995).

J. Lear, *Aristotle: The Desire to Understand* (Cambridge, 1988).

G. E. R. Lloyd, *Aristotle* (Cambridge, 1968).

J. M. E. Moravcsik (ed.), *Aristotle: A Collection of Critical Essays* (Garden City, 1967).

C. Shields (ed.), *The Oxford Handbook of Aristotle* (Oxford, 2012).

Aristotle: Logical Works

P. Crivelli, *Aristotle on Truth* (Cambridge, 2004).

J. Hintikka, *Time and Necessity: Studies in Aristotle's Theory of Modality* (Oxford, 1973).

B. Jones, "An Introduction to the First Five Chapters of Aristotle's *Categories*," *Phronesis*, 20 (1975), 146–72.

J. Lear, *Aristotle and Logical Theory* (Cambridge, 1980).

W. Leszl, "Aristotle's Logical Works and His Conception of Logic," *Topoi*, 23 (2004), 71–100.

Aristotle on Epistemology

P. Adamson, "*Posterior Analytics* II.19: A Dialogue with Plato?," in V. Harte, M. M. McCabe, R. W. Sharples, and A. Sheppard (eds.), *Aristotle and the Stoics Reading Plato* (London, 2010), 1–19.

J. Barnes, *Aristotle: Posterior Analytics* (Oxford, 1996).

M. F. Burnyeat, "Aristotle on Understanding Knowledge," in E. Berti (ed.), *Aristotle on Science: The* Posterior Analytics (Padua, 1981), 97–139.

M. Ferejohn, *The Origins of Aristotelian Science* (New Haven, 1980).

M. Frede, "Aristotle's Rationalism," in M. Frede and G. Striker (eds.), *Rationality in Greek Thought* (Oxford, 1996).

Aristotle on Substance

M. F. Burnyeat, *A Map of* Metaphysics Zeta (Pittsburgh, 2001).

D. Charles, *Aristotle on Meaning and Essence* (Oxford, 2000).

M. Frede, *Essays in Ancient Philosophy* (Oxford, 1987).

M. L. Gill, *Aristotle on Substance* (Princeton, 1989).

M. J. Loux, *Primary Ousia: An Essay on Aristotle's* Metaphysics Z and H (Ithaca, NY, 1991).

T. Scaltsas, D. Charles, and M. L. Gill (eds.), *Unity, Identity, and Explanation in Aristotle's Metaphysics* (Oxford, 1994).

C. Shields, *Order in Multiplicity: Homonymy in the Philosophy of Aristotle* (Oxford, 1999).

M. Wedin, *Aristotle's Theory of Substance: The* Categories *and* Metaphysics Zeta (Oxford, 2000).

Aristotle on the Four Causes

J. Annas, "Aristotle on Inefficient Causes," *Philosophical Quarterly*, 32 (1982), 311–26.

D. Charles, "Aristotle on Hypothetical Necessity and Irreducibility," *Pacific Philosophical Quarterly*, 69 (1988), 1–53.

A. Code, "The Persistence of Aristotelian Matter," *Philosophical Studies*, 29 (1976), 357–67.

K. Fine, "Aristotle on Matter," *Mind*, 101 (1992), 35–57.

M. Johnson, *Aristotle on Teleology* (Oxford, 2005).

M. Leunissen, *Explanation and Teleology in Aristotle's Science of Nature* (Cambridge, 2010).

S. S. Meyer, "Aristotle, Teleology and Reduction," *Philosophical Review*, 101 (1992), 791–825.

Aristotle: *Physics*

D. Bostock, *Space, Time, Matter and Form: Essays on Aristotle's* Physics (Oxford, 2006).

U. Coope, *Time for Aristotle* (Oxford, 2005).

A. Falcon, *Aristotle and the Science of Nature: Unity without Uniformity* (Cambridge, 2005).

L. Judson (ed.), *Aristotle's Physics: A Collection of Essays* (Oxford, 1991).

B. Morison, *On Location: Aristotle's Concept of Space* (Oxford, 2002).

R. Sorabji, *Time, Creation, and the Continuum* (London, 1983).

R. Sorabji, *Matter, Space, and Motion* (London, 1988).

S. Waterlow, *Nature, Change, and Agency in Aristotle's* Physics (Oxford, 1982).

Aristotle: *On the Soul* (*De Anima*)

M. Durrant (ed.), *Aristotle's De Anima in Focus* (London, 1993).

S. Everson, *Aristotle on Perception* (Oxford, 1997).

T. K. Johansen, *Aristotle on the Sense-Organs* (Cambridge, 1998).

R. Polansky, *Aristotle's De Anima* (Cambridge, 2007).

A. W. Price, "Aristotelian Perceptions," *Proceedings of the Boston Area Colloquium in Ancient Philosophy*, 12 (1998), 285–309.

S. Menn, "Aristotle's Definition of Soul and the Programme of the De Anima," *Oxford Studies in Ancient Philosophy*, 22 (2002), 83–139.

M. C. Nussbaum and A. O. Rorty (eds.), *Essays on Aristotle's* De Anima (Oxford, 1992).

C. Shields, "Soul and Body in Aristotle," *Oxford Studies in Ancient Philosophy*, 6 (1988), 103–37.

J. Whiting, "Locomotive Soul: The Parts of Soul in Aristotle's Scientific Works," *Oxford Studies in Ancient Philosophy*, 22 (2002), 141–200.

Aristotle on Biology

D. Devereux and P. Pellegrin (eds.), *Biologie, logique et métaphysique chez Aristote* (Paris, 1990).

A. Gotthelf, *Teleology, First Principles, and Scientific Method in Aristotle's Biology* (Oxford, 2012).

A. Gotthelf and J. G. Lennox (eds.), *Philosophical Issues in Aristotle's Biology* (Cambridge, 1987).

D. Henry, "Aristotle on the Mechanism of Inheritance," *Journal of the History of Biology*, 39 (2006), 425–55.

J. G. Lennox, *Aristotle's Philosophy of Biology* (Cambridge, 2001).

G. E. R. Lloyd, *Aristotelian Explorations* (Cambridge, 1996).

Aristotle: *Ethics*

D. Bostock, *Aristotle's Ethics* (Oxford, 2000).

S. Broadie, *Ethics with Aristotle* (Oxford, 1991).

J. M. Cooper, *Reason and Human Good in Aristotle* (Cambridge, Mass., 1975).

P. Gottlieb, *The Virtue of Aristotle's Ethics* (Cambridge, 2009).

R. Kraut (ed.), *The Blackwell Guide to Aristotle's* Nicomachean Ethics (Malden, Mass., 2006).

J. Miller, *Aristotle's* Nicomachean Ethics: *A Critical Guide* (Cambridge, 2011).

A. W. Price, *Love and Friendship in Plato and Aristotle* (New York, 1989).

A. O. Rorty, "The Place of Pleasure in Aristotle's Ethics," *Mind*, 83 (1974), 481–93.

A. O. Rorty, *Essays on Aristotle's Ethics* (Berkeley, 1980).

D. Scott, "Aristotle on Well-being and Intellectual Contemplation," *Proceedings of the Aristotelian Society*, supplementary volume (1999), 225–42.

S. Stern-Gillet, *Aristotle's Philosophy of Friendship* (Albany, NY, 1995).

J. O. Urmson, *Aristotle's Ethics* (Oxford, 1988).

Aristotle on Mind and God

M. F. Burnyeat, *Aristotle's Divine Intellect* (Milwaukee, 2008).

V. Caston, "Aristotle on Consciousness," *Mind*, 111 (2002), 751–815.

T. De Koninck, "Aristotle on God as Thought Thinking Itself," *Review of Metaphysics*, 47 (1994), 471–515.

M. Frede and D. Charles (eds.), *Aristotle's* Metaphysics Lambda (Oxford, 2000).

R. Heinaman, "Aristotle and the Mind–Body Problem," *Phronesis*, 35 (1990), 83–102.

T. Irwin, "Aristotle's Philosophy of Mind," in S. Everson (ed.), *Psychology* (Cambridge, 1991), 56–83.

R. Wardy, *The Chain of Change: A Study of Aristotle's* Physics VII (Cambridge, 1990).

Aristotle on Political Philosophy

D. Keyt and F. D. Miller, Jr. (eds.), *A Companion to Aristotle's* Politics (Oxford, 1991).

R. Kraut, *Aristotle: Political Philosophy* (Oxford, 2002).

R. Kraut and S. Skultety (eds.), *Aristotle's* Politics: *Critical Essays* (Lanham, Md., 2005).

C. Lord and D. O'Connor (eds.), *Essays on the Foundations of Aristotelian Political Science* (Berkeley, 1991).

G. Patzig, (ed.), *Aristoteles' Politik* (Göttingen, 1990).

P. L. Phillips Simpson, *A Philosophical Commentary on the* Politics *of Aristotle* (Chapel Hill, NC, 1998).

C. J. Rowe and M. Schofield (eds.), *The Cambridge History of Greek and Roman Political Thought* (Cambridge, 2000).

Aristotle: *Rhetoric* and *Poetics*

J. Dow, "A Supposed Contradiction about Emotion-Arousal in Aristotle's *Rhetoric*," *Phronesis*, 52 (2007), 382–402.

W. W. Fortenbaugh, "Aristotle's *Rhetoric* on Emotions," *Archiv für Geschichte der Philosophie*, 52 (1970), 40–70.

D. J. Furley and A. Nehamas (eds.), *Aristotle's* Rhetoric (Princeton, 1994).

S. Halliwell, *Aristotle's* Poetics (Chapel Hill, NC, 1986).

C. Rapp, "The Nature and Goals of Rhetoric," in G. Anagnostopoulos (ed.), *A Companion to Aristotle* (Oxford, 2009), 579–96.

A. O. Rorty (ed.), *Essays on Aristotle's* Poetics (Princeton, 1992).

A. O. Rorty (ed.), *Essays on Aristotle's* Rhetoric (Berkeley, 1996).

Women in Ancient Philosophy

J. Annas, "Plato's *Republic* and Feminism," *Philosophy*, 51 (1976), 307–21.

C. A. Freeland (ed.), *Feminist Interpretations of Aristotle* (University Park, Pa., 1998).

C. A. Freeland, "Feminism and Ideology in Ancient Philosophy," *Apeiron*, 33 (2000), 365–406.

R. Mayhew, *The Female in Aristotle's Biology: Reason or Rationalization* (Chicago, 2004).

M. E. Waith, *A History of Women Philosophers*. Volume 1: *600 BC–500 AD* (Dordrecht, 1987).

J. K. Ward (ed.), *Feminism and Ancient Philosophy* (New York, 1996).

Followers of Plato and Aristotle

H. Baltussen, *Theophrastus Against the Presocratics and Plato* (Leiden, 2000).

J. Dillon, *The Heirs of Plato: A Study of the Old Academy* (Oxford, 2003).

W. W. Fortenbaugh, P. M. Huby, R. W. Sharples, and D. Gutas, *Theophrastus of Ephesus: Sources for his Life, Writings, Thought and Influence* (Leiden, 1992).

D. Gutas, *Theophrastus: On First Principles* (Leiden, 2010).

L. Tarán, *Speusippus of Athens* (Leiden, 1981).

H. Tarrant, "Speusippus' Ontological Classification," *Phronesis*, 19 (1974), 130–45.

INDEX